THE CAMBRIDGE COMPANION TO

EARLY MODERN PHILOSOPHY

The Cambridge Companion to Early Modern Philosophy is a comprehensive introduction to the central topics and changing shape of philosophical inquiry in the seventeenth and eighteenth centuries. It explores one of the most innovative periods in the history of Western philosophy, extending from Montaigne, Bacon, and Descartes through Hume and Kant. During this period, philosophers initiated and responded to major intellectual developments in natural science, religion, and politics, transforming in the process concepts and doctrines inherited from ancient and medieval philosophy. In this *Companion*, leading specialists examine early modern treatments of the methodological and conceptual foundations of natural science, metaphysics, philosophy of mind, logic and language, moral and political philosophy, and theology. A final chapter looks forward to the philosophy of the Enlightenment. This will be an invaluable guide for all who are interested in the philosophical thought of the early modern period.

DONALD RUTHERFORD is Professor of Philosophy at the University of California, San Diego. He is the author of *Leibniz and the Rational Order of Nature* (1995), editor (with J. A. Cover) of *Leibniz: Nature and Freedom* (2005), and editor and translator (with Brandon Look) of *The Leibniz–Des Bosses Correspondence* (2007).

OTHER VOLUMES IN THE SERIES OF CAMBRIDGE COMPANIONS

ABELARD *Edited by* JEFFREY E. BROWER *and* KEVIN GUILFOY
ADORNO *Edited by* THOMAS HUHN
ANSELM *Edited by* BRIAN DAVIES *and* BRIAN LEFTOW
AQUINAS *Edited by* NORMAN KRETZMANN *and* ELEONORE STUMP
ARABIC PHILOSOPHY *Edited by* PETER ADAMSON *and* RICHARD C. TAYLOR
HANNAH ARENDT *Edited by* DANA VILLA
ARISTOTLE *Edited by* JONATHAN BARNES
AUGUSTINE *Edited by* ELEONORE STUMP *and* NORMAN KRETZMANN
BACON *Edited by* MARKKU PELTONEN
SIMONE DE BEAUVOIR *Edited by* CLAUDIA CARD
BERKELEY *Edited by* KENNETH P. WINKLER
BRENTANO *Edited by* DALE JACQUETTE
CRITICAL THEORY *Edited by* FRED RUSH
DARWIN *Edited by* JONATHAN HODGE *and* GREGORY RADICK
DESCARTES *Edited by* JOHN COTTINGHAM
DUNS SCOTUS *Edited by* THOMAS WILLIAMS
EARLY GREEK PHILOSOPHY *Edited by* A. A. LONG
FEMINISM IN PHILOSOPHY *Edited by* MIRANDA FRICKER *and* JENNIFER HORNSBY
FOUCAULT *Edited by* GARY GUTTING
FREUD *Edited by* JEROME NEU
GADAMER *Edited by* ROBERT J. DOSTAL
GALILEO *Edited by* PETER MACHAMER
GERMAN IDEALISM *Edited by* KARL AMERIKS
GREEK AND ROMAN PHILOSOPHY *Edited by* DAVID SEDLEY
HABERMAS *Edited by* STEPHEN K. WHITE
HEGEL *Edited by* FREDERICK BEISER
HEIDEGGER *Edited by* CHARLES GUIGNON
HOBBES *Edited by* TOM SORELL
HUME *Edited by* DAVID FATE NORTON
HUSSERL *Edited by* BARRY SMITH *and* DAVID WOODRUFF SMITH
WILLIAM JAMES *Edited by* RUTH ANNA PUTNAM

KANT *Edited by* PAUL GUYER
KANT AND MODERN PHILOSOPHY *Edited by* PAUL GUYER
KEYNES *Edited by* ROGER BACKHOUSE *and* BRADLEY BATEMAN
KIERKEGAARD *Edited by* ALASTAIR HANNAY *and* GORDON MARINO
LEIBNIZ *Edited by* NICHOLAS JOLLEY
LEVINAS *Edited by* SIMON CRITCHLEY *and* ROBERT BERNASCONI
LOCKE *Edited by* VERE CHAPPELL
MAIMONIDES *Edited by* KENNETH SEESKIN
MALEBRANCHE *Edited by* STEVEN NADLER
MARX *Edited by* TERRELL CARVER
MEDIEVAL JEWISH PHILOSOPHY *Edited by* DANIEL H. FRANK *and* OLIVER LEAMAN
MEDIEVAL PHILOSOPHY *Edited by* A. S. MCGRADE
MERLEAU-PONTY *Edited by* TAYLOR CARMAN *and* MARK HANSEN
MILL *Edited by* JOHN SKORUPSKI
MONTAIGNE *Edited by* ULLRICH LANGER
NEWTON *Edited by* I. BERNARD COHEN *and* GEORGE E. SMITH
NIETZSCHE *Edited by* BERND MAGNUS *and* KATHLEEN HIGGINS
OCKHAM *Edited by* PAUL VINCENT SPADE
PASCAL *Edited by* NICHOLAS HAMMOND
PEIRCE *Edited by* CHERYL MISAK
PLATO *Edited by* RICHARD KRAUT
PLOTINUS *Edited by* LLOYD P. GERSON
QUINE *Edited by* ROGER F. GIBSON
RAWLS *Edited by* SAMUEL FREEMAN
THOMAS REID *Edited by* TERENCE CUNEO *and* RENE VAN WOUDENBERG
ROUSSEAU *Edited by* PATRICK RILEY
BERTRAND RUSSELL *Edited by* NICHOLAS GRIFFIN
SARTRE *Edited by* CHRISTINA HOWELLS
SCHOPENHAUER *Edited by* CHRISTOPHER JANAWAY
THE SCOTTISH ENLIGHTENMENT *Edited by* ALEXANDER BROADIE

ADAM SMITH *Edited by* KNUD HAAKONSSEN
SPINOZA *Edited by* DON GARRETT
THE STOICS *Edited by* BRAD INWOOD
TOCQUEVILLE *Edited by* CHERYL B. WELCH
WITTGENSTEIN *Edited by* HANS SLUGA *and* DAVID STERN

The Cambridge Companion to EARLY MODERN PHILOSOPHY

Edited by Donald Rutherford
University of California, San Diego

CAMBRIDGE UNIVERSITY PRESS
Cambridge, New York, Melbourne, Madrid, Cape Town, Singapore, São Paulo

CAMBRIDGE UNIVERSITY PRESS
The Edinburgh Building, Cambridge CB2 2RU, UK

Published in the United States of America by Cambridge University Press, New York

www.cambridge.org
Information on this title: www.cambridge.org/9780521529624

First published 2006

Printed in the United Kingdom at the University Press, Cambridge

A catalogue record for this book is available from the British Library

ISBN-13 978-0-521-82242-8 hardback
ISBN-10 0-521-82242-4 hardback
ISBN-13 978-0-521-52962-4 paperback
ISBN-10 0-521-52962-X paperback

CONTENTS

FIGURES

NOTES ON CONTRIBUTORS

STEPHEN DARWALL is John Dewey Collegiate Professor of Philosophy at the University of Michigan. He has written widely in moral philosophy and the history of ethics, and is the author of *Impartial Reason* (1983), *The British Moralists and the Internal "Ought": 1640–1740* (1995), *Philosophical Ethics* (1998), *Welfare and Rational Care* (2002), and *The Second-Person Standpoint* (2006).

DENNIS DES CHENE is Professor of Philosophy at Washington University in St. Louis. He is the author of *Physiologia: Natural Philosophy in Late Aristotelian and Cartesian Thought* (1996), *Life's Form: Late Aristotelian Conceptions of the Soul* (2000), and *Spirits and Clocks: Machine and Organism in Descartes* (2001).

STEPHEN GAUKROGER is Professor of History of Philosophy and History of Science and ARC Professorial Fellow at the University of Sydney. He is author of *Explanatory Structures* (1978), *Cartesian Logic* (1985), *Descartes: An Intellectual Biography* (1995), *Francis Bacon and the Transformation of Early-Modern Philosophy* (2001), *Descartes' System of Natural Philosophy* (2002), and *The Emergence of a Scientific Culture in the West, 1210–1685: Science and the Making of Modernity*, volume I (forthcoming).

SUSAN JAMES is Professor of Philosophy at the Birkbeck School of Philosophy, University of London. She is author of *The Content of Social Explanation* (1984) and *Passion and Action: The Emotions in Seventeenth-Century Philosophy* (1997), and editor (with Gisela Bock) of *Beyond Equality and Difference* (1992).

NICHOLAS JOLLEY is Professor of Philosophy at the University of California, Irvine. He is the author of *Leibniz and Locke: A Study of the New Essays on Human Understanding* (1984), *The Light of the Soul: Theories of Ideas in Leibniz, Malebranche, and Descartes* (1990), *Locke: His Philosophical Thought* (1999), and *Leibniz* (2005). He is the editor of *The Cambridge Companion to Leibniz* (1995) and co-editor of Nicolas Malebranche's *Dialogues on Metaphysics and on Religion* (1997).

THOMAS M. LENNON is Professor of Philosophy at the University of Western Ontario. He is the author of *The Battle of Gods and Giants: The Legacies of Descartes and Gassendi, 1655–1715* (1993), *Reading Bayle* (1999), and (with Patricia Easton) *The Cartesian Empiricism of François Bayle* (1992), editor and translator of *Against Cartesian Philosophy: Pierre-Daniel Huet's Censura Philosophiae Cartesianae* (2003), and (with P. J. Olscamp) Nicolas Malebranche, *The Search after Truth* and *Elucidations of the Search after Truth* (1997), and editor of *Cartesian Views: Essays Presented to Richard A. Watson* (2003).

MICHAEL LOSONSKY is Professor of Philosophy at Colorado State University. He is author of *Linguistic Turns in Modern Philosophy* (2005) and *Enlightenment and Action from Descartes to Kant: Passionate Thought* (2001), and editor of Wilhelm von Humboldt's *On Language* (1999). He is co-author (with Heimir Geirsson) of *Beginning Metaphysics* (1998) and co-editor (with Geirsson) of *Readings in Language and Mind* (1996).

DONALD RUTHERFORD is Professor of Philosophy at the University of California, San Diego. He is the author of *Leibniz and the Rational Order of Nature* (1995), editor (with J. A. Cover) of *Leibniz: Nature and Freedom* (2005), and editor and translator (with Brandon Look) of *The Leibniz–Des Bosses Correspondence* (2007).

TAD SCHMALTZ is Professor of Philosophy at Duke University. He is the author of *Malebranche's Theory of the Soul* (1996) and *Radical Cartesianism* (2002), and has edited *Receptions of Descartes* (2005). He currently is editor of the *Journal of the History of Philosophy*.

J. B. SCHNEEWIND, Professor Emeritus of Philosophy, Johns Hopkins University, is the author of *Sidgwick's Ethics and Victorian Moral Philosophy* (1977) and *The Invention of Autonomy* (1998). He has also edited an anthology, *Moral Philosophy from Montaigne to Kant* (1990), and written numerous articles on the history of ethics.

A. JOHN SIMMONS is Commonwealth Professor of Philosophy and Professor of Law at the University of Virginia. He has been an editor of the journal *Philosophy & Public Affairs* since 1982. He is the author of *Moral Principles and Political Obligations* (1979), *The Lockean Theory of Rights* (1992), *On the Edge of Anarchy* (1993), *Justification and Legitimacy* (2000), *Is There A Duty to Obey the Law? For and Against* (with C. H. Wellman) (2005), and many articles in political, moral, and legal theory. He has also edited *International Ethics* (1985) and *Punishment* (1995).

M. W. F. STONE is Professor of Philosophy at the Higher Institute of Philosophy, Catholic University, Leuven, Belgium. He is the author of many articles on late medieval and early modern scholasticism, and a forthcoming two-volume history of casuistry, *The Subtle Arts of Casuistry: An Essay in History of Moral Philosophy*. His present research is on ideas of grace and nature in early modern philosophy.

PREFACE

This *Cambridge Companion* aims to serve as an introduction and guide to what has come to be known as "early modern philosophy"– roughly, philosophy spanning the period between the end of the sixteenth century and the end of the eighteenth century, or, in terms of figures, Montaigne through Kant. Its intended audience includes both students of philosophy and those with a general interest in the period who wish to know more about how philosophy relates to contemporary developments in science, religion, and politics. At the same time, it is hoped that the chapters are framed in such a way that even specialists will be offered a fresh look at the philosophical thought of early modern Europe.

Many people have contributed to the production of this *Companion*. Besides the individual authors, to whom I owe a special debt, I would like to thank several anonymous reviewers for the Press, who provided useful suggestions about the contents of the volume. In early work on it, I was aided by Matthew Kisner; valuable assistance was provided later by Kristen Irwin, who also collaborated on the short biographies that are included as an appendix. Helpful advice was offered along the way by Richard Arneson, David Brink, Daniel Garber, Steven Nadler, and Alison Simmons. Throughout the editorial process, Hilary Gaskin has been a source of encouragement and good counsel, for which I am grateful.

My greatest thanks are reserved, as always, for Madeleine Picciotto, who created space, time, and other conditions for the possibility of this book.

ABBREVIATIONS

Full references appear in the bibliography under Primary Sources.

BACON

New Org.	*New Organon* (Bacon 2000)

BOYLE

Origin	*The Origin of Forms and Qualities According to the Corpuscular Hypothesis* (in Boyle 1991)

DESCARTES

AT	*Œuvres de Descartes*, Adam and Tannery (Descartes 1974–86)
CSM	*The Philosophical Writings of Descartes*, Cottingham et al. (Descartes 1984–91)
Passions	*The Passions of the Soul* (in AT XI and in CSM I)
Princ.	*Principles of Philosophy* (in AT VIIIA [Latin] and IXB [French] and in CSM I)

HOBBES

Lev.	*Leviathan* (Hobbes 1994)

HUME

Treatise	*A Treatise on Human Nature* (Hume 2000)
Enquiry	*Enquiry concerning Human Understanding* (in Hume 1975)

KANT

Ges. Schr.	*Gesammelte Schriften*, Königlich preussischen (later: Berlin) Akademie der Wissenschaften (Kant 1910–).

LEIBNIZ

AG	*Philosophical Essays*, Ariew and Garber (Leibniz 1989)
GP	*Die philosophischen Schriften*, Gerhardt (Leibniz 1875–90)
L	*Philosophical Papers and Letters*, Loemker (Leibniz 1969)
M	*The Leibniz–Arnauld Correspondence*, Mason (Leibniz 1967)
Discourse	*Discourse on Metaphysics* (in AG and L)
New Ess.	*New Essays on Human Understanding* (Leibniz 1981)
Theod.	*Theodicy: Essays on the Goodness of God, the Freedom of Man and the Origin of Evil* (Leibniz 1952)

LOCKE

Essay	*An Essay concerning Human Understanding* (Locke 1975)

MALEBRANCHE

OC	*Œuvres complètes*, Robinet (Malebranche 1958–84)
Dial.	*Dialogues on Metaphysics and on Religion* (Malebranche 1997a)
Search	*The Search after Truth* (Malebranche 1997b)
TNG	*Treatise on Nature and Grace* (Malebranche 1992)

SPINOZA

Ethics	*Ethics Demonstrated in Geometrical Order* (in Spinoza 1985)
TTP	*Theological-Political Treatise* (Spinoza 1998)

SUÁREZ

Disp. met.	*Disputationes metaphysicae* (in Suárez 1856–78, XXV–XXVI)

DONALD RUTHERFORD

Introduction

The seventeenth and eighteenth centuries have long been recognized as an especially fruitful period in the history of Western philosophy. Most often this has been associated with the achievements of a handful of great thinkers: the so-called "rationalists" (Descartes, Spinoza, Leibniz) and "empiricists" (Locke, Berkeley, Hume), whose inquiries culminate in Kant's "Critical philosophy."[1] These canonical figures have been celebrated for the depth and rigor of their treatments of perennial philosophical questions, concerning, for example, existence, modality, causality, knowledge, obligation, and sovereignty, as well as for their efforts to push philosophy in new directions, challenging many of the assumptions of ancient and medieval philosophy. In this connection, it has been argued that epistemology assumes a new significance in the early modern period as philosophers strive to define the conditions and limits of human knowledge. Yet early modern philosophers make major contributions in almost every area of philosophy, and in many cases their conclusions continue to serve as starting points for present-day debates. The chapters in this *Companion* are designed to acquaint the reader with the most important developments in early modern philosophy and to point the way toward more advanced studies in the field.

THE NEW HISTORY OF EARLY MODERN PHILOSOPHY

Few would challenge the notion that the early modern period is a rich and even revolutionary era in the history of philosophy. Nevertheless, scholarship published during the last thirty years has led to a revision in our conception of the scope and significance of early modern philosophy. Four developments are noteworthy, all of them associated with an increased emphasis on a contexualized understanding of the practice of philosophy and of the knowledge it produces.

First, historians have challenged the assumption that early modern philosophy can be adequately comprehended in terms of the major published works of its most famous figures. It is now a commonplace that to understand a philosopher's views – expressed in the well-honed sentences of a book such as Descartes's *Meditations* or Kant's *Critique of Pure Reason* – requires understanding them in relation to the entire corpus of the philosopher's writings, published and unpublished. Correspondences, preliminary drafts, and subsequent revisions of published texts are all seen as important sources of evidence. In addition, it is increasingly acknowledged that our understanding of a canonical text can be deepened by reading it in conjunction with the works of a philosopher's immediate predecessors and contemporaries – works that often supply an illuminating background for its interpretation.[2] In short, even if a published treatise carries an imprimatur as the authoritative expression of a philosopher's position on a given topic, understanding that position often is facilitated, and sometimes is only possible, by relating it to other pieces of textual evidence.

A second and more profound challenge has targeted the privileged status accorded to the philosophers making up the traditional canon of early modern philosophy. In recent years, the cast of leading characters has expanded to include an array of figures who are significant thinkers in their own right and whose thought intersects at vital points with that of the canonical seven. These figures include Michel de Montaigne, Francisco Suárez, Hugo Grotius, Francis Bacon, Pierre Gassendi, Thomas Hobbes, Henry More, Ralph Cudworth, Anne Conway, Antoine Arnauld, Nicolas Malebranche, Blaise Pascal, Pierre Bayle, Samuel Pufendorf, Francis Hutcheson, Thomas Reid, Adam Smith, Jean-Jacques Rousseau, and Christian Wolff – to mention only some of the authors whose writings have been subject to intensive analysis in the secondary literature. By attending to their works, historians have arrived at fuller and more nuanced accounts of philosophy's development in the early modern period.

One result of these efforts to map more accurately the landscape of early modern philosophy has been a growing skepticism concerning traditional interpretative categories (e.g. "rationalist" versus "empiricist"). Such dichotomies have been criticized as inadequate for understanding the relationships among the views of early modern philosophers. Moreover, they have tended to reflect a bias in the history of philosophy toward epistemology and metaphysics and away from ethics, political philosophy, and theology. Recent scholarship has sought to counter this bias both through detailed studies of the practical philosophy of the early modern period, and through studies that aim to deliver a synoptic picture of the views of particular thinkers, emphasizing the close connections between, for example, metaphysical theories and ethical theories.[3]

Finally, the development of early modern philosophy increasingly has been recognized to be inseparable from, and in many cases dependent upon, a larger set of intellectual and cultural changes, which include the emergence of modern natural science, theological conflicts within and between the Catholic and Protestant churches, and the movement toward the modern nation-state. Within the early modern period, philosophy retains a distinct identity as a discipline whose concerns are continuous with those of ancient and medieval philosophy, on the one hand, and later modern philosophy, on the other. What the new history of early modern philosophy has stressed, however, is that abstract philosophical problems acquire a determinate content within a specific intellectual context – one that must be appreciated in order to understand the theories and arguments of the philosophers in question. In most cases one finds no sharp line dividing philosophical debates concerning, for example, the nature of matter or freedom of the will, and related debates in physics or theology. Thus, again, one is forced to take a more expansive view of the relevant textual evidence than previously was common in the history of philosophy.

The present volume reflects these priorities of the new history of early modern philosophy. Its focus is the changing shape of philosophical inquiry in the early modern period, with emphasis placed on the transformation of concepts and doctrines inherited from ancient and medieval philosophy and the arguments used to justify these transformations. Unlike other guides to the philosophy of the period, this *Cambridge Companion* is not organized by individual philosophers but rather by areas of inquiry. Following an opening chapter that looks broadly at the character and defining tensions of early modern philosophy (Donald Rutherford), the volume proceeds systematically through chapters dedicated to the methodological and conceptual foundations of natural science (Stephen Gaukroger; Dennis Des Chene), metaphysics (Nicholas Jolley), philosophy of mind (Tad Schmaltz), logic and language (Michael Losonksy), ethics (Susan James; Stephen Darwall), political philosophy (A. John Simmons), theology (Thomas M. Lennon), and the enduring vitality of scholastic thought (M. W. F. Stone). A final chapter looks ahead to the end of the early modern period through the lens of the Enlightenment philosophy of Kant (J. B. Schneewind).

THE PHILOSOPHICAL LIFE

Early modern philosophers come in many stripes.[4] Some were university teachers, some were not. Some were clerics, some were not. As one might expect, almost all were men, but a number of women are now recognized as making notable contributions to the philosophy of the early modern period.[5] With the exception of Spinoza, all the major figures of seventeenth- and eighteenth-century philosophy were professed Christians, though what exactly such a profession meant was a point of contention, reflecting the continued prominence of religious discord and theological debate in the period.

Although some early modern philosophers chose to pursue careers as university teachers, many were wary of following such a path for fear of the restrictions that might be placed on their freedom to philosophize. Spinoza famously turned down the offer of a professorship in Heidelberg for this reason, choosing to support himself as a lens grinder. In the middle of the eighteenth century, Christian Wolff was forced to flee his position at Halle, because rumors had spread to the king of the dangerous political consequences that could be inferred from his doctrines. For the most part, it was thought that a philosophical life could best be pursued outside the university. In some cases, this was made possible by a private income (Descartes, Shaftesbury); in others it depended upon securing a religious office (Gassendi, Malebranche, Berkeley) or other employment (Bacon, Hobbes, Leibniz) that left one with sufficient time and freedom to pursue one's own reflections.

For those philosophers who eschewed a university career, philosophy was for the most part a solitary endeavor. From the beginning of the seventeenth century, however, concerted attempts were made to share ideas and intelligence about the latest developments in natural philosophy – a pattern of cooperation that culminated in the establishment of the first scientific societies in Florence, Paris, and London. Prior to this, Marin Mersenne had convened gatherings that brought together many of the leading thinkers in Paris, including at different times Descartes, Gassendi, Hobbes, and Grotius.[6] Mersenne also carried on an extensive correspondence that connected scholars from across Europe, an activity in which he was followed by Henry Oldenburg, secretary of the Royal Society of London during the 1660s, and by Leibniz. In these ways, philosophers who were not university teachers were nonetheless drawn together in informal intellectual communities.

The world of early modern philosophy was an intimate one. Through his friend Nicolas-Claude Fabri de Peiresc, Gassendi obtained one of Galileo's new telescopes, with which he made a series of important observations. In 1634, while traveling through Italy, Hobbes paid a personal visit to Galileo, then under house arrest near Florence. Through the offices of Mersenne, Descartes's *Meditations* were published in 1641 with objections by Arnauld, Gassendi, and Hobbes. When Leibniz arrived in Paris in 1672, he made the acquaintance of Malebranche and Arnauld. On departing Paris four years later, he spent a week in discussion with Spinoza in Holland. In his early life, he had written to a then elderly Hobbes; he engaged in important correspondences with Arnauld and Wolff; he wrote books responding to works by Bayle and Locke; and near the end of his life he was drawn into a bitter feud with Newton over their rival claims to priority in the discovery of the calculus. Such patterns of contact continued in the eighteenth century with philosophers such as Hume, who composed much of his *Treatise of Human Nature* in France at La Flèche, where Descartes had studied over a century earlier. Hume was a friend of the Scottish philosophers Francis Hutcheson and Adam Smith, and late in life made an abortive attempt to arrange refuge for Jean-Jacques Rousseau in England.

Despite the largely solitary nature of their own activity, then, philosophers in the seventeenth and eighteenth centuries actively studied, disagreed with, and responded to the views of their contemporaries and recent predecessors. This makes the period an especially attractive one in which to study the development of philosophical ideas through the active engagement of thinkers with one another. Such an approach has served as a starting point for much recent research. Moving beyond the question of whether a given philosopher may or may not have read the works of an influential precursor, historians of philosophy have endeavored to disentangle and reconstruct lines of argument that link the views of successive thinkers, illuminating in this way the sources of philosophical creativity and the standards of rationality that guide the progress of philosophy.

LOOKING AHEAD

The seventeenth century is a period of sweeping intellectual change. From the groundbreaking works of Bacon and Galileo to the crowning achievement of Newton's *Principia*, the century ushers in a radically new conception of the natural world and the place of human beings in it. Equally dramatic are the searching reexaminations of the foundations of law, liberty, and political sovereignty carried out by such thinkers as Grotius, Hobbes, and Locke. Philosophy is transformed at every level by these developments. Well-entrenched assumptions about causality, matter, mind, knowledge, language, law, and even God are subject to reappraisal and in many cases revision. The result is the body of philosophical theories we today think of as the first examples of early modern philosophy, distinguishing them in this way from the inherited synthesis of ancient Greek philosophy and Christianity that had prevailed to that point.

Many of the chapters in this *Companion* begin from a view of early modern philosophy as defined by the efforts of early seventeenth-century thinkers to throw off the "yoke of Aristotle." Often, it was not the philosophy of Aristotle himself whom these thinkers were reacting against, but a version of scholastic Aristotelianism (or "scholasticism") which prevailed in university teaching through the seventeenth century, and in some locations well into the eighteenth. Fostered by the innovators themselves (e.g. Bacon, Hobbes, Descartes), the dominant narrative of the history of early modern philosophy remains that of a revolutionary movement that aims to illuminate the darkness of a sterile orthodoxy with the sharp light of a new critical reason.

The chapters by Donald Rutherford ("Innovation and orthodoxy in early modern philosophy") and M. W. F. Stone ("Scholastic schools and early modern philosophy") argue in different ways for the need to qualify this narrative. Rutherford shows that, with a few exceptions, the leading innovators of early modern philosophy were committed to maintaining a harmony between the conclusions of philosophical reason and the tenets of Christianity. However radical their challenges to Aristotelian natural philosophy, logic, and epistemology, they sought to preserve the compatibility of their views with Christian orthodoxy, much as their medieval predecessors had done. From the other direction, Stone details how early modern scholastic philosophy is far from the moribund tradition that it is often depicted as being. There is considerable innovation and critical reflection here as well, highlighted by the widely influential works of the Jesuits Luis Molina and Francisco Suárez. Thus, it is an oversimplification to think of early modern philosophy exclusively in terms of the replacing of the old by the new. Other chapters extend this picture of the complexity of the play of the old versus the new in the early modern period. In the apt image offered by Nicholas Jolley in his chapter "Metaphysics," early modern philosophers often can be seen as delivering new wine in old bottles – bottles that later are found to hold with difficulty the potent vintage that has been poured into them.

A further point to keep in mind is that during the early modern period, 'philosophy' does not designate a unitary enterprise. Both diachronically and synchronically, it is a constellation of loosely related investigations of fundamental questions about nature, humanity, and God. We can helpfully distinguish three stages in the evolution of early modern philosophy, corresponding roughly to the three centuries encompassed by the period. Extending a pattern that begins in the Italian Renaissance, the sixteenth century witnesses the reemergence of a host of ancient philosophical views – Platonism, Pyrrhonian skepticism, Epicureanism, Stoicism – along with a variety of attempts to synthesize their insights and to render them consistent with Christianity. The results are, by ancient lights, eclectic mixtures of ideas, but such mixtures make for a fertile soil from which grow many of the innovations of the next century.

The seventeenth century is best known for landmark advances in the understanding of nature, both those that we take as defining the beginnings of modern natural science and those that we see as characteristically philosophical reflections on the nature of mind and body, and the relation of human beings to God. Here the philosopher who casts the longest shadow is Descartes, whose views stimulate the inquiries of a succession of followers – Malebranche, Arnauld, Pascal, Spinoza, Leibniz – dedicated to extending or correcting his ideas. Yet Descartes is by no means the only seminal philosophical thinker of the seventeenth century. During his lifetime, his greatest rival is Gassendi, whose efforts to defend a Christianized Epicureanism help to make respectable the revival of ancient atomism. Equally significant are the contributions of Hobbes, a friend and ally of Gassendi, who along with Spinoza formulates the most serious challenge in the seventeenth century to received ideas in moral and political philosophy, and Locke, who is instrumental in moving philosophy's center of gravity away from speculative metaphysics.

Where the advances of seventeenth-century philosophy are often tentative attempts to reconceive the broadest outlines of reality, the eighteenth century builds on the secure foundations of Newton's unified theory of the mathematical structure of nature. For eighteenth-century philosophers, consequently, there is comparatively little mystery about the operation of nature. With this issue settled, the weight of philosophical interest shifts from theoretical philosophy to practical philosophy – above all, to the question of the grounds of the moral and political obligations of human beings. Underlying many of the debates of the century is the question that might be seen as the most significant legacy of early modern philosophy: Can human life, and whatever we judge to be of value about it, be defined independently of reference to God, conceived according to biblical teaching as humanity's creator, lawgiver, and judge? The previous centuries had revealed the deep and bloody rifts that could open between men who disagreed about religion. Consequently, the motivation to rise above these differences and to understand human beings in purely secular terms was strong. How precisely to do this, however, was by no means obvious. Can human beings be understood merely as a part of nature, as Spinoza had suggested already at the end of the seventeenth century? Is there a nontheological yet universal conception of reason in terms of which we can define the common moral identity and value of human beings? These are the questions with which the leading philosophers of the Enlightenment struggled, and to a large extent they remain questions for us today.

NOTES

1 For a recent study that conforms to this pattern, see Bennett 2001.
2 See the contributions to the Cambridge Philosophical Texts in Context series, beginning with Ariew, Cottingham, and Sorell 1998.
3 Renewed emphasis on the practical philosophy of the early modern period has been associated especially with the work of J. B. Schneewind (1998, 2003, 2004). For other contributions, see Tuck 1982, 1993; Darwall 1995; Haakonssen 1996; Krasnoff and Brender 2006.
4 Over the past decade a number of excellent biographies and biographical studies of early modern philosophers have appeared in English: Gaukroger 1995; Martinich 1999; Nadler 1999; Kuehn 2001; Malcolm 2002.
5 See the new editions of works by Anne Conway (1996) and Margaret Cavendish (2001), as well as the texts collected in Atherton 1994.
6 Similar informal intellectual circles, which served as forerunners of later scientific societies, existed in other European countries. See Lux 1991; Feingold 1991.

DONALD RUTHERFORD

1 Innovation and orthodoxy in early modern philosophy

A NEW BEGINNING?

What we know today as early modern philosophy was forged in the opening years of the seventeenth century, in the writings of such thinkers as Francis Bacon, Thomas Hobbes, and René Descartes. We think of this period as the beginning of modern philosophy in part because these philosophers saw themselves as the vanguard of an intellectual revolution, whose goal was to break with the philosophy of the past. Here they identified their most important target as Aristotle, whose teachings in logic and metaphysics had dominated educated opinion in Europe through most of the previous millennium. Almost all of the best-known philosophers and scientists of the seventeenth century saw Aristotle's views as a significant impediment to the advance of knowledge, and believed that progress could only begin once the edifice of Aristotle's system had been razed and philosophy could begin to rebuild on solid foundations. The metaphor of demolishing the old to make room for the new is familiar to students of philosophy from Descartes's First Meditation, but the English philosopher Francis Bacon had employed it some twenty years before Descartes. In his *New Organon* (another allusion to Aristotle, whose logical works were known as the *organon*, or "instrument"), Bacon declares: "It is futile to expect a great advancement in the sciences from overlaying and implanting new things on the old; a new beginning has to be made from the lowest foundations, unless one is content to go round in circles for ever, with meagre, almost negligible, progress" (*New Org.*, I.31).[1]

Among leading thinkers of the seventeenth century, the belief took root that progress was at last possible in philosophy, but that it required a thorough sweeping out of old patterns of thought. The progress that Bacon and others envisioned is closely associated with the emergence of modern natural science: empirically supported knowledge of the structure and laws of nature, and techniques for manipulating nature so as to produce beneficial effects for human beings. Collectively, these innovations make up what has come to be known as "the Scientific Revolution."[2] It is important, however, to avoid anachronism in our use of the term "science." Prior to the seventeenth century, there was no clear distinction between philosophy and science. Science takes its name from the Latin word *scientia*, which signifies a systematic body of knowledge such as was traditionally sought by philosophy. What we know as natural science was originally simply a branch of philosophy: natural philosophy. This way of characterizing the discipline survives well into the seventeenth century, as illustrated by Hobbes, who follows the ancients in defining "philosophy" *or* "science" as demonstrative knowledge concerning the causes of things, and then draws a division within this highest category of knowledge between "natural philosophy" and "civil philosophy" (see Fig. 1).

Accepting this point about the classification of knowledge, the fact remains that many of the most important intellectual breakthroughs of the early modern period occur in the area of natural philosophy and that these breakthroughs are responsible for redefining the discipline of philosophy. By the end of the seventeenth century, a distinction had begun to emerge between, on the one hand, natural science, characterized by experimentation, measurement, and mathematical representations of natural order, and, on the other, philosophy, conceived more or less traditionally as a speculative discipline. Although Newton's *magnum opus* is entitled *Mathematical Principles of Natural Philosophy*, Newton himself is one of the people most responsible for drawing a methodological boundary between natural science and speculative philosophy. The boundary is marked by his famous assertion "hypotheses non fingo" ("I do not feign hypotheses"). For Newton, the domain of science, or "experimental philosophy," is confined to explanatory propositions that can be "deduced from the phenomena." What cannot be deduced in this way is merely a hypothesis, and "hypotheses, whether metaphysical or physical, or based on occult qualities, or mechanical, have no place in experimental philosophy."[3]

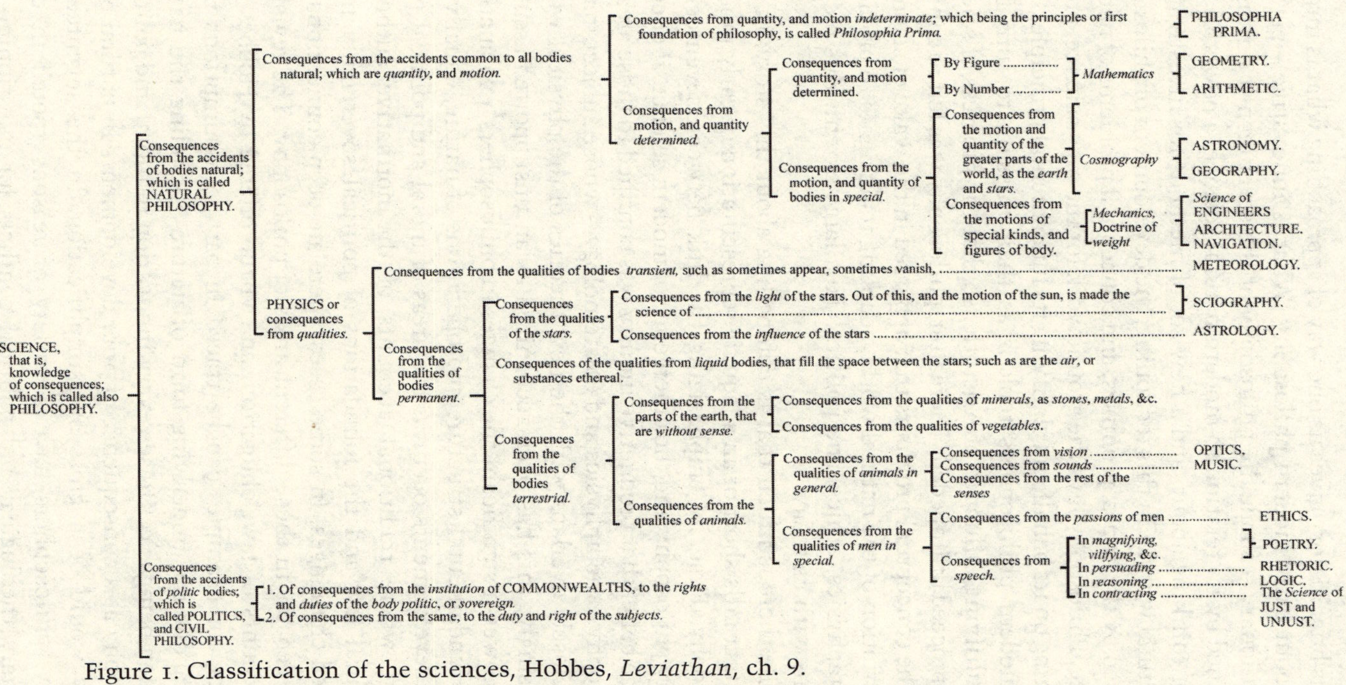

Figure 1. Classification of the sciences, Hobbes, *Leviathan*, ch. 9.

This brief history gives us one way of approaching what is innovative about early modern philosophy. What is innovative – perhaps revolutionary – about the philosophy of the seventeenth century is explained by its relation to modern natural science: a powerful new way of thinking about, and a new set of methods for investigating, the natural world. On this reckoning, the development of philosophy is driven by the hopes, promises, and conceptual problems of natural science. Philosophy lays the groundwork for the new science, propagandizing on its behalf and clarifying its fundamental principles. The first modern philosophers took it as their mission to turn back the stultifying influence of Aristotle, so that the progress of science could proceed unimpeded. Thereafter, philosophy was left to contend with the conceptual problems that appeared in the wake of science's redescription of the natural world, adapting its insights to problems in metaphysics, ethics, and politics. To a large extent, this picture remains with us today.

While there is much that is compelling about this story, in two respects it falls short of an adequate representation of early modern philosophy. First, by emphasizing the link between seventeenth-century philosophy and the emergence of modern science, it encourages the belief that productive inquiry was confined to those areas of philosophy – metaphysics and epistemology – whose subject matter most closely overlaps with the new theories of the physical world. Increasingly, this has been recognized as an unsupported assumption. However significant the changes in philosophers' explanations of the fundamental structure and operations of nature, equally decisive developments occur in the areas of moral and political philosophy, where traditional accounts of the normative authority of natural law and the foundations of political sovereignty meet repeated challenges. In some cases, there are deep connections between debates in these different areas of philosophy. The revisionary accounts of law, obligation, and virtue offered by Hobbes and Spinoza, for example, can be traced in part to assumptions they make about the underlying form of nature, including the nature of human beings. Yet to see every innovation in moral and political philosophy as a consequence of prior developments in natural philosophy would be a gross oversimplification. In the seventeenth century, philosophers have a variety of reasons rooted in contemporary theological and political conflicts for questioning the coherence of traditional explanations of normative authority. Independent of contemporary developments in the natural sciences, these supply ample impetus for philosophy's movement in new directions.[4]

The account of early modern philosophy as making a radical break with its past – whether as a result of the new science or for other reasons – must also be qualified. While some of its best-known figures describe their projects in revolutionary terms, recent scholarship has documented the extent to which even these philosophers remain tied to the ideas and arguments of their predecessors. Philosophical theories are rarely, if ever, entirely new creations. More often, they are built with bricks and timber scavenged from philosophy's past. Thus, while the innovators depicted themselves as razing the edifice of Aristotle's system in order to begin anew, what they built in its place was a structure assembled with materials borrowed from other ancient schools and from Aristotle himself. In no case was there a simple rupture with the past – the old replaced with an entirely novel way of thinking.

Furthermore, there was by no means universal support in the seventeenth century for the idea that philosophy needed to move in a radically new direction. Opposing those philosophers who argued for a sharp break with the past were others who urged a continuity between ancient and modern thought.[5] For the latter, contemporary developments in natural philosophy could, and should, be incorporated into a theoretical framework that upheld traditional teachings, particularly in the areas of theology and moral and political philosophy. For these philosophers, nothing was more disturbing than the possibility that innovations in natural philosophy might lead to the undermining of the ancient model, shared by almost all Western religious and philosophical traditions, of an orderly universe, ruled by an omnipotent and provident deity.

Such conservative tendencies play a critical role in shaping philosophical debate in the seventeenth century. As we shall see, it is a period in which massive effort is devoted to holding on to the past by interpreting the concepts and theories of the new science in terms of traditional metaphysical and theological categories. In many cases this effort is exerted by the very same individuals who contribute significantly to the emergence of modern science. The lesson we may take from this is that the development of early modern philosophy cannot be explained solely in terms of the new picture of nature that forms the basis of seventeenth-century natural science. Most philosophers of the period, in fact, were determined to understand the new science in a way that would render it consistent with a traditional, biblically based conception of human beings and their dependence on God. The exception is a handful of radical thinkers – above all, Spinoza – who, working through the implications of the ideas that precipitated the new science, as well as novel conceptions of moral and political authority, were prepared to challenge the interpretative framework of Judeo-Christian theology as a starting point for the understanding of nature and human society.

THE MEDIEVAL SYNTHESIS

The innovations of early modern philosophy occur against the backdrop of a rich tradition of medieval thought, whose foundations were laid in the thirteenth century in the writings of Thomas Aquinas. Aquinas is by no means the only medieval philosopher whose views are consequential for the development of early modern philosophy; nevertheless, the scholastic Aristotelianism against which early modern philosophers react is most clearly traceable to Aquinas's comprehensive synthesis of Aristotle's natural philosophy and Christian theology. Aquinas's singular achievement was to show how, through a division of intellectual labor, these two very different systems of thought could be seen as supporting one another. The key was to accept that Aristotle was generally right about philosophy and the details of the natural world, and the Catholic church right about matters spiritual and divine.

Three features of Aristotle's natural philosophy are relevant for our purposes. First, Aristotle conceives of the cosmos as consisting of a closed set of concentric spheres, at the center of which is the earth. A sharp distinction is drawn between the properties of things enclosed within the innermost sphere, the sublunary world, and those located on outer spheres, celestial objects such as planets and fixed stars. Celestial objects are eternal and unchanging; those that move, move with perfect circular motions around the earth. By contrast, objects in the sublunary world are subject to generation and corruption, and move with a natural motion that is rectilinear and perpendicular to the earth's surface.

Second, on Aristotle's account, all natural substances (rocks, plants, animals, people) are *hylomorphic*, or composites of form and matter. Matter is the stuff from which everything is made. By itself, however, matter has no specific characteristics; it is "pure potentiality." In each case, a substance's qualities are supplied by form, which makes it the kind of thing that it is. Form gives a substance its characteristic shape, properties, and power to act. Aristotle identifies the latter power with the substance's *nature*, which is "a sort of source and cause of change and remaining unchanged in that to which it belongs primarily and of itself" (*Physics* 192b20–22). Every kind of substance has a specific nature, which is responsible for its being able to do whatever it can do, from purely physical motion to sensation and rational thought. A substance's form also determines that its natural motions have an intrinsic end or goal (*telos*). Rocks naturally fall downward to the earth; fire rises upward from the earth. Plants naturally grow toward the sun and reproduce themselves through seed. Animals naturally move toward what they sense as agreeable to their constitution and away from what they sense as disagreeable to it, and like plants, they naturally seek to reproduce themselves.

Third, according to Aristotle, human beings are hylomorphic substances that are distinguished from other animals by the possession of rationality. Because we possess the power of reason, we are able to regulate our actions by choosing to act or not act on the basis of rational conceptions of our good, and we are able to know and contemplate the order of the universe. Through philosophy, Aristotle believes, we can come to understand reflectively that our highest good, or happiness, is a life of rational activity, that is, a life spent exercising theoretical and practical reason.

The details of Aristotle's philosophy are of concern to us only insofar as they inform the view of the natural world that modern philosophy reacts against. Christian theology was able to take on almost all of Aristotle's philosophy, with the exception of the eternality of matter (which the doctrine of creation *ex nihilo* excludes) and the limitation of the human good to rational activity. On the account defended by Aquinas, only God can be identified with the highest or unqualified good; hence human happiness must consist in union with God, which can be achieved only in another, nontemporal life. For the rest, Aquinas and other medieval thinkers saw Aristotle's philosophy as fitting coherently with the Christian view that human beings are composed of an immaterial soul and a material body, and that all things have been created by God to fulfill a natural purpose within a well-organized, hierarchical cosmos. At the apex of this hierarchy are human beings, who dominate the rest of creation in a manner analogous to the way in which they themselves are ruled by God. Authority for this conception of the place of human beings in creation is found in Genesis 1:26, which serves as a touchstone for philosophers throughout the early modern period: "And God said, Let us make man in our image, after our likeness: and let them have dominion over the fish of the sea, and over the fowl of the air, and over the cattle, and over the earth, and over every creeping thing that creepeth upon the earth."[6]

CHALLENGES TO THE SYNTHESIS

The union of Aristotle and Roman Catholic theology was extraordinarily successful in Europe, fostering a long period of fruitful inquiry. By the end of the fifteenth century, however, events were occurring that would eventually lead to its overthrow:

- The period we know as the Renaissance (roughly the fourteenth through sixteenth centuries) witnessed the rediscovery of a wide range of classical texts offering alternatives to Aristotle's views in natural philosophy, metaphysics, and ethics.
- The invention and rapid spread of mechanical printing in the late fifteenth century allowed for the dissemination of these new texts, containing a variety of unorthodox ideas, to a wider public.
- The Reformation, initiated by Martin Luther (1517), issued a fundamental challenge to the authority of the Roman Catholic church, which included an insistence on the right of individual conscience and political self-determination.
- Copernicus's heliocentric cosmology (1543) removed the earth from the center of the cosmos and rejected Aristotle's picture of the world as a closed set of concentric spheres.

These developments had a decisive impact on the course of Western philosophy, culminating in the groundbreaking works of Galileo, Bacon, Hobbes, and Descartes at the beginning of the seventeenth century. At every turn, however, efforts were made to isolate the impact of new ideas, so as to preserve the integrity of Christianity. Presented with an array of new texts containing competing claims of ancient wisdom, philosophers were forced to reexamine the support for Aristotle's teachings. Where criticisms were offered of Aristotle's views, they were invariably accompanied by attempts to demonstrate the compatibility of other pagan philosophies – Platonism, Stoicism, ancient skepticism, Epicureanism – with the revealed truth of Christianity. Given the content of the ancient views, some syntheses were more successful than others. As had happened in the past, numerous efforts were made to unite aspects of Platonism and Stoicism with Christian theology. While some rejected outright such attempts at accommodation – here the influence of Augustine was strongly felt – many found in Platonism and Stoicism productive avenues for articulating metaphysical and ethical theories which they believed to be consistent with the truth of Christian teachings. At the same time, specific theses, e.g. the Stoic conception of fate and the identification of God with the world soul, were almost universally judged to be at odds with the core tenets of Christianity; hence some attempt had to be made to minimize their role within any alternative, anti-Aristotelian theory of nature.[7]

Since the beginning of the sixteenth century, the revival of ancient skepticism had offered a powerful tool for loosening the grip of Aristotelian philosophy. In the eyes of some, it pointed the way toward a purified Christianity, founded on faith alone, independent of philosophical reason. For others, however, the unrestricted application of skeptical arguments could only result in the fostering of a broad climate of doubt, and hence the weakening of Christianity.[8] Even more unsettling from the point of view of Christian orthodoxy was the growing attraction of Epicurean philosophy, known principally through Lucretius' *De rerum natura*. In natural philosophy, Epicurean atomism represented a compelling alternative to Aristotle's hylomorphism, but it brought with it metaphysical commitments (a denial of divine providence and teleology, the thesis of the plurality of worlds) that many saw as antithetical to Christianity. Epicurean ethics, founded on the doctrine of hedonism, i.e. that pleasure is the only noninstrumental good and pain the only noninstrumental evil, was viewed by most Christians as a cover for moral corruption, despite the fact that Epicurus himself recommended a life of virtue as necessary for the attainment of the highest good: mental contentment or tranquility.[9]

The effort to turn back the perceived pernicious influences of Epicureanism, skepticism, and to a lesser extent Stoicism, was a central preoccupation of writers in the late sixteenth and early seventeenth centuries. The publications of Descartes's friend Marin Mersenne are prominent examples of such works, which help to establish a context within which Cartesianism can be represented as the only defensible alternative to Aristotelian natural philosophy.[10] Running parallel to this are the efforts of Pierre Gassendi to rehabilitate Epicureanism in a form acceptable to Christianity. Although Cartesianism is generally seen as triumphing in "the battle of the gods and giants," Gassendi succeeded in removing much of the opprobrium from the doctrines of atomism and hedonism, which subsequently acquire a new prominence in the philosophies of Hobbes and Locke.[11]

One of the most significant consequences of this vigorous play of ideas was a heightening of philosophy's awareness of issues concerning human knowledge. Broadly, this can be posed as a problem about the grounds of epistemic authority. What ultimately supports the claim of a given individual, text, or method to be an authoritative source of knowledge? Where rival authorities present themselves, how are the competing claims to be adjudicated? Throughout the sixteenth and seventeenth centuries, such concerns were bound up with larger moral and political issues. Most pointedly, the Reformation raised questions about the authority of religious teaching. Whom is one to believe in matters of scriptural interpretation: the Catholic church, one of the new Protestant sects, or one's own conscience – an inner testimony that answers to no human authority? But following closely on this was the question of the grounds for accepting religious figures as authorities in matters of government, law, or morality.[12]

In the seventeenth century, the same concern extends to the challenge mounted by the new science to the received synthesis of Aristotelian natural philosophy and Christian theology. The issue initially arises in the wake of Copernicus's heliocentric hypothesis, which disputes Aristotle's conception of the cosmos. Soon, however, the question is applied across the board: What case in general can be made for Aristotelian philosophy as against the array of new (and old) ideas that challenge its supremacy? The attempt to address this question is a primary motivation for the development of early modern philosophy: its efforts to articulate foundational concepts of nature, methods by which reliable knowledge can be obtained, and the aptness of the human mind for acquiring such knowledge. Nevertheless, in all of these inquiries the answers philosophy gives continue to be subject to the test of religious orthodoxy – even while the demands of orthodoxy themselves are as fiercely debated as any other claims to authority.

RECONCILING SCIENCE AND RELIGION: GALILEO AND BACON

The imperative to accommodate the innovations of the new science to Christianity is felt throughout seventeenth-century philosophy. Yet it manifests itself in different ways, depending upon the interests and objectives of the philosopher and the religious context in which he finds himself. This can be briefly illustrated by considering two of the most influential proponents of the new science, Galileo and Bacon.

The question of authority lies at the heart of Galileo's confrontation with the Catholic church. In 1616, following a trial conducted by the Congregation of the Holy Office, the church publicly censured two key propositions of Copernicanism:

- The sun is the center of the world, and is completely immobile by local motion.
- The earth is not the center of the world and is not immobile, but moves as a whole and also with a diurnal motion.

The judgment on the first of these propositions was particularly harsh. It was deemed "formally heretical," because it contradicted the approved (literal) meaning given to certain scriptural passages by the church. In the background to this verdict was the declaration of the Council of Trent in 1546 that only the church had the authority to interpret the "true sense and meaning" of scripture. The immediate targets of this assertion were Protestant reformers who claimed for themselves the right to interpret scripture as they saw fit, but the point applied equally to those who, in affirming the truth of the Copernican hypothesis, thereby implied that the relevant parts of scripture had to be understood differently from how the church had declared them to be understood.[13]

Immediately following the 1616 condemnation of Copernicanism, the church had extracted from Galileo a promise not to "hold, teach or defend in any way whatsoever, verbally or in writing" the censured propositions. The pretext for Galileo's subsequent trial and conviction by the Congregation of the Holy Office in 1633 was that, with the publication of his *Dialogue concerning the Two Chief World Systems* in the previous year, he had openly flouted the church's authority by violating the ban on the public discussion of Copernicanism. Seen in this light, it was not so much how Galileo represented the respective strengths and weaknesses of the Aristotelian and Copernican systems in his *Dialogue* (or that the defender of the former system is called "Simplicio"), but simply that he had challenged the church's right to decide what could and could not be discussed publicly.[14]

In the background to these events, however, was a more profound challenge Galileo had earlier issued to the church's claim to be the sole judge of the meaning of scripture. On the basis of this claim, it inevitably followed that the church also set itself up as a judge of scientific truth, since where hypotheses concerning the natural world were found to contradict the approved meaning of scripture, the church claimed the right to declare such hypotheses false. In 1615, prior to the condemnation of Copernicanism, Galileo composed a detailed response to the church's position, his *Letter to the Grand Duchess Christina.*[15] There he argued that regarding the operations of nature, reason is the only authoritative judge of truth. If reason supports the truth of Copernicus's hypothesis, then it should be accepted, and a literal reading of the contested scriptural passages rejected.[16]

Although Galileo's stance inevitably set him on a collision course with the church, his defense of the authority of scientific reason occurs within a framework that upholds both the foundational truth of scripture and the orthodox conception of humanity as made in God's image. In this, he does not move far beyond the parameters established by Aquinas's synthesis. The Bible is the revealed word of God expressed in a form that all can understand, not just those adept at scientific reasoning. Hence we should not expect to be bound by a strict literalism in our interpretation of scripture. In matters relating to faith and salvation, the Catholic church is the undisputed authority on what we should believe. At the same time, reason is a gift of God, and in fact a more prized gift than the senses, since it is the way in which we are most clearly made in God's image. Thus, if reason leads us to understand nature differently from the way the senses present it to us (i.e. as Copernicans rather than Aristotelians), we should accept reason's verdict as authoritative. Although Galileo here directly challenges the authority of the Catholic church, he does so in a way that reinforces the harmony between the claims of the new science and the tenets of Christianity. His *theological* defense of reason's right to judge of scientific truth supports the conclusion that although the theories and methods of natural philosophy undergo a fundamental revision in his hands, these changes come against the backdrop of a stable set of assumptions about the relation of human beings to God.

A different attempt to reconcile the claims of science and religion is found in the writings of Galileo's contemporary Francis Bacon. Bacon is an outspoken critic of what he perceives as the obfuscation and vain speculation of scholastic Aristotelianism. He argues for a rejection of Aristotle's philosophy and its replacement by his own inductive method and the new scientific theories that will be developed through its employment. Yet despite the revolutionary tenor of his writings, Bacon is concerned to make his innovations fit within a biblical understanding of human beings and their place in creation. This means showing above all how the advancement of science can be reconciled with Adam's Fall and the limitations this has placed on human nature.

Bacon's most important philosophical work, *The New Organon* (1620), is an extended argument on behalf of the possibility of scientific progress. The book's frontispiece is an image of a ship sailing forth from the pillars of Hercules, below which is quoted Daniel's prophecy on the last days of the world: "Many shall pass through, and knowledge will be increased" (12:4).

Bacon expounds on his choice of motto in *New Organon*, I.93: it "signifies enigmatically" that it is providence, or God's will, "that the circumnavigation of the world . . . and the increase of the sciences should come to pass in the same age." Bacon is aware that few of his readers see in the future an ever-expanding horizon of human knowledge. That the "increase of the sciences" should lead to an unprecedented mastery of nature is for most an idle dream, or an expression of sinful pride. On Bacon's analysis, this pessimism is a significant obstacle to the advance of scientific inquiry; progress in the sciences is impeded by the absence of *hope* for their future success. Consequently, he sees his central task as providing reasons for hope, in the form of concrete signs of a new age (voyages of discovery, useful inventions), a method for the "true interpretation" of nature, and diagnoses of errors that have hindered the advance of knowledge. Reiterating his appeal near the end of the first book of the *New Organon*, Bacon writes:

> [E]ven if the breeze of hope blew much more weakly and faintly from *this New Continent*, still we believe that the attempt has to be made (unless we want to be utterly despicable). For the danger of not trying and the danger of not succeeding are not equal, since the former risks the loss of a great good, the latter of a little human effort. But from what we have said and from other things which we have not said, it has seemed to us that we have abundance of hope, whether we are men who press forward to meet new experiences, or whether we are careful and slow to believe.
>
> (*New Org.*, I.114)

In stressing the necessity of an attitude of hope, Bacon transforms a Christian theological virtue into a scientific one. The Christian hope for better things to come, which from St. Paul onward signifies a confidence in an eternal life after death,[17] becomes in Bacon's hands the hope for a steady expansion of our ability to master nature in this life. On the face of it, such a goal appears resolutely secular, but Bacon's understanding of it is, in fact, profoundly theological. The mastery of nature is to be understood as the restoration of humanity's rightful place in creation: the reordering of a world that has been disordered by Adam's Fall. As Bacon writes in an earlier work, *Valerius terminus*:

> [I]t is not the pleasure of curiosity, nor the quiet of resolution, nor the raising of the spirit, nor victory of wit, nor faculty of speech, nor lucre of profession, nor ambition of honor or fame, nor inablement for business, that are the true ends of knowledge; some of these being more worthy than other, though all inferior or degenerate: but it is a restitution and

reinvesting (in great part) of man to the sovereignty and power (for whensoever he shall be able to call animals by their true names he shall command them) which he had in his first state of creation.[18]

The received explanation of humanity's loss of dominion over nature is the disorder that results from the Fall. But if Bacon prescribes the pursuit of science as a means of rectifying the natural order, is he also suggesting that we can through our own efforts expunge Adam's sin? Here Bacon must walk a fine line. No orthodox Christian, Protestant or Catholic, could accept that original sin might be erased, and human beings justified in the eyes of God, without the aid of divine grace. Accordingly, Bacon can make only a limited claim on behalf of the advancement of knowledge. In reacquiring mastery over nature we do not thereby remove the guilt that was incurred by Adam's disobedience; that is addressed only by faith and religion. Bacon concludes the *New Organon* on this note, reassuring his readers that the improvement of the material conditions of life through the progress of science is consistent with the Bible's representation of humanity's destiny:

We intend at the end (like honest and faithful guardians) to hand men their fortunes when their understanding is freed from tutelage and comes of age, from which an improvement of the human condition must follow, and greater power over nature. For by the Fall man declined from the state of innocence and from his kingdom over the creatures. Both things can be repaired even in this life to some extent, the former by religion and faith, the latter by the arts and sciences. For the Curse did not make the creation an utter and irrevocable outlaw. In virtue of the sentence "In the sweat of thy face shalt thou eat bread" [Genesis 3:19], man, by manifold labors (and not by disputations, certainly, or by useless magical ceremonies), compels the creation, in time and in part, to provide him with bread, that is to serve the purposes of human life.

(*New Org.*, II.52)

For Bacon, the significance of the new science is that it offers the means of repairing creation and of returning human beings to their rightful dominion over the rest of nature – the position they lost as a result of the Fall. A modern reader might suppose that Bacon is here simply paying lip service to conventional ideas: in 1620 the pressures to appear religiously orthodox in England were so great that he could not afford not to reassure his readers on this point. A more plausible explanation is that Bacon, like most of the leading intellectuals of the seventeenth century, does not think twice about the truth of the Christian biblical narrative of creation, fall, and redemption. For these early modern thinkers, what science has to tell us about the world fails to threaten in any fundamental way the reality of the defining events of Christianity or their significance for human beings.[19]

DESCARTES'S REVOLUTION

More than any other early modern thinker, Descartes has been seen as revolutionizing philosophy – of making it, in effect, a different form of intellectual inquiry than it was for the ancients or medievals. While there is some truth to such claims, there are also clear limits to how far Descartes is prepared to go in transforming philosophy. These limits are set by his concern to preserve the consistency of his philosophy with the Christian conception of God and the teachings of the Roman Catholic church.[20] In the end, I suggest, what is most consequential about Descartes's philosophy is that it prepares the way for a set of more radical conclusions about the relationship of God to nature – conclusions that Descartes himself does not draw.

By the time Descartes appears on the intellectual scene in the late 1620s, the overhaul of Aristotle's cosmology had largely been completed. Now critics were beginning to focus attention on Aristotle's theory of substance. Recall that in Aristotle's philosophy, *form* plays a critical role in explaining the essential properties of a thing: what it is capable of doing as the kind of thing it is, including the natural end or goal of its activity. Proponents of the new science – figures such as Galileo, Gassendi, and Hobbes – rejected the existence of substantial forms. They argued that it is absurd to attribute a goal or purpose to inanimate things like rocks; that forms do nothing to explain why natural changes occur in the way they do; and that in any case, forms are unnecessary in science, since there is a better way of explaining (and predicting) natural change by means of mathematical laws. In place of Aristotle's theory, the new scientists embraced the doctrine of *mechanism*: the view that all natural changes can be explained in terms of changes in the sizes, shapes, and motions of particles of matter alone, in accordance with necessary mathematical laws.

Descartes was a strong proponent of the doctrine of mechanism. However, he went beyond many mechanists in formulating a larger metaphysical theory that took account of the existence of human beings as creatures whose actions cannot be explained solely in mechanistic terms. Descartes defends a *dualist* metaphysics whereby the created world is made up of two entirely different and independent types of substance: matter and mind. Every substance is either mind or matter; no substance is both. Matter (or body) is identified with real, three-dimensional Euclidean space. Mind is defined in terms of the mental powers of consciousness, rational thought, and freedom of the will. What is distinctive about human nature, according to Descartes, is that it consists of the *union* of these two separate substances. Furthermore, aside from angels, the only minds in the world are human ones, which have the capacity to choose freely and to guide the actions of their respective bodies. Everything else, including animals, is only matter, which operates according to necessary laws. Apart from human minds, the natural world is a complex machine devoid of purpose, thought, or feeling.

In addition to his new metaphysics of substance dualism, Descartes initiated a new approach in epistemology, which he saw as critical for defending the superiority of mechanistic science over its Aristotelian rival. In Descartes's view, the main source of the errors of Aristotle's philosophy was its willingness to take the evidence of sense experience at face value. When we rely on our senses in thinking about the world, we inevitably draw false conclusions about it. We suppose that such things as colors, odors, and flavors are real properties of bodies, and we attribute human wants, needs, and purposes to inanimate objects. According to Descartes, the way to avoid such errors is to begin our search for knowledge by turning inward toward the mind itself. Our most certain knowledge is of the existence of our own mind ("I think, therefore I am"), of the mind's essence (it is a "thinking thing"), and of the innate ideas contained in the mind. Through the latter we acquire knowledge of God and of the essence of matter. This effectively reverses traditional views about the order of knowing. For Aristotle, form is a part of the natural world, which we know through sense experience. For Descartes, what we know first is the mind itself; on the basis of what we find within us, we are able to proceed to knowledge of other things.

Although the senses have a role to play in science (e.g. in selecting among physical hypotheses), the foundations of philosophy must be established independently of sense experience. Our most certain knowledge of reality is derived through the mind's own "natural light," i.e. reason.

In his most famous work, *Meditations on First Philosophy*, Descartes describes a line of thought by which he hopes his readers will be brought to accept this new view of the world. As he writes in a letter to Mersenne, "I may tell you, between ourselves, that these six Meditations contain all the foundations of my physics. But please do not tell people, for that might make it harder for supporters of Aristotle to approve them. I hope that readers will gradually get used to my principles and recognize their truth, before they notice that they destroy the principles of Aristotle" (CSM III 173). At the level of natural philosophy, there is no doubt that Descartes regards his project as revolutionary: his objective is nothing less than the complete overthrow of Aristotle's views. But Descartes is equally forthright in affirming his support for the teachings of the Catholic church. Indeed, one may see his larger goal as a new synthesis, in which his own philosophy would replace that of Aristotle as the secular counterpart to Catholic theology. For this reason, Descartes places strict limits on the scope of his inquiry. He insists that his concerns are restricted to natural philosophy and metaphysics, and he disavows any claim to have arrived at new knowledge about theology or politics. In these matters he promises complete orthodoxy.

Descartes was justified in believing that deviations from orthodoxy carried significant risks: the philosopher Giordano Bruno was burned at the stake as a heretic in 1600, and in 1633 Galileo was forced to recant his support for the Copernican hypothesis. The latter event had a profound impact on Descartes, who decided not to go ahead with the publication of his book *The World*, and lived much of his later life in more liberal Holland, although even there his philosophy was censured by the authorities.[21] None of this, however, gives us any reason to think that Descartes may have been dissimulating in his professions of religious orthodoxy, or that God is not absolutely central to his philosophy.[22] The latter point can be supported in a number of ways. I will consider just one argument, which bears directly on Descartes's defense of mechanism, the most innovative part of his philosophical system.

The assumption of the existence and agency of God is indispensable to Descartes's worldview. This conclusion follows directly from his identification of the essence of matter with geometrical extension. Descartes touts his definition of matter as one that meets the highest standards of "clarity and distinctness." In contrast to the Aristotelian account of matter as "pure potentiality," Descartes's definition is fully intelligible to reason. Furthermore, by identifying matter with extension, Descartes guarantees the applicability of mathematics to nature. The mathematical representation of the properties of matter will be no more difficult than the representation of the properties of geometrical figures. Yet one important element is missing in Descartes's account of matter: an explanation of the source of its motion and of the principles by which motion is transferred from one body to another. With respect to the former, Descartes has no choice but to invoke God. There is no other way for motion to be in matter – an unchanging, homogeneous plenum – except that God has chosen to give one region of extension a motion relative to another. Furthermore, God is responsible for sustaining the same motion in a body, unless it is acted on by another body (a version of the principle of inertia), and for preserving the same total quantity of motion and rest in the universe (a version of a conservation principle). As Descartes writes in his *Principles of Philosophy*:

> God imparted various motions to the parts of matter when he first created them, and he now preserves all this matter in the same way, and by the same process by which he originally created it; and it follows from what we have said that this fact alone makes it reasonable to think that God likewise always preserves the same quantity of motion in matter.
>
> (*Princ.*, II.36, CSM I 240)

On Descartes's account, either the laws of motion are identical with God's regular and immutable action on matter, or those laws are immediate effects of God's action and serve "as secondary and particular causes of the various motions we see in particular bodies" (*Princ.*, II.37, CSM I 240). Either way, there can be no Cartesian physics without God playing an ineliminable causal role in nature.[23]

This line of reasoning is pushed to its logical conclusion by Descartes's most prominent follower, Nicolas Malebranche.

According to Malebranche, God's essential role as the creator and sustainer of finite things entails that God is the only true cause of natural change. Created things (minds and bodies) that appear to act on one another and to change each other's states, in fact, are only "occasional causes," which is to say, occasions for God acting on the world, recreating it in a new state of existence. In Malebranche's philosophy, which he sees as a consistent development of Descartes's position, created nature is causally impotent: nature itself can do nothing, and nothing can happen in nature, unless God does it.

Malebranche regards this as an entirely happy result that confirms a fundamental truth of Christianity: that we are utterly dependent on God for our existence and for everything that happens in the world. Indeed, Malebranche thinks that any other causal theory which accorded a modicum of activity to finite things would be tantamount to a kind of paganism, in which we end up worshiping bodies – loving and fearing them – for the good and evil they may bring us. In a famous chapter of his *Search after Truth* entitled "The Most Dangerous Error of the Philosophy of the Ancients," Malebranche writes: "We therefore admit something divine in all the bodies around us when we posit forms, faculties, qualities, virtues, or real beings capable of producing certain effects through the force of their nature; and thus we insensibly adopt the opinions of the pagans because of our respect for their philosophy" (*Search*, VI.ii.3). Like any confirmed mechanist, Malebranche is convinced that there are good philosophical reasons for rejecting the Aristotelian theory of forms. However, he believes that there are even better theological reasons, which point to the conclusion that created nature is devoid of all causal power, and that consequently everything that happens in nature must be ascribed to God's action.

The debate over the source of the apparent causal powers of created things is a defining one in seventeenth-century philosophy.[24] Invariably, however, arguments about which theory can best account for the phenomena are subordinated to arguments that assess the acceptability of different theories in terms of their theological consequences. Descartes and Malebranche both insist that the God of their philosophies is identical to the revealed God of Christianity. Malebranche, a Catholic priest, develops this point at length in his writings. Descartes is less explicit about it, but there is no reason to think that he seriously questions it. Nevertheless, despite their efforts to uphold the claims of religion, the writings of Descartes and Malebranche failed to win widespread support within the Catholic church. Descartes's works were placed on the Index of Prohibited Books in 1663, and through the efforts of Arnauld, Malebranche's were added in 1690 (*Treatise on Nature and Grace*) and 1709 (*The Search after Truth*).[25] The fundamental objection in both cases was that the philosophers had elevated the authority of reason above the revelation of scripture and the apostolic teachings of the Catholic church. Pascal pinpointed what many found objectionable about Descartes's world view: "I cannot forgive Descartes: in his whole philosophy he would like to do without God; but he could not help allowing him a flick of the fingers to set the world in motion; after that he had no more use for God."[26]

Pascal's complaint identifies the core criticism, from a Christian point of view, of Cartesian attempts to reconcile the domains of religion and philosophy. If reason is the final arbiter of what one should believe, and if reason requires God only as a foundational principle of the causal order of nature, then supporters of orthodoxy are forced to assume a defensive position, making the case that scripture and tradition demand more than this. The difficulty of mounting such a defense from within the perspective of reason was apparent to thinkers such as Pascal and Pierre Bayle. Consequently, they saw Descartes's philosophy as containing the seeds of the most potent threat to religion in the early modern period.

THE SPECTER OF NATURALISM

Painting with a broad brush, seventeenth-century philosophers can be distinguished as either *compatibilists* with respect to the relation of religion and philosophy, or *incompatibilists*. The vast majority of early modern thinkers were compatibilists. They believed that contemporary developments in the natural sciences and in moral and political philosophy could be reconciled with the traditional biblical account of human beings and their place in creation. As we have seen, Galileo, Bacon, Descartes, and Malebranche fall into this group, as do Gassendi, Hobbes, Boyle, More, Cudworth, Leibniz, Locke, and Newton.[27] One conclusion to draw from this is that innovations in natural philosophy by themselves were not viewed by most philosophers as a serious threat to the integrity of Christianity. Most assumed that Aquinas's ideal of a synthesis of secular philosophy and Christian theology could be preserved, provided that a suitable substitute for Aristotle's philosophy could be found. Nowhere is this clearer than in the case of Newton, who in the General Scholium to his *Principia* includes a final discussion of God as "a part of natural philosophy":

> This most elegant system of the sun, planets, and comets could not have arisen without the design and dominion of an intelligent and powerful being . . . He rules all things, not as the world soul but as the lord of all . . . And from true lordship it follows that the true God is living, intelligent, and powerful; from the other perfections, that he is supreme, or supremely perfect . . . We know him only by his properties and attributes and by the wisest and best construction of things and their final causes, and we admire him because of his perfections; but we venerate him because of his dominion. For we worship him as servants, and a god without dominion, providence, and final causes is nothing other than fate and nature. No variation in things arises from blind metaphysical necessity, which must be the same always and everywhere. All the diversity of created things, each in its place and time, could only have arisen from the ideas and the will of a necessarily existing being.[28]

Incompatibilists are far fewer in number among early modern philosophers, and they fall into two distinct groups. In one are those like Pascal and Bayle who detected in Descartes's thought the beginnings of a downward spiral into irreligion. To the extent that one makes reason the final arbiter of truth concerning reality – including the existence and actions of God – one undermines the foundations of Christianity. As Bayle frames the problem:

> One must necessarily choose between philosophy and the Gospel. If you do not want to believe anything but what is evident and in conformity with the common notions, choose philosophy and leave Christianity. If you are willing to believe the incomprehensible mysteries of religion, choose Christianity and leave philosophy. For to have together self-evidence and incomprehensibility is something that cannot be. The combination of these two items is hardly more impossible than the combination of the properties of a square and a circle. A choice must necessarily be made.[29]

For incompatibilists of this kind, the attempt to ground religion in reason, or to argue for the equal authority of religion and philosophy, could only spell disaster for Christianity as a religion based on faith and revelation. Consequently, they urged a curtailing of the authority of philosophy. While accepting that the new science offered innovations of practical value, they denied that it was the basis of a fundamentally new understanding of reality.

A second group of incompatibilists likewise recognized the impossibility of a reconciliation of philosophy and revealed religion, but they drew from this exactly the opposite conclusion. For these thinkers, the path that philosophy had embarked on at the beginning of the seventeenth century could only terminate in the rejection of the truth of revealed religion. This might take the form of a defense of *deism*, which recognizes the existence of an impersonal transcendent God: a being that is causally responsible for the creation of the world but thereafter is uninvolved in its operation or in the unfolding of human history. Or it could go beyond this. Followed to its logical conclusion, rational inquiry might be seen to support the metaphysical stance of *naturalism*, according to which existence is limited to the totality of nature, with no appeal made to a transcendent creator God. A naturalism of this sort might include the idea of God as an immanent and eternal intelligence, or principle of order, but so understood, God would be identical to nature itself. The danger of openly espousing such a position in the seventeenth century was very real. To deny the existence of God as defined by Jewish and Christian scripture was to deny the existence of God altogether. Consequently, deists and naturalists (or materialists) were routinely denounced as atheists.

The doctrine of naturalism finds its most potent expression in the seventeenth century in the writings of Benedict de Spinoza. Spinoza is unique among the central figures of early modern philosophy. He is the only major modern philosopher whose religious background is Jewish rather than Christian. And he is one of the few philosophers prior to the nineteenth century who openly challenges the central claim of Judeo-Christian theology: that the world has been freely created by a transcendent God, who is the lawgiver to, and judge of, human beings. Against this orthodoxy, Spinoza advances in his *Ethics* the bold thesis that God is simply an eternal and infinite power, from which all things necessarily follow and in which all things exist as modes of the one divine substance.[30]

What we call the created world is, for Spinoza, nothing but an infinitely varied determination of God's power. God does not choose to create: God simply is (and we are "in" God). This alternative to the orthodox doctrine of creation brings with it other novel claims. If everything follows necessarily from God, then there is no contingency in the world and no freedom of the will. Everything is the way it is necessarily, because of the way God necessarily is. Whatever power finite things possess, they possess because they are modes of the one substance. Thus, there is no problem about how God "gives" his power to something different from himself. Finally, Spinoza's philosophy neatly resolves the Cartesian problem of mind–body interaction. On his account, God is both a thinking substance and an extended substance (these are two of the infinite attributes through which God's power is expressed). Consequently, any finite thing is simultaneously a mind and a body. In Spinoza's philosophy, there is no interaction between minds and bodies, because mind and body are identical.

Spinoza, it should be clear, does not eliminate God from philosophy. On the contrary, he makes nature nothing less than an immediate expression of God's infinite and eternal power. In advancing this position, however, he draws a sharp contrast between the God of philosophy and the God of Jewish and Christian scripture. In his *Theological-Political Treatise* he argues that the core of biblical religion is not a set of truths about God but an ethical injunction: "to obey God with all one's heart by practising justice and charity" (*TTP*, preface). Religion prescribes this moral law as a command that must be obeyed. Obedience to divine authority, as communicated by scripture, defines for Spinoza the province of religion. Religion thus regards human beings as essentially servile, subordinate to the command of God. In the *TTP* and more fully in the *Ethics*, Spinoza aims to transform this understanding of the ground of moral norms, representing them as dictates of *reason*, as opposed to the commands of a sovereign God.

Spinoza's philosophy is, then, in the broadest terms an Enlightenment project, whose goal is the release of human beings from intellectual servitude.[31] Distinctive about his approach is that it defines the conditions of Enlightenment against the background of an uncompromising metaphysical naturalism. Describing the position of those with whom he disagrees, Spinoza writes in the preface to Part Three of the *Ethics*:

> Most of those who have written about the affects, and men's ways of living, seem to treat not of natural things, which follow the common laws of Nature, but of things which are outside Nature. Indeed they seem to conceive man in Nature as a dominion within a dominion. For they believe that man disturbs, rather than follows, the order of Nature, that he has absolute power over his actions, and that he is determined only by himself.

Rejecting the assumption that human beings possess an absolute power over their actions, Spinoza insists that we conceive of them as bound by the same "common laws of nature" that govern the operations of other things. There is but a single "order of nature," and human beings are no less a part of that order than plants or other animals.

Condemnation of Spinoza's thought was nearly universal in the early modern period. Many dismissed it with the blanket charge of atheism, but some such as Leibniz treated it with great seriousness and devoted themselves to a philosophical refutation of its principles. Like Newton, with whom he otherwise disagreed deeply, Leibniz's principal reservation concerning the identification of God and nature was its consequence that a "blind metaphysical necessity" ruled all things. Such a conclusion was unacceptable in his eyes, chiefly because it entailed that the universe was without an inherent moral order: a norm of justice that would serve both as a standard of right action and as an end to be realized through the course of human history. If God is not a wise and just creator in whose image human beings have been made, then there is no special place reserved for human beings in nature, nor can we look to God's example for moral principles by which to guide our actions.[32]

The implications of this possibility resonate throughout the eighteenth century, culminating in the influential naturalist and non-naturalist conceptions of humanity defended by Hume and Kant. From this perspective, it is Spinoza who most clearly points toward a new philosophical era. Although earlier thinkers paved the way with a new picture of nature, they held fast to the assumption that this picture must be reconcilable with the truth of scripture and with the idea that human beings are in some significant way above, or independent of, nature. Not until Spinoza is a comprehensive attempt made to challenge this assumption. Applying the same critical reason that fostered the new science to basic questions of human existence, Spinoza reaches the conclusion that the assumption must be abandoned. That Spinoza's revolution leaves many problems unresolved (consciousness, freedom, normativity) goes without saying, but these are now the problems distinctive of modern philosophy.

NOTES

1 Nor is Bacon the first to call for a new beginning, based on a break with the teachings of scholastic Aristotelianism. In the preface to his *De magnete* (1609), Walter Gilbert stresses the need for "a new style of philosophizing," for men "who look for knowledge not in books only, but in things themselves" (quoted in Hill 1965, p. 86).
2 For a broad-ranging critique of the idea of a "Scientific Revolution," see Shapin 1996.
3 Newton's remarks appear in the General Scholium, added as a conclusion to the second (1713) edition of the *Principia*. For a discussion of its significance, see I. Bernard Cohen, "A Guide to Newton's *Principia*," ch. 9, in Newton 1999.
4 See Schneewind 1998, pp. 6–9; and in this volume, the chapters by Darwall and Simmons.
5 Some claims for continuity were based on adopting a different historical antecedent, e.g. Epicurus (in the case of Gassendi) or Plato (in the case of More and Cudworth). Others such as Leibniz argued for an underlying agreement between the claims of the new science and the principles of Aristotle's philosophy.
6 For a development of this theme, see Craig 1987.
7 A typical attempt to reconcile Stoic fate with the Christian notion of providence is found in Justus Lipsius's *De constantia* (1584). Levi 1964 offers a good account of how early modern moralists tend toward eclectism, drawing at will from Christian, Platonic, and Stoic sources, among others. Two recent collections include a number of studies on the influence of Stoic ideas in the early modern period: Miller and Inwood 2003; Strange and Zupko 2004.
8 On the influence of ancient skepticism in the early modern period, see Popkin 2003. For a detailed account of the reception of ancient skeptical texts, see Schmitt 1983b.
9 Wilson 2003 surveys the reception of, and reaction to, Epicureanism among early modern philosophers.
10 On Mersenne, see Lenoble 1943; Dear 1988.

11 The competing legacies of Descartes and Gassendi are examined in Lennon 1993. On Gassendi's rehabilitation of Epicureanism, see Joy 1987; Osler 1993, 2003; Sarasohn 1996.

12 This challenge is raised by Luther in his 1520 *Appeal to the Christian Nobility of the German Nation*. That religious figures lack any legitimate political authority is one of the principal points argued for by Hobbes in *Leviathan*.

13 For a full discussion, see Blackwell 1991, ch. 5 and app. I, which reproduces the decree of the Council of Trent.

14 See Blackwell 1991, pp. 125–34. This is not to say that leading church figures did not also find the contents of the *Dialogue* objectionable. They clearly did, especially pope Urban VIII, whose published declaration that the Copernican hypothesis is "neither true nor conclusive" and that "it would be excessive for anyone to limit and restrict the divine power and wisdom to one particular fancy of his own" is assigned to Simplicio (Shea 1986, pp. 130–31).

15 This document circulated widely in manuscript before its eventual publication in Strasbourg in 1636. It is translated in Galileo 1957, pp. 157–216.

16 At least two lines of argument run through Galileo's letter. One distinguishes science and religion in terms of their respective domains: science is authoritative in the investigation of nature; scripture, as interpreted by the church, is authoritative in moral and spiritual matters. A weaker stance grants a presumptive authority to scripture as interpreted by the church, unless contradicted by *demonstrated* scientific truth. To the extent that Galileo accepts the latter point of view, his position remains vulnerable, since the church disputed whether the Copernican hypothesis had been demonstrated, according to standards that Galileo himself accepted. See Shea 1986, pp. 126–27, and the detailed analysis of McMullin 1998.

17 Romans 8:24–25; Aquinas, *Summa theologiae*, IIaIIae, q. 17, a. 5.

18 Bacon 1857–74, vol. III, p. 222 (quoted in Gaukroger 2001, p. 78). For a development of this point, see Gaukroger 2001, ch. 3.

19 As Gaukroger notes (2001, pp. 74–75), Bacon accepts a history of philosophy, popularized by Renaissance thinkers such as Giovanni Pico della Mirandola, that traces its origins to a secret wisdom revealed by God to Adam, and subsequently transmitted through a succession of hermetic figures before being developed by Pythagoras, Democritus, and Plato. On such an account, the history of philosophy, including natural philosophy, is part of the esoteric history of Christianity; hence there is no division between the two that needs to be bridged.

20 See e.g. the "Dedicatory Letter to the Sorbonne" that prefaces the *Meditations*, and the letter to Father Dinet, appended to the Seventh Objections and Replies in the second edition of the *Meditations*: "As far as theology is concerned, since one truth can never be in conflict with another, it would be impious to fear that any truths discovered in philosophy could be in conflict with the truths of faith. Indeed, I insist that there is nothing relating to religion which cannot be equally well or even better explained by means of my principles than can be done by means of those [Aristotelian principles] which are commonly accepted" (CSM II 392).
21 See Verbeek 1992.
22 For more on this point, see Lennon's chapter in this volume.
23 Des Chene's chapter in this volume provides a fuller discussion of Descartes's physics.
24 The problem is actively engaged by Descartes, Malebranche, More, Cudworth, Boyle, Locke, Leibniz, and Newton, to mention only some of the most prominent contributors to the debate.
25 Nadler 2000a, p. 6.
26 From "Sayings Attributed to Pascal" (Pascal 1966, p. 355).
27 This is not to say that all these figures held theological views that religious authorities would have regarded as orthodox, but simply that they were theists who remained committed to the truth of Christianity as revealed in scripture. The inclusion of Hobbes within this group is controversial. For contrasting interpretations of his attitude toward religion, see Martinich 1992 and Jesseph 2002.
28 Newton 1999, pp. 940–42. Some see an important distinction between such public expressions of Christian piety and Newton's private speculations about religion (Westfall 1986, p. 226). The latter center on his interpretation of scriptural prophecy and defense of Arianism, the fourth-century heresy that denies the full divinity of Christ and hence the doctrine of the Trinity. For further discussion, see Manuel 1973; Force and Popkin 1998; Mamiani 2002.
29 *Dictionary*, Third Clarification, IV, in Bayle 1991, pp. 428–29.
30 For an account of the development of Spinoza's views and the circumstances of his expulsion from the Amsterdam Jewish community, see Nadler 1999.
31 See Israel 2001; and Schneewind's chapter in this volume.
32 For further discussion and references, see the editors' introduction to Rutherford and Cover 2005.

STEPHEN GAUKROGER

2 Knowledge, evidence, and method

The understanding of what knowledge consists in, how it is to be secured, the means by which discoveries are to be made, and the means by which purported knowledge is to be legitimated or confirmed were all questions that were disputed intensely in the course of the sixteenth and seventeenth centuries.[1] These disputes were partly the outcome of developments in natural philosophy, but in some cases they lay partly at the source of these developments. They began, in the early sixteenth century, with reflection on Aristotle's doctrine of method and scientific explanation,[2] but soon turned into increasingly radical revisions to this doctrine. By the beginning of the seventeenth century, they took the form of a search for a wholly new approach, with several different, novel methodological models being advocated. The search for a satisfactory method is not a wholly linear development, however, and two sets of factors serve to overdetermine what is already quite a complex issue. The first turns on the fact that questions of method not only have direct connections to substantive developments in natural philosophy itself, but also to the relation between natural philosophy and the other disciplines (most notably metaphysics and theology), as well as to the question of what kinds of skills and virtues the practitioner of natural philosophy requires. Secondly, questions about the appropriate method for scientific disciplines become translated into questions about the legitimation of the scientific enterprise as a whole.

These concerns come together at certain crucial junctures, shaping what are taken to be the core methodological questions. It is important that we are able to at least glimpse how this shaping takes place, for the context in which it occurs is different from the concerns that shaped questions of method in the work of Whewell and Mill and their nineteenth- and twentieth-century successors. The concerns that emerged from this latter development put questions of induction and hypothetico-deductivism at the fore; and while inductive and hypothetical procedures were discussed and contrasted with one another in the seventeenth and eighteenth centuries, they were pursued in a rather different way. Above all, one of the crucial differences was that, in the nineteenth and twentieth centuries, methodological questions were concerned largely with the attempt to reconstruct how successful scientific developments had occurred, to identify the methodological conditions for these successful outcomes, and to draw general methodological lessons. By contrast, in the sixteenth and seventeenth centuries, there weren't any successful models of the kind that Newtonian mechanics or Newtonian optics, for example, were to provide, and the aim of the exercise was to explore various methodological strategies with a view to discovering whether they did in fact yield anything of value. It is fundamental to an understanding of early modern concerns with method to grasp that the aim was to discover something which would aid one in pursuing natural philosophy, for example, not to rationalize, with hindsight, some scientific achievement. In the seventeenth century, above all, method was considered a practical, pressing question which enabled one to get started on the scientific enterprise in the first place. It was not something one reconstructed in retrospect, and at several removes from the enterprise that embodied that method, and it is important that we avoid importing considerations appropriate to this kind of enterprise into one in which methodological considerations are a core part of the scientific enterprise itself.

THE RENOVATION OF ARISTOTLE IN THE RENAISSSANCE

In his earlier writings such as the *Topics*, Aristotle had elaborated procedures for the "discovery of knowledge." These procedures were designed to guide one in uncovering the appropriate evidence, discovering the most fruitful questions to ask, and so on, and they did this by providing devices or strategies for classifying or characterizing problems so that they could be posed and solved using set techniques. In his later works such as the *Prior* and *Posterior*

Analytics, however, there is a marked change of emphasis. Aristotle now pursues the question of the presentation of results, as his interests shift to the validity of the reasoning used to establish conclusions on the basis of accepted premises: syllogistic. In other words, his concerns shifted from questions of discovery to questions of demonstration. What happens in the sixteenth-century development of the Aristotelian account of method turns in large part on a basic confusion about the method of discovery, in that Aristotle's original method of discovery, the topics, becomes lost, at least in the context of scientific discovery, and his method of demonstration – syllogistic – comes to be construed as method per se, that is, as a method of discovery as well as a method of presentation.[3]

In the sixteenth century this gave rise to two opposing tendencies. Defenders of Aristotle, such as the *regressus* theorists, tried to understand how syllogistic could be construed so that it could be used as, or at least be part of, a method of discovery. Critics of Aristotle, by contrast, argued that syllogistic could not possibly be part of a method of discovery, that many of the problems in Aristotle's account of a whole range of philosophical matters were traced to his having attempted to employ this useless method. These critics sought a genuine method of discovery in rhetoric, which was the area in which the study of the topics had been developed after the death of Aristotle, principally by those Roman thinkers who stood at the foundations of early modern rhetoric, Cicero and Quintilian. There were both conservative and radical advocates of this approach, the conservatives, such as Peter Ramus (1515–72), seeing a method of discovery as being a guide to the storehouse of knowledge built up since antiquity, and the radicals, such as Bacon, seeing it as offering an opportunity to replace traditional learning with something completely new.

As an example of the defenders of Aristotle, we can take those early sixteenth-century Paduan Aristotelians such as Jacopo Zabarella (1533–89) and Agostino Nifo (ca. 1469–1538) who developed an account of the demonstrative syllogism as a method of discovery known as *regressus* theory. The basic issue to which *regressus* theory was directed was the informativeness of the procedure of building up knowledge syllogistically, and, although this was not clearly recognized at the time, there was in effect a double problem. First, Aristotle's procedure seemed to require that we start from sense perception, abstracting more and more general principles from what we observed, and then deducing our observations from those basic principles; and this seemed circular and uninformative. Second, there was the question of how a purely formal device like the syllogism could yield new information, how it could go beyond the information contained in the premises.

Aristotle had presented scientific demonstrations syllogistically, and he had argued that some forms of demonstration provide explanations or causes whereas others do not. This may occur even where the syllogisms are formally identical. Consider, for example, the following two syllogisms:

The planets do not twinkle
That which does not twinkle is near

The planets are near

The planets are near
That which is near does not twinkle

The planets do not twinkle

In Aristotle's discussion of these syllogisms in his *Posterior Analytics* (I.13), he argues that the first is only a demonstration "of fact," whereas the second is a demonstration of "why," or a scientific explanation. In the latter, we are provided with a reason or cause or explanation of the conclusion: the reason why the planets do not twinkle is that they are near. In the former, we have a valid but not a demonstrative argument, since the planets' not twinkling is not a cause or explanation of their being near. So the first syllogism is in some way uninformative compared to the second: the latter produces understanding, the former does not.

This is the key to understanding how the syllogism can be informative for the *regressus* theorists. It is true that we start with observations, proceed to general principles, and then deduce observations, but the grasp of the observations that we have at the end of the process is very different from that which we have at the beginning. We start by grasping *that* something happens, but at the end of the process we grasp *why* that same thing happens. On this reading, the syllogism is not a discovery of new facts so much as a discovery of the reasons underlying the facts. However, what it looks like is a way of articulating the facts in terms of the principles underlying them, rather than a means for discovery of the facts. This was in fact Aristotle's own view. For Aristotle, the epistemic and the consequential relations in demonstrative syllogisms run in opposite directions. That is to say, it is knowing the premises from which the conclusion is to be deduced that is the important thing as far as providing a deeper scientific understanding is concerned, not discovering what conclusions follow from given premises. The demonstrative syllogism was simply a means of presentation of results in a systematic way, one suitable for conveying these to students.[4] The conclusions of the syllogisms were known in advance, and what the syllogism provided was a means of relating those conclusions to premises that would explain them.

Regressus theory incorporates this kind of understanding into a larger theory of scientific demonstration. *Regressus* combines an inference from an observed effect to its proximate cause with an inference from a proximate cause to an observed effect, and it is this peculiar combination that produces the knowledge required. The most usual scheme employed is a fourfold one, although there are a number of variants.[5] First, we obtain "accidental" knowledge of an effect through observation; second, through induction and demonstration of the fact, we obtain "accidental" knowledge of the cause of the fact; third, via a form of reflection referred to as *negotiatio*, we grasp the necessary connection between the proximate cause and its effect; and finally, fourth, we demonstrate the fact from the cause that necessitates it.

Regressus theory was subject to a number of problems. One of these derives from Aristotle, namely that of distinguishing demonstrative from nondemonstrative syllogisms. The two syllogisms given above, for example, are formally identical: both are in Barbara mode, which means that the way in which the conclusion is deduced from the premises is identical. The fact that one of the syllogisms gives us a cause of the effect is not due to a formal difference, and in any case there are other kinds of syllogism in which cause is related to effect. Aristotle himself refers us to a form of intellectual insight (*nous*) by which we distinguish the difference between demonstrative and nondemonstrative syllogisms, but he does not give us an account of what difference it is that we are supposed to recognize. Nevertheless, what he was trying to achieve is clear enough. He was seeking some way of identifying those forms of deductive inference that resulted in epistemic advance, that advanced one's understanding. Realizing that no purely logical criterion would suffice, he attempted to show that epistemic advance depended on some nonlogical but nevertheless internal or structural feature that some deductive inferences possess. But he was unable to provide any account of just what gave rise to this feature.

The *regressus* account has a related problem. In the crucial third stage of the *regressus*, we are supposed to grasp the necessary connection between cause and effect through a *negotiatio*. In contrast to Zabarella and to his own account in early publications, Nifo, in his later writings, begins to show some skepticism about *negotiatio*, suggesting that the best we can hope for in some cases is conjectural knowledge.[6] And indeed *negotiatio* does remain a mysterious process, although the idea of inspecting the contents of one's mental states for guidance as to the truth or certainty of a proposition is something we shall see reappear in Descartes, even though its source is very different.

THE HUMANIST RESPONSE

Those who rejected the idea that the syllogism could play any role in scientific understanding tended to assume (along with many supporters of Aristotle) that, for Aristotle, the demonstrative syllogism was a method of discovery, a means of deducing novel conclusions from accepted premises. Conceived as a tool of discovery, there is some justice in the claim that the demonstrative syllogism looks trivial, but, as I have indicated, this was never its purpose for Aristotle: discovery was something to be guided by the "topics," which were procedures for classifying or characterizing problems so that they could be solved using set techniques. More specifically, they were designed to provide the distinctions needed if one was to be able to formulate problems properly, as well as supplying devices enabling one to determine what has to be shown if the conclusion one desires is to be reached. Now the topics were not confined to scientific inquiry, but had an application in ethics, political argument, rhetoric, and so on, and indeed they were meant to apply to any area of inquiry. The problem was that, during the middle ages, the topics came to be associated very closely and exclusively with rhetoric, and their relevance to scientific discovery became at first obscured and then completely lost. The upshot of this was that, for all intents and purposes, the results of Aristotelian science lost all contact with the procedures of discovery which produced them. While these results remained unchallenged, the problem was not particularly apparent. But when they came to be challenged in a serious and systematic way, as they were from the sixteenth century onward, they began to take on the appearance of mere dogmas, backed up by circular reasoning. It is this strong connection between Aristotle's supposed method of discovery and the unsatisfactoriness not only of his scientific results but also of his overall natural philosophy that provoked the intense concern with method in the seventeenth century.

The first stage of this revision took the form of what might be termed a humanist backlash. If the defenders of Aristotle had ignored (because they misrecognized) his method of discovery, humanists such as Ramus ignored his method of presentation. The topics had been pursued with vigor and refined in rhetoric and law in the Renaissance, and served there as the means of discovery or invention. The humanist critics of Aristotle held up the topics as constitutive not just of discovery but of the whole process of cognitive understanding.

The *regressus* theorists had believed that we cannot simply demonstrate an effect through its proximate cause since, although causes are better known "in nature," effects are better known "in us," because our knowledge always starts from sensation. This distinction was crucial to orthodox Aristotelianism. It draws a sharp line between what is "better known to us," which is a function of our limited experience, and what is "better known in nature," that is to say, the most general precepts underlying the discipline under consideration, precepts which enable us to grasp the universal principles around which the discipline is structured. This distinction motivates Aristotelian accounts of pedagogy, invention or discovery, and judgment, the idea being that we must start from what is better known to us and work toward, or – in the all-important case of the pedagogical context – be guided toward, what is better known in nature. This guidance takes the form of the methods of resolution (analysis of a problem into its elements) and composition (construction of a solution out of these elements), all this being done on the basis of a syllogistic formulation of all knowledge. Disputes between Aristotelians and their opponents on the question of scientific demonstration in the sixteenth century generally took place in a pedagogical context. Ramus thinks of knowledge in exclusively pedagogic terms, transforming the topics into a system of pedagogic classification of knowledge: the point of the exercise is to enable us to refer any question back to the storehouse of ancient wisdom, the role of the topics being to provide us with points of entry into this storehouse.[7] Ramus's approach had no monopoly on attempts to deal with this question, but it did manage to engage a very broad range of questions – about the relative standing of various disciplines, the aims of pedagogy, and the nature of knowledge – which had become problematic in the course of the sixteenth century.

An important ingredient in the Ramist response to the Aristotelians is an outright rejection of the distinction between "better known to us" and "better known in nature": one kind of knowledge can be said to be prior to another only if the one is needed to explain the other, and such priority resides resolutely with the most general precepts. Instead of trying to combine them, Ramists prized apart discovery and demonstration, maintaining that the former had nothing to do with the syllogistically motivated procedures of resolution and composition, but depended simply on observation and inferences from such observation (induction). Demonstration is irrelevant to how knowledge is acquired, on this view: all that matters is how it is best conveyed, and this will be the same in all pedagogic circumstances, for it will always consist in the move from the more general to the less general.

A NEW METHOD OF DISCOVERY: BACON

The idea that there is no independent method of presentation of results, only a method of discovery, encouraged the idea that the only effective way of demonstrating something was to reproduce how it was discovered. This proved to be a very powerful idea, and combined with an attack on the sterile nature of scholastic book-learning, fostered a renewed concern with methods of discovery, a concern that was to be at the forefront of philosophy in the seventeenth century. One of the key figures in this development was Francis Bacon.[8]

Bacon's concern was above all to make natural philosophy a practical, productive discipline, and he used insights gained from the study of rhetoric and its application in legal reasoning to this end. Following the Roman rhetorical tradition, he thought of epistemology in psychological terms, and his methodological project has two main parts: one aims to rid the mind of preconceptions, while the other aims to guide the mind in a productive direction. These components are interconnected, for until we understand the nature of the mind's preconceptions, we do not know in what direction we need to lead its thinking.

Bacon's radical view is that various natural inclinations of the mind must be purged before the new procedure can be set in place. His approach here is genuinely different from that of his predecessors, as he realizes. Logic or method in themselves cannot simply be introduced to replace bad habits of thought, which Bacon identifies as "idols," because it is not simply a question of replacement.[9] The simple application of logic to one's mental processes is insufficient. In his doctrine of the idols of the mind, Bacon provides an account of the systematic forms of error to which the mind is subject, and here the question is raised of what psychological or cognitive state we must be in to be able to pursue natural philosophy in the first place. Bacon believes an understanding of nature of a kind that had never been achieved since the Fall is possible in his own time, because the distinctive obstacles that have held up all previous attempts have been identified in what is in many respects a novel theory of what might traditionally have been treated under a theory of the passions, one directed specifically at natural-philosophical practice.

One of the great values of Bacon's account of the idols is that it allows him to make the case for method in a particularly compelling way. Bacon argues that there are identifiable obstacles to cognition arising from innate tendencies of the mind (idols of the tribe), from inherited or idiosyncratic features of individual minds (idols of the cave), from the nature of the language that we must use to communicate results (idols of the marketplace), or from the education and upbringing we receive (idols of the theater). Because of these, we pursue natural philosophy with seriously deficient natural faculties, we operate with a severely inadequate means of communication, and we rely on a hopelessly corrupt philosophical culture. In many respects, these are a result of the Fall and are beyond remedy. The practitioners of natural philosophy certainly need to reform their behavior, overcome their natural inclinations and passions, etc., but not so that, in doing this, they might aspire to a natural, prelapsarian state in which they might know things as they are with an unmediated knowledge. This they will never achieve. Rather, the reform of behavior is a discipline to which they must subject themselves if they are to be able to follow a procedure which is in many respects quite contrary to their natural inclinations.

In the first instance, then, what is needed is a purging of those features of the mind that lead us astray. Once we have achieved this, or at least have made some significant advances along these lines, we can pursue Bacon's method of discovery. What Bacon is seeking from a method of discovery is something that modern philosophers would deem impossibly strong: the discovery of causes which are both necessary and sufficient for their effects. Showing his Aristotelian heritage, what Bacon is seeking are the ultimate explanations of things, and it is natural to assume that ultimate explanations are unique. Bacon's method is designed to provide a route to such explanations, and the route takes us through a number of proposed causal accounts, which are refined at each stage. The procedure he elaborates, eliminative induction, is one in which various possibly contributory factors are isolated and examined in turn, to see whether they do in fact make a contribution to the effect. Those that do not are rejected, and the result is a convergence on those factors that are truly relevant. The kind of "relevance" that Bacon is after is, in effect, necessary conditions: the procedure is supposed to enable us to weed out those factors that are not necessary for the production of the effect, so that we are left only with those that are necessary.

He provides an example of how the method works in the case of color.[10] We take, as our starting point, some combination of substances that produces whiteness, i.e. we start with what are in effect sufficient conditions for the production of whiteness, and then we remove from these anything not necessary for the color. First, we note that if air and water are mixed together in small portions, the result is white, as in snow or waves. Here we have the sufficient conditions for whiteness, but not the necessary conditions, so next we increase the scope, substituting any transparent uncolored substance for water, whence we find that glass or crystal, on being ground, become white, and albumen, which is initially a watery transparent substance, on having air beaten into it, becomes white. Third, we further increase the scope, and ask what happens in the case of colored substances. Amber and sapphire become white on being ground, and wine and beer become white when brought to a froth. The substances considered up to this stage have all been "more grossly transparent than air." Bacon next considers flame, which is less grossly transparent than air, and argues that the mixture of the fire and air makes the flame whiter. The upshot of this is that water is sufficient for whiteness, but not necessary for it. He continues in the same vein, asking next whether air is necessary for whiteness. He notes that a mixture of water and oil is white, even when the air has been evaporated from it, so air is not necessary for whiteness, but is a transparent substance necessary? Bacon does not continue with the chain of questions after this point, but sets out some conclusions, namely that bodies whose parts are unequal but in simple proportion are white, those whose parts are in equal proportions are transparent, proportionately unequal colored, and absolutely unequal black. In other words, this is the conclusion that one might expect the method of sifting out what is necessary for the phenomenon and what is not to yield, although Bacon himself does not provide the route to this conclusion here.

This being the case, one can ask what his confidence in his conclusion derives from, if he has not been able to complete the "induction" himself. The answer is that it derives from the consequences he can draw from his account. There are two ways in which the justification for the conclusions can be assessed: by the procedure of eliminative induction that he has just set out, and by how well the consequences of the conclusions so generated match other observations. In other words, there is a two-way process, from empirical phenomena to first principles (induction), and then from first principles to empirical phenomena.

THE METHODOLOGICAL IMPLICATIONS OF A NEW MATHEMATICAL NATURAL PHILOSOPHY

Radically anti-Aristotelian though he is, Bacon is in some ways still very much within the Aristotelian tradition. Explanation for Bacon still takes the form of the discovery of essential natures, and such explanation is not quantitative. Yet in the course of the early decades of the seventeenth century, the principal source of dissatisfaction with Aristotle derived from the resistance of his followers to the use of mathematics in physical explanation, and many of the key issues in questions of method in the early to mid-seventeenth century lay in the area of how quantitative, mathematical explanations were to be secured in physical theory.

The guiding principle behind Aristotle's approach to understanding natural processes lies in his classification of the different types of knowledge in book E of the *Metaphysics*. He offers a threefold classification of the "sciences" into the practical sciences, which concern themselves with those variable, contingent, and relative goods that are involved in living well; the productive sciences, which enable us to do or make things; and the theoretical sciences, which are concerned with understanding how things are and why they are as they are. The division of the theoretical sciences works in terms of two variables: whether the phenomena falling under the science are changing or unchanging, and whether their being or "existence" is dependent or independent. Aristotle defines metaphysics, physics, and mathematics in terms of their subject matters. Metaphysics is concerned with whatever does not change and has an independent existence. Physics is concerned with those things that change and have an independent existence, that is, all natural phenomena. Finally, mathematics deals with those things that do not change and do not have an independent existence, that is, those quantitative abstractions we make: numbers (discontinuous magnitudes) and geometrical shapes (continuous magnitudes). The aim of scientific inquiry on his account is to determine what kind of thing the subject matter is by establishing its essential properties. The kinds of principles one employs to achieve this are determined by the subject matter of the science. To establish the essential properties of a natural object, one needs to use principles consonant with that subject matter, i.e. principles that are designed to capture the essence of something which is independent and changing.

This has a very significant bearing upon the connections between the theoretical sciences, and it is particularly marked in the complex question of the relation between physics and mathematics, for it leads to the idea that physical principles must be used in physical inquiry, and mathematical principles in the very different kind of subject matter that constitutes mathematics. The two cannot be mixed, for physical and mathematical principles are essentially concerned with different kinds of subject matter. Although there are many qualifications we need to make to this in exploring the Aristotelian account in detail, the general thrust of the Aristotelian position is that physical inquiry or demonstration cannot be pursued mathematically, any more than mathematical inquiry can be pursued physically. The point can be made in a different way by asking what one does in a physical explanation, and in particular by asking what it is that makes a physical explanation informative. Aristotle, and the whole ancient and medieval tradition after him, thought that one has explained a physical phenomenon when one has given an account of why that event occurred in the way it did, and that this ultimately comes down to providing an account of why bodies behave as they do. In accounting for this behavior, one needs to distinguish between accidental features of a body and its essential properties, and any behavior which can be said to be due to the body itself is due to the essential properties it has. These essential properties explain its behavior. Such properties are physical, and Aristotle argued that they cannot be captured by employing mathematical or quantitative concepts.

As well as natural philosophy, there also existed another discipline in antiquity, which, although it was classed under practical mathematics, dealt with physical devices: this was mechanics, the science of machines. The devices that mechanics investigated – the lever, the inclined plane, the pulley, the screw, gears – were problematic from the Aristotelian point of view in two respects. First, they were non-natural devices, that is, they added to nature rather than making manifest a natural process: as such, they came under the category of "violent motions" rather than "natural motions" and were not properly the subject of natural philosophy at all. Bacon had drawn attention to this feature of Aristotelianism, noting that useful devices were actually excluded from its domain of investigation, whereas these were, in Bacon's view, exactly what investigation should be directed toward. Second, the mechanical disciplines were neither wholly mathematical nor wholly physical, and fell under the rubric of what Aristotle and his followers called "mixed mathematics." A physical account of something – such as why celestial bodies are spherical – is an explanation that works in terms of the fundamental principles of the subject matter of physics, that is, it captures the phenomena in terms of what is changing and has an independent existence, whereas a mathematical account of something – such as the relation between the surface area and the volume of a sphere – requires a wholly different kind of explanation, one that invokes principles commensurate with the kinds of things that mathematical entities are.[11] In *On the Heavens*, for example, we are offered a *physical* proof of the sphericity of the earth,[12] not a mathematical one, because we are dealing with the properties of a *physical* object. In short, distinct subject matters require distinct principles, and physics and mathematics are distinct subject matters. However, Aristotle also recognizes subordinate or mixed sciences, telling us in the *Posterior Analytics* that "the theorems of one science cannot be demonstrated by means of another science, except where these theorems are related as subordinate to superior: for example, as optical theorems to geometry, or harmonic theorems to arithmetic."[13] Whereas physical optics – the investigation of the nature of light and its physical properties – falls straightforwardly under physics, for example, geometrical optics "investigates mathematical lines, but qua physical, not qua mathematical."[14] The question of the relation between mixed mathematics, on the one hand, and the "superior" disciplines of mathematics and physics, which did the real explanatory work on this conception, remained a vexed one throughout the middle ages and the Renaissance, but so long as the former remained marginal to the enterprise of natural philosophy the problems were not especially evident. By the beginning of the seventeenth century, however, the disciplines of what were conceived of as mixed mathematics were attracting a significant amount of attention, above all on the question of whether they might have any explanatory force in their own right.

In its most general form, the problem was how to integrate mechanics into matter theory. Mechanics deals with physical processes in terms of the motions undergone by bodies and the nature of the forces responsible for these motions. Matter theory deals with how the physical behavior of a body is determined by what it is made of, and in the seventeenth century it typically achieves this in a corpuscularian fashion, by investigating how the nature and arrangement of the constituent parts of a body determine its behavior.

Mechanical and matter-theoretic approaches to physical theory are very different: they engage fundamentally different kinds of considerations, and on the face of it offer explanations of different phenomena. We don't explain how levers, inclined planes, screws, and pulleys work in terms of matter theory. Correlatively, it is far from clear that the appropriate form of explanation of the phenomena of burning, fermentation, and differences between fluids and solids is in terms of mechanics.

Traditionally, matter theory had been constitutive of natural philosophy, and it was generally assumed from the Presocratics up to the seventeenth century that the key to understanding physical processes lay in understanding the nature of matter and its behavior, whether this understanding took the form of a theory about how matter is regulated by external immaterial principles, by internal immaterial principles, or by the behavior of the internal material constituents of macroscopic bodies. The traditional disciplines of practical mathematics included such areas as geometrical optics, positional astronomy, harmonics, and statics, the latter being the only area of mechanics that had been developed in antiquity. Statics, along with the other disciplines, was considered very much as a branch of mathematics, which meant – on the prevailing Aristotelian conception – that it dealt with abstractions and hypotheses rather than with physical reality. In other words, it was not part of natural philosophy; it was not something that one would use to explore the nature of the physical world.

Around the beginning of the seventeenth century, however, there was an attempt to draw on the traditional disciplines of practical mathematics and to incorporate these into natural philosophy. In particular, mathematical astronomy had traditionally been considered able to provide mathematical models of the cosmos, but had not been considered to be in a position to establish the physical reality of any of them. There were some Aristotelians, such as the Jesuit mathematician Christopher Clavius (1538–1612), who tried to accommodate a quantitative approach in terms of "mixed mathematics,"[15] and a number of natural philosophers, such as Galileo in his early writings, had attempted to pursue this line of inquiry, but it came to nothing, above all because Aristotle's nonquantitative, matter-theory driven natural philosophy simply carried too much baggage.[16]

Galileo had pushed hard for the incorporation of mathematical astronomy into natural philosophy, and had sought to rid it of the merely hypothetical standing that it had had up to that point.[17] The kind of account of celestial motion he offered was very different from that we find in Aristotle, or in sixteenth-century scholastic writers on cosmology and astronomy. Galileo attempted to develop a mechanical theory, above all a dynamics, that made natural-philosophical sense of Copernicanism, in the way that Aristotelian natural philosophy had been used to ground and make physical sense of the Ptolemaic system. The single greatest obstacle from the methodological point of view was the objection that mechanics dealt only with mathematical idealizations, not with reality, and this objection had to be cleared out of the way before the project for a quantitative natural philosophy could proceed. This was, in fact, the greatest methodological problem of the first half of the seventeenth century.

GALILEO AND THE PROBLEM OF IDEALIZATIONS

In *Two New Sciences* (1638), Galileo provides the first modern full-scale kinematical treatment of motion: in particular, he presents and justifies laws concerning free fall and projectile motion. These he presents in the form of mathematical descriptions of what happens in a void. Now the motion of bodies in a void is something we never experience and something to which we have no direct access. The motions of bodies in resisting media is something we regularly experience, yet these motions differ from the motions those same bodies would undergo in a void. Galileo's law of free fall tells us that all bodies undergo a uniform acceleration in a void, but this is clearly not the case in a resisting medium. At first sight, therefore, the law appears to suffer from two drawbacks: it appears to tell us something about a situation that may never occur, and it appears not to tell us about situations that do normally occur. Hence there seem to be problems both about the relevance of the law and about whether it could receive any evidential support.

Galileo's solution is to set out the relations that hold between a body falling in a void and that body falling in a resisting medium.[18] He takes the fall of bodies in a resisting medium as his starting point and then describes a series of experiments, including thought experiments, designed to decide what factors are operative in determining the rate of fall of a body and how these factors operate.

He deals first with the traditional Aristotelian view that rate of fall is directly proportional to absolute weight. He has two arguments against this. The first is empirical: if two bodies made of the same material but of different absolute weights are dropped simultaneously from the top of a tower to the ground, they arrive at the ground simultaneously. The second is a thought experiment. If we drop, say, two lead spheres of different weights, then on the Aristotelian account the heavier will fall faster. But, suppose we tie the spheres together. The slower one would then surely slow down the faster one, and the faster one would speed up the slower, so that the resultant speed would be somewhere between the two original speeds. But the aggregate weight is greater than the weight of the heavier body. Hence, rate of fall cannot be directly proportional to absolute weight. Now, Aristotle had also held that the rate of fall is inversely proportional to the density of the medium. Against this another thought experiment is proposed. If we let the density ratio of water to air be $n:1$, where $n>1$ (since the specific weight of water is greater than that of air), and take a body that falls in air but floats in water (e.g. a wooden sphere), and say that this has a rate of fall of one unit in air, then it would follow that it has a rate of fall of $1/n$ units in water. But, we have already said that it floats – i.e. would rise and not fall – in water. So rate of fall cannot be inversely proportional to the density of the medium.

Next, Galileo makes an important generalization. Instead of thinking simply in terms of rate of fall determined with respect to one body in two media or with respect to two bodies in one medium, he considers the case of any body in any medium. First, he describes an experiment which shows that the ratio between the rates of fall of bodies is not the same as the ratio of their specific weights. Gold and lead, which fall at approximately the same rate in air, behave quite differently in mercury, the former sinking, the latter rising to the surface. This experiment indicates that differences in rate of fall of bodies diminish as the density of the medium decreases. This prompts him to ask what would happen in the limiting case of a void: he raises the possibility that in such a case the rate of fall of all bodies would be equal. But, until we know the precise connection between speed, specific weight, and resistance, we will not be able to establish this. Galileo therefore proposes an experiment in which the buoyancy effect of the medium can be distinguished. The buoyancy effect is the ratio between the specific weight of the body and that of the medium. The problem is to determine precisely what effect this ratio has on rate of fall. He compares the buoyancy effect of two media (air and water) on two bodies (ebony and lead). Given the specific weights of these substances, the buoyancy effect can easily be calculated. It turns out that the buoyancy effect varies much more radically than the specific weight of the body: if we let the specific weights of air, water, ebony, and lead, be 1, 800, 1,000, and 10,000 respectively, then it turns out that whereas the buoyancy effect of air has a negligible effect on rates of fall of ebony and lead, the buoyancy effect of water on ebony is huge (it loses four-fifths of its effective weight) whereas its effect on lead is very small (less than one-tenth). It is the specific weight ratios that determine rate of fall, not the specific weights themselves. Since a void has no specific weight, it cannot bear a ratio relation to the specific weight of the falling body; i.e. this ratio which determines differences in the rate of fall cannot be operative in the case of a void. So we must conclude that all bodies – whatever their specific weight – fall in a void with the same "degree of speed" (i.e. as it turns out, degree of uniformly accelerated motion). This conclusion is particularly important, since on the basis of the equality of rates of fall of all bodies in a void we can proceed, at least in principle, to calculate the differences in speeds between any two bodies in any media by determining the amount by which the theoretical speed in a void will be diminished; and we do this by comparing the specific weight of bodies with that of the media. To this end, Galileo takes us through (largely unsuccessful) experiments to measure the specific weight of air.

There remains one problem. Bodies falling in media do not in fact accelerate uniformly. Neither specific weight nor the buoyancy effect can account for this, since they are both constant (the latter being a constant for any particular body and any particular medium). This leads Galileo to invoke a form of resistance to fall which is distinct from the buoyancy effect: the friction effect. The friction effect increases with the acceleration of the body, since larger and larger amounts of resisting medium have to be traversed, and equilibrium is reached when the body ceases to accelerate because of friction. This state of equilibrium occurs much earlier in rarer bodies, not because the friction effect bears a direct relation to specific weight, but because the buoyancy effect is much greater in bodies of lower density, and hence their motion is already greatly retarded. For this conclusion to go through, however, two things have to be shown: first, that the friction effect is greater for rarer bodies; second, that it increases with speed. In order to show the first, we need to isolate the friction effect experimentally from the buoyancy effect. Free fall does not allow us to do this. Galileo suggests rolling two bodies, e.g. one of cork and one of lead, down a plane which is gently inclined so as to make the motions as slow as possible and thereby to reduce the buoyancy effect. The trouble here is that the more gentle the incline, the greater the surface friction, which would interfere with our isolating the friction effect (which is totally different from surface friction, since it is an effect of the medium). He resolves these difficulties by proposing an ingenious experiment in which a cork and a lead sphere are suspended on threads of equal length and set in oscillation. The periods of oscillation remain identical for both spheres, but in the case of the cork sphere, the amplitude of swing is considerably reduced very quickly. This cannot be due to the greater specific weight of the lead causing it to move faster: we can begin the experiment by swinging the cork through a greater arc so that it initially moves faster, but the same thing will happen. Moreover, since the buoyancy effect is simply the specific weight ratio, it cannot be due to this, either. It must therefore be due to the friction effect. Finally, all that remains to be shown is that the friction effect increases with speed. Again, no direct experiment on freely falling bodies is possible because of the great distances that would be involved and the difficulties in measurement that would ensue. Hence the consequence, that bodies projected at artificially high speeds will be retarded until they reach their natural maximum speed for that medium, is of crucial importance, since an experimental situation in which this can be tested can be realized in a relatively easy and straightforward way. We simply fire a gun vertically downward from a great height and measure the penetration of the bullet into the ground. We then fire the gun close to the ground and measure that penetration. The first is less than the second, which means that the bullet has been retarded.

In sum, Galileo shows, by means of a series of actual experiments and thought experiments, that rate of fall bears a complex relation to specific weight, buoyancy effect, and friction effect. By determining exactly how these factors are related to one another, he is able to determine what happens when the medium is removed entirely, and this forms the content of his law of free fall. Now Galilean kinematics is the model for much seventeenth-century mechanics, providing the model which, when developed further by Huygens and others, will be fleshed out by Newton in dynamical terms in the *Principia*. If there is any method by which the *Principia* proceed, it is built on Galileo's procedure in the *Two New Sciences*. But what is the method? None of the standard methodologies of science seem to fit the bill.

Since we do not experience bodies falling in a void, for example, we cannot arrive at Galileo's law by cumulative induction, that is, by comparing instances of falling bodies and isolating what they have in common. On the other hand, since, if the law holds, its truth is contingent – bodies may just as easily have fallen at different rates in a void, or may have fallen with an unaccelerated or nonuniformly accelerated motion – it is impossible that a priori arguments will lead us to the law. To maintain that the law is a hypothesis open to empirical tests is of no real help, either. First, the problem simply reappears at a different level. The situation described in the law does not naturally occur and cannot be experimentally induced, so in what way is it open to empirical test? And, even if the situation *could* somehow be experimentally induced, that would still leave the problem of how the law could be at all relevant to the case of bodies falling in resisting media. Second, the presumption behind the hypothetical construal is that the theory itself is somehow developed at a purely conceptual level and then tested empirically to determine whether it is true or not. But, it is clear that here experiment is an integral part of scientific discovery, not an added extra. This has important consequences for our understanding of methodological questions, because it suggests the inappropriateness of any general distinction between invention and presentation (or its modern analogue, context of discovery and context of justification). Rather, in the present case (hardly a unique case in this respect), there seems to be a continuous integration of discovery and justification. There may indeed be cases in which a separation of discovery and justification is possible, but no general lesson can be drawn from such cases about best methodological practice.

DESCARTES: "UNIVERSAL METHOD" VERSUS HYPOTHESES

The most formative figures in seventeenth-century discussions of method are Bacon and Descartes, and Descartes's contribution is by far the deeper and more complex.[19] There are in fact a number of different strands in Descartes's work on method, and it will be helpful here to distinguish between questions of discovery and questions of presentation, as this was a distinction basic to his project, although, as we shall see, there is a blurring of the distinction on the crucial questions of hypotheses.

We must distinguish two distinct phases in Descartes's thinking on questions of discovery. During the 1620s, Descartes believed he had hit upon a general method of discovery that had its origins in mathematics; but this encountered problems around 1628, and during the 1630s, he advocated a less ambitious account of discovery in natural philosophy that was experimental, and not unlike the procedure in Galileo which we have just looked at.[20]

In 1620, Descartes made an important mathematical discovery. From the beginning of the century, there had been an interest in an implement called the proportional compass, which had a variety of uses. Galileo wrote a pamphlet showing how to use a proportional compass to calculate compound interest, and proportional compasses were used to solve geometrical problems that were not soluble using a ruler and ordinary compass, such as the division of angles into as many equal parts as one chooses. For Descartes, the fact that the proportional compass could be used to solve both arithmetical and geometrical problems suggested that these were not, perhaps, fundamental disciplines at all. Since the principle behind the proportional compass was continued proportions, he realized that there was a more fundamental discipline, which he initially identified with a theory of proportions, later with algebra. This more fundamental discipline had two features. First, it underlay arithmetic and geometry, in the sense that, along with various branches of practical mathematics such as astronomy and the theory of harmony, these were simply particular species of it, and for this reason he termed it *mathesis universalis*, "universal mathematics." Its second feature was that this universal mathematics was a problem-solving discipline: indeed, an exceptionally powerful problem-solving discipline whose resources went far beyond those of traditional geometry and arithmetic. Descartes was able to show this in a spectacular way in geometry, taking on problems, such as the Pappus locus problem, which had baffled geometers since late antiquity, and he was able to show how his new problem-solving algebraic techniques could cut through these effortlessly. In investigating the problem-solving capacity of his universal mathematics, however, Descartes suspected that there might be an even more fundamental discipline of which universal mathematics itself was simply a species, a master problem-solving discipline that underlay every area of inquiry, physical and mathematical. This most fundamental discipline Descartes termed "universal method," and it is such a method that the *Rules* sought to set out and explore.[21]

The general feature that underlies universal mathematics, which Descartes hoped to isolate and make the subject of universal method, was the clear and distinct representation of ideas. In the case of mathematics, for example, Descartes was led to reject both geometrical and arithmetical representations of problems: the former because geometrical proofs often offered only an indirect connection between premises and conclusions and lacked transparency because they often had, of necessity, to proceed through auxiliary constructions and the like, and the latter because relations between numbers were not apparent in their usual arithmetical representation. In the case of arithmetical operations, for example, the truth of the proposition $2 + 3 = 5$ is not immediately evident in this form of representation, but it is evident if we represent the operation of addition as the joining together of two line lengths (see Fig. 2).

In this case, we can see how the quantities combine to form their sum (and this is just as evident in the case of very large numbers the numerical value of whose sum we cannot immediately compute).

In fact, the project collapsed in the case of mathematics, because there was simply no line-length representation of some of the more sophisticated operations opened up by Descartes's algebra.[22] But Descartes was loath to abandon the idea that there were ways of presenting ideas clearly and distinctly to ourselves in such a way

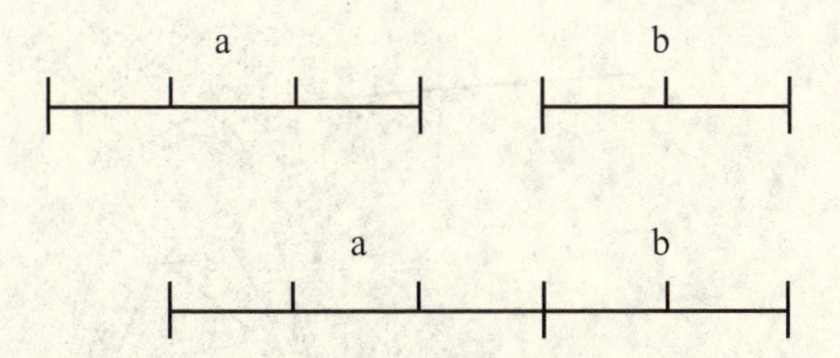

Figure 2. Representation of addition, Descartes, *Rules*, 18 (AT X 464: CSM I 73).

that we could immediately grasp the truth or falsity of their content. The new paradigm for clear and distinct grasp now shifts from mathematics to epistemology, and it is the *cogito* that comes to stand in as the archetypical form of clear and distinct idea: simply by reflecting on the content of the idea, we grasp that it must be true. But while reflection on clear and distinct ideas provides a basis for setting out truths in a systematic way, it is not presented by Descartes as a method of discovery.

If anything has a claim to being his proposed method of discovery in natural philosophy it is, as he tells Antoine Vatier in a letter of 22 February 1638, to be found in his account of the rainbow.[23] This is presented in book 8 of his *Météores*, which is devoted to explaining the angle at which the bows of the rainbow appear in the sky. He begins by noting that rainbows are also in fountains and showers in the presence of sunlight, which leads him to formulate the hypothesis that the phenomenon is caused by light reacting on drops of water. To test this hypothesis, he constructs a glass model of the raindrop, comprising a large glass sphere filled with water, and, standing with his back to the sun, he holds up the sphere in the sun's light, moving it up and down so that colors are produced (see Fig. 3).

Then, if we let the light from the sun come

> from the part of the sky marked AFZ, and my eye be at point E, then when I put this globe at the place BCD, the part of it at D seems to me wholly red and incomparably more brilliant than the rest. And whether I move toward it or step back from it, or move it to the right or to the left, or even turn it in a circle around my head, then provided the line DE always marks an angle of around 42° with the line EM, which one must imagine to

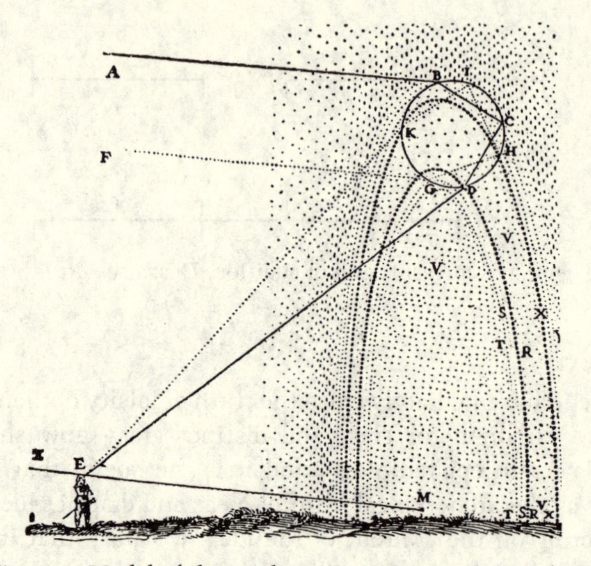

Figure 3. Model of the rainbow, Descartes, *Météores* (AT VI 326).

extend from the center of the eye to the center of the sun, D always appears equally red. But as soon as I made this angle DEM the slightest bit smaller, it did not disappear completely in the one stroke, but first divided as into two less brilliant parts in which could be seen yellow, blue, and other colors. Then, looking toward the place marked K on the globe, I perceived that, making the angle KEM around 52°, K also seemed to be colored red, but not so brilliant.

(AT VI 326–27)

Descartes then describes how he covered the globe at all points except B and D. The ray still emerged, showing that the primary and secondary bows are caused by two refractions and one or two internal reflections of the incident ray. He next describes how the same effect can be produced with a prism, and this indicates that neither a curved surface nor reflection are necessary for color dispersion. Moreover, the prism experiment shows that the effect does not depend on the angle of incidence, and that one refraction is sufficient for its production. Finally, Descartes calculates from the refractive index of rainwater what an observer would see when light strikes a drop of water at varying angles of incidence, and finds that the optimum difference for visibility between incident and refracted rays is for the former to be viewed at an angle of 41° to 42° and the latter at an angle of 51° to 52°, which is exactly what the hypothesis predicts (AT VI 336).

Hypotheses here figure very much as a method of discovery, but there is also a use of hypotheses in Descartes where they are part of a method of presentation. Both *The World* and the *Treatise on Man*, for example, purport to describe hypothetical imaginary worlds rather than real worlds,[24] and in the *Principles of Philosophy* he prefaces his account of the formation of the Earth with the statement that he is describing a way in which the Earth might have been formed by purely natural processes, not the way in which it was in fact formed, by an act of creation,[25] and again he explicitly calls his account a hypothesis. In each of these cases, Descartes is introducing an extremely contentious thesis – heliocentrism, the doctrine of animal machines, and an account of the formation of the Earth that eschews any mention of ends – which he wants to present in such a way as to obtain for it the greatest possible hearing. In the case of at least the first two (and possibly all three), he does not genuinely believe that what he is offering is merely hypothetical, but an account of what really happens, and in each case it is crucial to his project that the outcome of the "hypothetical" processes he invokes is something identical to what we find in the real world.

In the late seventeenth- and early eighteenth-century disputes over the merits of Cartesian and Newtonian natural philosophy, one of the central issues was that of the role of hypothesis, Newtonians contrasting the certainty of the results achieved in Newton's *Principia* with the merely hypothetical standing of those of Descartes.[26] The questions here are complex. While those natural philosophers who identified themselves as Cartesians in the second half of the seventeenth century were in fact very experimentally orientated,[27] by the eighteenth century, Cartesianism was identified with an analytical/mathematical approach to mechanics.[28] But confining our attention to Descartes himself, it is clear that a good deal of the polemic against him would have been neutralized if the role of hypotheses in discovery (even though discovery and justification are in some respects indistinguishable in his investigation of the rainbow, for example, just as they were in Galileo's investigation of free fall) had been distinguished from the hypothetical mode of presentation of contentious theories and results, for much of the criticism rests on the view that even Descartes admits that his main results are merely hypothetical, which is a misunderstanding of the role of hypotheses in the presentation of results.

METHOD MAKETH THE MAN

Concern with method is not just a question of how one goes about doing natural philosophy in the seventeenth century. Both Bacon and Descartes urged that natural philosophy lay at the core of the philosophical enterprise, and both of them combined a concern with method with a concern for what kind of person is best equipped to carry out this method. Moreover, both of them believed that the traditional philosopher, and traditional philosophical training, were woefully inadequate to the task they envisaged. In effect, what Bacon and Descartes were concerned with was the transformation of philosophers into what, in the nineteenth century, would become known as scientists. This is a recurrent theme in Bacon's work, and Descartes touches upon it primarily in his *Search after Truth*.[29] The problem was not only that a traditional core area of philosophy might be pursued in a completely novel way, but that philosophy itself was going to be a very different kind of enterprise once this core area had been removed. The new natural philosophy had a clear purpose, and what distinguished it above all was the method (disputed as this was) by which it was to realize that purpose.

By the end of the seventeenth century, there was widespread consensus that the speculative methods that philosophy had traditionally employed had failed it in natural philosophy. The new natural philosophy and the other traditional philosophical concerns had to be realigned. This inevitably raised the question of what the purpose of philosophy per se was, with Locke maintaining in the "Epistle to the Reader" at the beginning of *An Essay concerning Human Understanding*, that "every one must not hope to be a Boyle, or a Sydenham; and in an Age that produces such Masters, as the Great Huygenius, and the Incomparable Mr. Newton, with some other of that strain; 'tis Ambition enough to be imploy'd as an Under-Laborer in clearing Ground a little, and removing some of the Rubbish that lies in the Way to Knowledg."[30] The view of the reformed natural philosopher/scientist as the master builder and the philosopher as under-laborer was not universal. The great tradition of German systematic metaphysics from Leibniz to Kant was very much one of scholastic philosophy radically reformed and renewed, for example, one in which metaphysics, which had its own distinctive way of proceeding, provided the foundations which, among other things, allowed one to make sense of the natural philosophy and mechanics that had developed their results by quite different methods.

NOTES

1 Although now somewhat dated, the best general coverage of these questions is Gilbert 1960. There was also an extensive legal and medical literature on questions of evidence that bear on method, which I do not discuss here. On the legal literature, see Franklin 1963 and Maclean 1992. On the medical literature on these questions, see Maclean 2001.
2 On the very varied impact of Aristotle in the sixteenth century, see Schmitt 1983a and Di Liscia et al. 1997.
3 See Gaukroger 1989, ch. 1.
4 See Barnes 1975.
5 See Jardine 1988, pp. 687ff.
6 See the discussion in Jardine 1976.
7 See the discussion in Ong 1983.
8 For a detailed discussion of Bacon on these questions, see Gaukroger 2001, Urbach 1987, and Anderson 1971.
9 The chief discussion of the doctrine is in *New Organon,* which is to be found in vol. I (Latin) and vol. IV (English trans.) of Bacon 1857–74, and in Bacon 2000.
10 See Bacon's *Valerius terminus* (1857–74, vol. III, pp. 235–41).
11 See Aristotle, *Posterior Analytics* 75a28–38: "Since it is just those attributes within every genus which are essential and possessed by their respective subjects as such that are necessary, it is clear that both the conclusions and the premises of demonstrations which produce scientific knowledge are essential . . . It follows that in demonstrating we cannot pass from one genus to another." Cf. 76a23ff. and *On the Heavens* 306a9–12.
12 *On the Heavens*, 297a9ff.
13 *Posterior Analytics* 75b14–16.
14 *Physics* 194a10.
15 See Dear 1995.

16 See Gaukroger and Schuster 2002.
17 For details see Biagioli 1993.
18 Galileo, *Two New Sciences* (1974, pp. 65–108). See the discussions in Gaukroger 1978, ch. 6; Clavelin 1974, parts III and IV.
19 The most general treatment is Clarke 1982.
20 For details see Gaukroger 1995.
21 See Rule 4 of *Rules for the Direction of the Native Intelligence* (AT X 371–79: CSM I 15–20).
22 See Gaukroger 1995, pp. 172–81.
23 Descartes, AT I 559–60: CSM III 85; see also the *Discourse* (AT VI 63–65: CSM I 143–44), and *Météores* (AT VI 325).
24 *The World* at AT XI 31–32, 36: CSM I 90, 92; and *Treatise on Man* at AT XI 120: CSM I 99.
25 *Principles*, IV.1 (AT IXB 201: CSM I 267).
26 See Laudan 1981, ch. 4.
27 See McClaughlin 2000; and more generally Clarke 1989.
28 See Blay 1992.
29 On the construction of a new scientific persona in Bacon, see Gaukroger 2001. On the construction of a new scientific persona in Descartes, see Gaukroger 2002.
30 Locke 1722, vol. I, p. ix.

DENNIS DES CHENE

3 From natural philosophy to natural science

In 1619, after one of his first encounters with Descartes, Isaac Beeckman, pleased to find a kindred spirit, noted that "physico-mathematici" are "paucissimi" – very few.[1] Aside from himself, Descartes, and perhaps Galileo, Beeckman knew of no others. A half-century later, Leibniz noted that "recent philosophers all wish to explain physical matters mechanistically (*mechanice*)."[2] The period between witnessed a transformation in the concepts, methods, and institutions of natural philosophy, so remarkable that it is tempting simply to grant that Bacon's promised "new instauration" – in later language, a revolution – was accomplished, and the philosophy of the schools wholly superseded.

That transformation was uneven and incomplete. Even in physics, though there was undoubtedly profound change in fundamental concepts, explanations of particular phenomena were sometimes almost rote "mechanizations" of explanations already found in scholastic works. At the outset, many of the phenomena themselves were not new. Even more so does this hold in chemistry and physiology. Descartes's *Treatise on Man*, written in the early 1630s, though it "mechanizes" physiology, does so almost entirely on the basis of the anatomy and physiology of his nonmechanist predecessors. The program of the *Treatise* could have proceeded perfectly well without Harvey's discovery of the circulation of the blood and Kepler's new theory of vision. Adherents of Aristotelianism, moreover, were not without resources to accommodate some, if not all, of the novelties of their rivals. Honoré Fabri rejected both Cartesianism and Gassendism. Nevertheless he was an "experimental philosopher," and quite capable of formulating corpuscular explanations of optical and mechanical phenomena. Not only could new concepts happily coexist with old data; but the concepts themselves by no means composed an indissoluble whole.

The changes, moreover, now bundled under the heading of the "Scientific Revolution," were, though roughly contemporary, only loosely related. The uses of experience – and especially the creation of new phenomena by artificial means – changed even as the concepts employed to explain them did. But neither was dependent on the other. The same holds for the new institutional arrangements for the production and dissemination of scientific results established in the second half of the century. The three streams – conceptual, experimental or practical, and institutional – though often mingled, had their own tempi, their own terrains. Even if there was a kind of unity in their progression, talk of a single emerging scientific worldview does not do justice either to the heterogeneity of change or to the multiplicity of its causal conditions.

In this chapter, I concentrate on the conceptual. The story has two parts. First of all, scholastic matter and form give way to a "mechanical" matter, to which only a few primary accidents are attributed. Scholastic form, for its part, is supplanted by *figure* – the shapes attributed to elementary parts or corpuscles of matter – and *texture* or *configuration* – the various manners of combination of those elementary parts. It is by reference to the hypothetical figures and configurations of matter that the reduction of material accidents is made good. So-called "secondary" qualities, including not only the sensible but also the dispositional – flexibility and transparency as well as taste and color – are to be *explained*, where "explanation" means a more or less speculative causal account by which it is shown that matter thus configured *would have* the effects to be explained. This, the "mechanical hypothesis" of Boyle, though not an entirely new mode of explanation, became the means by which the imputedly profligate and obscure scholastic forms and qualities were dismissed.

The second part of the story concerns laws and ends. By the time of Newton, the primary object of natural philosophy is no longer powers and operations, but the laws of nature. At first, the laws in question are only the fundamental laws of motion. But gradually the notion of law is extended to cover almost any universal generalization – Boyle's law, for example, or Hooke's – until "science" and "knowledge of laws" become, as in Kant, virtually identical. It is by way of the notion of law, which is only with difficulty extractable from its theistic origins, that the scholastic distinction between chance and *ends* is supplanted by a distinction between chance and causal *laws*, which, conjoined with suitable hypotheses about material figures and configurations, yield an efficient-causal account of order in the natural world.

This conception of science, impressed firmly upon philosophical reflection by Kant, would have seemed quite alien to a scholastic. Scholastic natural philosophy does gather generalizations. But the source of natural order is a community of *natures*, defined in terms of active and passive *powers*, subordinated to a hierarchy of ends. What mediates between the old and new conceptions is the ascription to God of those ends, which are not, as Aristotle would have it, intrinsic to things; the new philosophy goes on to deny to the things of nature not only ends but active powers. *Force* is either God himself or from God. It is not surprising, then, that occasionalism should have experienced a revival in seventeenth-century thought; that revival makes evident the difficulty of retaining, in a science based on passive matter actuated by the power of God according to laws, a notion of efficient cause with more meat on its bones than the Humean.

What follows is primarily a coarse-grained description of historical change. Explanations are harder to come by. Those I offer are for the most part in terms of motivations internal to the disciplines I examine. It is, in my view, not evident why the school philosophy should have given way so quickly, or at all; nor why experiment, and especially the deliberate *production* of new phenomena by art (by what we would call technological means), should have taken on the importance it did. An internal dynamic develops in the sciences by which hypotheses are made to yield experimental setups the realization of which will put those hypotheses to the test, and conversely by which new devices and the phenomena produced by them are thought to demand theoretical explanation. That dynamic is largely absent from the schools. It cuts across conceptual disagreements, and is perhaps a better diagnostic of the newness of the new philosophy than any one theoretical or methodological innovation. But that is only to push the problem back a step: it is again not evident why that dynamic should have taken hold when it did. One can see, perhaps, that a rational agent, endowed with certain aims, would prefer the new way to the old, and for what reasons. The real and the rational, however, do not coincide as a matter of course. Even if a "rational reconstruction" could be given a role in explaining the triumph of the new science, the fact that reason was in this instance *effective* would itself require explanation.

MATERIAL SUBSTANCE

Aristotelian views

(1) *Prime and proximate matter*. Matter and form are for the Aristotelian the basic components of all material substances. *Prime* matter is the basic stuff underlying all such substances; for each kind of substance, there is a corresponding *proximate* matter, the qualities of which are those required to support the operations characteristic of things having its form. That much was common to all Aristotelians, whether Scotist or Thomist or eclectic. In disputed questions on matter, which are found in both *Physics* and *Metaphysics* commentaries, one finds on almost every other point significant differences.

The principal argument for the existence of prime matter is that in every natural change there must be something that persists through the change. Otherwise we would have not change but annihilation and creation. It was generally believed that creation is the prerogative of God, because to bring something out of nothing requires infinite power. Natural agents cannot create. They can only produce new forms in a preexisting (and persistent) matter.

But is there *one* stuff that underlies *all* change, and that is therefore common to all material things? Disputations on this point record the opinion that celestial and terrestrial matter differ even in their underlying stuff, but the predominant opinion is that in all bodies there is unique "prime" or first matter that persists through every natural change. In particular, the transmutation of elements, as of water into air under the action of fire, seems to require such a matter, bereft of all qualities though perhaps not of quantity. In transmutation, nothing remains of the old substantial form and the elemental qualities associated with it. Yet since this is a natural change, effected by a natural agent, the new element is not *created*.

Its form is introduced into (or "educed from the *potentia* of" – see below) a matter that persists through the change.

(2) *Prime matter and quantity*. The relation of prime matter to quantity was a vexed question. The orthodox Thomist held that matter is *pura potentia*, a "pure potency" to take on any material substantial form. In particular, matter is not essentially endowed with quantity, although no material thing exists naturally without quantity. Against those nominalists who held that matter and quantity are one (on the grounds that matter and quantity have, naturally, the same effects), the Thomist argued that in transsubstantiation, the quantity of the host remains even after its substance – its matter and its substantial form – is annihilated. Quantity can therefore exist without matter, and is therefore distinct from it.[3]

Nevertheless, matter seems to have a natural affinity for quantity. Divine intervention is required to deprive it of quantity altogether. Natural change – in particular, the corruption of a complex substance into its elements – cannot do so. Suárez, here departing from the Thomist view (represented in the seventeenth century by John of St. Thomas and the various authors based at Salamanca: see Martin Stone's chapter in this volume), held that matter is not *pure* potency – it is *essentially in potentia* to quantity, even if by divine act that *potentia* can be prevented from being actualized. That *potentia*, moreover, distinguishes it as matter: spiritual substances do not have a *potentia* to quantity.

(3) *Matter and form*. The new philosophers, when they took note of prime matter, dismissed it as unintelligible and otiose; but most of their criticisms were directed against form. An Aristotelian material individual is a "complete substance" with two components, each of which is an "incomplete substance." Prime matter and its complement, substantial form, are "substantial" insofar as each is the subject of inherence for certain accidents; they are "incomplete" because neither can exist naturally without the other.

Among the accidents of material substance, quantity was by most philosophers held to inhere in matter. Also inhering in matter, according to some, were the qualities that together made the matter fit to receive a particular form. The soul of a human being, for example, requires a certain "temperament" or combination of elemental qualities in the body joined with it. Rather than say that the soul itself is hot or cold or wet or dry, it was thought that those qualities inhere in the matter by virtue of the soul joined with it. In a human being, warmth inheres in the body. But, as changes after death prove, the presence of that warmth depends on the soul.

Habits, desires, and volitions, on the other hand, inhere in the soul. The remembering of a tree, for example, requires the use of a bodily organ – a ventricle in the brain or the animal spirits residing therein – but is itself a quality of the soul. Similarly the various powers of the soul, which belong to the Aristotelian category of quality, inhere in the soul alone, even if their exercise requires the use of bodily organs.

The resulting picture is one in which the accidents of complex material substances are divided into those that inhere immediately in form, and those that, though produced by form, inhere immediately in matter. The active powers of a thing inhere in its form, its passive powers and qualities in its matter, or in quantity which itself inheres immediately in matter.

In a complex substance, the "order of production" is from form to powers and from powers to operations (which are the *actus* or actualizations of underlying *potentiae* or powers). Substantial form is thus twice removed from experience: what affects our senses is not form but accidents. Substantial form, like prime matter, is an inferred entity. It would, however, be misleading to take matter or form to be analogous to the "theoretical" entities referred to in current philosophy of science. Theoretical entities like atoms or genes, though not immediately accessible to the unaided senses, are typically not ontologically separate *kinds* in the way that substance, matter, and form are ontologically separate from quality and quantity. An atom is a body, a very small body; it is a constituent of those macroscopic bodies that do affect the senses, not a component.

The closest counterpart in modern science to Aristotelian form is *structure* or *function*. Like form, these are not accessible to the senses except through concrete realizations (in the case of structure) or actual operations (in the case of function). They enter into explanations not as efficient causes or constituents of observables, but as ways of describing concrete individuals or collections of individuals, which are not, however, necessarily reducible to any one such realization. The Aristotelians were inclined to credit form and matter with distinct existence; they admitted a more generous ontology than most recent philosophers are willing to countenance. But that difference should not obscure the likeness of role in explanation. It is not my purpose here to defend the use of structure or function in scientific explanation. It suffices to point out that if they have a legitimate use, then an analogous case can be made for the inferred entities of Aristotelian natural philosophy. The issue between the schools and us, or between the schools and the new philosophers, is not solely one of utility in explanation; it is a question of existence.

(4) *Qualities.* Substantial form was one of the two most frequent targets of criticism among the *novatores* (or moderns). Quality was the other. The Aristotelian admitted among the primary, irreducible qualities of material substances the proper sensibles of each of our five senses, the four elemental qualities (hot, cold, wet, dry), and various "occult" qualities like those thought to underlie the attraction of iron to lodestones. Figure, which is an entirely passive quality, has no role in explaining the qualities of homogeneous substances like blood and bone. It comes into its own in explaining certain dispositional qualities like transparency and flexibility. In such explanations, the Aristotelian and the mechanical philosopher tend to converge.

The new philosophers criticized their predecessors on two main points. The first was the doctrine of "real qualities." Though rhetorically prominent, it has more the character of a debating point than of a genuine issue. To show how it is possible that the host should continue to affect our senses in the same way even when its substance is annihilated and replaced by the body of Christ, Thomas Aquinas had supposed that the accidents of the host could persist even when its substance was annihilated. Not surprisingly, philosophers like Descartes and Boyle found the doctrine of Thomas unintelligible. Accidents are *defined* in terms of inherence: an accident depends on something else to exist, namely the substance it inheres in. "Accident without substance" is a contradiction in terms.

Aristotelians in their defense of the doctrine distinguish the essence of accidents, defined as *potential* inherence, from their existence. The whiteness of the host remains in its essence an accident even if, by divine intervention, it happens to exist without inhering in any substance. The issue is not, as Descartes would have it, whether an accident can be a substance – it can't – but rather the invoking of the distinction between potential and actual. The defenders of Thomas treat their account of the essence of accidents as a natural extension of that distinction; Descartes and the other new philosophers tend to reject it, not only here but everywhere in natural philosophy.

The second, and more important, point of criticism was that the Aristotelians' list of primary qualities was too big. Of the qualities recognized in Aristotelian physics, only figure is in fact required to explain what we experience in nature. Hot, cold, wet, dry, and the "occult" qualities can be reduced to the figures and motions of the parts of matter. The new philosopher demanded, in other words, an *explanation* of what the Aristotelian understood to be in no need of explanation, and itself the starting point for explaining the less fundamental properties of mixtures. I will return to this point in the discussion of the mechanical philosophy.

(5) *Change.* Aristotle appeals to the distinction between the potential and the actual in defining natural change. Natural change is the actuality (*actus*) of what was at first only potential (*in potentia*): when water spontaneously cools after being heated, its potential coldness becomes actual. It cools because it is in the nature of water to have a *potentia* toward coldness that will, if not hindered, express itself in actually being cold. Similarly, a seed is *in potentia* the mature plant or animal it will become, and it will become mature, given the materials it needs to do so and the absence of any hindrance.

Change in this sense can occur in substance, quantity, quality, and place. Change of substance is *generation* or *corruption*. Change of quantity is *growth* or *diminution*. Change of quality is *alteration*, as in heating or cooling or changing color. Change of place is *local motion* or *locomotion*. The distinction between *potentia* and *actus* applies to place as it does in the other cases. A heavy body which is not at the center of the world is only potentially in its natural place. Were it to reach the center it would have actualized that *potentia*. There are, of course, many cases of local motion that do not consist in falling or rising; these may be contranatural or "violent" from the standpoint of a body's heaviness or lightness, but from the standpoint of the agent that causes the local motion they may be natural changes necessary to or constitutive of, say, growth or generation. In principle, every change not itself natural (or purely miraculous) can be subsumed under some change which is, and so all change can be fitted into an overall teleology of the natural world.

Cartesian bodies

Descartes's physics was not the first new physics of the seventeenth century. Atomists like Thomas Harriot, Sebastian Basso, and Daniel Gorlaeus preceded him; Hobbes and Gassendi were developing their natural philosophies at roughly the same time; and in Italy, Bernardino Telesio, Francesco Patrizi, and Tommaso Campanella had already presented new, comprehensive alternatives to the school philosophy; Galileo had argued that Aristotelian qualities and forms were to be replaced by a single, mathematically describable matter.[4] Nevertheless Descartes's natural philosophy, and that of his rival Gassendi, taking advantage of discontent with Aristotelianism, came to dominate the field of alternatives by 1660. Their heyday, as it turned out, was short; but it was decisive.

(1) *Res extensa*. The principles of Descartes's physics fall under two headings: a new ontology of the natural world, and a new means of explaining change. The new ontology, which I treat here, was that of *res extensa* and *res cogitans*: extended stuff and thinking stuff are, with God, the three *summa genera* of Descartes's world. The new means was the laws of nature, the topic of the next section. Already in *The World*, written in the early 1630s but not published until 1664, Descartes writes of his new world that in it there are no forms, no elemental qualities, no sensible qualities, and no prime matter. Instead, the matter of this new world is to be conceived "as a true body, perfectly solid, which fills equally all the lengths, widths, and depths of this great space in the middle of which we have, in thought, come to rest."[5]

In Aristotelian physics, matter cannot naturally exist without quantity. But matter and quantity are held, except by nominalists, to be distinct. Quantity considered in itself is entirely passive; the active powers of material things are qualities. The modes of quantity are size and figure, and like quantity itself, they are entirely inert. When Descartes identified matter with extension, and the qualities of material things with the modes of extension, he was effectively ruling out any appeal to active powers in physical explanation. He was also eliminating any sort of change other than local motion – change of place. Not only is change of place the only one of the four sorts of Aristotelian change for which we have a clear and distinct idea, it is also the only one which, in the schools, was commonly studied in abstraction from ends. Already medieval philosophers, especially the so-called *calculatores*, had treated uniform and accelerated local motion in mathematical terms, independently of considerations about ends. Descartes's early work with Beeckman can be seen as a continuation of that tradition.

(2) *Against forms and qualities*. The positive agenda of Descartes's physics was to explain all natural phenomena using only extended stuff, local motion, and the laws of nature – in short, "mechanistically." The negative agenda was to ensure that appealing to substantial forms or qualities (aside from figure) would no longer be a serious alternative. In aid of that goal, a variety of arguments were brought forward, together with rejoinders to standard scholastic arguments on behalf of form and qualities.

The best known of Descartes's antischolastic arguments are no doubt the epistemological. Cartesian method allows certainty only to judgments on objects perceived clearly and distinctly. The forms and qualities attributed to bodies in Aristotelian physics are obscure and confused; certain knowledge of them, even if they existed, could not be attained. Although clarity and distinctness are taken up by later philosophers and applied to the same purpose of eliminating unwanted entities, the epistemological argument was not Descartes's primary reason for rejecting forms and qualities. Even setting aside the obvious issue of defining clarity and distinctness without begging the question, sensible qualities are, as Descartes himself admits, clear; so the only question is that of their distinctness. If measurability or geometrical representability were the criterion, then some "intensive qualities" (heat, for example) admitted of degrees; Nicole Oresme and others had already used geometric figures to represent temporal and spatial distributions of intensive as well as extensive quantities.[6]

It would seem, rather, that a commitment to considering matter as extension alone (and thus figure and size as the only modes of matter) motivated the search for arguments against forms and qualities. Already in the collaboration with Beeckman, Descartes had decided upon a "mechanistic" ontology, in which bodies are stripped of all but those qualities that admit of an *immediate* geometric representation (though even this requires that one treat the representation of intensive quantities by lines and figures as indirect or metaphorical).

What one might call a "physical" line of argument is found in Descartes's *Principles* and in Boyle's *Origin of Forms and Qualities* (1666). It is that even if, say, colors really existed in bodies, they could have no physical effects; in particular, they could not affect the senses. The argument rests on the supposition that one body can act on another only by local motion; local motion can bring about only change of size and figure. Hence either colors are just modes of extension (or the more complicated arrangements Boyle calls "textures"), in which case our ideas of color, which represent them as qualities distinct from any mode of extension, are systematically misleading – hence "obscure and confused"; or else there are no colors except in our thought.

The supposition that one body can act on another only by local motion remains to be defended. Here the positive agenda comes into play: if indeed all natural phenomena can be explained mechanistically, then forms and qualities, which for the purposes of this argument are taken not to be included among the mechanistic properties of matter, are *inert*. Once the mechanical properties of matter have been set apart, the production of forms and qualities by them, or their being affected by such forms and qualities, becomes difficult to conceive.[7] These arguments serve only to dislodge the assumption that forms and qualities are *required* in natural philosophy; they do not establish their nonexistence.

It is worth considering in greater detail the case against substantial forms. In Aristotelian texts on physics, the primary arguments on behalf of form are these.

First, the Aristotelian distinguishes between "substantial" change, in which an individual, or rather its matter, ceases to be of one kind and instead becomes another, and "accidental" change, in which the individual remains of one kind throughout. Death is a substantial change, fever merely accidental. The best way to account for that difference is to distinguish two sorts of form: substantial form, which determines what kind a thing is, and accidental form, which includes all other sorts of property.

Second, one pervasive feature of the natural world is that the features of bodies come in bundles. The same collocations recur: the coolness, wetness, transparency, and odorlessness of water, for example; or the capacities and structures proper to cats. Not only are those features found to exist together in single individuals time and again, but they come to be and pass away simultaneously. Burning paper loses not only its color but its flexibility and its durability. The best way (so the Aristotelian argues) to account for the bundling of features is to suppose that they have a common principle, that in each individual a single substantial form underlies all the features charateristic of its kind.

Finally, some substances have preferred states toward which they spontaneously tend if not perturbed. Water, if heated (but not to the boiling point), cools again once the source of heat is removed. A sick animal returns to health. Various arguments were marshaled to show that the spontaneous reversion to a particular quality, say, could not have another quality as its cause, but only the form. In more current terms: some changes are *reversible*, and are reversed when a thing is left to itself, and some are *irreversible*, as when water changes to steam under intense heat.

If, as Descartes and Boyle believe, matter is extended stuff (Boyle adds impenetrability to the list of fundamental properties of matter), and the only qualitative differences among bodies are differences of size and figure, then there can be no distinction between substantial and accidental change. Figures can vary indefinitely, continuously. The needle-like corpuscles that Descartes supposes water to consist in could be continuously transformed into the branched particles of oil.

Boyle, who devotes quite a few pages of the *Origin* to refuting scholastic arguments on form, substitutes for the distinction between substantial and accidental change a functional analogue compatible with the Cartesian or "mechanical" hypothesis: matter has no form, but it can be endowed with a "convention" of "mechanical affections" which will explain everything that the scholastics had explained by way of form (*Origin*, 40). That convention is to be explained by reference either to the shapes of individual corpuscles or to the "textures" or "configurations" formed by combining them (30). The collocation of observable features in an individual is thus a consequence of what Boyle calls its "essential modification" or "stamp." Those features will come and go together when the stamp is changed. The point of replacing form with "stamp" is ontological: the stamp of an individual is nothing additional to its mechanical properties, but only a subset of those properties that exhibits a certain stability.

As for the argument from preferred states, Boyle first notes that, since on his view natural change consists in alterations of figure and size brought about by the collision of bodies in local motion, he is "not so fully convinced that there is such a thing as nature's designing to keep such a parcel of matter in such a state that is clothed with just such accidents, rather than with any other" (*Origin*, 61). What the Aristotelian calls the natural state is either "*the most usual state*, or *that wherein that which produces a notable change in them finds them*," as when silver, which begins as flexible (i.e. as retaining whatever shape it is bent into), after hammering becomes "springy" (i.e. returns to its original shape after being bent) (61–62). There are no preferred states: water kept in the cellar will be cool, water kept in the attic will be warm, not because the one or the other is natural, but owing to the temperature of the surrounding air (60).

Two points merit emphasis. The Cartesian or mechanical conception of matter undermines any fundamental distinction between the natural kind of an individual, which is necessary to its existence, and merely contingent or accidental features which that individual can gain or lose without ceasing to be of the same kind. Nevertheless, Boyle (and, less explicitly, Descartes) not only wants to save some such distinction, but needs it to show why it should even *appear* that there are natural kinds. Even so, Boyle's arguments tend to support a view according to which kinds are arbitrary and relative to us – water is "naturally" cool because it is *usually* cool in the environments we live in.

The second point is that the fate of forms is tied to that of ends. Were things to have, as Aristotle seems to have thought, intrinsic ends, then it is quite reasonable to expect that they should "prefer" one state to another. Christian Aristotelians tended to substitute divine ends for intrinsic ends; nevertheless, most of them found themselves bound, for doctrinal reasons, not to deny that there are active powers in things. But if a thing has an intrinsic *power*, conceived in Aristotelian fashion as a potency awaiting actualization or perfection, then it is as if it were intrinsically directed toward actualization or perfection.

That intrinsic directedness toward what is not yet, as of the seed toward the state of maturity, runs contrary to what might be called a principle of isolation. Consider Boyle's argument for the "relative nature of physical qualities":

> We may consider, then, that when Tubal Cain, or whoever else were the smith that invented *locks* and *keys*, had made his first lock . . ., that was only a piece of iron contrived into such a shape; and when afterwards he made a key to that lock, that also in itself considered was nothing but a piece of iron of such a determinate figure.
>
> (*Origin*, 23)

We are asked to consider the lock without the key, and the key without the lock: what we see is that *keyness* and *lockness* are relative (we would say "relational"), and that "being a key" is nothing at all in addition to having "such a shape." That separate existence, actual or possible (hence "isolation"), is the basis of the argument is apparent when we turn to the question of the status of sensible qualities.

(3) *Sensible qualities*. The term 'secondary qualities' in the period could be used to refer to any property of bodies that was not one of the primary properties of matter: flexibility, for example, or transparency. It has since come to refer almost exclusively to the subset of secondary qualities that are first perceived by the senses – the "proper sensibles" of Aristotelian psychology. Aristotle's physics begins with sensible qualities (in particular, the tangible qualities of the elements) in keeping with his maxim of starting with "what is best known to us (*quoad nos*)." It takes those properties to be, as Boyle puts it, real and physical. They exist and are what they are independently of the manner in which we conceive them, and they can be causes or effects of natural change.

Early modern natural philosophers, whatever their disagreements about the primary properties of matter, almost all denied that secondary qualities, as they present themselves to the mind, are real. Echoing Descartes, Boyle writes:

> we have been from our infancy apt to imagine that these sensible qualities are real beings in the objects they denominate, and have the faculty or power to work such and such things, as gravity hath a power to stop the motion of a bullet shot upwards . . .; whereas indeed . . . there is in the body

to which these sensible qualities are attributed nothing of real and physical but the size, shape, and motion or rest, of its component particles, together with that texture of the whole which results from their being so contrived as they are.

(*Origin*, 31)

These remarks follow upon a thought experiment in which we are to conceive "that all the rest of the universe were annihilated, except any of these entire and undivided corpuscles" whose existence Boyle has supposed. It will then be "hard to say what could be attributed to it besides matter, motion (or rest), bulk, and shape" (*Origin*, 30). In particular, if all animals were to vanish from the world, "those bodies that are now the objects of our senses would be but *dispositively*, if I may so speak, endowed with colours, tastes, and the like, and *actually* but only with those more catholic affections of bodies – figure, motion, texture, &c." (34). The "disposition" here is the arrangement and order of the corpuscles in those bodies that affect the senses. Disposition in that sense is real and physical, but so named it is a *relative* quality, relative to the senses as being a lock is to keys.

Color as presented to us is a quality we take to be distinct from any mode of matter – from figure, motion, texture, and so on. In bodies there are no such qualities; they are "nothing real or physical." On the other hand, there are real and physical differences in bodies that account for the differences in our sensations. These are differences in what those bodies are "dispositively," that is, in orders and arrangements that have stable, determinate effects on the senses. In the *Météores*, Descartes proposes that those parts of subtle matter that "tend to rotate with more force than [the force with which] they move in a straight line" cause the colors red or yellow; those that rotate with less force cause blue or green. That proposal is part of an explanation of what we see when light passes through a prism, which is in turn part of an explanation of the rainbow.[8]

It should be clear that Descartes has no explanation of why any of the various ratios of angular to rectilinear force should yield that sensible quality which they in fact produce in the mind. That red corresponds to a large ratio and blue to a small one follows from the observed order of spectral colors in the spectrum produced by a prism and from a hypothesis about the effects of passing through the prism on the rotation of particles of subtle matter. But the relation of the "dispositive" quality of light that gives rise to sensations of red to the quality presented by those ideas to the mind – in Descartes's view, a quality which we take to be distinct from any mode of extension – is arbitrary. Hence the argument, found at the beginning of *The World* and in Boyle's *Origin* (31), that our sensations do not "resemble" their efficient causes in nature. The violent motion of particles that causes the sensation of heat does not resemble the quality presented in that sensation; it only *corresponds* to it by what Descartes calls, in the Sixth Meditation, an "institution" of God, a relation established toward the end of providing us, in sensation, with a guide to benefit and harm in the world around us.

LAWS AND THE FORMAL CONDITIONS OF WISDOM

A still prevalent conception of natural science would have it that the primary object of natural science is to discover the laws of nature. Those laws are universal and modally distinct from mere generalizations (they "support counterfactuals," for example); the universe is "closed" under those laws in the sense that every event can be subsumed under one or another law. They form a system which is subject to requirements of consistency, simplicity, richness of consequence, and so forth. In explanation they play the role of axioms, on the basis of which less fundamental (but still lawlike) generalizations, like the law of falling bodies, are derived.

That conception, crystallized in the work of Kant, is a creation of the seventeenth century. It is absent from scholastic philosophy. Scholastic philosophers were certainly interested in discovering and stating regularities in nature; they might even speak of nature in the large as a system or (in cosmology) a machine. Its rise coincides with great difficulties concerning causation. Active powers in bodies had been ruled out by Descartes; others, like Henry More, attempted to reinstate them, but in the context of an otherwise mechanist physics, those powers, like Newtonian gravitation, were universalized, no longer capable of supplying the basis for a classification of natural kinds. Necessary connection – the determination of effects by the *internal* character of their causes – likewise became problematic. In Malebranche, for example, the only cause whose internal character yields a neccessary connection to its effects is the divine will. Every other causal relation must be mediated by a law of nature.

In what follows, I first sketch a conception of efficient causality found in Suárez, which for the purposes of this discussion I take to be representative of Aristotelianism. I then examine the treatment of causal relations in Descartes, Malebranche, and Leibniz. This is not the only strand one could follow in the skein of early modern thought on causation. But it has had – by way of Hume and Kant – the largest role in determining recent theories of causation.

Cause and intentio

The treatment of the efficient cause in Suárez, as in his Aristotelian contemporaries, rests on a treatment of causes in general. From that we take the following conclusions.

There must be something in the nature of the cause by which it causes the effect; otherwise we have a mere *per accidens* cause. When I see Socrates, for example, what acts *per se* on my visual organ is his visible qualities, his whiteness, for example. His being called 'Socrates' is incidental to my sense of sight being affected by him: I see a white thing *per se*, a thing called 'Socrates' only *per accidens*. That condition implies intentionality in the causal relation, that is, in exhibiting the cause of a particular effect we must be able to point to something in the nature of the cause by which the effect is determined. The causal relation itself rests on a real connection, which Suárez calls "influx,"[9] between cause and effect; influx occurs when and only when the cause is actually causing its effect. There is in Suárez's way of thinking a distinction between necessary consecution (the effect, given the cause, must follow) and the real connection he calls "influx." Necessary consecution holds whether the cause is causing or not; only when there is a real connection is the cause *actually* a cause.

The Aristotelians, like their successors, tend to insist that where there is a real causal connection, there must be a demonstratively necessary connection. This can be seen in discussions of causality *per se* and *per accidens*. Of this distinction Suárez writes:

> A cause *per se* is that upon which the effect directly depends according to its own proper being, insofar as it is an effect, as the statue-maker is the cause

of the statue . . . A cause *per accidens*, since it is not a true cause, but is called so only by some habitude or similitude or conjunction with the cause, has no single definition but is said in various ways.[10]

When we say "the musician builds," the relation is *per accidens*. The musicality of the builder is incidentally conjoined with that which in the builder determines the effects of his activity as builder. "Fire heats" is not *per accidens*, because "fire radically and by its own virtue includes the proper reason of heating"; i.e. fire is the *per se* cause of something's being heated, because fire is by its nature hot. Similarly *per se* are "the animal moves," "the man reasons."

So-called chance events, which are brought about by the incidental concurrence of several causes, a concurrence having itself no "certain and definite cause" (so that eclipses are not chance events), are said to be "outside the intention of the agent." When a stone falls on Peter, that event is outside the intention Peter had in going where he was going, and also outside the intention of the stone or its progenitor (the object of that intention is the center of the universe).[11] More generally, in a *per accidens* relation, the effect (being visible, say) lies outside the intention of the feature under which the cause is described (being called 'Socrates').

This talk of intentions can be traced back to the basic conception of natural change in Aristotelian natural philosophy. Natural change is paradigmatically directed. The *actus* of a *potentia* has a definite *terminus a quo*, a starting point, and a definite *terminus ad quem*, a point of completion. The *terminus ad quem* of a power is part of its definition. Every power, exercised or not, has an object toward which it is directed – its *intentio*. This holds not only for agents that can represent goals to themselves as we do, but even, say, in plants where the *intentio* cannot possibly be represented. In knowing, therefore, the nature of a thing – hence its active and passive powers – we know the *intentiones* of its powers. We know, for example, of a human being that its generative powers intend offspring, that its will intends the good.

Neither the influx which is the basis of actual causation, nor the necessary connection between cause and effect, is based on laws. Aristotelian physics is replete with regularities; their basis is the shared natures of individuals. Powers come first, and define natures; the instantiation of natures in commonly occurring individuals gives rise to regularities.

Descartes on laws

"Rules" or "laws" of motion are present from the beginning in Descartes's physics. Beeckman's notes from 1619 record laws similar to those set forth by Descartes himself in 1630 and again in the *Principles* of 1644.[12] My interest here is in the derivation of those laws.

In the *Principles*, II.36, Descartes divides the causes of motion into the "universal and primary" cause, God, and the "secondary and particular causes" – the laws of motion laid out in subsequent sections of the *Principles*. The operation of the first cause is governed by the principle of the conservation of the total quantity of motion in the world; this is supposed to follow from the immutability of God's will, hence of his operation. The existence of any created thing requires an act of conservation (or "continued creation") on the part of God. Motion in particular, even though "it is nothing other in the matter moved than one of its modes," can be conserved in quantity. The measure of that quantity is volume times speed. That quantity of motion which, as part of the total act of creation, God gives the world at the beginning is conserved by God, so far as this is possible. Since the volume of matter remains constant, what God conserves is speed, which is distributed over bodies in such a way that the total quantity remains constant.

The conservation principle is a consequence of the immutability of divine operations. Diversity in the world does not imply diversity in its creator; God's will remains constant, but its effects may vary with the varying locations and speeds of bodies. The three laws of motion which are supposed to follow from the principle of conservation "localize" that principle in such a way that, given any interaction among bodies, one can show that within some finite region the total quantity of motion is conserved. The first and second laws apply to single bodies, the third to the collision of two bodies. Only in collision, where neither body can maintain its state of motion, does any redistribution of speed occur; all *change* in the world is a consequence of the third law or of the fragmentation and fusion of bodies (about which the laws have nothing to say directly).

The three laws are given in the Latin version of the *Principles* as follows:

[First law.] Each thing, insofar as it is simple and undivided, remains, insofar as it is in itself (*quantum in se est*), in the same state always, nor is it ever changed except by external causes.

(II.37, AT VIII.1, 62)

[Second law.] Each part of matter, considered separately, never tends in such a way that it would continue to move according to any curved lines, but only according to straight lines, even though many [parts] are often made to turn aside through their encounter with others.

(II.39, AT VIII.1, 63)

[Third law.] When a body that moves meets another, if it has less force to continue according to a straight line than the other has to resist it, then it is deflected in some other direction, and while retaining its motion gives up only its determination [i.e. its tendency to move in a particular direction]; but if it has more force, then it moves the other body with it, and however much it gives the other of its own motion, it loses the same amount.

(II.40, AT VIII.1, 65)

In the derivation of the first and second laws, not only the constancy but the *simplicity* of God's act is invoked. It is invoked explicitly in the derivation of the second: a body in motion, unimpeded by others, will move in a straight line because "of all movements, the straight line is the only one which is entirely simple and whose nature is comprised in an instant."[13] In the derivation of the first, Descartes, holding that motion in a body is something real and that change of motion is a genuine change, argues that a spontaneous change in the motion of a body, without its being acted upon by others, would entail a mutation in the divine operation by which it is conserved. That simplicity is invoked here to prove that constancy of operation implies constancy of motion can be seen if one considers that God could have willed, in what would seem like a single and immutable volition, that the speed of a body left to itself should always increase. That, however, would be less simple than to will that its speed remain the same.

The laws, then, are consequences of God's will (that the laws hold is of course a consequence also of his power). The character of the laws is inferred from necessary features of the divine will: immutability, simplicity. The laws result from a *single* divine act – namely, that of creating the material world; they hold universally of that world if we consider it apart from minds and from God himself. Even more: since they are derived from necessary features of the divine will, the laws must hold in every world God creates – if God creates bodies and motion at all.

It is worth contrasting three ways in which, in Descartes's world, the truth of a universal proposition about created things may be fixed.

1. It may be fixed in the manner of the eternal truths of arithmetic and geometry, by a free act of God. We cannot conceive other truths than those created by God; but the doctrine of their creation implies that other truths could have been created.[14]
2. It may be fixed in the manner of the laws of nature. The basis of the necessity of those laws is the necessity of the divine attributes, and in particular of God's immutability.
3. It may be fixed in relation to a divine end which, being an object of the divine will, we know to be universal and invariant. In the Sixth Meditation, Descartes observes that the relations instituted by God between particular motions in the brain and particular sensations are ordered to the end of health – that is, to keeping the body fit to serve in the union of body and mind. The resulting generalizations, I take it, are more than mere empirical generalizations. It doesn't just happen to be the case that every instance of *M* gives rise to an instance of *S*. There is a reason, namely, that this promotes the end of health, and that God willed that end in constructing the mind–body union. It would be wrong to call these generalizations "laws" on a par with the laws of nature. But neither are they entirely contingent.

For the Aristotelian, order in nature is derived from the presence in matter of forms whose powers, active and passive, are oriented to ends. This is most evident in living things, where the highest end of organisms is, by way of reproduction, to confer upon their specific form a kind of eternal existence, and thus to assimilate themselves to God.[15]

In Cartesian physics, we see the beginnings of what will eventually become the developmental or historical approach to explaining the existence of order. Descartes's historical cosmology and his theory of the earth, presented in the third and fourth parts of the *Principles*, are, however imperfect, examples of the production of complex structures according to the laws of nature. Those laws themselves are indifferent to order or the absence of order: the chaotic initial state adverted to in *The World* ("the most confused and tangled chaos that the Poets could describe"), and the boring uniform division of the world into little cubes assumed in the *Principles*, are equally consistent with the laws of nature.[16]

The derivation of the laws is from divine attributes. We will see that both Malebranche and Leibniz restore to physics the relation to the good which is rejected by Descartes. But already in Descartes the derivation of the laws adduces not only the immutability of the divine will but also the simplicity of the divine operations. Slogans like *natura nil facit frustra* ("nature does nothing in vain") had, of course, been part of natural philosophy for a long time – the one just quoted is found in Aristotle (*On the Heavens*, II.11). In Cartesian physics, what was attributed by Aristotle to nature is attributed instead to God; which is to say, the origin of simplicity is out of this world, transcendent if not transcendental.

Malebranche on laws

Causes. Suárez, to whom Malebranche refers in the elucidation on second causes (*Search*, Eluc. 15), recognizes four views on the efficacy of second causes.

1. That God is the unique efficient cause (one argument for which is that since God himself can bring about every effect, and since *natura nil facit frustra*, God "did not confer any operative virtue on creatures").[17]
2. That spiritual creatures are efficient causes, but corporeal creatures are not.
3. That corporeal creatures can be efficient causes of accidents but not of substances; and spiritual creatures of both those substances which are inferior to them and of accidents.
4. That "created agents truly and properly bring about those effects that are connatural and proportionate to them."[18]

The last of these is the orthodox view among Aristotelians. The view I attribute to Descartes is the second. *Res extensa* is inert. Moreover, if stones, say, really had a power that drew them toward the center of the earth, they would have to be capable of cognizing that end; but if they could cognize that end they would have to have minds.[19] The latter argument precludes only "directed" active powers; it is the definition of body as *res extensa* that precludes corporeal active powers in general.

Malebranche holds that God is the unique efficient cause. The argument of the *Search* on this point is this. The idea of body, first of all, precludes attributing efficacy to bodies. Hence only spirits can move bodies. But "when one examines the idea one has of all finite spirits, one sees no connection between their will and the movement of any body whatever" (*Search*, VI.ii.3), because the volitions of finite spirits have no *necessary* connection to their objects. The active power or force we attribute to the will in an impulsion toward the good properly belongs to God, not to the mind itself.

What remains is infinite spirit – God. "When one thinks of the idea of God . . ., one recognizes that there is a connection between his will and the movement of all bodies, that it is impossible to conceive that he should will that a body be moved and yet this body not be moved." Malebranche later calls that connection a "necessary" connection (*Search*, VI.ii.3). It is necessary by virtue of the definition of omnipotence: the inference from 'God wills that *p*' to '*p*' is valid, given that God is perfect.

Malebranche here treats the relation of cause to effect, in keeping with the scholastic tradition, as intentional. But he insists that the relation of cause to effect be one of necessity. Any defeasibility of the connection between cause and effect entails that the cause is only what Malebranche calls a "natural" or "occasional" cause – something that determines the particular effect of a genuine cause. Since the connection between any finite cause and its effect is defeasible (by God, at least), all finite causes are "natural."

Ends. Descartes denies that divine ends have any role in natural philosophy. The laws of nature are derived not from God's goodness but from his immutability. Neither in the laws themselves nor in their derivation is there any reference to the good. Only when we consider minds do ends (and normative notions like health) enter the picture. The moral and the physical order of the world are thus quite distinct.

For Malebranche, the contrary is true. God, in establishing the natural laws, "had to combine the physical and the moral in such a way that the effects of these laws would be the best possible" (*Dial.*, XIII.3). The source of this disagreement is that Malebranche, unlike Descartes, holds that the divine wisdom has priority over the divine will; the moral order likewise has priority over the physical. For example, "if man . . . had not sinned . . ., then since order would not permit him to be punished, the natural laws of the communication of movements would not have been capable of rendering him unhappy." The law of order is "essential to God," and so the arbitrary law of the communication of movements "must necessarily be submitted to it" (*TNG*, I.i.20). Adam before he sinned had, by virtue of the law of order, the power of *suspending* the laws of motion so as to avoid distraction from his end. From the standpoint of physics, Adam performed miracles; with respect to order, his feats were not miraculous, but rather the fulfillment of God's wisdom.[20]

Formal conditions of wisdom. God's wisdom precedes his will; the laws of nature are subordinate to order. Order itself consists largely in the preponderance of the "formal conditions of wisdom." From a portion of the argument of the *Treatise on Nature and Grace* (I.i.12–18), it will be seen that those conditions turn out to include just what are now sometimes called the "theoretical virtues," that is, the conditions thought to be required of good scientific theories.

The wisdom of God, for Malebranche as for Leibniz, encompasses all possible designs and all means of execution. The design and means God actually chooses will be those that bear "most strongly the character of the divine attributes." That character imposes upon God's means the formal conditions of wisdom – simplicity, generality, uniformity, and proportionality of means to ends. I call them "formal" because, taken in themselves, they yield no specific ends, no particular goods to be realized in creation. In that respect they resemble immutability, according to which *whatever* God wills, he wills eternally.

There is a tradeoff between means and ends. Elsewhere Malebranche writes that sometimes the wisdom of God "resists his volitions" (*TNG,* Eluc. 3, arts. 22–23): he wants all men to be saved, for example, but to do so would require him "to perform miracles at all moments"; this he is prevented from doing by his wisdom. If we abstract from the means, we can see ways in which the world could be more perfect. But in such a world, "there would not have been the same proportion between the action of God and this so perfect world as between the laws of nature and the world we inhabit" (*TNG*, I.i.14). Our world is the best in expressing not only the substantive goodness of God, but also the formal quality of simplicity.

Malebranche denies that there is any necessary connection between finite causes and their so-called effects. Hume, of course, would take over that claim (and Malebranche's example of the collision of two balls) in his argument against necessary connections, thereby raising the question of whether laws (their theistic backing having been removed) are at all distinct from mere generalizations, except in the degree to which they are confirmed in experience.

What I have called the "formal conditions of wisdom" are preponderant not only over the outcomes they entail in particular cases (because general volitions have priority over particular in God's will), but also over the perfection of the world taken absolutely, in abstraction from means. Given that we take other laws to be, logically speaking, possible, and that we do not know at the outset which laws God has established, it is to the formal conditions that we must turn in discovering the laws, first of all, and then in showing *why* they are as they are. The formal conditions provide a principle of selection among hypotheses, *and* (by virtue of their relation to the divine will) reason to believe that such a principle is a guide to truth.

Leibniz on laws

Like Malebranche, and unlike Descartes, Leibniz holds that the divine understanding preexists the act of creation. Each possible world is an entirely determinate collection of mutually defining individual concepts. Whatever lawlike relations obtain among individuals in the actual world obtain also among the corresponding individual concepts as they were understood all at once by God prior to creation (see, for example, *Theod.*, §225). Though not "geometrically necessary" – the contrary of a law is no contradiction – they are not arbitrary in relation to the divine nature. They are "born from the principle of perfection and order; they are an effect of the choice and of the wisdom of God" (*Theod.*, §349). Rather than being independent generalizations, they are subject to what we would call global constraints; they fit together into a harmonious whole.

Laws and wisdom. To act out of wisdom, to act reasonably, is to act according to principles or rules. Having the perfection of the entire universe in mind, God prescribed laws to himself, even though the inevitable consequence (as we know from experience) is that some individuals suffer, because "laws and reason make order and beauty; and because acting without rules would be acting without reason" (*Theod.*, §359). The argument here is that the creation of the world was a rational act, a choice of means to an end; to act rationally is to act according to rules, because from them (it's not clear whether Leibniz would say from them *alone*) order and beauty arise; since order and beauty are included in the end toward which God acts in creation, it follows that God must prescribe laws to himself, hence to the operations of his creatures.

The primacy of rules can be seen in the case of miracles. In explicit agreement with Malebranche, Leibniz holds that God does all according to order. Miracles may lie outside the customary order of nature; they may exceed the natural powers of individuals; but they are still encompassed within the design that God judged best. Leibniz takes this, he says, a "little further" than Malebranche. God, he says, *never* acts according to "primitive particular volitions," not even in producing miracles. Indeed, he "cannot have a primitive particular volition," independent from laws or general volitions; "it would be unreasonable." "The wise man acts always by principles; he acts always by *rules* and never by exceptions" (*Theod.*, §337). Apparent exceptions, for example when rules conflict, will have been generated by rule and will be settled by rule – rules of precedence among rules, say, according to which "weaker" rules give way to " stronger."

Thus the formal conditions on wisdom *must* be observed by God if he is to act wisely and well. Those conditions apply to the one adequate object of God's good intention – the entire world. It is, in other words, the whole system of universal laws that is subject to the formal conditions. In assessing the fulfillment of those conditions by a single law or special theory, we must always bear in mind the possibility that an apparent violation of those conditions in one part of science (natural *and* moral) may be compensated by greater perfection elsewhere.

By way of conclusion

In the view of Malebranche and Leibniz, Descartes's God is not a rational agent. For Descartes, God's freedom rests on the absolute indifference with which he acts. That condition sets the divine will apart from the human: our freedom, as creatures, rests on the determination of our will by reason. Descartes, however, compromises his position somewhat by invoking simplicity in the derivation of the laws of motion. That would seem to require an antecedent understanding of what is to be willed, and reasoned choice among alternatives.

Malebranche's God, and even more Leibniz's, is a rational agent. God's will, unlike ours, cannot fail to be effective; he has the foresight necessary to govern the world by particular volitions. Nevertheless, the formal conditions of wisdom apply equally to him and to us. The laws of nature "are a choice made by the most perfect wisdom," neither absolutely (that is, logically) necessary nor entirely arbitrary; their necessity is "a moral necessity, which arises from the free choice of wisdom in relation to final causes" (*Theod.*, §345).

Because the laws of nature are the results of rational acts of God, the scientist, who is himself or herself a rational agent, can employ in discovering the laws of nature the same formal conditions of wisdom that God was constrained by in creating the world. Those formal conditions are justified by reference to the rational agency which accounts for the existence and character of the natural world.

The evident question, then, is: what becomes of those formal conditions – and, more importantly, what justifies invoking them – when the theistic backing falls by the wayside? One answer is Kant's. The formal conditions of wisdom are the conditions of the possibility of scientific knowledge of the world; we derive them not from theology but from reflection on rational agency itself – a possibility already hinted at in Malebranche and Leibniz. The other, which with suitable qualifications one could call voluntarist, if not Cartesian, is the pragmatic answer. The formal conditions of wisdom have no foundation – neither in nature (by virtue of its being created by a rational agent) nor in a priori conditions on the rational search for truth. They are, as Descartes's position would imply, arbitrary; but since the pragmatist denies to any particular conceptions the normative force Descartes attributes to clear and distinct ideas and to the truths revealed to us by the light of nature, what remains to justify the application of those conditions is, in those cases where experience is not decisive, only utility or aesthetic preference.

NOTES

1 Beeckman 1939, vol. I, p. 244; AT XI 52.
2 *Theoria motus concreti*, art. 58 (GP IV 210–11).
3 Fonseca, *Commentarium . . . in libros metaphysicorum Aristotelis*, bk. 5, ch. 13, q. 1, §2 (1615, vol. II, p. 648A).
4 Galileo 1952, p. 13. See Biener 2004.
5 *The World*, ch. 6, AT XI 33: CSM I 90–91.
6 Oresme, *Tractatus de configurationibus*, bk. 3, ch. 5, in Oresme 1968. See Murdoch and Sylla 1978, pp. 231–41.
7 Descartes, *Princ.*, IV.198, AT VIIIA 322: CSM I 284–85.
8 *Météores*, disc. 8 (AT VI 333–34).
9 *Disp. met.*, disp. 12, §2, n. 4 (Suárez 1856–78, vol. XXV, p. 384).
10 *Disp. met.*, disp. 17, §2, n. 2 (Suárez 1856–78, vol. XXV, p. 583).
11 *Disp. met.*, disp. 19, §12, n. 3 (Suárez 1856–78, vol. XXV, p. 742).
12 *The World*, ch. 7, AT XI 41–43: CSM I 94–96; *Princ.* II.37–40, AT VIIIA 62–65: CSM I 240–43.
13 *The World*, ch. 7, AT XI 45: CSM I 96–97.
14 See Descartes's letters to Mersenne of 6 May and 27 May 1630, AT I 149–50, 152: CSM III 24–25.
15 Coimbra, *Commentarii . . . in octo libros physicorum Aristotelis*, bk. 4, ch. 9, q. 1, a. 3 (1594, vol. II, p. 62). See Des Chene 2000, p. 174.
16 *The World*, ch. 6, AT XI 34: CSM I 91; *Princ.*, III.46–48, AT VIIIA 100–104: CSM I 256–58.
17 *Disp. met.*, disp. 18, §1, n. 2 (Suárez 1856–78, vol. XXV, p. 593).
18 Ibid. n. 5 (p. 594).
19 See Garber 1992, pp. 98–99.
20 Ibid. The *Search* (I.5) seems not to have required the suspension of the laws of motion.

NICHOLAS JOLLEY

4 Metaphysics

According to the Gospels, men do not put new wine in old bottles. Metaphorically speaking at least, philosophers of the early modern period tend to be exceptions to this rule. Descartes and his successors inherited a rich metaphysical vocabulary and set of categories from the ancient and medieval world; particularly in the work of Aristotle and his scholastic disciples, this conceptual framework had been devised to articulate a metaphysical picture of the universe very different from any which was likely to commend itself to philosophers in the age of the Scientific Revolution. Nonetheless, instead of rejecting this inherited framework wholesale, philosophers of the period tend to retain it in large measure while infusing it with radically new content. Such content was of course adapted to the task of providing metaphysical foundations for the new scientific world picture. And in the case of many philosophers it was also adapted to the goal of providing new bases for doctrines of traditional natural theology such as the immortality of the soul.

The contrast between the new wine and the old bottles may help to throw light on one difficulty posed by metaphysics of the early modern period. Readers approaching the metaphysical systems for the first time are struck by the fact that philosophers often seem to be announcing "news from nowhere"; the great metaphysical systems tend to be full of strange and extravagant claims, typified by Spinoza's insistence that there is only one substance, Malebranche's insistence that there is only one cause, and Leibniz's insistence that no created substances causally interact with one another. There is no doubt that, fortified by confidence in the power of human reason, philosophers of the period are often led to advance theories of reality that are radically at variance with the dictates of common sense and which can retain an air of strangeness even after prolonged familiarity. It is of course important to remember that in many cases they draw on a tradition, at least as old as Plato, which emphasizes that there is a fundamental difference between the world of appearances or phenomena and the world of ultimate reality. It is also possible to dispel the air of mystery surrounding such metaphysical claims by seeing that their authors are often seeking to articulate new philosophical insights within a traditional vocabulary and set of concepts. As the Gospels remind us, the danger of putting new wine into old bottles is that it may burst the leather skins. At times, as we shall see, the new insights of early modern philosophers regarding such issues as substance, laws, and causation seem similarly in danger of exploding the traditional metaphysical framework.

Although the leading philosophers of the early modern period are often content to practice metaphysics within a traditional set of categories, it would be misleading to suggest that there were no dissentient voices. John Locke, for example, is famous for his skepticism about whether the concept of substance deriving from Aristotle retains any point or value on the new scientific picture of the world. And even Malebranche, though he claims to be rejecting only natural causality, might be read as advocating that the concept of causality in general should be jettisoned altogether from philosophy. Moreover, some philosophers of the period, of whom Locke is again a prime example, extend their skepticism beyond particular metaphysical concepts to the whole enterprise of metaphysics; that is, they call into question the power of the human mind to understand and articulate the fundamental nature of reality.

METAPHYSICS: ITS METHOD AND PROSPECTS

One of the most famous works of early modern philosophy is entitled *Ethics Demonstrated in the Geometrical Manner*. Even a superficial inspection of this work, which is as much a contribution to metaphysics as to moral theory, reveals the accuracy of its full title. Spinoza's *Ethics* employs throughout the rather intimidating apparatus of Euclid's *Elements*: the reader is immediately confronted with an impressive array of numbered axioms, definitions, postulates, and theorems to be proved. Spinoza's *Ethics* may seem merely to embody in an extreme and uncompromising form a conviction that was rather widespread among early modern philosophers, particularly in the first half of the period: philosophy should seek to emulate the practice of geometry. It is not difficult to understand why geometry exercised such a hold over the imagination of philosophers in the period. Ever since Descartes in the *Discourse on the Method* had written admiringly of the long chains of reasoning of the geometers (CSM I 120), philosophers had been impressed by the possibility of achieving certain and demonstrative knowledge in geometry; such certainty seemed to contrast favorably with the obscurity, sterility, and inconclusiveness of debates in scholastic philosophy. Moreover, philosophers of the period did not have to look back to the ancients to find impressive contributions to mathematical knowledge. Near the beginning of the period, the discovery of coordinate geometry revolutionized mathematics by synthesizing geometry and algebra; near the end of the period, Leibniz and Newton independently advanced the subject with the discovery of the differential calculus.

The hold that geometry in particular exercised over the imagination of some early modern philosophers is further illustrated by a celebrated anecdote about Hobbes's discovery of the subject:

> Being in a Gentleman's library Euclid's Elements lay open, and 'twas the *47 El. libr. 1* [i.e. the Pythagorean theorem]. He read the Proposition. *By G –*, sayd he . . . *this is impossible*! So he reads the Demonstration of it, which referred him back to such a Proposition, which proposition he read. That referred him back to another, which he also read. *Et sic deinceps* [and so on] that at last he was demonstratively convinced of that trueth. This made him in love with Geometry.[1]

Obviously Aubrey's story about the origins of Hobbes's love affair with geometry shows that one reason for the attraction was the prospect of achieving demonstrative certainty. But the anecdote also brings out another aspect of Hobbes's attraction to geometry which is no less revealing: it illustrates the possibility of deriving initially counterintuitive conclusions from previous theorems and ultimately from axioms and definitions which are beyond dispute.[2] Thus it is not a conclusive objection to a geometrical theorem that it appears counterintuitive or surprising: criticism must focus on the reasoning or the premises from which it is derived. Clearly this moral of the anecdote is relevant to Hobbes's own political philosophy: Hobbes recognizes that his main conclusion to the effect that nothing less than absolute sovereignty is a properly constituted state will appear shockingly counterintuitive to many of his readers. But it is no less relevant to the metaphysics of the period. The results of metaphysical systems such as those of Spinoza and Leibniz are highly counterintuitive at first sight. Confronted with an objection to this effect, Spinoza and Leibniz could respond in part by observing that our sense of surprise and shock is a function of our bondage to preconceived opinions and the confused ideas of common sense; once we succeed in attaining clear and distinct or adequate ideas, this reaction will disappear. But they could also respond by drawing the same moral from Euclid that Hobbes clearly did: the counterintuitiveness of a conclusion is not a decisive objection to a proposition validly derived from incontestable axioms and definitions.

The Euclidean method may thus seem peculiarly well adapted to the presentation of metaphysical systems that propose serious revisions of commonsense views. But it remains the case that Spinoza's *Ethics* is the only major work of early modern philosophy which adopts the Euclidean model in a pure and thoroughgoing way. Impressed by this fact, some recent writers have tended to question whether even the rationalist philosophers were really committed to the view that metaphysics could achieve the demonstrative certainty of geometry. Indeed, it has even been claimed in the case of Spinoza that the Euclidean apparatus is something of a sham.[3] It is certainly true that neither Descartes nor Leibniz made more than intermittent or perfunctory use of the apparatus of Euclidean geometry when writing metaphysics. But it would be a mistake to infer from this that they were not committed to the ideal of geometrical demonstration.

In the case of Descartes, it should be particularly easy to determine his position, for he was pressed on the point by the authors of the Second Objections who invited him to "set out the entire argument [of the *Meditations*] in the geometrical fashion starting from a number of definitions, postulates, and axioms" (CSM II 92). In reply, Descartes claims that there is a sense in which he *has* written the *Meditations* in the geometrical manner. For one thing, the work is written in geometrical order, "which consists simply in this":

> The items which are put forward first must be known entirely without the aid of what comes later; and the remaining items must be arranged in such a way that their demonstration depends solely on what has gone before. I do try to follow this order very carefully in my *Meditations*.
>
> (CSM II 110)

It is true, Descartes concedes, that he has not employed the Euclidean apparatus in the *Meditations* (and, we might add, did not do so even in the *Principles*), but here Descartes justifies his practice by means of a distinction between two kinds of geometrical method. The method of Euclid in his *Elements* is the method of synthesis: with its array of definitions, postulates, and axioms it bullies the reader into submission, as it were: "if anyone denies one of the conclusions it can be shown at once that it is contained in what has gone before, and hence the reader, however argumentative or stubborn he may be, is compelled to give his assent" (CSM II 111). But there is also the method of analysis, which shows the true way by means of which the thing in question was discovered. The method of analysis, which is the true method of instruction, is more appropriate to metaphysics than the Euclidean or synthetic method, and it is for this reason that Descartes adopted it in the *Meditations*.[4]

In one way Descartes's explanation of why the synthetic method is not appropriate in metaphysics is somewhat surprising. The explanation turns on an alleged difference between the concepts of geometry and metaphysics: in the former, the concepts at issue are accepted by everyone and accord with the use of our senses; in the latter field, by contrast, they conflict with so many preconceived opinions derived from the senses that it is difficult to make them clear and distinct; indeed, this difficulty is the principal obstacle to doing metaphysics, and can be overcome only by the kind of sustained reflection practiced by the solitary inquirer in the *Meditations*. One might suppose that from a Cartesian perspective the concepts of geometry and metaphysics were epistemically on a par; in each case what is at issue is a body of innate ideas that can be accessed only by turning away from the data of the senses and the imagination. But there is a strand in Descartes's theory of mathematics which tends to emphasize the positive role of the imagination. Even in the Sixth Meditation, Descartes may not wish to deny such a role: he may simply wish to put us on our guard against supposing that geometrical concepts actually are mental images. Whether or not we think that Descartes's preference for the analytic method is simply ad hoc and self-serving, we should note that he was not insuperably opposed to the method of synthesis in metaphysics; for Descartes at least makes a concession to the authors of the Second Objections by casting part of the argument of the *Meditations* in geometrical (i.e. Euclidean or synthetic) form.

Leibniz, like Descartes, seems to have held that the Euclidean or synthetic method was less than ideal for the presentation of metaphysics. But whereas Descartes stresses facts about the nature of metaphysical concepts as a reason for avoiding this method, Leibniz offers, at least officially, a more straightforward explanation: the mathematical style repels people. It is thus inappropriate for a philosopher who seeks to gain widespread agreement to his principles. Yet such explanations tend to be accompanied by uncompromising statements to the effect that his metaphysics achieves the demonstrative certainty of mathematics. Thus in the same breath Leibniz tells a correspondent: "I never write anything in philosophy that I do not treat by definitions and axioms" (GP III 302). More uncompromisingly, Leibniz earlier informs another correspondent: "I ruled decisively on these general philosophical matters a long time ago, in a way that I believe is demonstrative or not far from it" (GP III 474).[5]

Although the issue is controversial, it is possible that there is a deeper explanation of Leibniz's avoidance of the Euclidean apparatus. None of Leibniz's major expositions of his metaphysics is cast in Euclidean form, but arguably in the *Discourse on Metaphysics* (and some related texts) Leibniz approximates this form more than in later works such as the *New System*, the *Monadology*, and the *Principles of Nature and Grace*. The *Discourse on Metaphysics* is certainly much richer in deductive philosophical arguments than those later writings; moreover, it is not too difficult to see how its arguments could be recast in the form of axioms, definitions, and theorems to be proved. Yet the foundational doctrines in the *Discourse on Metaphysics* included Leibniz's concept-containment theory of truth, and we know that when Leibniz submitted a summary of the work to Arnauld, the latter believed that this theory had wholly unacceptable consequences for human and divine freedom. It is striking that in the later presentations of his metaphysics, the theory of truth makes no appearance. Thus we cannot discount the possibility that fear of being charged with unorthodoxy lay behind Leibniz's avoidance of the Euclidean method.

Although they may not all embrace the Euclidean method, Descartes, Leibniz, and Spinoza share the same confidence in the possibility of demonstrative metaphysics. In the last decade of the seventeenth century, a major challenge to the claims of dogmatic metaphysics was mounted by John Locke in his great *Essay concerning Human Understanding*. In the introduction to this work, Locke diagnoses the apparent failure of the metaphysicians in terms of their adoption of the wrong method; they had simply assumed without questioning that the human mind was adequate to the task of discovering the ultimate nature and structure of reality:

> For I thought that the first Step towards satisfying several Enquiries, the Mind of Man was very apt to run into, was, to take a Survey of our own Understandings, examine our own Powers, and see to what Things they were adapted. Till that was done I suspected we began at the wrong end, and in vain sought for Satisfaction in a quiet and secure possession of Truths, that most concern'd us, whilst we let loose our Thoughts into the vast Ocean of *Being*, as if all that boundless Extent were the natural, and undoubted Possession of our Understandings, wherein there was nothing exempt from its Decisions, or that escaped its Comprehension.
>
> (*Essay*, I.i.7)

In a way that anticipates Kant, Locke thus calls for a reorientation of philosophy toward a critique of the mind's powers.

To say, however, that Locke is skeptical of the possibility of demonstrative metaphysics is not to say that he is skeptical about the possibility of demonstrative knowledge in general. Locke, no less than Descartes or Leibniz, believes that we can achieve such knowledge a priori in the case of mathematics; he is far from subscribing to an extreme empiricism which regards mathematics as an inductive science. Indeed, ironically, Locke is in agreement with Spinoza that "*morality [is] capable of demonstration*" (*Essay*, IV.iii.18). Why, then, is Locke pessimistic about the prospects of demonstrative certainty in metaphysics?

Locke offers a principled answer to this question which strikes deep roots in his theory of knowledge: it turns on the nature of the objects of study in the different disciplines. At the cost of some oversimplification, Locke's answer is this. In the case of mathematics and morality we are concerned with entities such as triangles and gratitude whose real essences are transparent to the intellect because they are creations of the human mind. In metaphysics, by contrast, as in natural science, we are dealing with entities, such as material substances, whose essences are opaque to us; they are opaque to us because the entities in question are the products of nature, not the human mind. Despite his admiration for the achievements of Boyle and Newton, Locke thus classifies the natural sciences, as we would call them, alongside metaphysics as disciplines in which demonstrative knowledge is for ever beyond our reach (*Essay*, IV.iii.26).

Locke's call for a reorientation of philosophy toward a critique of the human understanding represents one way in which philosophers could react against the enterprise of speculative metaphysics. It is this form of reaction which Hume develops in his *Inquiry concerning Human Understanding*, the title of which is a clear allusion to Locke's great work; indeed, Hume goes much further than Locke in his attempt to expose the illusions of speculative metaphysics (e.g. *Enquiry*, XII.3). But there is another side to Hume's philosophy which turns away from metaphysics and the Euclidean paradigm in a direction which has no real precedent in Locke. Hume's *Treatise of Human Nature*, his early masterpiece, resembles the works of the metaphysicians in the sense that it draws its inspiration from a nonphilosophical model; but the model in question is not Euclidean geometry but the experimental method of the new science: the *Treatise* is, as its subtitle says, an attempt to introduce the experimental method into moral subjects. Hume's professed aim is thus the naturalistic one of seeking to discover laws of human psychology by the same method as Newton and others had discovered laws governing physical phenomena. It is true that in the course of executing his project Hume reveals a deep familiarity with seventeenth-century metaphysical debates about substance, causality, and the like. Officially, at least, however, he is interested not in making a direct and novel contribution to such debates, but rather in explaining why human beings hold the beliefs about the world that they do.

SUBSTANCE

Perhaps nowhere is the tendency of early modern philosophers to pour new wine into old bottles more apparent than in their doctrines of substance. The concept of substance is undoubtedly the most prominent concept in the metaphysical systems of Spinoza and Leibniz: with some qualifications, it plays an important role in Descartes's philosophy, too. The fact that the concept is so prominent in early modern metaphysics reflects the legacy of Aristotle above all, for Aristotle regards metaphysics as that science which is principally concerned with the question: What is substance or being? That is, metaphysics, for Aristotle, is a quest to discover what is ultimately real. But though early modern philosophers are indebted to Aristotle for the term 'substance,' they typically employ it to articulate a very different metaphysical vision of the world from that which is found in Aristotle and his successors. Moreover, even when they retain or echo Aristotelian definitions of 'substance,' they tend to infuse such definitions with new content. As we shall see, in some cases the traditional connotations of the term 'substance' may set up tensions with the metaphysical picture which they wish to articulate.

Of the leading philosophers of the early modern period, at least before Locke, it is perhaps Descartes who is least enthusiastic about the terminology of 'substance'; in some of his more popular writings, such as the *Discourse on the Method*, Descartes comes close to dispensing with the term altogether in favor of the more familiar, everyday word 'thing.'[6] As we shall see, Descartes's decision to retain the term in the more formal expositions of his system is a source of difficulty for understanding his philosophy. But it would be wrong to dwell on such problems at the outset, for it is the strengths of Descartes's ontology, not its difficulties, that are most immediately apparent and that obviously impressed many of his earliest readers. The attractions of the new Cartesian ontology are not unlike those of the Copernican system in astronomy, in comparison with its rivals: Descartes's ontology is striking by virtue of its simplicity and elegance. In place of the complex Aristotelian picture of a world of substances which are all compounds of matter and form, Descartes substitutes a very different account: the created universe consists of two kinds of thing or substance, each of which has a principal attribute that constitutes its nature. The nature of body or matter is constituted by the principal attribute of extension, that is, by the property of being spread out in three dimensions. The nature of mind is constituted by the principal attribute of thought or consciousness. The further, more specific properties of body and mind are simply modes, that is, ways of being, of the respective principal attributes: the modes of extension are such properties as being square or triangular; the modes of thought are such properties as willing, doubting, and sensing. It is true that, for all its simplicity and elegance, Descartes's ontology is far removed not only from the Aristotelian–scholastic picture of the world, but also from untutored common sense which that picture was able in part to accommodate; according to Descartes, for example, strictly speaking bodies have no sensible qualities such as color, taste, odor, and sound. But in this respect, too, the parallel with the Copernican revolution in astronomy holds: the Copernican hypothesis that the earth rotates daily on its axis and revolves annually around the sun was similarly less in tune with common sense than the system it replaced. But Descartes, like Copernicus of course, has arguments to persuade the reader that the departure from common sense is not a weakness of his system, for common sense is the repository of preconceived opinions and prejudices.

The attractions of the Cartesian ontology are obvious: its problems appear only when we start to probe beneath the surface. The most famous problem perhaps is that of giving a coherent account of the status of human beings within this system, but there is also a more general difficulty: Descartes seems curiously undecided on the issue whether his dualistic system is symmetrical in respect of the number of substances. There is no question that Descartes subscribes to the thesis that there is a plurality of minds or thinking substances: such a thesis is of course required by Christian orthodoxy, and it is also one datum of common sense which Descartes never appears to challenge. But to the question whether there is similarly a plurality of extended substances, Descartes has often seemed to return an ambiguous answer. Common sense would suggest that there are indeed many extended substances, and Descartes sometimes writes as if particular bodies, such as the lump of wax described in the Second Meditation, do indeed qualify as such substances. But there are pressures in his philosophy to maintain that the dualism is asymmetrical with respect to this issue: whether this means that there is only one extended substance remains to be seen.

Descartes's difficulties with regard to this issue may spring in part from his decision to cast his system in the traditional terminology of 'substance'; they are arguably compounded by the fact that Descartes offers not one, but two definitions of 'substance' which seem clearly nonequivalent. In the "Arguments in Geometrical Fashion" appended to the Second Replies, Descartes defines 'substance' in a way which, despite the rather convoluted language, is clearly traditional:

> *Substance.* This term applies to every thing in which whatever we perceive immediately resides, as in a subject, or to every thing by means of which whatever we perceive exists. By 'whatever we perceive' is meant any property, quality or attribute of which we have a real idea. The only idea we have of a substance itself, in the strict sense, is that it is the thing in which whatever we perceive . . . exists, either formally or eminently. For we know by the natural light that a real attribute cannot belong to nothing.
>
> (CSM II 114)

Such a definition is a recognizable descendant of Aristotle's conception of substance as an ultimate subject of predication: that is, a substance is a bearer of properties but is not itself a property of something else (in contrast, say, to yellowness or honesty). In terms of such a definition it may seem obvious that particular, finite bodies, such as the lump of wax in the Second Meditation, for example, are extended substances. As Descartes notes, the piece of wax is extended, flexible, and changeable; it thus seems clearly to be a bearer of properties which is not itself predicable of anything else.

In the *Principles of Philosophy*, however, Descartes offers a definition of 'substance' which seems to have different implications for the status of bodies. In this work he defines 'substance' in terms of independence, and though he does not explicitly add the qualification, the independence in question seems to be causal: "By *substance* we can understand nothing other than a thing which exists in such a way as to depend on no other thing for its existence" (*Princ.*, I.51, CSM I 210). Descartes immediately proceeds to recognize that, taken strictly, this definition rules out all created substances, and a fortiori all extended substances; strictly, only God satisfies the definition, for all other things exist only with the help of divine concurrence. But Descartes then says that, taken in a weaker sense, the definition does leave room for created substances: "as for corporeal substance and mind (or created thinking substance), those can be understood to fall under this common concept: things that need only the concurrence of God in order to exist" (*Princ.*, I.52, CSM I 210). But if corporeal substance is said to depend only on divine concurrence for its existence, it seems clear that no finite body – whether macroscopic or microscopic – can be a corporeal substance by this definition. The piece of wax, for example, obviously depends for its existence on other finite bodies such as the body of the bee. By contrast, the entire physical universe would seem to satisfy the conditions for substantiality in the weaker sense. Although Descartes does not draw the consequence explicitly in the *Principles*, he seems committed by his definition to denying that there is a plurality of corporeal substances.

It is tempting to conclude that Descartes's real view is that there is only one extended or corporeal substance – the entire, indefinitely extended physical universe.[7] Such a thesis has indeed often been attributed to Descartes, but the attribution may rest on a misconception. For it is possible that for Descartes, 'corporeal substance,' like 'matter,' is in technical jargon a mass noun rather than a count noun.[8] Just as we cannot meaningfully ask how many golds or waters there are, so we cannot meaningfully ask how many extended or corporeal substances there are: there is just indefinitely extended or corporeal substance. Thus on this reading, the term 'substance' is more akin to 'stuff' than it is to 'thing.' We can still of course say that there are finite, particular bodies, such as the pen on my table, but it is not such countable items which are candidates for extended or corporeal substance: such items would rather be parts of extended or corporeal substance (in the way that water drops are parts of water). That this is Descartes's view is suggested by a passage from the Synopsis to the *Meditations* where he contrasts body, in the general sense, with the human body in relation to the issue of the incorruptibility of substance:

> Secondly, we need to recognize that body, taken in the general sense, is a substance, so that it too never perishes. But the human body, insofar as it differs from other bodies, is simply made up of a certain configuration of

limbs and other accidents of this sort: whereas the human mind is not made up of any accidents in this way, but is a pure substance.

(CSM II 10)

If Descartes does implicitly treat 'extended substance' as a mass noun, we can see again how the new wine of his metaphysics is in danger of bursting the old Aristotelian bottle. For in the Aristotelian tradition, the term 'substance' was surely a count noun: individual substances, for Aristotle, are paradigmatically the sort of things that can be counted.

There are powerful pressures in his philosophy, then, which push Descartes in the direction of recognizing that there is an asymmetry at the heart of his dualism. As we have seen, this asymmetry may take one of two forms: Descartes may hold that the asymmetry is simply with respect to number – whereas there is only one extended substance, there are many thinking substances. More interestingly and more radically, Descartes may hold that the asymmetry is a matter of logical grammar captured in the distinction between count nouns and mass nouns: whereas there is extended substance (or stuff), there are many thinking substances (or things). Whether Descartes consistently recognizes the presence of either asymmetry in his dualism may be disputed, but the idea of some such asymmetry is still highly instructive for an understanding of Descartes's leading rationalist successors: it is tempting to say that Spinoza and Leibniz develop the different sides of the dualism and, with due qualifications, present it as the whole truth about the universe. Whereas Spinoza develops the first side, Leibniz develops the second side.

It is Leibniz who makes one of the most illuminating remarks about Spinoza's philosophical relationship to Descartes: Spinoza, says Leibniz, merely cultivated certain seeds in Descartes's philosophy (GP II 563). Part of what Leibniz has in mind here involves an issue that will come up in the next section: Spinoza goes further than Descartes in his rejection of teleological explanation, that is, explanation in terms of purposes. But the most obvious illustration of Leibniz's point involves the doctrine of substance. In the *Principles of Philosophy*, Descartes, as we have seen, defines 'substance' in terms of causal independence, and infers from this that, strictly speaking, there is only one substance, God. But Descartes immediately takes the point back again, as it were, by allowing that there is a weaker sense in which there can be created substances. Spinoza, by contrast, will tolerate none of Descartes's qualifications: Spinoza is unequivocal that there is no other substance than God.

There is no doubt that at some level Leibniz must be right that Spinoza's pantheistic metaphysics grows out of a seed that Descartes himself sows in the *Principles*. The difficulty is to know whether Spinoza reaches this doctrine by a strictly Cartesian route. The issue is highly controversial, but it does not seem that Spinoza, like Descartes in the *Principles*, seeks to define 'substance' in terms of causal independence: rather, in the early propositions of the *Ethics*, Spinoza appears to regard causal independence or self-sufficiency as a derivative truth about substance which needs to be established by philosophical argument.[9] It is true that Spinoza's definition of 'substance' does not wear its meaning on its face, but it seems correct to say that it has Aristotelian roots: by defining 'substance' as "that which is in itself and conceived through itself" (*Ethics*, I, def. 3), Spinoza seems to mean, in part at least, that substance is a bearer of properties or an ultimate subject of predication. As many writers have noticed, it is possible to express this idea in the terminology of 'independence,' but the independence in question is not causal, but logical: properties are logically dependent on substance, but substance is not dependent on, but prior to, its properties or modes. Spinoza's strategy in the early propositions of the *Ethics* seems to be to show that that which is a genuine bearer of properties or an ultimate subject of predication must also be causally independent or self-sufficient. Thus Spinoza can agree with Descartes about this last point, but not because he subscribes to Descartes's definition of 'substance' in the *Principles*.

If Spinoza finds it necessary to argue for the causal independence of substance, he also finds it necessary to argue further for the thesis that there is no other substance than God; for Spinoza, unlike Descartes, the thesis is not a trivial consequence of the initial definition of 'substance.' Spinoza's strategy has two parts. First, by means of a version of the ontological argument, he seeks to show that God, or absolutely infinite substance, necessarily exists (*Ethics*, I, prop. 11); for to deny the existence of a God whose essence involves existence is absurd. Further, Spinoza then argues that no other substance can exist. For since God has infinitely many – that is, all possible – attributes, if there were another substance, it would have to share an attribute with God, and Spinoza has earlier claimed to have established that there cannot be two substances with a shared attribute. The proof of this proposition relies on a principle accepted also by Leibniz: there cannot be two substances with all their properties in common.

Spinoza is thus led to argue for the thesis that there is no other substance than God. But is this a monistic doctrine? Spinoza's metaphysical system has been traditionally described in these terms, and there is clear textual support for the traditional description; in the corollary to *Ethics*, I, prop. 14, Spinoza says: "it follows quite clearly that God is one; that is, in the universe there is only one substance." But our earlier discussion of Descartes may lead us to wonder whether there is not a hint in Spinoza of a different doctrine; in places Spinoza, like Descartes, may implicitly treat 'substance' as a mass noun rather than a count noun. Just as Descartes may be saying not that there is just one extended substance, but rather that there is extended stuff or substance, Spinoza may be saying not that there is one substance, but that there is substance which is both extended and thinking. As in the case of Descartes, Spinoza's metaphysics of substance may be in danger of bursting its Aristotelian bottle.

Although, especially in his later philosophy, Leibniz seems to move far away from Aristotle's metaphysics, he is much more concerned than Descartes or Spinoza to maintain essential continuity with the Aristotelian tradition. Unlike Descartes or Spinoza, for instance, Leibniz never abandons the Aristotelian thesis that the world consists ultimately of individual substances: substances, for Leibniz, as for Aristotle, are items that can in principle be counted. Moreover, Leibniz seeks to accommodate Aristotelian assumptions concerning substances, such as that they are compounds of matter and form. It is one of Leibniz's constant complaints against the Cartesians and their fellow moderns that they had needlessly abandoned the valuable metaphysical insights in the Aristotelian–scholastic tradition. A main aim of Leibniz's philosophy is to show how a metaphysics of essentially Aristotelian inspiration can also provide a proper grounding for the new mechanistic physics.

Leibniz's metaphysics is perhaps most famous for its insistence that an individual substance is a genuine unity or *unum per se*. At times Leibniz may be tempted to define 'substance' in these terms, but it is important to see that he is not throwing over the traditional definition of 'substance' as an ultimate subject of predication. Leibniz shows his respect for the Aristotelian definition in *Discourse on Metaphysics*, §8, when he remarks that "when several predicates are attributed to a single subject, and this subject is attributed to no other, it is called an individual substance" (AG 40–41). When Arnauld charged Leibniz with simply introducing a stipulative definition of 'substance' as 'that which has true unity,' Leibniz protested that he was being unfair: the conception of substance as a true unity is equivalent to the Aristotelian definition of 'substance' as a bearer of properties or ultimate subject of predication. As Leibniz explains, "To be brief, I hold as axiomatic the identical proposition which varies only in emphasis: that which is not truly *one* entity is not truly one *entity* either. It has always been thought that 'one' and 'entity' are interchangeable" (M 121). On the basis of this conception, Leibniz insists that no mere aggregate can be a substance, and in his middle period he seems attached to the idea that all, and perhaps only, organisms are substances since, unlike inanimate bodies, they are genuine unities by virtue of being informed by a soul or substantial form. Such a thesis drew inspiration from the invention of the microscope and the discoveries that it made possible: it is also true to the teachings of Aristotle in his *Metaphysics*.

Although Leibniz treats the Aristotelian conception of substance with respect, he also insists that it does not go deep enough. In *Discourse on Metaphysics*, §8, Leibniz argues that we can gain more insight into the nature of individual substances by seeing that they have complete concepts which contain everything that can be truly predicated of them; thus it is part of the complete concept of Julius Caesar (located in the mind of God) that he crossed the Rubicon and was assassinated in the Capitol. Although the issue is controversial, it seems that from this thesis Leibniz seeks to derive some of the main doctrines of his metaphysics: individual substances do not causally interact; rather, each is the causal source of all its states which evolve in a harmony with one another that has been preestablished by God.

Leibniz's obsession with the idea that substances are genuine unities finds its most mature expression in the theory of monads. (The term 'monad' derives from the Platonic term for unity.) Perhaps the most important point to make about this difficult and counterintuitive theory is that it is a form of atomism; as Leibniz says, monads are the true atoms of nature.[10] But monads are of course not physical atoms for Leibniz, for in his view nothing purely material can be a genuine unity: rather, they are spiritual atoms or soul-like entities endowed with perception and appetition. Many of the doctrines which Leibniz had earlier formulated in connection with corporeal substance reappear in a new form in the theory of monads.

Even in the theory of monads, Leibniz seeks to accommodate Aristotelian doctrines; sometimes this accommodation seems rather strained, as in Leibniz's insistence that even monads are in a sense compounds of matter and form. But Leibniz's final metaphysics draws its inspiration far more from the Platonic and neo-Platonic tradition than from the Aristotelian one. The theory of monads, for instance, is a striking illustration of the ancient Platonic thesis that there is a fundamental contrast between the world of appearance and reality. The bodies which we see around us belong to the realm of phenomena: only monads are ultimately real. Nonetheless, there is an important connection between the two realms: bodies are grounded in monads in a quite specific sense. The forces of bodies which are the object of investigation by physicists derive from the primitive forces at the level of monads (L 529–30).

"[Spinoza] would be right if there were no monads" (GP III 575). Despite his professed hostility to Spinoza's "atheism," Leibniz in this famous remark at least pays Spinoza the compliment of regarding his system as the only alternative to his own. Such a judgment is perhaps not surprising, for the two systems represent two very different ways of developing Descartes's legacy. But it would be a mistake to notice only the contrasts between the two systems, which are indeed sufficiently striking. In fact, it is more fruitful to see Leibniz and Spinoza as engaged in a dialogue on the basis of some important shared commitments. Leibniz, like Spinoza, accepts the principle of the Identity of Indiscernibles, but believes that it does not have the consequences Spinoza claims for it. For Spinoza, the principle excludes the possibility of a plurality of substances of the same nature; for Leibniz, it does not have this consequence, for substances can share the same abstract nature while being individuated in terms of their points of view. Leibniz, like Spinoza, accepts that a substance is essentially causally self-sufficient, but whereas Spinoza draws the consequence that there can be no other substance than God, Leibniz, like Descartes, accepts a somewhat weaker version of this principle which allows for created substances: such substances are as causally self-sufficient as is consistent with their status as creatures.

For all their differences, the philosophers we have discussed agree in according the concept of substance a prominent role in their philosophy, even if they adapt it to accommodate new metaphysical insights. Yet there were other philosophers such as Gassendi and Locke in particular who openly question whether there is a place for the category of substance on the new scientific picture of the world. Locke's contemporaries had, after all, broken entirely with the Aristotelian conception of a world of individual substances ranged into natural kinds according to forms or essences. In place of such a world picture, Locke tentatively accepted the corpuscularian hypothesis according to which the physical world was ultimately made up of tiny corpuscles or particles endowed with the primary qualities of size, shape, solidity, and motion. In the eyes of Locke and others, it was by no means obvious that a concept of substance deriving from Aristotle retained its philosophical value and usefulness. As we shall see here and in the final section, it is not only the Aristotelians who are the targets of Locke's polemics.

Locke's critique of the concept of substance is directed against a line of thinking that can be traced back to a passage in Aristotle's *Metaphysics*. As we have seen, substances, for Aristotle, are ultimate subjects of predication, and such subjects are normally taken to be such items as individual human beings and horses. But in one passage, Aristotle suggests that the ultimate subject of predication is not the individual horse, for example, but rather the ultimate substratum which is opposed to all properties whatever.[11] It is this concept of substance as substratum of all properties that is the target of Locke's famous polemic.

From the beginning, Locke's critique of the concept of substance as substratum has intrigued and puzzled his readers. For one thing, Locke's critique is marked by a certain systematic ambivalence: Locke maintains that the idea of a substratum is natural and even indispensable to us, while also deploring its uselessness.[12] Moreover, the critique seems to include two components which are not obviously consistent with one another. On the one hand, Locke complains that the idea of a substratum which is the bearer of properties but itself propertyless is empty of content; for this reason, it can play no useful role in philosophy. On the other hand, Locke complains that the idea of substance, far from being clear and distinct as the Cartesians suppose, is obscure and confused: it is the idea of something we know not what. In the same vein he complains that substance in general has a nature which is "secret and abstract" (*Essay*, II.xxiii.6). It is natural to object, as Leibniz did, that Locke is here needlessly making difficulties for himself. "If you distinguish two things in a substance – the attributes or predicates and their common subject – it is no wonder that you cannot conceive anything specific in this subject. This is inevitable, because you have already set aside all the attributes through which details could be conceived" (*New Ess.*, II.xxiii). In other words, it is perverse to complain that the idea of such a substratum is obscure and confused, for to do so suggests that there is more to be known. But if the idea of a substratum is the idea of a bare particular opposed to all properties whatever, then there is nothing that could in principle be known. This apparent tension in Locke's teachings about substance can be resolved, I think, by seeing that he is working with an implicit contrast between the divine and human levels of knowledge. Our idea of substance is indeed empty of content: it is the idea of a propertyless substratum. God has the idea of substance in the sense that he knows what it is to be a genuine thing; it is relative to this perfect divine idea that our own idea of substance is obscure and confused.

The most obvious target of Locke's polemic may seem to be the Aristotelians, and there is no doubt that they are one of Locke's targets. But there is also no doubt that Locke, following Gassendi, has the Cartesians in his sights: Locke thinks that he can exploit the poverty of our concept of substance in order to undermine the dogmatic substance dualism of Descartes and his disciples. Thus Locke appeals to the obscurity of our idea of substance in order to argue that, though it may be natural for us to think in dualistic terms, we cannot rule out the possibility that one and the same substratum supports both mental and physical properties. But there is also a hint, perhaps, of a more radical critique. Drawing on the emptiness of the concept of substratum, Locke suggests that the debate between substantial dualists and their opponents has no real content to it, at least at the level of our ideas. Whether we say that one and the same substratum supports mental and physical properties, or that different substrata play this role, is a matter of convention and custom only: in terms of our imperfect ideas, there is no fact of the matter to be discovered.

Locke's teachings about substance are so rich and ambivalent that they lent themselves to being developed in different philosophical directions. It is traditional to portray Berkeley as one philosopher who developed the negative, critical side of Locke's teachings for his own, very distinctive purposes. In one way this is correct: Berkeley saw how this side of Locke could be exploited in the interests of attacking the doctrine of material substance – that is, that there is a realm of mind-independent physical objects conceived along corpuscularian lines. In a vein that is obviously influenced by Locke, Berkeley insists on the unhelpfulness and indeed incoherence of saying that extension is supported by a substratum. If the claim is taken literally, it leads to an infinite regress of such substrata, for the substratum, being itself extended, will need to be supported by a further substratum, and so on; if it is taken metaphorically, it is unintelligible.[13]

Berkeley's debt to Locke is beyond question, but it would be wholly misleading to portray Berkeley simply as a critic of the concept of substance. Famously, although Berkeley insists that the concept of material substance is incoherent, he also insists that no such difficulties plague the concept of spiritual or mental substance. One of Berkeley's reasons for this asymmetry turns on the notion of support or substratum. In the case of material substance, there is no way of cashing out the metaphor of a support or substratum of properties. In the case of spiritual substance, however, this is far from being so: spiritual substances support their properties – ideas – by perceiving them.[14] Berkeley is thus led to a form of idealism according to which the created universe consists entirely of spiritual substances. Thus, although Berkeley is able to make use of Locke's critique, he is no more led to dispense with the concept of substance altogether than is Leibniz in his own somewhat similar metaphysics. Berkeley is at least prepared to retain some of the old bottles for the new wine of his uncompromisingly idealistic metaphysics.

CAUSALITY

Modern philosophical discussion of the nature of causality has traditionally been traced back to Hume, and it is certainly true that

Hume gave a new direction to philosophical thought about the topic. But it is now realized that Hume himself was building on the work of his predecessors: philosophical theories, such as occasionalism, which were formerly dismissed as extravagant, ad hoc solutions to particular problems are now seen as general theories of great interest which played a pivotal role in the development of thought about causality between Descartes and Hume.[15] On the whole, the philosophers who made the most important contributions to the debate about causality seem to have believed that Descartes's own thinking on this topic remained too conservative. Despite his boast that he was beginning philosophy again on new foundations, in this area of his thought Descartes seemed to accept scholastic assumptions about causality which had no place in his own very different picture of the physical world. For a number of philosophers, the task before them was to complete the Cartesian revolution in this area; they sought to draw out the implications of the new theory of matter and to show that traditional claims about natural causality could no longer be upheld. In some cases, such as the occasionalists, they came close to suggesting that the concept of causality in general should be jettisoned from philosophy.

In the Aristotelian tradition, the term 'cause' (or its Greek and Latin equivalents *aitia* and *causa*) was used in a much broader sense than is current today. In general, a cause was whatever answered a Why? question, and it is in terms of this fact that we must understand why the Aristotelian tradition recognizes four kinds of causes: the efficient, formal, material, and final causes are supposed to correspond to four different kinds of Why? question.[16] Thus to answer the question: Why is the statue so heavy? by citing the fact that it is made of bronze, is to appeal to the material cause. To answer the question: Why is the angle A, inscribed in a semicircle, a right angle? by citing the fact that it is equal to an angle B which is half of a straight angle, is to appeal to the formal cause. In general, with the possible exception of Leibniz, early modern discussions of causality tended to focus on the notion of efficient cause, that is, the kind of cause that brings about a change of state in another thing; it is the efficient cause that is at issue when we say, for example, that the stone caused the window to break. But as we shall see toward the end of this section, there was also a lively debate about the place of final causes, that is, causes that appeal to goals or purposes, in the new mechanistic picture of the physical world. First, we must turn to the debate over efficient causality.

"Now it is manifest by the natural light that there must be at least as much reality in the efficient and total cause as in the effect of that cause" (CSM II 28). In these terms Descartes states his most explicit principle concerning the nature of efficient causation in the course of proving the existence of God in the Third Meditation. (Although Descartes proceeds to apply this principle to ideas, it is clear that it is intended to be of wholly general application.) Despite Descartes's claim that it is self-evident, the principle has seemed far from intuitive and vulnerable to counterexamples. Some insight into the principle can be gained by seeing that it is associated with, and indeed follows from, what has been called an heirloom model of efficient causation: in causal transactions, the effect inherits a property, or strictly a property instance, from the cause (CSM II 192). It is perhaps more natural to think of this model of efficient causation in terms of a different metaphor: causation is pictured as a process of contagion. Thus when the lighted gas causes the water in the kettle to become hot, it does so by infecting the water with its own property of heat.

The heirloom or contagion model of causation has often seemed like a relic of the scholastic tradition which remains unassimilated in Descartes's philosophy. Whether this model of causation was actually embraced by the scholastics has recently been disputed.[17] Nonetheless, it was certainly so regarded by Leibniz, who attacks the doctrine of influx, as he terms it, vigorously throughout his career: for Leibniz, the doctrine is particularly associated with Suárez. According to Leibniz, it is utterly unintelligible to suppose that properties or individual accidents could pass over from one substance to another. "Strictly, it can be said that *no substance exercises on another a metaphysical action or influx* . . . [I]t is impossible to explain how anything passes from one thing into the substance of another."[18] Leibniz is thus led to the denial of causal interaction between created substances. It is striking that in attacking the doctrine of influx here, Leibniz does not call for a new understanding of efficient causation which would allow us to preserve the intuition that substances causally interact; rather, he seems to hold that influx is the only available model of causal interaction. Yet in his earlier writings, Leibniz had hinted at a different strategy; he had criticized the scholastic Suárez for badly defining 'cause' in terms of influx (GP IV 148). But if Suárez's definition of 'cause' is a bad one, it seems reasonable to suppose that a better definition might open the way to a defense of causal interaction or transeunt causation.

Leibniz's denial of influx may throw light on a vexed issue concerning the scope of his denial of causal interaction. The doctrine is most famous as a thesis concerning relations between substances, and it is in these terms that it is generally introduced in Leibniz's main expositions of his metaphysics: indeed, some of his arguments depend explicitly on assumptions about the nature of individual substances. The denial of interaction thus applies to monads and perhaps also organisms. But Leibniz can also be found insisting that the doctrine is a thesis in physics which applies to all bodies, whether animate or inanimate: "no impetus is transferred from one body to another, but each body is moved by its innate force which is determined only on the occasion, i.e. in respect of another. For eminent men have already recognized that the cause of the impulse one body receives from another is the body's elasticity itself, by which it recoils from another."[19] Yet if items such as billiard balls are at issue, these are not strictly substances but aggregates of substances for Leibniz. Leibniz seems to be suggesting that causal interaction between such bodies in collision would involve an objectionable form of influx, and is thus impossible.

The heirloom principle, or the doctrine of influx, as Leibniz terms it, thus seems to be a point on which Descartes and Leibniz are sharply divided. There is less disagreement over the status of a weaker, but related principle – the Causal Likeness Principle – to the effect that there must be a likeness between cause and effect. Although Descartes never makes this principle a cornerstone of his philosophy, he is certainly capable of appealing to it implicitly; as we shall see in the next section, he invokes it in connection with the issue of the causation of sensory ideas. However, the form in which Descartes accepted the principle is unclear and has been a subject of debate. In the case of Spinoza, by contrast, there is little ambiguity. His acceptance is prominently proclaimed early on in the *Ethics* (I, prop. 3): "Things which have nothing in common cannot be the cause of one another." For Spinoza, the Causal Likeness Principle serves as the basis for excluding the production of one substance by another of a different attribute: it thus excludes the creation of matter by God as envisaged by Descartes and indeed many Christian philosophers. As we shall see, the principle also serves as the basis for excluding causation across attributes of the one substance, God or Nature.

Perhaps the principle concerning causality which had the most fruitful results was to be stated by Malebranche in his *Search after Truth*: "A true cause," according to Malebranche, "is one such that the mind perceives a necessary connection between it and its effect" (VI.ii.3). (Although Malebranche does not say so explicitly, it is clear that he understands 'necessary connection' here in a strong logical sense.) In the hands of Malebranche, this principle is a key premise in his most interesting and powerful argument for occasionalism. The principle serves to establish the positive thesis that God is indeed a true cause, for the mind does perceive a necessary connection between the will of an infinite being and its upshots. It is a necessary truth that if God wills a logically possible state of affairs, that state of affairs obtains. The principle also serves to establish the striking negative thesis that is at the heart of occasionalism: no creature is a genuine cause, for the mind does not perceive a necessary connection between any such being and its alleged upshots. It is logically possible, for instance, that one billiard ball should collide with another at rest, and that the stationary ball should fail to move following the collision. It is also logically possible that I should will to raise my arm and that it should fail to move. Particular events in the created world, such as the collision of billiard balls, are thus simply the occasions on which God's genuine causality is exercised; it is in this way that the doctrine gets its name.

The insistence on necessary connection as an essential component of genuine causality was to be taken up and developed in different directions by two of Malebranche's successors. Berkeley employed Malebranche's principle in order to argue for a form of semioccasionalism. Berkeley agrees with Malebranche that the mind does not perceive a necessary connection in the case of bodies, construed, as his immaterialism requires, in terms of collections of ideas: that food nourishes and fire burns is known not a priori, by means of a necessary connection, but by observing regularities.[20] But at least in his published writings, Berkeley cannot agree with Malebranche that finite minds or spirits are on a par with bodies.

According to Berkeley, it seems that we do know a priori, by perceiving a necessary connection, that our arm will go up when we decide to raise it. Berkeley's insistence on this asymmetry needs to be understood in terms of his theological commitments. If the human mind in the exercise of its will were not a genuine cause, it could hardly be said to be made in the image of God. Berkeley seems to have believed that, for all their piety, the occasionalists were prepared to sacrifice the teachings of Genesis.

Like Berkeley, Hume agrees with the occasionalists that necessary connection is an essential component of causality; but unlike Berkeley, he agrees with Malebranche's occasionalism in his insistence on the symmetry of the mental and physical cases. In the *Inquiry concerning Human Understanding*, Hume is explicit that we are no more able to perceive a logically necessary connection in the case of voluntary physical movement than in the case of the collision of two billiard balls (*Inquiry*, VII.1). Indeed, within the framework of his own very different, empiricist theory of ideas, Hume adopts and refines the negative Malebranchian arguments. But despite his acknowledged debt to the doctrine, Hume of course is no occasionalist. Hume parts philosophical company with Malebranche by insisting that the necessary connection which is an essential component of our concept of causality must be construed in psychological, not logical, terms. To say that events of type A cause events of type B is to say not only that they are constantly conjoined in our experience; it is to say also that, after sufficient exposure to such regularities, the human mind feels compelled to expect an event of type B on the occasion of an event of type A. As Hume says, upon the whole, necessity exists in the mind, not in objects (*Treatise*, I.iii.14). Insofar as Hume writes as a metaphysician rather than a naturalist, he thus makes his most distinctive contribution to the debate over causality by offering a reductionist or deflationary account of causality which allows us to preserve the intuition that there are causal connections in nature.

The appeal to necessary connection thus not only provided the basis for Malebranche's most powerful and intriguing argument for occasionalism; it also proved a source of inspiration to successors such as Berkeley and Hume. But though the argument from necessary connection is Malebranche's most powerful argument for occasionalism, it is by no means the only one. Malebranche offers two other important arguments for the doctrine which show him to be engaged in a dialogue with Descartes; in their different ways, both arguments seek to develop the implications of Cartesian theses more fully and consistently than Descartes had done. One such argument for occasionalism is theological: it turns on Descartes's doctrine that God conserves the world by continuously creating it. According to Malebranche, when properly understood this doctrine leaves no room for genuine causal powers on the part of creatures. In recreating bodies, God does not simply will that a billiard ball, for instance, be somewhere or other; his volitions are fully specific or determinate with regard to such variables as location and velocity (*Dial.*, VII.11). Thus there is no need for God to endow created substances, whether minds or bodies, with genuine causal powers of their own; and since God always acts in the simplest way, we can be sure that he has not done so. Although most naturally illustrated with reference to bodies, this argument is of wholly general application; it applies to created minds as well as bodies. Another argument is more modest in scope inasmuch as it has no implications for the status of minds: it turns on the new Cartesian conception of matter. Malebranche rightly observes that on the Cartesian account, matter, being defined in geometrical terms, is purely passive and devoid of active force; it is subject, for instance, to the law of inertia. So understood, matter is incapable of being a genuine cause (*Dial.*, VII.5; cf. OC X 47). It is in this argument, perhaps, that the connection between metaphysics and the new physics is tightest.

Final causes

Whether Descartes was entitled to say that bodies are genuine efficient causes may be disputed, but there is no doubt that he sought to banish all causes but efficient causes from the new physics. In particular, Descartes sought to argue that appeals to final causes have no place on the new mechanical conception of the physical world. Descartes, in other words, seeks to banish from physics any explanations which appeal to divine or cosmic purposes: for example, it is wholly inappropriate to say that the rain fell in order that the crops might grow.[21] In the *Meditations*, Descartes justifies the exclusion of final causes from physics on theological grounds:

> Since I now know that my own nature is very weak and limited, whereas the nature of God is immense, incomprehensible and infinite, I also know without more ado that he is capable of countless things whose causes are beyond my knowledge. And for this reason alone I consider the customary search for final causes to be totally useless in physics; there is considerable rashness in thinking myself capable of investigating the impenetrable purposes of God.
>
> (CSM II 39)

It is tempting to say that Descartes is somewhat disingenuous here. His real reasons for banishing final causes from physics turn on the sufficiency of mechanical explanations of phenomena and on the fact that, unlike teleological explanations, they appeal only to clear and distinct ideas. But Descartes is not above seeking to legitimate his revolutionary redirection of physics by appealing to considerations of piety.

We saw in an earlier section that according to Leibniz, Spinoza merely cultivated certain seeds in Descartes's philosophy. With the possible exception of his teachings concerning substance, none of Spinoza's doctrines illustrates the truth of Leibniz's dictum better than his stance on final causes. It is important to notice that Descartes does not go so far as to deny that God has purposes; he simply says that they are impenetrable, and that it is for this reason that they should not be invoked in physics. Spinoza, by contrast, converts Descartes's negative epistemological claim into an ontological one: God has no purposes (*Ethics*, I, appendix). Such a thesis is consistent with his conception of God as an impersonal being devoid of will and intellect; indeed, it follows from that doctrine in conjunction with the further assumption that only persons can have purposes. Spinoza's strong thesis, of course, like Descartes's weaker one, has implications for physics, for if God (or Nature) has no purposes at all, then it trivially follows that it is misguided to seek to explain physical phenomena in terms of divine or natural purposes. Some readers have supposed that Spinoza takes the even stronger position that teleological explanation is misguided in principle.[22]

A self-consciously rearguard action in defense of final causes was mounted by Leibniz, who characteristically holds that teleological explanation is not in competition with explanation in terms of efficient causes. Leibniz insists, like Malebranche, that God acts from final causes, for God is a benevolent person whose goal in creation is to maximize the good. In opposition to Descartes, Leibniz further insists that there is a place for teleological explanation even on the new anti-Aristotelian physics. Leibniz's underlying idea here seems to be that in the conduct of scientific research, it is often helpful to adopt the divine perspective at least as a heuristic device; that is, scientific discovery will be aided by reflection on the fact that God aims always to produce his effects "by the easiest and most determinate ways" (*Discourse*, §21, AG 54). Leibniz is fond of citing Snell as a prominent modern example of a scientist who followed the method of final causes, for Snell sought the easiest or most determinate path by which rays of light might pass from a given point in a medium to a given point in another (*Discourse*, §22, AG 55). Leibniz's rehabilitation of final causes is typically ingenious, but it may be doubted how far his own conception of teleological explanation agrees with the Aristotelian one.[23]

SUBSTANCE, CAUSALITY, AND THE MIND–BODY PROBLEM

The tendency of early modern philosophers to put new wine into old bottles is strikingly illustrated by Descartes's attempt to explain the unity of a human being in terms of his dualistic metaphysics. One of the strengths of the old Aristotelian–scholastic tradition was its ability to give a convincing account of such unity; the soul was regarded as a substantial form which unifies and organizes the matter of the human body. Descartes, of course, broke with this tradition with his revolutionary insistence that the mind is a purely thinking substance which is really distinct from its body; the body, if not a substance in its own right, is at least part of a substance which is wholly different in nature from mind. On Descartes's account, then, a human being seems to be a mysterious compound of two utterly heterogeneous entities. Yet Descartes insists in the *Meditations* that in fact on his metaphysics the mind and its body form a very tight union (CSM II 56). In correspondence with his wayward disciple Regius, Descartes even goes so far as to instruct him to say that the human being is a "true *ens per se*, and not an *ens per accidens*" (CSM III 206). Indeed, Descartes has seemed to some readers to be suggesting that the mind–body union is a genuine third substance which is the true subject of properties, such as sensation and imagination, which cannot be properly attributed to either the mind or the body alone.[24] At the very least Descartes claims to believe that his new dualistic metaphysics can do justice to the old Aristotelian–scholastic doctrine that a human being is an *ens per se*, or genuine unity. In general, Descartes's successors did not share his confidence that he had solved the problem of unity or the related problem of mind–body interaction.

Of Descartes's major successors, it is Leibniz who is most sympathetic to the Aristotelian–scholastic approach to the problem of unity. As we have seen, Leibniz is attracted by the thesis, deriving from Aristotle, that the paradigm substances are organisms, and in terms of this thesis Leibniz is capable of articulating a standard Aristotelian–scholastic theory of the status of the soul. In some notes responding to Fardella, Leibniz writes in a purely Aristotelian–scholastic vein that "the soul, properly and accurately speaking, is not a substance but a substantial form, or the primitive form existing in substances, the first act, the first active faculty" (AG 105). Yet it is uncharacteristic of Leibniz to take such a purely scholastic position. More typically, even during the period in which he recognizes the existence of corporeal substances, Leibniz modifies Aristotelian–scholastic teachings in order to accommodate Platonic and Cartesian intuitions. A living organism such as Alexander the Great is indeed a substance, and his soul plays the unifying role which it plays for Aristotle and his scholastic disciples, but Leibniz also wants to insist that the soul is a substance in its own right. Moreover, toward the end of his career, Leibniz moves even further away from Aristotelian–scholastic teaching. According to the doctrine of monads, not only is the human soul (or mind) a substance in its own right, but the human body is itself an aggregate of such substances (i.e. monads) whose states evolve in a preestablished harmony with those of the soul. It is true that Leibniz still wishes to say that it is the presence of the soul that confers unity on the human being, but he is now driven to explain such unity by saying that the soul is the dominant monad with respect to the aggregate of subordinate monads which constitute the human body. The claim that the human soul is the dominant monad is unpacked in terms of relations of clarity and distinctness among perceptual states.

Spinoza was no less dissatisfied than Leibniz by Descartes's account of the unity of a human being; indeed, he is even more unsparing in his ridicule of Descartes's position. But, as we should expect, his own proposed solution to the problem owes little or nothing to the Aristotelian–scholastic tradition. In outline, Spinoza's solution to the problem is remarkably simple: mind and body are one and the same thing. This thing is not of course a substance, but a finite mode of the one substance, God or Nature. Stated thus baldly, Spinoza's thesis that mind and body are identical may seem indistinguishable from the outright materialism of Hobbes, but it would be misleading to assimilate their positions too closely. It is true that Hobbes and Spinoza are alike in rejecting the view that the human mind is an immaterial substance; they are thereby able to circumvent all the problems that Descartes had found in explaining how such a substance is united to its body. But the difference between Hobbes and Spinoza is suggested by the way in which the former qualifies his bald statement of identity: mind and body are one and the same thing, conceived now under the attribute of thought, now under the attribute of extension (*Ethics*, III, prop. 2 schol.). Spinoza regards the mental and the physical as irreducibly different – indeed, really distinct – aspects under which a human being may be conceived; the attributes of thought and extension run through the whole of nature, and neither attribute has primacy over the other. Hobbes, by contrast, is a reductive materialist: the mental is simply a subdomain of the physical, and it is the physical which is ontologically basic.

A third solution to the problem of the unity of a human being may have its roots in Descartes's own teachings. Descartes has sometimes been read as saying that the unity of a human being is constituted simply by the fact of interaction between body and mind. In the *Dialogues on Metaphysics* and elsewhere, Malebranche develops this thesis in an occasionalist direction. As an occasionalist, Malebranche cannot hold that there is any genuine causal interaction between mind and body, but he can and does say that mental and physical events are occasional causes. Moreover, Malebranche also expresses this idea in terms of the existence of "laws of the union of mind and body," or as we might say, psychophysical laws:

Thus it is clear that in the union of the soul and the body there is no other connection than the efficacy of the divine decrees: decrees which are immutable, and efficacy which is never deprived of its effect. God has therefore willed, and he wills unceasingly, that the various disturbances of the brain are always followed by various thoughts of the mind united to it. And it is the constant and efficacious will of the Creator which, properly speaking, effects the union of these two substances. For there is no other nature, that is, there are no other natural laws except the efficacious volitions of the Almighty.

(*Dial.*, IV.11)

Malebranche thus invokes the idea of divinely decreed laws to offer a deflationary account of the union of mind and body.

The problem of interaction

Whether or not Descartes tries to cash out the union of mind and body in terms of interaction may be disputed, but it was widely agreed by Descartes's successors that he faced an insuperable problem in explaining how such interaction is possible on his ontological principles. In the *New System*, for example, Leibniz writes that "how the body makes anything happen in the soul, or vice versa . . . Descartes had given up the game at this point, as far as we can determine from his writings" (AG 142–43; cf. Spinoza, *Ethics*, V, pref.). Indeed, it is sometimes thought that the great metaphysical systems such as Malebranche's occasionalism and Leibniz's doctrine of preestablished harmony were devised as ad hoc solutions to this one problem. But it should be clear by now that this view is misleading. As we have seen, such systems address more basic and general problems about whether there is a place for natural causality on the new mechanistic scientific world picture, and if so, how it can be accommodated. The challenge which Malebranche, Spinoza, and Leibniz faced was to devise principled solutions to the problem of interaction on the basis of their general commitments concerning the nature of substances and of efficient causality.

Descartes's successors may have found problems in his apparent commitment to the interaction of mind and body, but was Descartes himself aware of a problem? Here, as elsewhere, Descartes seems to speak with an ambiguous voice. Sometimes, as in correspondence with Arnauld, Descartes writes in such a way as to suggest not only that mind and body do interact, but that such interaction is unproblematic: "That the mind, which is incorporeal, can set the body in motion is something which is shown to us not by any reasoning or comparison with other matters, but by the surest and plainest everyday experience" (CSM III 358; cf. CSM II 275). There has been a tendency among commentators to suppose that Descartes is not entitled to such confidence. But in fact it is by no means obvious that mind–body interaction is inconsistent with Descartes's own official pronouncements concerning causality.[25] As we have seen, his most explicit principle concerning causality maintains that there must be at least as much reality in the total efficient cause as in the effect. Descartes is not without resources for reconciling this principle with two-way interaction of mind and body. On Descartes's scale of reality, substances rank higher than modes. If, then, in the interaction of mind and body, substances are causes of the modes in another substance, there will be no violation of this admittedly rather obscure principle regarding efficient causality.

At other times, however, Descartes seems more willing to concede that the interaction of mind and body is problematic on his principles. To Princess Elisabeth, for instance, he writes that the question of how the soul can move the body is "the one that can be most properly put to me in view of my published writings" (CSM III 217). On occasion, indeed, Descartes seems prepared to abandon in part his commitment to such interaction on the grounds that it would conflict with accepted causal principles. In the *Comments on a Certain Broadsheet,* for instance, Descartes argues against the existence of strictly adventitious ideas (that is, ideas that are caused by external physical objects) by appealing to the fact that there is no likeness between sensory ideas and corporeal motions; there is, for instance, strictly no color in the external physical world (CSM I 304). Here, then, Descartes is prepared to appeal implicitly to a Causal Likeness Principle in order to rule out at least the action of body on mind.

It is this side of Descartes that is developed by his leading successors who advanced positive metaphysical systems of their own. Malebranche, Spinoza, and Leibniz all deny that there is, strictly speaking, any causal interaction between mind and body.[26] Such an approach to the problem of mind–body interaction may seem initially surprising, but further reflection suggests that it should not be. In the first place, such philosophers seek to derive their denial of mind–body interaction from their general commitments concerning efficient causality. Moreover, in the case of Spinoza and Leibniz, a further motivation for their approach to the problem of interaction was their desire to uphold the principle of the causal closure of the physical world; that is, every physical event has exclusively physical causes. Clearly, this principle cannot be consistently combined with both the recognition of interaction and the dualistic thesis that the mental and the physical are different in nature. Since, in contrast to Hobbes, their commitment to this last thesis is nonnegotiable, they avoid an inconsistent triad of propositions by denying mind–body interaction. In the eyes of Leibniz, in particular, acceptance of the principle of causal closure is essential to any satisfactory physics. Indeed, Leibniz complains that even Malebranche's occasionalist adjustment of Descartes's ontology threatens to introduce a troublesome "disturbance" of the laws of physics (*Theod.*, §61). Leibniz's worry here is that to hold, as Malebranche does, that mental events may be even occasional causes of physical events is inconsistent with the principle of the conservation of momentum.

Of the three solutions to the problem of interaction proposed by Malebranche, Leibniz, and Spinoza, it is perhaps Spinoza's position that is most puzzling. The source of the problem lies in Spinoza's insistence that mind and body are one and the same thing conceived under different attributes – the attributes of thought and extension. The attempt to combine this thesis with the further thesis that the mental and physical realms are alike causally closed, appears to lead to paradox. For it seems intuitive that if A is the cause of B, and B is identical with C, then A is the cause of C. Thus, for example, if the stinging action of the bee causes a state of the brain and this state of the brain is identical with pain, then the bee's sting causes pain. But Spinoza cannot accept this causal principle, for in conjunction with his identity thesis it entails a conclusion which is inconsistent with his denial that there is any causal flow between the mental and physical realms.[27] The solution to this paradox seems to lie in a proper understanding of Spinoza's conception of cause, which is alien to the post-Humean mind. For Spinoza, the link between cause and effect is one that is perspicuous to the intellect; to say that A is the cause of B is to say at least that A explains B in an illuminating way. When causation is understood in these terms, the general principle that Spinoza's philosophy seems to violate no longer appears intuitive. In technical jargon, for Spinoza, causal contexts are not referentially transparent but opaque.[28]

In common with Descartes's other major successors, Locke addresses not only the issue of the ontological status of the mind, but the further question of whether it interacts with the body; like them, he sees these issues as related in interesting ways. But in other respects, here as elsewhere, Locke stands apart, for in his case the direction of the argument is quite different. The philosophers we have examined so far tend to argue from the heterogeneity of mind and body to the impossibility of causal interaction between them. Locke, by contrast, like Descartes himself on occasion, accepts the interaction of mind and body as a fact of experience which cannot be sensibly denied, and exploits this fact as a basis for undermining an immaterialist theory of mind. Locke can agree with others that it is difficult to conceive of interaction between heterogeneous substances, but for him this serves as a reason for doubting that mind and body are such substances. "What certainty of Knowledge can anyone have that some perceptions, as *v.g.* pleasure and pain, should not be in some bodies themselves, after a certain manner modified and moved, as well as that they should be in an immaterial substance, upon the Motion of the parts of Body: Body as far as we can conceive being able only to strike and affect body, and Motion, according to the utmost reach of our *Ideas*, being able to produce nothing but Motion" (*Essay*, IV.iii.6). It is true that Locke never entertains the possibility of reductive materialism; that is, he never entertains the hypothesis that mental states are simply identical with brain states. But while he is committed to property dualism, he does exploit the fact of mind–body interaction in order to question the truth of substantial dualism. Here, as so often in his philosophy, Locke appeals to the deliverances of common sense in the service of a rather subtle and systematic attack on Cartesian dogmatism about the essences of mind and matter.

SPACE AND TIME

For obvious reasons, philosophers up to the time of Kant tended to debate the nature of space and time in tandem. Yet it is also noticeable that they tended to focus more sharply on the case of space; philosophical theories that seem primarily tailored to space are often said to apply *mutatis mutandis* to the case of time. This tendency to focus on space at the expense of time is particularly prominent in the early modern period. Accordingly, in this section we shall devote more attention to space than to time.

Philosophical debate about space centered on a cluster of issues which were not always sharply distinguished. One such issue concerns the place of space within the system of ontological categories favored by early modern philosophers: is space a substance, an attribute, or a relation? As we shall see, each of these options could boast distinguished advocates. A related issue concerned the actuality and even the possibility of empty space or the void. Philosophers who were united in their rejection of scholastic physics and their adherence to the new mechanical philosophy could be sharply divided over whether the physical universe was a plenum. Although they would have deplored its anthropomorphic phrasing, some philosophers continued to agree with Aristotle's dictum that nature abhors a vacuum, while others sought to revive the Epicurean theory of atoms in a void. A final issue concerning the infinity or finitude of space was particularly sensitive for theological reasons, for traditionally only God was supposed to be strictly infinite. Thus philosophers who cared about theological orthodoxy had to tread carefully around this issue.

The first two issues concerning space are tightly related in the case of Descartes and Spinoza. In his *Principles of Philosophy*, Descartes explains that there is only a rational distinction between space and corporeal substance:

> There is no real distinction between space, or internal place, and the corporeal substance contained in it: the only difference lies in the way in which we are accustomed to conceive of them. For in reality the extension in length, breadth and depth which constitutes a space is exactly the same as that which constitutes a body.
>
> (*Princ.*, II.10, CSM I 227)

Descartes thus answers the purely ontological question by saying that space is in effect a substance which differs from matter only in our way of conceiving it. And from the ontological thesis, Descartes proceeds to derive an answer to the related question about the vacuum: since space and corporeal substance are one and the same under two descriptions (merely rationally distinct), a vacuum or empty space is strictly impossible.

The impossibility of a vacuum, in the philosophical sense of that in which there is no substance whatsoever, is clear from the fact that there is no difference between the extension of a space, or internal place, and the extension of a body.

(*Princ.*, II.16, CSM I 229–30)

Although Descartes's commitment to the impossibility of a vacuum is uncompromising, a complicating factor is introduced by his extreme doctrine of divine omnipotence. In correspondence with Arnauld, Descartes explains that he would not dare to say that God could not bring about the existence of wholly empty space (CSM III 358–59). But at the same time he makes it crystal clear that a vacuum involves a "contradiction in my conception." For Descartes, it is no less impossible that there should be a vacuum than that two plus one should not be equal to three.

Spinoza's thinking about space involves a characteristic attempt to accommodate Cartesian themes within a pantheistic metaphysics. Like Descartes, Spinoza holds that space is only conceptually distinct from extended or corporeal substance; like Descartes, too, for this reason he is committed to the impossibility of a vacuum (with no Cartesian qualifications stemming from reflection on divine omnipotence). But Spinoza's abandonment of the transcendent God of orthodox theology allows and even in some cases dictates a departure from Cartesian principles. For reasons of theological caution, Descartes had been reluctant to deify space, as it were, by proclaiming it to be infinite; instead, Descartes had preferred to say that it was boundless or indefinite (*Princ.*, I.27, CSM I 202). Spinoza, of course, has no such scruples about saying that space as extended substance is infinite; indeed, a major inspiration of his whole pantheistic metaphysics was the insight that space, on the new science, was taking on an attribute which had traditionally been ascribed to God alone. Spinoza's readiness to deify extended substance lies behind a further departure from the Cartesian framework: Spinoza holds that this substance is indivisible. The philosophical point behind this attempt to accommodate a traditional property of God within his system seems to be that space is logically prior to its regions: such regions can only be identified as regions of space. Thus space is not built up of regions in the way that a whole is built up of parts.[29]

The same tendency to take up a dogmatic stand on the ontological status of space is visible in the work of Newton's prominent philosophical spokesman, Samuel Clarke. Newton himself tended to be averse to philosophical speculation, which he believed had corrupted Christian theology, but Clarke had no such scruples; in correspondence with Leibniz and elsewhere, Clarke was prepared to explore the metaphysical and even theological underpinnings, as he saw them, of the Newtonian theory of absolute space and time. According to this theory, which is motivated by complex scientific arguments, absolute space and time are like giant, indeed infinite, containers for bodies and events respectively: space is logically prior to bodies, and time is logically prior to events or processes.[30] To say that absolute space and time are containers might suggest that in ontological terms they are substances, but this is not in fact Clarke's view. According to Clarke, space and time are not substances but attributes; indeed, they are attributes of God himself.[31] Infinite space is the divine attribute of immensity; infinite time is the divine attribute of eternity. Clarke's insistence that space and time are attributes may seem philosophically unmotivated, but it no doubt reflects his religious concerns. Clarke, like Spinoza, wishes to exploit the theological associations of infinity, but unlike Spinoza, he does not wish to stray far from Christian theological orthodoxy. Clearly Clarke could not have identified absolute space and time with the very substance of God without falling into heresy.

The Newtonian theory of absolute space and time has some implications for the other main issue debated by philosophers in the period. As we have seen, for Newton, space does not depend logically on matter for its existence; for this reason empty space is at least a logical possibility. But the Newtonian theory of empty space does not of itself imply that there actually is such empty space; as far as the theory is concerned, it is conceivable that absolute infinite space is everywhere full of matter. But Newton and his disciple in fact agree with the Epicurean tradition in recognizing the existence of atoms and the void.

In their different ways, Descartes, Spinoza, and Clarke all accord a fundamental place to space in their ontologies; Spinoza and Clarke even agree in linking space with God. It is obvious that Leibniz, especially in his mature metaphysics, is not in a position to do the same, for according to the doctrine of monads the only true substances are immaterial souls whose basic properties or attributes are perception and appetition. Indeed, Leibniz cannot find any place for either space or time at the ground floor of his metaphysics. Here it is helpful to recall that, more clearly than Descartes or Spinoza, Leibniz operates with a sharp distinction between appearance and reality. Space and time, for Leibniz, are purely phenomenal; they belong to the realm of appearances, and not the realm of what is truly real, namely monads.

To say that space and time are appearances, however, does not settle the question of their ontological status. In the correspondence with Clarke, Leibniz provides a clear answer to this question which contrasts sharply with the Newtonian and Cartesian views: space and time, for Leibniz, are neither substances nor attributes, but relations. "I hold space to be something merely relative as time is . . . I hold it to be an order of coexistences, as time is an order of successions" (*Third Letter*, §4, AG 324). Thus for Leibniz, space and time depend logically on the existence of bodies and events respectively. If there were no bodies there would be no space; if there were no events there would be no time.

In correspondence with Clarke, Leibniz defends a further ontological thesis: space and time are not merely relational but ideal. The thesis that space and time are ideal follows from the relational theory in conjunction with Leibniz's doctrine that only substances are fully real, everything else, including relations, being an *ens rationis* or mental construct. The reference to mental constructs serves to show that the ideality of space and time is to be sharply distinguished from the idealism of the theory of monads. To say that space and time are ideal is to say that, as relations, they are contributed by the perceiving mind; to say that the theory of monads is a form of idealism is to say that the basic substances are mental or quasi-mental in nature. Moreover, the claim that space and time are ideal has no tendency to imply that reality is constituted by such quasi-mental substances. Even if, as in his middle period, Leibniz accepted the existence of corporeal substances, he would still be committed to the ideality of space.

Philosophers such as Leibniz and Clarke were divided, then, on the merits of the relational and nonrelational theories of space. Although he was writing before the famous correspondence, in his *Essay* Locke reveals his awareness not only of the issues in this debate but also of its theological dimensions. Characteristically, Locke refuses to arbitrate between these two main positions: "But whether any one will take Space to be only a relation resulting from the Existence of other Beings at a distance; or whether they will think the Words of the most knowing King *Solomon, The Heaven and the Heaven of Heavens, cannot contain Thee*; or those more emphatical ones of the inspired Philosopher *St. Paul, In Him we live, move, and have our Being,* are to be understood in a literal sence I leave everyone to consider" (*Essay*, II.xiii.26). Although Locke himself prefers to remain agnostic, some readers have supposed that there was a development in his thought on the issue; under the influence of Newton he may have moved away from the relational theory to the doctrine of absolute space and time.[32]

Locke may have come to favor the absolute theory, but there is no reason to suppose that he felt himself thereby committed to either a substantive or attributive theory. Locke's tendency to question the value of traditional ontological categories is evident in his discussion of the one issue concerning space and time on which he was concerned to defend a positive stance, namely the theoretical possibility of a vacuum. Locke's defense of this position is of course integral to his whole polemic against Cartesian dogmatism which, on this issue, recognizes only a rational distinction between matter and space and concludes that a vacuum is absolutely impossible. Locke attacks the Cartesian dogma in various ways: he appeals to conceptual considerations about the evident distinctness of our ideas of body and space, and he rehearses some traditional arguments, which go back to the Epicureans, to establish the theoretical possibility of empty space (*Essay*, II.xiii.21). But his most distinctive method of attack on the Cartesian dogma emerges in response to one familiar ontological objection: "If it be demanded (as usually it is) whether this *Space* void of matter, be *Substance* or *Accident* I shall readily answer, I know not, nor shall be ashamed to own my Ignorance, till they that ask, shew me a clear distinct *Idea* of substance" (*Essay*, II.xiii.17). Thus Locke seeks to remove the sting of the standard objections to the possibility of a vacuum (space void of matter) by questioning the value of the categories of traditional orthodoxy.

Locke is skeptical not only about the value of traditional ontological categories such as that of substance; he is skeptical also about the whole enterprise of demonstrative metaphysics. Here, as in other areas of his philosophy, Locke anticipates and no doubt helps to shape the spirit of the succeeding age. The eighteenth century was to witness a reaction against the construction of metaphysical systems such as those of Descartes, Leibniz, and Spinoza. No doubt the multiplication of very different systems, all making the same claims to demonstrative certainty, helped to bring the enterprise into discredit. Moreover, the divergence of the metaphysicians contrasted unfavorably with the success of the experimental scientists; the scientists may have had their disagreements about the theoretical foundations of their work, but they were able nonetheless to boast solid achievements. In any case, Locke's insistence that philosophers should begin by taking a survey of their understandings was not to go unheeded in the following century; it was to be the guiding spirit of the Critical philosophy of Kant.[33]

NOTES

1 Aubrey 1972, p. 230.
2 The point is well made by Watkins 1973, p. 13.
3 See Bennett 1984, pp. 16–20. Bennett argues that Spinoza's method is hypothetico-deductive rather than demonstrative (pp. 20–23).
4 For further discussion of Descartes's distinction between the analytic and the synthetic method, see Curley 1986.
5 For Leibniz's views on metaphysics as a demonstrative science, see Rutherford 1995a, pp. 73–79.
6 Cf. Cottingham 1993, p. 159.
7 See, for instance, Williams 1978, p. 253.
8 Cf. Woolhouse 1993, pp. 45–50.
9 The view that Spinoza defines 'substance' in terms of causal independence is defended by Curley 1969. For criticisms of Curley's thesis, see Bennett 1984, pp. 92–96.
10 *Monadology*, §3 (AG 213).
11 *Metaphysics*, 1028b. This Aristotelian anticipation of Locke's account is noted by Woolhouse 1993, p. 7.
12 Locke's ambivalence toward the idea of substance in general has been noted by many commentators; see, for example, Bennett 1987. In recent years Locke's teachings concerning substance have been the subject of great controversy. For a very different account of Locke's position than the one defended here, see Ayers 1991, vol. II, pp. 15–128.
13 *Three Dialogues*, I, in Berkeley 1948–57, vol. II, pp. 197–99.
14 *Three Dialogues*, III, in Berkeley 1948–57, vol. II, pp. 233–34.

15 Commentators who have contributed to this reassessment of causality in the period include Loeb 1981, McCracken 1983, Clatterbaugh 1999, and Nadler 2000b.
16 For a helpful account of Aristotle's doctrine of the four causes in relation to early modern philosophy, see Mates 1986, pp. 158–60.
17 See O'Neill 1993.
18 *Primary Truths*, in Leibniz 1973, p. 90.
19 *A Specimen of Discoveries*, in Leibniz 1973, p. 79 (translation modified).
20 *A Treatise concerning the Principles of Human Knowledge*, §31, in Berkeley 1948–57, vol. II, p. 54.
21 This example comes from Bennett 1984, p. 213.
22 See Bennett 1983. For an opposing view, see Curley 1990 and Garrett 1999.
23 The differences between Aristotle's and Leibniz's conceptions of teleology are noted in Garrett 1999.
24 The thesis that the mind–body union forms a third substance is defended in Hoffman 1986. Cf. Cottingham 1986.
25 See Loeb 1981, ch. 3; Richardson 1982; Radner 1985.
26 For further discussion of their positions, see Schmaltz's chapter in this volume.
27 The issue is discussed in Delahunty 1985, p. 97.
28 See Della Rocca 1996, ch. 8.
29 Cf. Bennett 1984, p. 86.
30 For an illuminating discussion of the issues, see Broad 1981.
31 *A Demonstration of the Being and Attributes of God* (1705), props. V–VI, in Clarke 1738, vol. II, pp. 539–41.
32 See Lennon 1993, secs. 18, 276–88.
33 I am very grateful to Donald Rutherford and Sean Greenberg for their helpful comments on earlier drafts.

TAD SCHMALTZ

5 The science of mind

In *Philosophy and the Mirror of Nature*, Richard Rorty attributes to René Descartes the invention of a distinctively modern notion of the mind. According to Rorty, Descartes deviated from previous thinkers, both Aristotelian and Platonic, in taking the realm of the "mental" to include both the "sensory grasp of particulars" and the intellectual grasp of universals.[1] What makes these apparently heterogeneous kinds both count as mental is the fact that we have indubitable access to the various states. Thus, Descartes made indubitability the new mark of the mental. Rorty claims that this new mark was connected to a new conception of the mind as "an inner arena with its inner observer." This new conception in turn rendered knowledge of what exists outside of the inner arena problematic, and thus made it possible "to pose the problem of the veil of ideas, the problem which made epistemology central to philosophy."[2]

There can be no doubt that Descartes deviated in some significant ways from the psychology of Aristotle and the later scholastics. However, the deviations are linked less to epistemological preoccupations with external world skepticism than to a concern to articulate a new metaphysical conception of the mind and its relation to the material world.[3] The first of the three sections in this chapter considers the Aristotelian and scholastic accounts of the soul that serve as the foil for Descartes's discussions, and then takes up Descartes's view of the mind and its influence on his early modern successors. A prominent issue here will be the various reactions among these thinkers to the so-called "mind–body problem." In light of Rorty's remarks, it is significant that this problem is more metaphysical than epistemological.[4] The second section begins with a reaction to scholastic theories of cognition in Descartes that involves the positing of "ideas" in the mind that serve to represent objects. Here again, it turns out that early modern discussions of this reaction emphasize less the problem of external world skepticism than the question of what metaphysical view of the mind and its faculties is required for an adequate account of cognition. In the third section, I examine the role attributed to the mental faculty of the will in cognition. The starting point here is an account of this role in Descartes that differs significantly from what is found in his scholastic opponents. A further significant feature of Descartes's position, which is more closely connected to earlier scholastic discussions, is his insistence on the freedom of acts of our will. With one notable exception, the early modern thinkers surveyed here agreed with Descartes that such acts are free. However, they offered fundamentally different accounts of the nature of that freedom.

SOUL, BODY AND MIND

From the Aristotelian soul to the Cartesian mind

In *De anima*, Aristotle's account of the soul (*psukhe* or *anima*) starts from a hylomorphic theory on which a living organism is a composite of indeterminate matter and a determining form. The soul is then defined as the form of "a physical body having life potentially" and as the ground or principle of the various powers of the living body. The soul is the source not only of intellectual powers of human beings, but also of the vegetative powers of nutrition, growth, and reproduction common to all living things, as well as of the sensitive powers of external and internal sensation, appetition, and self-motion common to humans and other animals.[5]

Aristotelianism did not provide the only perspective on the soul and the nature of life at the beginning of the seventeenth century. There were alternatives that took into account competing Platonic/Augustinian, Epicurean, or Galenic views.[6] However, at this time the study of the soul was dominated by the commentaries on Aristotle's texts that issued from various religious orders and universities. Late scholastics such as Francisco Suárez, the Coimbrans, and Eustachius a Sancto Paulo (1573–1640) invariably read Aristotle in light of the "Christianized" version of his position in the thirteenth-century commentaries of Thomas Aquinas. In particular, there was broad sympathy among the late scholastics for the Thomistic attempt to temper the Aristotelian emphasis on the essential connection between soul and body with the Christian doctrine that human souls can exist apart from body. There was a consensus that all souls are "substantially united" to the bodies they vivify but that human souls are also immaterial and incorruptible since they have intellectual powers that – unlike the powers of vegetation and sensation – do not require bodily organs for their operation.[7]

In the letter dedicating his *Meditations* to the Paris Theology Faculty, Descartes emphasized his attempt in this text to follow the 1513 injunction of the Lateran Council that Christian philosophers refute by natural reason the claim of the twelfth-century Aristotelian commentator Averroes that the individual human soul is not immortal. But though Descartes agreed with the majority of his Aristotelian contemporaries that reason supports the conclusion that the human soul is naturally incorruptible, he differed radically from them in his understanding of what the soul is. Thus, in response to the complaint of his French critic Pierre Gassendi that the soul is responsible for vegetative and sensory functions in us as well as for our thought, Descartes insisted that the principle responsible for these bodily functions is distinct in kind from the principle in virtue of which we think. His proposal here is that the Aristotelian soul, the principle responsible for all of the functions of living beings, be replaced by the mind (*mens* or *esprit*), the thinking thing revealed by our reflection on the self. The dualist conclusion in the *Meditations* is that this mind is a substance that is really distinct from and can exist apart from body, the nature of which consists in extension alone.

It is Descartes's identification of matter with extension that provides the primary basis for his rejection of an Aristotelian account of life. For Descartes, explanations in physics are to be framed solely in terms of the sizes, shapes, and motions of the parts of matter. Likewise, he insisted on a physiology that does away with scholastic souls and their vegetative and sensitive powers. He offered a theory on which the operations of plants and animals would not differ in kind from the mechanistic operations of inanimate matter. Only in the case of thought did he find it necessary to posit a nonmechanistic principle that is distinct from extension and its modifications. In his *Discourse on the Method*, Descartes held that the fact that human beings can use language appropriately in an indefinite number of cases shows that they have the "universal instrument" of reason, the operations of which cannot be explained in terms of mechanistic bodily dispositions. In contrast, the operations of animals that lack reason can be explained entirely in terms of those dispositions (CSM I 139–41). The implication here that such animals are mere "beast machines" devoid of any sort of sensation or feeling provided a considerable source of opposition to Cartesianism both during Descartes's life and after his death. For Descartes, however, the inclination we have to attribute sensory thoughts to nonrational animals is akin to our inclination to attribute to bodies something similar to our sensations of colors and tastes. Both inclinations are to be eliminated by means of reflection on our clear and distinct idea of body.

On one point, however, Descartes did make a concession to the scholastics. In the Sixth Meditation, he claimed that the presence in us of the sensations of pain, hunger, and thirst reveal that our mind is not merely present in the body as a sailor is in a ship, but is "most closely joined" and "as if intermixed" with it (CSM II 56). The comparison of the soul to the sailor in a ship is from Plato, and most late scholastics followed Aristotle in protesting that our soul does not merely use the body as its instrument. Descartes even appropriated scholastic language at one point in claiming that our soul is substantially united with our body to form an *ens per se*, thus indicating that the soul–body union constitutes a single being (*ens*) that exists "through itself" (*per se*) (CSM III 206). When his sympathetic critic, Antoine Arnauld, objected that his account of mind reverts to the Platonic view of the soul, Descartes protested that his arguments for the substantial union are "as strong as any I can remember having read" (CSM II 160).

Soon after he wrote this, however, Descartes conceded in 1643 correspondence with Princess Elisabeth that he had said little about the precise manner in which the human soul is united with its body, since his main concern was to show that this soul is a thinking thing that is really distinct from body (CSM III 217–18). When discussing the union, he focused on confused sensory states that reveal most clearly the connection of our soul to the body. When discussing the real distinction, however, he tended to emphasize the purely intellectual faculty that he took to operate apart from the body. In holding that it is our intellectual powers that reveal the immateriality of our soul, Descartes was in agreement with the scholastics. What is somewhat obscured by his reference to the union, however, is a disagreement with the scholastic position connected to his claim that sensations are modes of thought. Whereas for the scholastics, sensations are powers manifested in the bodily sense organs of humans and other animals, for Descartes, they are modes of thought that can exist only in a thinking thing, albeit a thinking thing united to a body.

The mind–body problem: Malebranche, Leibniz, Spinoza

Among Descartes's followers, there was a stress on the distinctively mental nature of sensory consciousness. Descartes had introduced the view that thought involves consciousness (*conscientia* or *conscience*), though he appealed to this notion relatively infrequently. It was the French physician Louis de la Forge (1632–66) who, in his *Treatise on the Human Mind* (1666), insisted that consciousness or inner sensation (*intérieur sentiment*) is an essential feature of all thought. No doubt influenced by La Forge, Nicolas Malebranche claimed in his *Search after Truth* and subsequent writings that we know our soul through a "consciousness or inner sensation" (*conscience ou intérieur sentiment*) of its states. In the "Elucidations" (1678), a set of comments on his views in the *Search*, Malebranche further offered a Cartesian argument for mind–body distinctness from the fact that the sensible qualities we perceive have no relation to the states that we clearly conceive in body. This argument is reminiscent of recent claims about the irreducibility of sensory qualia to bodily states. However, it differs significantly from Descartes's suggestion to Elisabeth that we can best apprehend the immateriality of the mind by disregarding the sensory aspects of the union and focusing on our purely intellectual thoughts.[8]

With the emphasis in the work of the later Cartesians on the sensory aspects of mind comes a new understanding of the "mind–body problem." In the work of scholastics such as Suárez, there was the problem of how the sensory powers of the human soul, which require a union with the body, could influence its more "noble" intellectual powers, which do not require such a union. In contrast, the problem for Descartes's successors concerned the nature of the union between soul and body revealed in sensory experience. Descartes himself assumed that such experience shows that motions in our body cause sensory perceptions in our mind and that volitions in our mind cause motions in our body. However, this "fact" about interaction was problematic for Malebranche. He offered the "occasionalist" position that our experience reveals only certain correlations among mental and bodily states, and that the true cause of these various states is the will of God. For Malebranche, the presence of certain motions in our body merely provides the occasion for God to produce certain perceptions in our soul, whereas the presence of certain volitions in our soul provides the occasion for him to produce certain motions in our body.

In his *New System of the Nature and Communication of Substances*, Leibniz accused Malebranche of invoking a *deus ex machina* in order to explain the correlations among mental and bodily states (AG 143). This accusation is no doubt a source of the textbook view that Malebranche offered occasionalism as an ad hoc solution to difficulties internal to the Cartesian system concerning the relation between mind and body. However, Malebranche himself presented his occasionalism as an extension of Descartes's critique of the Aristotelian account of nature. He followed Descartes in rejecting the scholastic view that bodies have various "substantial forms" and "real qualities" that go beyond their quantitative features. But Malebranche saw more clearly than Descartes that the reduction of body to passive extension rendered problematic our purported experience both of the action of bodies on each other and of the action of body on our mind. Moreover, Malebranche insisted that there must be a necessary connection between an effect and its "true cause," and that there can be such a connection only in the case of the production of effects by the volition of an omnipotent being. Thus, in the case of our own volitional action on the body, or even of our volitional production of our own mental states, it must be God who brings about the relevant effects. Malebranche offered this occasionalist view as an alternative to the traditional scholastic position, which Descartes himself sometimes suggested, that God merely "concurs" with the action of creatures in bringing about natural effects.

Another objection that Leibniz offered in the *New System* is that Malebranche posited a series of "perpetual miracles" by means of which God brings about particular effects. Arnauld, in 1687 correspondence with Leibniz, and Pierre Bayle, in a note on the *New System* in his *Historical and Critical Dictionary*, responded with the legitimate point that this line of objection overlooks Malebranche's claim that God produces natural effects by means of a small set of "general volitions" or general laws. It is only in the case of genuine deviations from natural laws that he required "particular volitions" in God to bring about particular effects. In Malebranche's view, then, various changes in soul and body are natural rather than miraculous insofar as they derive from the general laws governing the soul–body union that are to be identified in turn with general volitions in God.

Even so, Leibniz's insistence in the *New System* that created substance must have its own power indicates a fundamental disagreement with Malebranche. Leibniz granted Malebranche that no power in a created substance can exert a causal influence on another created substance. However, he claimed that a created substance can have the power to bring about changes in its own states. The fact that these changes correspond with changes in other substances can be explained by the fact that God created the substances with causal powers that act independently of, and yet "harmonize" with, each other. This is Leibniz's "hypothesis of agreements," as he called it in the *New System* (AG 144), better known by his later label for it, the "preestablished harmony" (see e.g. AG 148).

Leibniz often proposed the preestablished harmony as a solution to the problem of the soul–body union. In a defense of the *New System*, for instance, he contrasted the interactionist view that soul and body cause changes in each other and the occasionalist view that God causes all such changes with his own view that the soul and body cause changes in themselves that correspond to changes in the other. He illustrated the differences by comparing the three views to three explanations of the synchronous operation of two watches. The interactionist view corresponds to the claim that this operation is to be explained by the fact that the watches have an inexplicable "natural influence" on each other. The occasionalist view of the soul–body relation is akin to the claim that the watches run in tandem since there is a craftsman who constantly adjusts them. Finally, the preestablished harmony is compared to the simplest and most intelligible explanation of the operation of the watches, namely, one that appeals to the fact that the craftsman has constructed the watches so perfectly that they run on their own but in conformity to each other (AG 147–48).

There is one respect, however, in which this characterization of preestablished harmony is misleading. The suggestion is that the soul and body, like the two watches, are self-contained entities that have the same status. Yet Leibniz indicated in the *New System* that body is not a substance but something composed of simple, unextended substances, which he later called "monads." The operations of these simple substances are to be modeled on the operations of our own souls; all have "something analogous to sensation and appetite," even though many lack the abilities for rational reflection and even consciousness that our souls possess (AG 139). Given this form of idealism, then, the preestablished harmony must ultimately explain the correspondence not of the states of mental and bodily substances, but rather of the perceptions of simple substances or monads. The body is involved insofar as the substances perceive themselves to have bodies related in a systematic manner to other bodies. Because of preestablished harmony, these various perceptions support a scientific story that explains bodily operations entirely in terms of the mechanistic interaction of parts of matter. However, the harmony ultimately relates only perceptual changes in simple substances that are produced in a teleological manner by their own appetites or strivings for the good. These aspects of Leibniz's complex position serve to explain his claim in the *New System* that whereas he holds, contrary to both the scholastics and the Cartesians, that the operations of human as well as animal bodies can be explained entirely in mechanistic terms, he also claims, with the scholastics but against the Cartesians, that animal as well as human bodies are animated by soul-like substances (AG 139, 141–42).[9]

In the *Theodicy*, Leibniz protested that by depriving creatures of any causal power, and thus of substantiality, Malebranche falls "into Spinozism, which is an exaggerated Cartesianism" (§393). Nevertheless, the account of the mind–body relation in the work of Spinoza provides a clear alternative both to Malebranche's occasionalism and to Leibniz's preestablished harmony. This account is grounded in the distinctive claim of Spinoza's masterwork, the *Ethics*, that God is the only substance, of which all other finite things are "modes" or "affections." Spinoza held that this substance has an infinity of attributes that "the intellect perceives as constituting the essence of substance" (*Ethics*, I, def. 4), of which we know only two, namely, thought and extension. There is a remnant of Descartes's view of mind here, insofar as Spinoza claimed that neither thought nor extension can be conceived in terms of the other. However, he explicitly rejected Descartes's substance dualism when he insisted in the *Ethics* that the attributes of thought and extension yield conceptually distinct ways of conceiving one and the same substance.

In addition to being conceptually distinct, thought and extension are causally isolated. For Spinoza, this causal isolation follows from the axiom that knowledge of an effect involves knowledge of its cause (*Ethics*, I, ax. 4; II, prop. 6). If a mode of extension were the effect of a mode of thought, then the understanding of extension would require a conception of thought, thus violating the conceptual distinction between the two attributes. In Spinoza's view, only modes of extension can be understood to cause changes in other modes of extension, and only modes of thought can be understood to cause changes in other modes of thought.

Yet just as Leibniz posited a preestablished harmony among causally isolated states of distinct substances, so Spinoza posited a parallelism among causally isolated modes of distinct attributes. Spinoza's parallelism begins with the claim that the attribute of thought must contain ideas that represent all modes in other attributes. Thus, for each mode of extension, there is a corresponding idea of that mode in thought. Given his doctrine of the causal isolation of the attributes, Spinoza could not explain the correspondence of these modes to their ideas by appealing to a causal relation between them. Instead, he claimed that the ideas are linked to their objects in virtue of the fact that the former have the same "order and connection" among themselves that the latter do. On the basis of this parallelism of the two modal chains, as well as his claim that the attributes of thought and extension express the essence of the same substance, Spinoza concluded that a mode of extension and its idea are "one and the same thing, but expressed in two ways" (*Ethics*, II, prop. 7 schol.). This identification of the mental and the physical differs from Leibnizian idealism in refraining from giving priority to the mental realm.

Even so, Spinoza agreed with Leibniz in rejecting certain features of a more orthodox Cartesian account of the mind. Leibniz's pre-established harmony requires that our perceptions "express" everything that occurs in our body. Influenced by the Cartesian view that mental states are by nature accessible to consciousness, Arnauld protested against the implication here that his soul perceives "an infinite number of . . . things occurring in my body, of which it is nevertheless ignorant, as for instance all the functions of digestion and nutrition" (M 105). But Leibniz responded that our soul does not have "a perfect apperception of what is going on in the parts of its body," and that "too many things occur in our body for them to be separately perceived" (M 113). This response is connected to his claim that we have *petites perceptions* that express states of our body and also motivate action, but that fall below the level of consciousness. Spinoza's parallelism also requires that "nothing can happen in [the human] body without its being perceived by the [human] mind" (*Ethics*, II, prop. 12). With Leibniz, however, Spinoza insisted that our ideas of our bodily changes for the most part yield only a very confused and inadequate knowledge. And with Leibniz again, he did not require that ideas of these changes be accessible to consciousness. Moreover, Spinoza and Leibniz both insisted against Descartes that the mental realm includes not only human perception, but also the wholly confused perception of minds or souls that possess nothing similar to our own consciousness.

However, Spinoza rejected one aspect of Leibniz's position that derives from the Cartesian tradition in the philosophy of mind. Leibniz followed both Descartes and Malebranche in emphasizing the simplicity and thus indivisibility of the immaterial thinking thing. After Leibniz, it became a standard task in "rational psychology" to argue that our soul has these properties. Though Spinoza agreed that mind can be conceived apart from extension, his parallelism led him to conclude that our mind has a complexity that matches the complexity of our body. Indeed, in Spinoza's view our mind is simply the collection of ideas that are identical to the various parts that make up our body. When this body is destroyed, so too is the mind that is identified with it. Spinoza admittedly spoke somewhat obscurely of the "eternity of the mind," but he indicated clearly enough that there can be no personal immortality that involves the continued existence of our individual consciousness after the death of our body.[10]

Hobbesian materialism and Lockean skepticism

Besides Spinoza, the other prominent early modern critic of the doctrine of the immortality of the immaterial soul was Hobbes. Unlike Spinoza, however, Hobbes based this rejection on the possibility of reducing mind to matter. He went so far as to claim that the very notion of an immaterial substance is incoherent. The argument in his *Leviathan* is that since our idea of substance is drawn entirely from our sensory experience of bodies, "*substance* and *body* signify the same thing; and therefore, *substance incorporeal* are words which, when they are joined together, destroy one another, as if a man should say, an *incorporeal body*" (ch. 34, par. 2). Toward the start of this same text, Hobbes noted that the sensory experience caused in us by motion is itself "but divers motions (for motion produceth nothing but motion)" (ch. 1, par. 4).

Hobbes wrote a set of objections to Descartes's *Meditations*, to which Descartes himself responded in a dismissive manner. This response is not too surprising given the fundamental differences in their respective theories of mind, among other issues. But though Hobbes is alone among the major early modern philosophers in endorsing an uncompromising form of materialism, his views are similar in certain respects to those of Leibniz and Spinoza. All three thinkers held that we can give an account of the material world (or at least of nonmiraculous events in this world) that is entirely mechanistic and involves no special intervention on the part of nonextended things, even in the case of the operations of the human body. Of course, there are still significant differences here. After all, Leibniz held that the mechanistic account must be grounded in an account of perceptual changes in simple immaterial substances, and Spinoza held that the mechanistic account parallels an account of the relation among unextended ideas. Nevertheless, their common insistence on a universal mechanism in the material world places them in opposition both to Descartes, who allowed for the nonmechanistic action of mind on body, and to Malebranche, who allowed that God produces effects in the material world that derive not only from laws of motion but also from laws governing the relation of immaterial substances to bodies.

Locke offered a skeptical alternative both to Hobbes's strong form of materialism and to the dogmatic insistence in the work of the Cartesians on the demonstrability of dualism. In his *Essay concerning Human Understanding*, Locke provided an implicit criticism of Hobbes's rejection of incorporeal substance when he noted that our idea of corporeal substance is no clearer than our idea of spiritual substance, since we take both ideas to signify the unknown "substratum" that we suppose to underlie spiritual or corporeal qualities or operations. Locke concluded that we can no more infer to the nonexistence of spirit from the lack of a clear idea of an immaterial substratum than we can infer to the nonexistence of matter from the lack of a clear idea of a material substratum (II.xxiii.4).

Locke was not alone in rejecting the claim that we have clear knowledge of the substratum that underlies our mental operations. In responding to Descartes's thesis in the Second Meditation that "the nature of mind is better known than body," Gassendi emphasized that what scientific study has revealed about the nature of body is far superior to anything that Descartes has revealed about the mysterious "inner substance" responsible for thought (CSM II 192–93). Even Malebranche, who was sympathetic to Cartesian dualism, rejected Descartes's thesis on the grounds that the knowledge of the nature of mind that we gain through consciousness or inner sensation is inferior in kind to the knowledge of body that derives from the clear idea of extension.

Locke's skeptical argument against Hobbesian materialism depends, however, on the claim that our knowledge of material substance is as deficient as our knowledge of immaterial substance. This skeptical argument also undercuts the argument in Malebranche and other Cartesians that a clear idea of body reveals that bodies can possess only modes of extension, and so cannot be thinking things. In a famous passage from the *Essay*, Locke claimed that our ideas of matter and spirit do not allow us to determine whether "GOD can, if he pleases, superadd to Matter a Faculty of Thinking, than that he should superadd to it another Substance with a Faculty of Thinking" (IV.iii.6). Locke did insist elsewhere that it is probable that God has superadded an immaterial substance with this faculty in our case. Nonetheless, Locke's English critic, the bishop of Worcester, Edward Stillingfleet

(1635–99), protested that Locke confounded matter and thinking in claiming that God can superadd to body something that conflicts with the essence of matter. In the course of his extended public debate with Stillingfleet, Locke defended himself by asserting that though God cannot superadd to body qualities that contradict the essence of matter, he can and does superadd qualities such as motion, beauty, and sense that go beyond what is contained in that essence. Locke further noted, correctly, that he said in the *Essay* not that God actually did superadd thought to matter, but only that we cannot see a contradiction in the claim that he can. However, the implication in his writings that purely material animals have sensory thoughts does seem to require a stronger commitment to the superaddition of thought to a material system than his official position indicates.[11]

The discussion of superaddition in the Locke–Stillingfleet correspondence prompted a further debate between Samuel Clarke and Anthony Collins (1676–1729).[12] Collins started the debate by taking issue, in a letter to Henry Dodwell (1641–1711), with Clarke's claim in his 1705 Boyle lectures that consciousness is distinct in kind from other bodily properties, and so cannot belong to a material system. For his part, Clarke argued that since unitary consciousness is not composed in any intelligible way from powers that inhere in the parts of a material system, consciousness itself cannot inhere in that system. Collins responded that consciousness can be attributed to the whole material system without being attributed to each part. In this dispute we see an anticipation of the emphasis in recent discussions of the philosophy of mind not only on the nature of consciousness, but also on the question of whether the mental can "supervene" on the physical.

IDEAS, INNATENESS, AND COGNITION

From scholastic species to Cartesian ideas

One way of understanding medieval and Renaissance theories of cognition is in terms of the distinction between Platonic and Aristotelian traditions. The Platonic tradition emphasized that intellectual knowledge does not depend on the senses. In Platonists such as Marsilio Ficino (1433–99), there was the view that such knowledge derives from elements innate to intellect. Another strain of Platonism, which is found in the work of Augustine and later Augustinians, involved the claim that the intellect requires the assistance of divine "illumination" in order to attain certain knowledge of necessary truths. Some passages in Augustine's writings even suggested that the body merely stimulates the soul to form sensations in itself. Later Augustinians drew on such passages, as well as on the Augustinian principle that something cannot act on what is more noble than it, in arguing that sensations are produced not by the action of the body on the soul, but rather by the activity of an "agent sense."

In contrast, there was an emphasis in the Aristotelian tradition on the dependence of the human intellect on passive sensory experience. This tradition is reflected in the view in Thomas Aquinas that all of our knowledge starts with the reception in the external sense organs of "sensible species" transmitted from sensible qualities in external objects. Here it is only the "form" of the quality that is transmitted, not its matter. Thus, the material sense organ does not become literally colored or odorous, say, but merely receives something that allows it to cognize colors or odors. The species is then stored as a "phantasm" in the internal senses, where it provides material for further sensory judgments concerning the relevant sensible quality. Finally, the presence of the phantasm leads the intellect to abstract away all of its accidental material conditions, thereby producing an "intelligible species" that reveals the essence or nature of the sensible thing. Thomas argued that such species provide all that is required for our natural intellectual knowledge, and thus that there is no need for either the sort of divine illumination posited by the Augustinians or the innate intellectual equipment posited by other Platonists.[13]

Among the later scholastics, there were disputes over the details of the Thomistic account of cognition. Ockham and his followers allowed for the sensible quality to act at a distance on the external sense organs, and thus rejected the need for the transmission of a species from the external object. Also, some later scholastics worried that the positing of sensible and intelligible species might compromise a direct realism that allows for immediate sensory or intellectual contact with external qualities. Finally, I have indicated that there were worries about the claim that the less noble material phantasm can trigger the action of the human intellect.[14] Despite these complications, there was a broad agreement among the later scholastics with Thomas's insistence on the sensory basis of human knowledge, so much so that scholasticism came to be associated with the maxim that "nothing is in the intellect that was not first in the senses" (*nihil est in intellectu quin prius fuerit in sensu*).

Descartes ridiculed scholastic views concerning the reception of species when he referred in the *Discourse* to "all those little images flitting through the air, called intentional species, which so exercise the imagination of the philosophers" (CSM I 153–54). Already in Thomas, however, there was a concern to distinguish the species involved in sensation from the imagistic *eidola* of the atomists. The deepest objection in Descartes was not that the scholastics posit flying images, but that they appeal to something other than modes of extension, such as shape and motion, in explaining the bodily alterations involved in sensation. For Descartes, our "clear and distinct" understanding that the nature of body consists in extension precludes any such appeal.

In pre-1640 writings, but also occasionally in later works, Descartes offered a replacement for scholastic sensible species when he identified "ideas" with certain figures composed of motions in the brain that derive from external objects. Yet in the *Dioptrics*, an essay appended to the 1637 *Discourse*, he asserted that "it is the soul that senses, not the body" (CSM I 164). Moreover, in post-1640 writings he tended to restrict the term 'idea' to features of the mind. Thus, in a 1641 response to Hobbes, Descartes noted that he took ideas to be "whatever is immediately perceived by the mind," and that he used this term because "it was the standard philosophical term used to refer to the forms of perception in the divine mind, even though we recognize that God does not possess any corporeal imagination" (CSM II 127). We have the shift here from the scholastic view that cognition starts with the reception of species in the material sense organs to the Cartesian view that it starts with the perception of ideas in the immaterial mind.

The Scottish philosopher Thomas Reid took this shift to have pernicious effects. Though he praised Descartes for rejecting the "sophistry" of the scholastics, Reid criticized him for offering an "ideal system" that undermines the commonsense belief in the external world insofar as it interposes ideas between our mind and external reality. For Reid, the ultimate result of the introduction of the ideal system was the external world skepticism of Berkeley and Hume. Reid's historiography provides a source for the view in Rorty, cited at the outset of this chapter, that Descartes's "invention of the mind" placed the epistemological problem of "veil-of-ideas" skepticism at the center of philosophical discourse. As I have noted, one problem for this view is that Descartes and his successors posited ideas as part of empirically based accounts of sensory and intellectual cognition. There are no doubt epistemological issues raised by their discussions of ideas, but these discussions also address issues that are not so far removed from those that now fall within the purview of the science of psychology.

Ideas, objective reality, and representation

Though offered as an alternative to scholasticism, Descartes's account of ideas relies in important ways on the views of his scholastic predecessors. This reliance is clear in the *Meditations* and related texts, in which Descartes drew on terminology similar to that found in late scholastic writings in distinguishing between the "formal reality" of an idea as a mode of mind and the "objective reality" of that idea as a representation of its object. Descartes's claim that this objective reality requires a cause is central to his argument in the Third Meditation that God must exist as the cause of the objective reality of his idea of infinite substance. When a scholastic critic, Johan de Cater, objected that objective reality does not need a cause since it is not distinct from the act of cognition itself (CSM II 67–68), Descartes responded that this reality is a genuine feature of the idea that serves to link that idea to a real or possible external object (CSM II 75).

Descartes's claim that ideas have objective reality in addition to having formal reality as a mode of mind raises the question of the precise relation between these two kinds of reality. Indeed, there was a famous dispute among his followers over how precisely to characterize this relation. Malebranche proposed that the objective reality be identified with "the immediate object, or the object closest to the mind, when it perceives something" (*Search*, III.ii.1). He also insisted that this object is something that is independent of our perception. Though he argued for this sort of distinction in different ways at different times, Malebranche was motivated to accept it primarily by his Augustinian view that we depend for our knowledge of objects on ideas in God that serve as the "exemplars" or "archetypes" for the creation of those objects. Even so, Malebranche's view that the objects of perception are distinct from the perception itself can be seen as a development of Descartes's claim that he has perceptions of "true and immutable natures" that are "not invented by me or dependent on my mind" (CSM II 45).

Malebranche's Cartesian critic Arnauld responded that "representative beings" distinct from our perceptions are not required for our knowledge of objects, since the perceptions themselves suffice to explain such knowledge. Arnauld did allow that the idea as a perceptual modification of mind is conceptually distinct from the idea as a representation with a particular amount of objective reality. However, he insisted that given Descartes's own definition of an idea as "the form of any given thought" (CSM II 113), there is no real distinction between the idea and the thought it informs.[15]

Descartes bequeathed to his successors not only the general problem of the nature of ideas as representative beings, but also the specific question of whether our sensations serve to represent objects. Descartes did not provide a clear answer to this question, claiming at certain times that our sensations "represent nothing residing outside our thought" (CSM I 219), but at other times that they allow for a "confused and obscure" grasp of bodies (e.g. at CSM II 55). Malebranche sided with the view that our sensations do not represent extra-mental objects. In contrast, Leibniz argued that our sensory perceptions can "express" or represent bodily states, since they have a complexity that matches these states. He was particularly concerned to oppose Descartes's suggestion toward the end of the *Meditations* that such perceptions are merely extrinsically linked to these states by means of an arbitrary "divine institution" (CSM II 60–61). For Leibniz, sensations can represent precisely because they do not bear this sort of arbitrary relation to the bodily states that serve as their objects. Thus, for instance, our sensation of color is a complex of perceptions of the individual motions that this sensation represents.

For Cartesians such as Malebranche and Arnauld, phenomenological considerations suffice to establish the simplicity of the qualitative features of such a sensation. However, Leibniz protested that the simplicity is an illusion, and that we in fact "confuse" the various perceptions of individual motions. Whereas Malebranche held that our intellectual perception of bodies through ideas is distinct in kind from our sensations of them, Leibniz claimed that the difference is only one of degree of distinctness in the perception. This dispute prepares the way for the later position of Kant that the faculties of sensibility and understanding are independent sources for our representation of the world. Kant's claim that the understanding makes a contribution to this sort of representation that goes beyond what is given in sensory intuition is further connected to discussions in the early modern period concerning the role of judgment in sense experience.[16]

Sensory judgment and the Molyneux question

As indicated above, the scholastics held that material "phantasms" of sensible qualities play a role in judgments concerning those qualities. Descartes agreed that judgment plays a significant role in sensory cognition, but not too surprisingly his account of this role differs fundamentally from a standard scholastic account. Descartes's view of sensory judgment is explicated most clearly in his Sixth Replies published with the *Meditations*, in which he distinguished three "grades" or stages of sensation (CSM II 294–96). The first and purely physical stage involves only the mechanical effects of external objects on the sense organs and brain. In the case of the vision of the stick, for instance, this stage involves not the reception of sensible species, as the scholastics held, but only "the motion of the particles of the organs, and the change of shape and position resulting from this motion." In animals, this is the only stage of sensation. In humans, however, there is a second psychophysical stage of sensation that includes "all that immediately results in the mind owing to the fact that it is united to a corporeal organ so affected [by motion]." Examples of such effects would be "perceptions of pain, pleasure, thirst, hunger, colors, sound, taste, heat, cold, and the like." In the case of the stick, this stage involves "the mere perception of the color and light reflected from the stick." Some commentators have taken this stage to be restricted to sensations of "secondary qualities" such as those of color. However, Descartes's claim in this text that we also perceive "the extension of the color and its boundaries" indicates that this stage involves as well the sensation of "primary qualities" such as shape. Finally, there is in us a third stage of sensation that includes "all those judgments which, occasioned by the motion of the corporeal organs, we have been accustomed to make from our earliest years." Here Descartes drew on his earlier claim in the *Dioptrics* that the calculation of size and distance involves "a kind of reasoning" that proceeds "as if by natural geometry" (CSM I 170). Though our awareness of the size, shape, and distance of the stick appears to be immediate, it requires the supplementation of stage two sensations with various judgments. Descartes noted that since the judgments are confused with the sensations, people fail to realize that they are properly attributed only to the intellect.[17]

There is some question, however, concerning the intellectual nature of the stage three judgments. Descartes's own remarks may suggest that such judgments derive from pure intellect. However, in the *Dioptrics* he had characterized them as deriving from "a simple act of imagination" (CSM I 170). A further difficulty is that these judgments are supposed to include not only clear and distinct determinations of size and distance, but also the confused judgment that external objects resemble our sensations of them. For Descartes, pure intellect is not the source of such judgments, but rather the faculty that serves to correct them. Finally, on Descartes's official view (considered below), judgment involves not only perception but also an act of will. Malebranche took this view into account when he held that our perception of size and distance involves inferences deriving from the comparison of various sensations to which we assent by means of "natural judgments." Malebranche went beyond Descartes, however, in holding that such judgments depend on features of our will that God causes in us "independently of us, and even in spite of us" (*Search*, 1.9), and that therefore are distinct from "free judgments" in us that issue from the free exercise of our will.

The view in Descartes and Malebranche that the perception of the three-dimensional world includes judgments that go beyond basic sensory experience is relevant to a famous early modern debate prompted by the question, in a 1693 letter to Locke from his Irish friend William Molyneux (1656–98), whether a newly sighted person who previously distinguished a globe and cube of similar sizes by touch would be able to do so at first by sight alone. In his *Essay*, Locke accepted Molyneux's own negative answer to this question on the grounds that though the newly sighted person "has obtain'd the experience of, how a Globe, how a Cube affects his touch," such a person "has not yet attained the Experience, that what affects his touch so or so, must affect his sight so or so" (II.ix.8). Locke connected this answer to his own view that the sensation of light and color is transformed into "the far different Ideas of Space, Figure, and Motion" by means of a habitual judgment that "is performed so constantly, and so quick," that we do not separate it from the initial sensations (*Essay*, II.ix.9). Apparently, then, what the previously blind person lacks is the sort of judgment that would allow him to derive the perception of a three-dimensional globe and cube from his sensation of two-dimensional bounded patches of color.

In his consideration in the *New Essays* of this discussion in Locke, Leibniz agreed that it takes some skill to discern three-dimensional objects on the basis of perception of two-dimensional images. Even so, he insisted that it must be possible at least in principle for Molyneux's newly sighted person to discern the difference between the globe and cube "by applying rational principles to the sensory knowledge which he has already acquired by touch" (*New Ess.*, II.ix.8). Even though the sensory images of these figures produced by sight and touch differ, there is a single mathematical idea that captures their true nature. Though Locke rejected the suggestion in Leibniz that mathematical ideas have a purely intellectual content, the point that there is something common to our various perceptions of the spatial features of objects has some force against him, given his own claim that the ideas of space, figure, and motion are "simple ideas of divers senses" that we receive "both by seeing and feeling" (*Essay*, II.v).

In contrast, Berkeley took Locke's acceptance of Molyneux's position to confirm his own view that there is nothing common to visual and tactile ideas. In his *New Theory of Vision*, he argued that if there were some content common to these ideas, the Molyneux man should be able to discern the difference between the cube and globe by sight alone.[18] Berkeley takes the fact that he cannot to reveal that visual and tactile ideas of these figures are related not by means of their content, but rather through an association that renders visual ideas signs of the tactile ideas. What the Molyneux man is missing is the experience required for such an association.[19]

Pure intellect and innatism

In the Second Meditation, Descartes addressed the common scholastic position that our knowledge starts with our sensory grasp of particular bodies by considering the case of our understanding of the nature of a piece of wax. He argued that our understanding that the wax is essentially an extended, flexible, and mutable thing does not derive directly from our sensory experience of the changing qualities of the wax. Such an understanding also cannot derive from the imagination, since we know that the wax can take on more shapes than we can imagine. Thus, the understanding must derive from a "pure mental scrutiny," that is, from an examination by a nonsensory faculty of pure intellect (CSM II 20–21).

In opposition to the scholastic "abstractionist" model of intellectual knowledge, Descartes insisted that our knowledge of the wax is informed by an innate idea of the "true and immutable nature" of extension. In the *Meditations*, Descartes distinguished this innate idea from "adventitious" ideas received directly from the senses and "factitious" ideas freely constructed by the mind. He complicated matters somewhat when he claimed in a later work, *Comments on a Certain Broadsheet* (1647), that even our sensory ideas must be innate, since the ideas we form do not exactly resemble the bodily motions that prompt their formation (CSM I 304).[20] Even in this text, however, Descartes distinguished between innate sensory ideas that are directly tied to bodily motions and innate intellectual ideas that are only indirectly tied to such motions. Moreover, it is clear that he took the innate intellectual ideas to be distinguished from sensory ideas by the fact that the former are rooted in the nature of a mental faculty that yields particular "clear and distinct" perceptions of the natures of objects.

Descartes's account of innate intellectual ideas bears some relation to the appeal to innate mental elements in the work of Platonists such as Ficino. However, Malebranche saw himself as adhering to a different form of Platonism. He accepted the basic Platonic point in Descartes that intellectual ideas are distinct from sensations. Indeed, his discussion of ideas in the *Search* is included in a section devoted to "the understanding, or pure mind," defined as "the mind's faculty of knowing external objects without forming corporeal images of them in the brain to represent them" (III.i.1). As we have seen, however, Malebranche concluded there that the ideas that represent these objects are not innate features of our minds, but rather archetypes in the divine mind. As he repeatedly stressed to Arnauld, his primary source for this account of ideas is the view of divine illumination in the writings of Augustine.

Despite their differences, Descartes and Malebranche agreed in favoring some form of Platonism over Aristotelian empiricism. Not all early modern critics of scholasticism followed them. In their published comments on the *Meditations*, both Hobbes and Gassendi repeatedly criticized the suggestion in Descartes that we have purely intellectual ideas that do not derive from sensation or imagination. Moreover, Hobbes and Gassendi alike accepted the basic scholastic position that sensation and imagination are merely operations of bodily sense organs. In Hobbes, more than Gassendi, the attack on innate ideas was part of a campaign against the doctrine of the immateriality of mind. However, Locke later combined an attack on innatism with his own skepticism concerning our knowledge of the ultimate nature of mind. In the first book of his *Essay*, he relied on the principle that only actually perceived ideas can be present in our mind to counter the possibility that there can be any unperceived innate ideas or truths. Locke responded to the further suggestion that such ideas or truths could be present merely potentially by claiming that it trivializes the doctrine. Since our mind must have the capacity to perceive all the ideas or truths it can perceive, this suggestion renders all such mental items innate (*Essay*, I.ii.5). Locke offered as an alternative the view that sensation and reflection fill the "empty Cabinet" of the mind with particular ideas, from which the mind abstracts the more general ideas that serve to explain its knowledge of general truths (*Essay*, I.ii.15).

In his *New Essays*, Leibniz responded to Locke's charge of triviality by claiming that innate truths are not present in "a bare faculty, consisting in a mere possibility of understanding these truths; it is rather a disposition, an aptitude, a preformation, which determines our soul and brings it about that they are derivable from it" (I.i.11). There is an obvious similarity here to Descartes's claim in the *Comments* that intellectual ideas are innate in the same way that certain diseases are innate in children who have a tendency to contract them (CSM I 303–4). For both Descartes and Leibniz, to say that we have innate knowledge of a triangle, for instance, is to say that our intellect has a tendency or disposition that leads it to clearly and distinctly perceive that the triangle has a particular nature.[21]

Just as Descartes indicated in the *Comments* that even our sensory ideas are innate in a certain sense, so Leibniz's doctrine of preestablished harmony led him to claim that all our ideas arise from our own soul. Yet Leibniz followed Descartes in distinguishing sensory ideas from those that are innate to intellect. In Leibniz, the distinction is between sensations that confuse different *petites perceptions* of motions, and intellectual perceptions that are distinct in the sense that they indicate the "marks" or essential characteristics of their objects that suffice to distinguish such objects from others. The recognition of these marks is tied in turn to the inborn dispositions that Leibniz, as well as Descartes, took to be essential to intellectual innateness.

Even so, Leibniz's view that there is a rigorous correspondence of the mental and bodily realms seems to compromise the Platonist suggestion in both Descartes and Malebranche that pure intellect can operate independently of body. In a similar way, such a suggestion seems to be incompatible with Spinoza's insistence on the parallelism between mental and bodily modes. However, Spinoza allowed that our mind is "disposed internally" to have "adequate" ideas that can be understood in terms of its nature as the idea of our body. Such ideas are to be contrasted with inadequate ideas that our mind is "determined externally" to have through fortuitous sensory encounters with external objects (*Ethics*, II, prop. 29 schol.). Though neither Leibniz nor Spinoza was able to accept a full-bodied Platonism, both nonetheless retained some semblance of the Platonist view in Descartes (not found in Malebranche) that adequate or distinct knowledge derives from the intellect's own nature.

WILL, FREEDOM, AND DETERMINATION

Will and judgment in the scholastics and Descartes

I have noted the Thomistic position that the intellect "abstracts" intelligible species from the sensible species received through sensory contact with external objects. Scholastics who accepted such a position held that intelligible species provide the material for three kinds of further intellectual operations. The first involves the simple apprehension of species, the second a judgment that affirms or denies a link between subject and predicate, and the third a process of discursive reasoning that involves the derivation of consequences. Thus, there is the simple apprehension of the humanity of Socrates, the judgment that Socrates is human, and the discursive reasoning reflected in the syllogism that since Socrates is human and all humans are mortal, Socrates is mortal.

For the scholastics, these three operations were acts of the intellect rather than of the will. They followed Thomas in accepting the Aristotelian definition of the will as rational appetite. As rational, the will is guided by the results of the three intellectual operations, but as appetite, it is directed primarily toward the good and not, as in the case of the intellect, toward the true. It was a matter of controversy, however, whether or how acts of will (*voluntas*) involve a free choice among alternatives (*liberum arbitrium*). There were of course difficult theological issues concerning the compatibility of free human choice with divine preordination and the workings of grace in salvation. But even apart from such issues, there was a split between intellectualists who followed Aristotle in emphasizing the role of rational determination in free choice and voluntarists who followed Scotus and Ockham in insisting that free choice requires that the will not be constrained by the intellect.[22]

In the Fourth Meditation, Descartes claimed that judgment involves contributions from two faculties, namely, "the faculty of knowledge," which contributes perceptions of ideas, and "the faculty of choice or the freedom of the will," which contributes the affirmation or denial of the ideas perceived (CSM II 39). He appealed to this account of judgment to explain how we can fall into error. In Descartes's view, error cannot arise simply from the perception of ideas, since strictly speaking such a perception carries with it no truth or falsity. Error requires in addition a volitional affirmation that relates these ideas to reality. Thus, the perception of redness cannot itself be false; what is false is rather the affirmation that redness resembles some real quality external to mind.

Descartes's main thesis in this section of the *Meditations* is that we are responsible for our errors since we are free to refrain from affirming whatever we do not clearly and distinctly perceive. Indeed, he held in the *Principles* that our experience of the power of our will to refrain from judgment in these cases is so self-evident that "it must be counted among the first and most common notions that are innate in us" (*Princ.*, I.39, CSM I 205–6). It is this sort of power that explains our ability to use Descartes's "method of doubt" to overturn beliefs that rest on perceptions that are less than clear and distinct.

That this account of the will marks a departure from scholastic orthodoxy is indicated by the fact that when the Jesuits condemned a list of Cartesian propositions in 1706, they included the theses that perception is "a purely passive faculty" and that "judgment and reasoning are acts of the will, not the intellect." Even so, a closer consideration of Descartes's account of our freedom of choice reveals certain difficulties concerning the relation between will and intellect that are familiar from earlier scholastic disputes among intellectualists and voluntarists. Such difficulties are important for the various discussions of the freedom of the will in the work of Descartes's early modern successors.[23]

Libertarian freedom: Descartes and Malebranche

In the Fourth Meditation, Descartes held that will consists in the fact that when the intellect puts something forward for affirmation or denial, pursuit or avoidance, "we sense that we are determined by no external force to it." He allowed for cases where there also is a lack of internal determination due to the fact that the intellect does not lead the will in one direction rather than another. In such cases, there is a balance of reasons that leaves the will "indifferent." However, Descartes insisted that this sort of indifference is merely "the lowest grade of freedom," and that the more his will is determined by his perceptions, "the freer is my choice." He noted that when he had clear and distinct perceptions, "a great light of the intellect was followed by a great propensity in the will, and thus the spontaneity and freedom of that belief were all the greater in proportion to my lack of indifference" (CSM II 40–41). It would seem, then, that in this case freedom is compatible with internal determination by the intellect.

In contrast, Descartes asserted in the *Principles* that "we are so conscious of the freedom and indifference which is within us, that there is nothing we comprehend more evidently and more perfectly" (I.41, CSM I 206). Whereas Descartes had suggested earlier that perfect freedom excludes indifference, here he practically equated freedom with indifference. However, Descartes's understanding of indifference shifted over time. This shift is indicated in his correspondence in the mid-1640s with a Jesuit friend, most likely Denis Mesland. Descartes began by repeating the view in the *Meditations* that indifference involves a balance of reasons that constitutes the lowest grade of freedom. However, he also granted his correspondent that indifference could be identified rather with "a real and positive power to determine oneself," and that such indifference is in fact essential to freedom (CSM III 233). He further held that though "morally speaking" the will must follow the clear and distinct perceptions of the intellect, "absolutely speaking" it can always do the opposite of what the intellect commands it to do (CSM III 245). This account of freedom is more clearly "libertarian" than the one offered in the Fourth Meditation insofar as it rejects even the internal intellectual determination of free acts.

Malebranche later insisted that a libertarian account of our freedom is required by "all the principles of religion and morality," since it is only in virtue of possessing this sort of freedom that we, rather than God, can be said to be the source of sin (*Search*, Eluc. 1). In the *Search after Truth*, he held that we have a "freedom of indifference" with respect to the will, since we have "the power of willing or not willing, or even of willing the contrary of that toward which our natural inclinations carry us" (I.1). Malebranche concluded that we are responsible for our sinful love of particular goods, since we are free to "suspend consent" to love of that which we do not distinctly perceive to be worthy of it.

The line of argument here obviously is drawn from Descartes's claim in the Fourth Meditation that we are responsible for our errors, since we are free to suspend judgment on whatever we do not clearly and distinctly perceive to be true. But the link to Descartes is revealed even more clearly by the fact that Malebranche sided with Descartes, against the standard scholastic view, in claiming that assent to a proposition, no less than consent to a good, involves an act of will. And again with Descartes, Malebranche insisted that our assent to a proposition not clearly and distinctly perceived to be true is indifferent in the sense that we have the power to refrain from judgment. Thus he concluded in the *Search*, in the spirit of Descartes's view in the *Principles*, that we should make use of our freedom of indifference in order "never to consent to anything until we are forced to do so, as it were, by the inward reproaches of our reason" (I.2).

Since Malebranche was more firmly committed than Descartes to the occasionalist thesis that God is the only true cause, however, the assertion of libertarian freedom is more problematic for him. In the *Search*, Malebranche attempted to address the difficulties by offering a sense in which our causally inefficacious will can be said to be active. He began by comparing the will to the faculty that matter has of receiving motion. Inclinations are conceived as a type of "mental motion" that is always directed toward "the good in general," since we are always inclined toward happiness. Whereas God alone can be the cause of the "quantity" of this mental motion, the will is free in the sense that it has the power to "turn" its inclinations toward particular objects that are pleasing (I.I).

One problem for this account of our free will is that Malebranche had indicated in the *Search* that our inclinations are initially directed to pleasing objects by nature, that is to say, by God. Such an indication is also connected to Malebranche's claim, mentioned above, that our "natural judgments" concerning sensory objects derive from God. Given this view, there would seem to be no room for any sort of "turning" of inclinations by our will. This problem may explain why Malebranche emphasized in a later Elucidation of his *Search* that our free consent to the inclination toward a particular good is a mere "repose," an inactivity that preserves an inclination already present in us (Eluc. I). However, he also indicated that freedom involves not only the power to consent, but also the power to "suspend" that consent by searching for other objects to love. This suspension is supposed to be an inactivity that causes nothing real. The question is how this one inactivity can be opposed to the inactivity of consent.

In his final work, *Reflections on Physical Premotion* (1715), Malebranche went some way toward addressing these difficulties when he distinguished between the natural love that God determines and the free love that is under the control of our will (OC XVI 17–18). He suggested that since suspension leaves the motion corresponding to our free love in an indeterminate state, it contrasts with a consent in us that determines that motion toward a particular object. Even though there is an opposition here, it remains the case that neither suspension nor consent is causally efficacious in the sense of producing new perceptions or altering the quantity of the mental motion directed toward the good.

Necessitation and nominalism: Hobbes and Spinoza

Whereas Descartes and Malebranche embraced a libertarian freedom of indifference, in *Leviathan* Hobbes endorsed the compatibilist position that "*Liberty* and *necessity* are consistent." He argued there that free actions are simply voluntary actions, that is, actions necessitated by the will. Since the will in turn "proceedeth from some cause, and that from another cause in a continual chain (whose first link is in the hand of God the first of all causes), they proceed from *necessity*" (ch. 21, par. 4). Hobbes's nominalism is reflected in his view that the will itself is not some general faculty or power, but rather the last appetite deriving necessarily from a process of deliberation that itself necessitates the free and voluntary action (ch. 6, par. 53).

Hobbes's account of liberty and necessity prompted an impassioned rebuttal from the Bishop of Derry, John Bramhall (1594–1663). As a follower of the Dutch dissident Calvinist Jacob Arminius (1560–1609), Bramhall accepted a libertarian view that precludes any sort of necessitation or determination in the case of free acts. But Bramhall also defended a more traditional view of the will as a power against Hobbes's nominalistic counterproposal. In his *Defense of the True Liberty of Human Actions from Antecedent and Extrinsicall Necessity* (1655), Bramhall urged that the will is a special power or faculty of the mind that has the ability to determine itself without being further determined by anything external to it. Though he admitted that intellectual considerations can induce the will to act in a certain manner, he also insisted that this "moral" necessitation differs from any sort of "absolute" necessitation involving natural determination.[24]

Hobbes objected to Bramhall's view on two counts. First, he held that the notion of any sort of necessity other than absolute necessity is unintelligible. Necessity is simply "that which is impossible to be otherwise," and since the claim that voluntary actions are necessitated says only that it is impossible that they not occur given the presence of the last appetite in deliberation that produces it, this sort of necessity is perfectly consistent with freedom.[25] Second, Hobbes claimed that "to confound the faculty of the will with the will were to confound a will with no will; for the faculty of the will is no will." The will is rather a particular volition, and to say that we are free to will is simply to say that we are free to do what we will, that is, what our last appetite in deliberation determines us to do.[26]

In contrast to Hobbes, Spinoza rejected the position that a free act can be necessitated by external causes. In the *Ethics*, he defined freedom as that "which exists from the necessity of its nature alone, and is determined to act by itself alone." Freedom here is contrasted with "necessary compulsion," defined as that "which is determined by another to exist and to produce an effect in a certain manner" (I, def. 7). Spinoza also argued that as the only being that is "in itself and conceived through itself," God alone can be said to be perfectly free. All other finite things are modes that must be conceived through God, and as such are effects determined by something external to them to exist and to produce their effects. In the appendix to part I of the *Ethics*, Spinoza further dismissed the belief in human freedom as a fiction deriving from ignorance of the external causes that determine our action.

Somewhat paradoxically, Spinoza spoke toward the end of part IV of the *Ethics* of the various qualities of a "free man" (props. 66–73), and he devoted part V of this text to a consideration of "human freedom." However, he made clear that the "free man," or an individual who "is led by reason" or "one who lives according to the dictate of reason alone," is an idealization. Actual human beings cannot be internally determined by reason alone, since they inevitably are affected by passions deriving from external causes. Even so, humans can approach the model of the free man insofar as they are able to control their passions and to follow reason.

Spinoza's admission that determined human actions can be said to have at least some degree of freedom shows that he did not reject entirely the sort of compatibilism that one finds in Hobbes. However, Spinoza was more clearly sympathetic to the nominalist aspects of Hobbes's account of the will. Thus, he urged in the *Ethics* that the will, understood as a power or faculty distinct from specific volitions, falls into the class of "complete fictions" that are "nothing but Metaphysical beings, or universals, which we are used to forming from particulars" (II, prop. 48 schol.). Indeed, Spinoza went beyond Hobbes in denying that there is any sort of distinction between will and intellect. Here his target was the view in Descartes that the perception of ideas is distinct from the volitional act of affirming or denying them. Spinoza's argument is that since a particular volitional affirmation of an idea cannot be conceived apart from that idea, and since the perception of the truth of an idea is simply the affirmation of the idea, the volition and the idea are one and the same (II, prop. 49). There is the objection from Descartes that the fact that one has the power to suspend judgment concerning a particular idea shows that the idea cannot be identified with a volitional judgment. However, Spinoza responded that suspense of judgment does not arise from a power, much less a free power, but is simply a second-order perception that the idea is not adequately perceived (II, prop. 49 cor. schol.).

Determined freedom: Locke and Leibniz

Locke's main account of freedom is found in the chapter of his *Essay* on the idea of power. This long chapter was extensively revised for the second (1694) edition, and includes later additions in the fourth (1700) and fifth (1706) editions. In contrast to Hobbes and Spinoza, Locke consistently claimed in this text that the will is a certain sort of faculty or power, in particular, an "active power" that enables the agent to act in accord with conscious choice. There may seem to be an even greater difference, given that Locke explicitly denied that actions deriving from the will can be necessary. Yet the difference here is largely verbal, since Locke defined necessary actions simply as those that do not derive from will or volition. Moreover, he consistently allowed that the will is itself determined by something external to it. In line with Hobbes, but not with Spinoza, he held that such external determination in no way precludes freedom of action.

Locke initially defined freedom as "the power a Man has to do or forbear any particular Action, according as its doing or forbearance has the actual preference of the Mind" (*Essay*, II.xxi.15). He emphasized that since freedom and will are both powers, freedom is not properly attributed to the will. Instead, freedom is simply the power of a rational agent to exercise the power of will in a certain manner.

Locke also insisted, against Hobbes, that free acts must be distinguished from voluntary acts. Though it is necessary that a free act be voluntary, that is, derive from the will, it is further necessary that other choices be open to the agent. Thus, Locke noted that a prisoner who remains in a locked room because he prefers to do so acts voluntarily but not with freedom, since to be free it must be open to him to leave the room if he so prefers. This precision is reflected in Hume's famous definition of liberty in the *Enquiry concerning Human Understanding*, according to which "if we choose to remain at rest, we may; if we choose to move, we also may" (VIII.1).

In the second edition of the *Essay*, Locke introduced a new element into his account of freedom when he noted that "the hinge on which turns the *liberty* of intellectual Beings" consists in the fact that such beings "can suspend this prosecution [of true felicity] in particular cases, till they have looked before them, and informed themselves, whether that particular thing, which is then proposed, or desired, lie in the way to their main end, and make a real part of that which is their greatest good" (II.xxi.52). There is an obvious resemblance to the view in Malebranche that our freedom requires that we are able to suspend consent to love of an object that we do not clearly understand to be worthy of it. Even so, Locke did not accept Malebranche's libertarian claim that our consent to love of a particular good is undetermined. This is clear from his 1701 correspondence with the Dutch Arminian, Philipp van Limborch (1633–1712). Limborch insisted that free acts require an "Indifferency" on which "when all the requisites for acting are present, it can act or not act."[27] Here he was repeating the definition of libertarian freedom in the work of the Spanish Jesuit, Luis Molina. In response, Locke rejected this "antecedent indifferency" on the grounds that once all of the requisites for action are present, the will "is determined by the preference of the preceding judgment of the understanding for either that action or forbearance from it."[28] In an addition to the fifth edition of the *Essay* that no doubt derives from the Limborch correspondence, Locke did concede that before being determined the agent was free to suspend choice. In his own view, however, this freedom consists only in the fact that the agent had the ability to suspend choice had he so desired.[29]

In his comments on Locke's account of freedom in the *New Essays*, Leibniz noted that "the understanding can determine the will, in accordance with which perceptions and reasons prevail, in a manner which, although it is certain and infallible, inclines without necessitating" (*New Ess.*, II.xxi.8). He held that free agents are determined to choose what appears to be best, but that this "inclining" determination is distinct from a "geometrical or metaphysical" necessitation that precludes any choice. In the preface to his *Theodicy*, Leibniz cited Hobbes and Spinoza as the two thinkers who have "extended furthest the doctrine of the necessity of things." Just as Hobbes advocated "absolute necessity" against Bramhall, he notes, so Spinoza posited "a blind and geometric necessity, with complete absence of capacity for choice, for goodness and for understanding in [the] first cause of things."

Although Hobbes differed from Leibniz in suggesting that determined free actions are logically necessitated, he nonetheless allowed as much as Leibniz that we are determined to choose what appears to us to be best. And whereas Leibniz differed from Spinoza in holding that "the first cause of things" selects the best among infinite possible worlds, there is a sense in which he accepted Spinoza's claim that freedom precludes external determination. Thus, Leibniz frequently emphasized that his system of preestablished harmony provides room for freedom insofar as it requires that all states of a substance arise spontaneously from that substance itself. All that is further required for a spontaneous act to be free, according to Leibniz, is that it derive from a deliberate choice of that which appears to be best.

At one point, Leibniz allowed that free choice involves a sort of "indifference." However, he held that such indifference requires only that the choice be indifferent in the sense that "neither I nor any other more enlightened mind could demonstrate that the opposite of this truth implies a contradiction" (AG 194). In contrast, he rejected the stronger Molinist claim that the free agent is indifferent in the sense that all the requisites for action being given, the agent is able to act or not to act. Leibniz insisted that there can be no "absolute indifference," since "choice always follows the greatest inclination," and thus the free agent is determined to choose what appears to be best. Even when we choose against what reason tells us is best, this choice must be determined by passions or even by "small impressions" too indistinct for us to recognize (AG 193–96). Here, then, Leibniz stands with Hobbes and Locke, and against

Descartes and Malebranche, in holding that we have a determined freedom that precludes any contracausal indifference.

NOTES

1 Rorty 1979, p. 54.
2 Ibid., p. 51. Rorty notes that he is simply relaying the "usual story" about the "emergence of epistemological skepticism out of a theory of representative perception created by Descartes and Locke" found in the work of Etienne Gilson and J. H. Randall (p. 49, n. 19).
3 For a critique of Rorty's narrative that emphasizes this line of argument, see Wilson 1999b.
4 Several recent works have emphasized the connections of Descartes's theory of mind to his views in metaphysics and natural philosophy. See, for instance, Rozemond 1998, Alanen 2003, and Clarke 2003.
5 See the material on Aristotle's view of the life sciences in Gotthelf 1985.
6 There is a helpful discussion of the various competing currents of early modern thought in Menn 1998.
7 For a consideration of the views on these matters in the texts of the early modern Jesuit scholastics, see Des Chene 2000.
8 I provide a more detailed treatment of the differences between Descartes and Malebranche on this point in Schmaltz 1996, esp. chs. 2 and 4.
9 For a discussion of the relation of Leibniz's account of preestablished harmony to his monistic metaphysics, see Rutherford 1995a, ch. 8.
10 On Spinoza's views concerning immortality and the eternity of the mind, see Nadler 2001, esp. chs. 5–6.
11 There is an important exchange over Locke's understanding of the possibility of the superaddition of thought to matter in Wilson 1999c, Ayers 1981, and Wilson 1999d.
12 See Clarke 1738, vol. III, pp. 719–913.
13 For a discussion of Thomas's view that sets it in its medieval context, see Mahoney 1982.
14 For a discussion of these medieval debates, see Pasnau 1997.
15 Moreau 1999 is a recent treatment of the Arnauld–Malebranche debate.
16 For a comparison of the different accounts of ideas in Descartes, Malebranche, and Leibniz, see Jolley 1990.
17 Wolf-Devine 1993 provides a treatment of Descartes's various discussions of visual perception.
18 For more on Berkeley's views in the *New Theory of Vision*, see Atherton 1990.

19 Berkeley 1975, pp. 49–50.
20 Schmaltz 1997 focuses on this argument in Descartes for sensory innateness.
21 On the debate between Locke and Leibniz on this issue, see Jolley 1984, ch. 9.
22 Kent 1995 considers debates in the later medieval period over the nature of the human will and freedom.
23 On the issues addressed in the following sections, see Sleigh, Chappell, and Della Rocca 1998. Notice, however, that in contrast to the libertarian reading of Descartes that I offer presently, the view in §II of that article (assigned to Chappell) is that he was a compatibilist who held that "everything apart from God is caused by factors other than itself" (p. 1,206).
24 Hobbes and Bramhall 1999, p. 52.
25 Ibid., pp. 72–73.
26 Ibid., pp. 73, 82.
27 Locke 1976–92, vol. VII, p. 367.
28 Ibid., p. 408.
29 For more on the complexities of Locke's account of the will and freedom, see Yaffe 2000.

MICHAEL LOSONSKY

6 Language and logic

In their monumental work, *The Development of Logic*, Martha Kneale and William Kneale maintain that during the seventeenth century logic was "in decline as a branch of philosophy."[1] But an era that included Leibniz, who according to the Kneales "deserves to be ranked among the greatest of all logicians,"[2] as well as Locke, who dismisses formal logic as "learned Ignorance" while writing "the first modern treatise devoted specifically to philosophy of language,"[3] suggests drama and excitement, not decline. While traditional logic was indeed in decline, logic itself was being transformed into modern mathematical logic. Moreover, the turn away from formal logic was also a dramatic turn to natural language for insight and solutions to the problems of philosophy. These two turns, the mathematical and linguistic turns of early modern philosophy, are defining features of seventeenth-century European philosophy.

EARLY MODERN LOGIC

In 1626, the Dutch logician Franco Burgesdijk maintained that there were three kinds of logicians: Aristotelians, Ramists, and Semi-Ramists. While Aristotelians continued to develop Aristotle's logic of categorical syllogisms and immediate inferences, Ramists sought alternative logics that captured reasoning that traditional Aristotelian logic ignored. Semi-Ramists, also called "Philippo-Ramists" after Luther's collaborator Philipp Melanchthon, sought a synthesis of traditional and alternative logics, which included the search for formal methods to capture nonsyllogistic reasoning.[4] It is useful to follow Burgesdijk and divide early modern logic into traditional logic, alternative logics, and attempts to synthesize the two.

Traditional logic: Aristotelians

By the thirteenth century, Aristotelian logic consisted of two parts: old and new logic. Old logic (*logica vetus*) consisted of Aristotle's *Categories* and *On Interpretation*, supplemented with Porphyry's *Isagoge* as a general introduction to the *Categories*. The remaining four texts of Aristotle's *Organon* were known as the new logic (*logica nova*): *Prior Analytics*, *Posterior Analytics*, *Topics*, and *On Sophistical Refutations*. These four texts were preserved in the original Greek in Sicily and southern Italy, and were also brought to Muslim Spain in the eleventh and twelfth centuries in Greek and in Arabic translations.

The *Prior Analytics* and *On Sophistical Refutations* were particularly influential. The former expanded on the meager discussion of syllogisms in the *logica vetus* and the latter focused on fallacies and paradoxes, which were mostly new topics. These fallacies and paradoxes based on syntactic and semantic ambiguities of ordinary language were discussed under the headings *Sophismata* and *Insolubilia*, and motivated syntactic and semantic studies that in the thirteenth century came to be known as "modern logic (*logica moderna*)" in order to distinguish it from "ancient logic (*logica antiqua*)," which hewed more closely to the traditional topics of terms, propositions, immediate inferences, and syllogisms. The most important "modern logic" text for three hundred years was Peter of Spain's *Summulae logicales*, written about 1245. It was still being used in the seventeenth century, by which time it had enjoyed no less than 166 printed editions.[5]

All the books of Aristotle's *Organon* were core texts of the European university curriculum during the fourteenth and fifteenth centuries except the *Topics*.[6] The *Topics* discussed practical problems of reasoning, specifically, how to find the materials "out of which arguments are constructed" (*Topics*, 105a20), and "how we are to become well supplied with these" materials (101b13–14). What characterizes the post-medieval period and informs seventeenth-century philosophy is that the practical and epistemological perspective of the *Topics* moves to center stage.

But the medieval logician's preoccupation with evaluating deductive arguments constructed from categorical propositions still thrived in the early modern period, particularly in Roman Catholic countries. As just mentioned, Peter of Spain's textbook was still being reprinted in the seventeenth century. Outstanding contemporary contributions to traditional logic include those of the Portuguese Jesuit Pedro Fonseca (1528–99), whose *Institutionum dialecticarum libri octo* was published in fifty-three editions between 1564 and 1625, the Polish Jesuit Martin Smiglecki (1563–1618), whose monumental 1,600-page *Logica* (1618) was reprinted three times in Oxford, and the Italian Jesuit Girolamo Saccheri (1667–1733), whose *Logica demonstrativa* was published in 1697.[7] Thomas Wilson (1524–81) introduced scholastic terminology, including the term 'proposition,' into English, in his *Rules of Reason* (1551), but major traditional logic texts continued to be written in Latin, particularly John Wallis's (1616–1703) *Institutio logicae* (1687) and Henry Aldrich's (1647–1710) *Artis logicae compendium* (1691).

Alternative logics: informal logic, induction, and scientific method

Traditional logic texts mentioned inductive reasoning, but generally had very little to say about it. Logicians in the early modern period saw this as a serious defect and sought alternative logics that would capture nondeductive argumentation. This search for alternatives during the period has been dismissed as not part of the development of logic in the sense of the study of deductive validity, but part of the "new study of heuristic methodology."[8] If we are guided by early modern conceptions of logic, however, it is a mistake to ignore the new study of methodology in a history of the period.

RUDOLPH AGRICOLA (1444–1485). Agricola's *De inventione dialectica libri tres,* written by 1480 and published in 1515, became a widely used textbook in the sixteenth century. This success marks the decline of traditional logic.[9] The title already captures important characteristics of the alternative logic movement. Traditionally, the term 'dialectic' was used narrowly for the study of probable reasoning, not demonstrative reasoning. Moreover, the art of judgment, which is the evaluation of deductive inferences, was the centerpiece of logic, as opposed to the art of invention, which focuses on the invention or construction of arguments. Agricola's title upsets these priorities. Dialectic now is used to cover all forms of argumentation, and invention becomes the centerpiece of dialectic, which Agricola characterizes as "the art of speaking with probability (*probabiliter*) on any question whatsoever, insofar as the nature of the subject is capable of infusing conviction."[10] This also includes deductive arguments, which he treats as limiting cases of probable reasoning, intentionally blurring the line between induction and deduction (242).[11]

For Agricola, invention is "thinking out the middle term or argument" (16). Guided by the traditional theory of syllogisms, Agricola sees the first step in argument construction as the search for true propositions that involve one of the terms of the conclusion and a new term. Agricola's project is to design a method for finding such propositions for a given conclusion. Once a list of propositions is generated, the arguer then tries various pairs of propositions until a syllogism for the conclusion is found.

The tool for locating propositions is a list of topics or *loci* that apply to all things. According to Agricola, each topic is a "common mark (*nota*) of a thing, through which it is possible to discover what can be shown, which is also what is probable, with regard to any particular thing." Each topic is "a refuge and treasure chest" wherein "all tools for fixing belief (*faciendae fidei*) are stored" (20). Agricola's list consists of twenty-four topics ordered hierarchically in order to make it easier for the arguer to work systematically through them.

To illustrate his method, Agricola considers the case of someone arguing for the proposition "A philosopher needs a wife" (414). Agricola runs through his twenty-four topics collecting various properties of philosophers, including that philosophers are pale and thin, but in the end settles on the property *aiming to live virtuously*. He then does the same for wife, focusing on various virtues of wives, including that they desire and can bear children. This suggests various propositions that together with the proposition that philosophers seek to live virtuously can be put together in a syllogism with the conclusion that philosophers need wives (414–22).

Agricola recognizes that this is not an automatic procedure for finding premises. "The value of these exercises," he writes, "is primarily this: the description (*descriptio*)" that can be built by going through the topics and that will be structured by the topics for easy overview (422). The arguer needs to build up a rich description involving the terms of the conclusion, and then the arguer will have a fund of information, "lined up for battle" (424). In this manner Agricola shifts the focus of logic to methods for generating descriptions of objects.

Agricola includes a brief discussion of induction by simple enumeration, but he distinguishes between a complete induction or enumeration of all instances, in which the conclusion must be true if all the premises are true, and an incomplete induction, where the conclusion need not be true even if the premises are true (322–28). There are good and bad incomplete inductions, and he suggests that the difference between a good incomplete and a complete induction is a matter of degree (318).

With the exception of including syllogisms involving singular propositions, which had been ignored by traditional Aristotelian logic, Agricola makes no contribution to the theory of deduction. But as we have seen, Agricola's significance lies elsewhere. By attending to informal reasoning and the problems of argument construction, Agricola can legitimately be seen as a precursor of the field of informal logic. Moreover, by turning to nondeductive reasoning and methods for discovering truths about an object, including empirical truths, Agricola tills the soil for the cultivation of inductive logic and the logic of scientific reasoning.

PETER RAMUS (1515–1572). Agricola's logic was taught at the University of Paris by Johann Sturm (1507–89), and it is likely that one of Sturm's students was Pierre de la Ramée, better known as Ramus. Legend has it that the title of his master's thesis was "Whatever Aristotle Stated Is False (*Commentitia*)," indicating Ramus's reputation as a radical critic of Aristotle which lasted well into the seventeenth century.[12] His *Dialectique* (1555), the first published logic book in French, and the Latin version *Dialecticae libri duo* published a year later, were very popular texts (nearly 250 editions were published) that took broad swipes at Aristotelian logic. However, it needs to be pointed out that Ramus follows tradition in important respects, more so than Agricola. For instance, his discussion of argumentation sharply distinguishes deductive and inductive arguments, and when discussing argumentation, he focuses almost exclusively on deduction.

But there are good reasons for Ramus's reputation. While he begins his logic in good Aristotelian fashion with a discussion of categories and classification, his list of nine basic categories (*cause*, *effect*, *subject*, *adjunct*, *opposite*, *comparative*, *name*, *division*, *definition*) departs significantly from Aristotle's ten categories (*substance*, *quantity*, *quality*, *relation*, *place*, *time*, *action*, *passion*, *situation*, *state*). The inclusion of *cause* and *effect* as main categories rather than a subdivision, as is the case in Aristotle's *Categories*, and the elevation of efficient cause over Aristotle's other three causes, mark the increasing importance of scientific reasoning. Also, Ramus's list includes linguistic categories such as *name* and *definition*, signaling the coming linguistic turn of early modern philosophy to be discussed below.

Ramus follows Agricola in confining rhetoric to matters of style, not argumentation, and placing all argumentation within the domain of logic. "Dialectic is the art of good disputation," he writes, adding that the term 'dialectic' has the "same sense as the name Logic" because they are about "nothing else but disputation or reasoning."[13] He also focuses on the art of invention, devoting forty pages of the *Dialectique* to the art of invention, whereas the discussion of the structure of propositions and syllogisms receives only twenty-nine pages. Like Agricola, Ramus allows for syllogisms with singular propositions, but he goes further by also classifying them. He also adds conditionals and disjunctions to his discussion of noncategorical propositions, which received little attention from his predecessors (134–41).

An innovation of Ramus's discussion of the theory of judgment is the addition of a section on method. Traditionally, method was treated as a part of rhetoric, but Ramus, along with Sturm and Melanchthon, was among the first logicians to locate a discussion of method under the rubric of logic.[14] During the medieval period, method (*methodus*) was primarily a pedagogical concept that included providing students with overviews, syllabi, and other aids or shortcuts that would make complex material more accessible.[15] Ramus elevates method to the systematic organization or arrangement (*disposition*) of all knowledge, and explicitly distinguishes his method from pedagogical shortcuts. He writes, "this name [method] signifies the whole subject . . . although commonly it is taken for . . . a shortcut" (144–45).

Ramus's arrangement anticipates important features of Descartes's concept of method. He divides method into the methods of nature and prudence, and the method of nature requires that all known propositions be arranged so that the first propositions are those that are the most evident or clear (*évident*) (145). The first propositions should also be the most general and universal propositions, assuming that general propositions are the most evident. Moreover, the propositions are to be arranged syllogistically so that the less general propositions are derivable from the more general ones. The method of prudence orders propositions relative to audiences that are being instructed and are not ready for scientific knowledge (150). Here propositions are not arranged deductively, but according to probability and induction.

Ramus not only elevates method to a branch of logic, but also gives it a symbolic apparatus. Ramus was looking for a simple technique for arranging propositions so that they would be visually attractive in a classroom textbook. To that end he adapted the branching tables that were widely used in medical textbooks.[16] These are tree-like diagrams that begin with one main concept, typically on the left, followed by brackets that terminate in additional concepts. Each of these concepts also branches into other concepts. Ramus at first does not limit the branches of his tables to dichotomies, but the Ramist tradition preferred binary trees, and it is these dichotomous tables that became the hallmarks of Ramist logic and pedagogy.

What was attractive about these tables was that they suggested a mechanical procedure for ordering information. Ramus's search for mechanical procedures is likely tied to his interest in mathematics. When Ramus was forbidden to teach philosophy, he turned to teaching and publishing textbooks in geometry and arithmetic. Ramus maintained that mathematics is the foundation of natural philosophy and an essential practical tool in astronomy and mechanics.[17] As Mahoney has observed, "by emphasizing the central importance of mathematics and by insisting on the application of scientific theory to practical problem solving, Ramus helped to formulate the quest for operational knowledge of nature that marks the Scientific Revolution."[18] Indeed the "stark triviality"[19] of Ramist tables is precisely the source of their historically significant role in the mathematization of logic.

FRANCIS BACON (1561–1626). Bacon is even more radical in his response to traditional logic than Agricola or Ramus.[20] For Bacon, logic simply is induction and scientific method and his boldness and ambition is captured in the title of his book on logic, *The New Organon, or True Directions for the Interpretation of Nature* (1620).

"We reject proof by syllogism," he writes, "because it operates in confusion and lets nature slip out of our hands." Instead, Bacon focuses on the process of arriving at judgments useful to scientific inquiry, and this he calls "induction": "For we regard *induction* as the form of demonstration which respects the senses, stays close to nature, fosters results and is almost involved in them itself."[21] Induction will be the method for establishing "degrees of certainty" on the basis of sensation and constructing "a new and certain road for the mind from the actual perception of the senses."[22]

Bacon also distances himself from his humanist predecessors by sharply distinguishing the delivery of knowledge, say in classroom instruction, from the discovery of new knowledge. Under the heading of *inventio*, Ramus and Agricola ran together delivery and discovery and, more importantly, focused primarily on delivery. For this reason, Bacon did not see his work as a contribution to the art of invention.

Induction aims to tie reasoning to the observation of nature, rather than to what is appropriate to social interaction.[23] Accordingly, the first step is to prepare the ground for induction by compiling "a good, adequate *natural* and *experimental* history," much as Agricola required a good *descriptio*. Bacon, however, designs a method for compiling a description, because without a method it will be so rich that it "confounds and confuses the understanding." Therefore "*tables* must be drawn up," and this must be done "in such a way and with such organization that the mind may be able to act upon them" (*New Org.*, II.10). These tables are not simply a matter of "convenience,"[24] but are necessary if the mind is to learn something from nature.

The ground is prepared by constructing three tables under the heading " Presentations of instances to the intellect" (II.15). First, "the table of existence and presence" collects all the "known *instances* which meet in the same nature" that is being investigated, or, in Bacon's words, interpreted (II.11). The second, the "table of divergences," presents negative instances. The third "table of degrees or comparison" collects instances in which the object under investigation is found in degrees (II.12–13).

Once the data is collected in these comparative tables, "*induction* itself has to be put to work" (II.15). The first inductive step is "*rejection* or *exclusion*," which is supposed to leave the interpreter of nature with a set of affirmative instances, which Bacon calls the "first harvest" (II.16, 20). Contrary to widespread characterizations of Bacon's induction, this is not the end of the inductive process. The first harvest is only a preliminary conclusion that needs to be refined and confirmed with "other aids to the intellect in the *interpretation of nature* and in true and complete *induction*." One such aid is to search for "*privileged instances*" (II.21). This consists in isolating instances where the phenomenon under investigation stands out or is particularly revealing or clear, for example, a heated thermometer, which is a "*revealing instance* of the motion of expansion" (II.24).

Bacon's own estimation that he develops a concept of induction that is superior to simple enumeration is accurate. He formulates principles of eliminative induction and anticipates Mill's Joint Method of Agreement and Difference and the Method of Concomitant Variations.[25] Moreover, Bacon's claim that rejection or exclusion is only the first step of induction, followed by eight steps of refinement, including finding privileged or revealing instances, shows that eliminative induction does not exhaust his concept of induction.[26] It is with justification that Bacon has been described as "the Father of Inductive Philosophy" whose account of inductive arguments broke "new ground."[27]

Synthesis: Gottfried Wilhelm Leibniz

As noted above, Philippo-Ramism sought a synthesis of traditional and alternative logics, and although Leibniz's work on logic transcends this trend, it also has its roots in it.[28] An important influence on Leibniz is the Semi-Ramist Joachim Junge (1597–1657), whose *Logica hamburgensia* (1638) Leibniz considered to be one of the greatest logic texts. This textbook presented traditional Aristotelian logic, but also included an extensive discussion of valid deductive inferences that traditional logic did not capture.[29]

Leibniz's own interests in logic were eclectic. He describes how as "a lad of thirteen years" he was fascinated by the various logics of classification and how he himself compiled "tabulations of knowledge" and so practiced the art of division and subdivision, "drawing heavily" on the topical logics of both the Ramists and Semi-Ramists (L 463–64). He believed these methods were not only useful for memorizing and recalling information, but also helped generate descriptions and explanations and thus could guide discovery. The logics that "serve discovery," Leibniz writes, also include "the art of inquiry into nature itself," which "Verulam Bacon began so ably" (L 465).

But traditional logic is also valuable. Determining the number of valid figures and modes of syllogisms is "no less worthy of our consideration than the number of regular bodies" (L 465). For Leibniz, syllogistic logic is "one of the finest, and indeed one of the most important inventions to have been made by the human mind" (*New Ess.*, IV.xvii.4). Aristotle's achievement, Leibniz maintains, was to be "the first actually to write mathematically outside of mathematics" (L 465). What stands out for Leibniz in Aristotle's logic is that "it is a kind of universal mathematics whose importance is too little known" (*New Ess.*, IV.xvii.4).

However, Leibniz saw defects in both the logic of discovery and judgment. For example, "Aristotle's work is indeed but a beginning, virtually the ABCs" of deductive reasoning because there are valid deductive inferences that are not captured by traditional logic (L 465). Leibniz has in mind conditional and disjunctive arguments as well as inferences involving propositions about relations, such as "If David is the father of Solomon, then certainly Solomon is the son of David," or "If Jesus Christ is God, then the mother of Jesus Christ is the mother of God" (*New Ess.*, IV.xvii.4).

Leibniz's remedy for the problems of logic was a unified logical calculus that would capture all valid inferences and serve both the arts of invention and judgment. His first attempt, *Dissertation on the Art of Combinations*, was published in 1666. It is guided by two main ideas. First, there are simple and indefinable concepts, or "first terms," and all other concepts, propositions, and chains of propositions that constitute inferences are various combinations or structures of concepts, and second, these structures of concepts can be represented mathematically.

Throughout his life, Leibniz proposed various ways to represent logical relations mathematically. In 1666, he assigned numbers to the simple concepts and represented the combination of concepts as the product of the values of its simpler components.[30] In 1679, Leibniz worked on a calculus of ideas in which every true universal affirmative proposition is one in which the number assigned to the subject can be divided exactly without any remainder by the number assigned to the predicate. If the subject cannot be divided by the predicate without remainder, the proposition is false.[31] His last proposal in 1690 attempted to capture logical operations in terms of addition and subtraction.[32] The underlying theme in all these proposals is that deductive relations of propositions can be calculated or computed mechanically just as we calculate in arithmetic or algebra. The central operation in all deductive proofs is the substitution of equivalents.

The representation of this conceptual structure with written signs would be a "universal writing," "universal polygraphy," or what he later calls "universal symbolistic" and "general characteristic."[33] This universal characteristic would be a symbol system that precisely represents the structure of all possible conceptual content.[34] This is why Gottlob Frege, who with George Boole founded modern mathematical logic, pays homage to Leibniz, characterizing his own *Begriffsschrift*, or *Conceptual Notation*, as a revival of Leibniz's project of a universal characteristic. But as Frege notes, his own project is much more modest. While Leibniz hoped to design a language that would express all possible content, Frege limits himself to logical form, that is, the content that is relevant for deductive validity.[35]

In practice Leibniz also had to restrict his project. While he never gave up his faith that with enough time, effort, and support he could make some headway in isolating the set of simple concepts and the rules for combining these into complex concepts and propositions, his interest steadily shifted to designing a "logical calculus" for deductive relations only, that is, a logical calculus that abstracts from specific content and is thus capable of diverse interpretations.[36]

It must be noted that the suggestion that deductive relations can be expressed mathematically is not original to Leibniz. He appropriately credits Thomas Hobbes, who in part 1 of *De corpore*, titled

"Computation or Logic," declares that to reason is to compute, and "to compute, is either to collect the sum of many things that are added together, or to know what remains when one thing is taken out of another," and he concludes that "*Ratiocination*, therefore, is the same with *addition* and *substraction*" (1.i.2).[37] Hobbes, however, takes only a few very small steps in working out the details of this declaration, and it falls to Leibniz to actually make progress in the reduction of logical relations to arithmetical operations and the development of the idea of a calculus that represents mathematically the formal structure of all valid inferences, irrespective of interpretation.

The importance of Leibniz's logic lies not only in the clarity of his vision of the mathematization of logic, but also in its breadth and depth. As Frege writes, "Leibniz in his writings strews such an abundance of seeds of ideas that in this respect hardly any other can measure up to him."[38] For example, Leibniz recognizes the importance of the concepts of necessity and identity for understanding deductive validity. His claims that the actual world is one of an infinity of possible worlds, and that contingent truths are propositions that are actually true but false in other possible worlds while necessary truths are ones "whose opposite is not possible," are foundational ideas of contemporary modal logic.[39] Similarly, Leibniz's principle of identity, "Those are the same of which one can be substituted for the other with truth preserved (*Eadem sunt, quorum unum alteri substitui potest salva veritate*)," persists in two forms in contemporary philosophy.[40] It appears as a principle for the identity of objects, often labeled "Leibniz's Law," namely, that if two things are identical, then anything true of the one is also true of the other: $x = y \rightarrow Fx \leftrightarrow Fy$.[41] It also appears as a principle for identifying content or synonymy, namely that two expressions have the same content if they can be substituted for each other in a sentence without changing its truth value.[42]

Finally, Leibniz's unified conception of logic included non-deductive inferences, an interest that dates back to his early work on legal reasoning. He believed that a complete logical calculus would include a logic of probability. "When we lack sufficient data to arrive at certainty," Leibniz writes, "the universal symbolistic would also serve to estimate degrees of probability" (L 654). The logic of probability would "establish the degrees of likelihood *on the evidence,"* that is, the probability of a proposition is a function of the overall weight of the available evidence (*New Ess.*, IV.ii.14). But the probability of a proposition relative to the evidence, according to Leibniz, "must be demonstrated through inferences belonging to the logic of necessary propositions" (*New Ess.*, IV.xvii.6). Thus the probability of a proposition relative to the available evidence is itself a necessary truth subject to deductive demonstration, which anticipates modern logical theories of probability.[43]

Leibniz's work in logic did not occur in an intellectual vacuum and it was not simply a product of his genius. Leibniz, a prolific correspondent, was also responding to, drawing on, and mirroring the intellectual ferment of his time. His achievements in logic, particularly his contributions to the mathematization of logic, are compelling evidence that the field of logic was not in decline during the early modern period.

EARLY MODERN LINGUISTIC TURNS

While for Leibniz, traditional logic is "one of the finest" achievements of the human mind, for John Locke, it is "a very useless skill," "a curious and unexplicable Web of perplexed Words" used to "cover . . . ignorance," an "endless Labyrinth," and "learned Ignorance." Worst of all, it destroys "the Instrument and Means of Discourse, Conversation, Instruction, and Society" (*Essay*, III.x.8–10). Locke's animus is not just directed at syllogistic logic, but at the twin ideas that symbols and formal rules guide human reasoning (IV.vii.11). Locke believed instead that natural language is "the Instrument and Means of Discourse, Conversation, Instruction, and Society." Language gets a starring role in the *Essay concerning Human Understanding*, and Locke concludes the *Essay* with the suggestion that "another sort of Logick" should replace formal logic, namely one that studies natural language (IV.xxi.4).

The turn to natural language begins with Renaissance humanism, where interest in language is so deep that it has been claimed that "Renaissance philosophers of language" share some of the "central philosophical concerns . . . of recent Anglo-American philosophy," particularly "turning to language as the main or only object of analysis" and examining language not simply for its own sake, but for the light it sheds on philosophical problems.[44] Renaissance critics rejected scholastic logic because they believed it clashed with customary speech (*usus loquendi*). For example, Lorenzo Valla (1407–57) exhorts the reader: "Let us conduct ourselves more simply and more in accordance with natural sense and common usage. Philosophy and dialectic . . . ought not to depart from the customary manner of speaking."[45] The Spanish humanist Juan Luis Vives (1492–1540) likewise criticizes the logician's use of variables and the rules that are "against every custom of speech."[46]

Humanism severed the tie between the study of logic and language. Relying on the gap between the apparent grammatical structure of natural language and formal logic, Renaissance humanists ridiculed the idea that logic had anything to do with natural language. Moreover, since human beings typically use natural language to express their thoughts, formal logic severed from language seemed irrelevant to human thinking. With formal logic in retreat, many early modern philosophers turned their attention to natural language to understand the human understanding.

Francis Bacon and Thomas Hobbes

The increasing importance of natural language in early modern philosophy is evident in the philosophies of Bacon and Hobbes. While critiquing traditional logic, Bacon affirms the Aristotelian view that words are "counters and signs of notions" and that the "notions of the mind . . . are like the soul of words, and the basis of every such structure and fabric." So if these notions are defective, then "everything falls to pieces," and hence a logic is needed that considers the formation of the notions that are the soul of language.[47] The first concern of such a logic is to locate and correct the sources of error.[48]

When Bacon turns to the sources of error, however, he rattles the traditional relationship between mind and language. These errors are Bacon's famous idols or illusions of the mind, and one of these involves language: the idols of the marketplace (*idola fori*), or more accurately, the idols of the forum, common or town square. Linguistic illusions are "the biggest nuisance of all," Bacon writes, "because they have stolen into the understanding." Human beings believe that their reason rules words, "but it is also true that words retort and turn their force back upon the understanding, and this has rendered philosophy and the sciences sophistic and unproductive" (*New Org.*, I.59). In *The Advancement of Learning*, Bacon makes this point even more dramatically: "although we think we govern our words . . . yet certain it is that words, as a Tartar's bow, do shoot back upon the understanding of the wisest, and mightily entangle and pervert the judgment."[49]

Bacon has next to nothing to say about the process by which language interacts with the human understanding. Moreover, his response to linguistic illusions is to find ways of strengthening the mind's independence from language. His remedy is to tighten the mind's bonds to the observation of nature and to pry it away from natural language infected by human intercourse. Bacon never considers that language may be essential to scientific reasoning and that the mind cannot be shielded from linguistic illusions.

While Bacon is unclear about the mind's ability to free itself from language, Hobbes explicitly affirms that reasoning cannot be pried apart from language. Without words or some other sensible marks for our thoughts, "whatsoever a man has put together in his mind by ratiocination . . . will presently slip from him, and not be revocable but by beginning his ratiocination anew."[50] Moreover, without the use of words we can reason only about particular things and particular causes (*Lev.*, ch. 5). Thus any reasoning about general causal relationships, which is essential to science, will require some sensible marks, and that is why Hobbes believes that science begins with the defining of words (ibid.). In fact, in *Leviathan* Hobbes seems to go so far as to declare language to be constitutive of all reasoning.[51] He writes that trains of thought are cases of reasoning when they are regulated by an acquired and artificial method, namely reason. Reason is acquired through "study and industry" and it depends on the "invention of Words, and Speech" (ch. 3).

As for Bacon before him, for Hobbes language is also a source of trouble, above all meaningless words. It is on account of this that Hobbes admonishes that "words are wise mens counters, they do but reckon by them: but they are the mony of fooles" (*Lev.*, ch. 4). Unfortunately, this advice does not address a central difficulty. Human beings need language to reason, Hobbes argues, because without language our thoughts "slip away." But if our thoughts are unstable and words are meaningful because they are tied to mental conceptions, we need an account of how language, on the one hand, is capable of providing stability to the mind and, on the other hand, acquires its own stability from the mind's unstable conceptions.

Descartes and the Cartesians

Descartes avoids this difficulty by denying that the mind without language suffers from instability that inhibits reason. This is evident in his reply to Hobbes's Fourth Objection to the *Meditations*. In response to Descartes's claim that the imagination does not play a role in the intellectual conception of a piece of wax, Hobbes argues that if "reasoning is simply the joining together and linking of names or labels by means of the verb 'is'," then "reasoning will depend on names, names will depend on the imagination, and imagination will depend (as I believe it does) merely on the motions of our bodily organs." Thus, Hobbes concludes, "the mind will be nothing more than motion occurring in various parts of an organic body" (CSM II 125–26).

Descartes rejects Hobbes's suggestion that we reason with language. Reasoning "is not a linking of names but of the things that are signified by the names, and I am surprised that the opposite view should occur to anyone" (CSM II 126). His opening defense is to distinguish imagination from "a purely mental conception." This is a recurring theme in Descartes's replies to Hobbes, most notably in his response to Hobbes's claim that "we have no idea or image corresponding to the sacred name of God." Images are part of the "corporeal imagination," Descartes writes, but ideas are "forms of perception" that even a divine mind without a body has (CSM II 127). This undercuts the need for language, because the instability Hobbes perceives is the instability of our mental images, not of the ideas of reason.

Hobbes's view is not only unmotivated, but it has what Descartes believes are two absurd consequences. First, it would mean that people speaking different languages could not reason about the same thing, but "a Frenchman and a German can reason about the same things, despite the fact that the words they think of are completely different." Second, and more importantly, if Hobbes is right, then "when he concludes that the mind is a motion he might just as well conclude that the earth is the sky, or anything else he likes" (CSM II 126). If the meaning of language is a function of "arbitrary conventions," Descartes argues, then if we reason with words, truth is arbitrary as well.

Accordingly, Descartes has little to say about natural language. There are only two other major passages where Descartes discusses language. The best known is his brief argument in *Discourse on the Method* that a human being, unlike a nonhuman animal, is able to "produce different arrangements of words so as to give an appropriately meaningful answer to whatever is said in its presence, as the dullest of men can do" (CSM I 140). The other is Descartes's letter to Mersenne in 1629 assessing the feasibility of a universal language. Descartes argues that a universal characteristic would require a "true philosophy" that breaks down all concepts into their simplest parts, but it is not likely that human beings will achieve this, even though it is possible (CSM III 13).

Although Descartes has little to say about language, his writings inspired important work on language. Descartes's fundamental assumption that the mind is wholly independent of language is preserved and developed in the *Port-Royal Grammar* (1660) and *Logic* (1662). According to the *Grammar*, language is simply the use of physical signs to express thoughts and "what occurs in our minds is necessary for understanding the foundations of grammar."[52] The primary concern of the *Grammar* is to show how grammatical distinctions common to diverse languages are a necessary consequence of the basic operations of the mind: conceiving, judging, and reasoning. The nature of these three operations, plus a fourth, ordering or method, is the subject of the *Port-Royal Logic*, which is even more explicit than the *Grammar* in its Cartesian submission of language to thought. If we did not have to communicate with other people, "it would be enough to examine thoughts in themselves, unclothed in words or other signs."[53]

The authors of the *Logic* also endorse Descartes's sharp divide between imagination and pure intellection, and conclude that "we can express nothing by our words when we understand what we are saying unless, by the same token, it were certain that we had in us the idea of the thing we were signifying by our words."[54] This conclusion is used against Hobbes's view that "reasoning will depend on words." Hobbes appeals to the conventionality of names, but if there are no ideas of things independent of the names of things, conventions are impossible.[55]

John Locke

Locke's thinking about the human understanding begins in a Cartesian fashion, paying little attention to language, but his *Essay* arrives at Hobbes's position that the mind relies on language. Locke expressly connected semantic inquiry with epistemology, and this has correctly been assessed as new and unique about Locke's discussion of language.[56] The stature of Locke's *Essay* as a work in epistemology is undeniable: it is recognized as a philosophical masterpiece that "inaugurates an 'epistemological turn' which was to launch philosophy on the road to Kant."[57] It is not an exaggeration to say that "Locke intended his epistemology as a solution to the crisis of the fracturing of the moral and religious tradition of Europe at the beginnings of modernity,"[58] and we can add that Locke feared that science was not immune from such fracturing.

What these assessments ignore is that Locke's epistemic concerns do not lead him straightaway to accounts of justification, belief, and knowledge. It is only in the last book of the *Essay*, book IV, that Locke turns to the theory of knowledge. He first discusses psychology in book II, called "Of Ideas," and Locke's original plan was that the next book be devoted to human knowledge. But Locke changed his plans, and the reason for this is that "there is so close a connexion between *Ideas* and Words; and our abstract *Ideas*, and general Words, have so constant a relation one to another, that it is impossible to speak clearly and distinctly of our Knowledge, which all consists in verbal Propositions, without considering, first, the Nature, Use, and Signification of Language; which therefore must be the business of the next Book," namely book III, "Of Words" (*Essay*, II.xxxiii.19; also III.ix.21). Locke then postpones the discussion of the nature, extent, and degree of human knowledge to book IV.

One reason Locke believes that all human knowledge "consists in verbal Propositions" is that human beings "in their Thinking and Reasonings within themselves, make use of Words instead of *Ideas*" (*Essay*, IV.v.4). This occurs primarily when people have thoughts involving complex ideas, which unlike simple ideas are not received passively, but instead are products of the workmanship of the understanding (*Essay*, II.xii.1).[59] In a complex idea, various simple ideas are tied together to form a new idea. For Locke, all ideas of substances are complex ideas, as are ideas of space, duration, number, power, and causality.

Unfortunately, complex ideas are unstable (*Essay*, IV.v.4). Their composition varies over time for individuals and it varies even more so across different individuals. Like Hobbes before him, Locke relies on language to make up for this instability, although Locke turns Hobbes's suggestion into a theory.[60] Because of the instability of ideas, human beings "usually put the Name for the *Idea*" and "reflect on the *Names* themselves because they are more clear, certain, and distinct, and readier to occur to our Thoughts, than the pure *Ideas*: and so we make use of these Words instead of the *Ideas* themselves, even when we would meditate and reason within ourselves, and make tacit mental Propositions" (IV.v.4). Accordingly, words "interpose themselves so much between our Understandings, and the Truth," and they are like a "*Medium* through which visible Objects pass" and "impose upon our Understandings" (III.ix.21). When we think with language, we rely on ideas of words rather than ideas of objects.[61]

Since it is complex ideas that require the support of language, the arena where language plays a key role in cognition is classification.[62] Against traditional Aristotelian accounts of species and natural kinds, Locke maintains that "this whole *mystery* of *Genera* and *Species*, which make such a noise in the Schools . . . is nothing else but abstract *Ideas*, more or less comprehensive, with names annexed to them" (*Essay*, III.iii.9).[63]

Locke's epistemological turn, then, leads him to psychology, which takes him to language, which becomes so important in Locke's mind that he not only devotes the third book of the *Essay* to linguistic topics, but in the concluding paragraphs of the *Essay*, where he gives his overall "Division of the Sciences," Locke recommends that one of the three branches of science is "σημειωτική, or *the Doctrine of Signs*, the most usual whereof being Words" (*Essay*, IV.xxi.4).

Needless to say, for Locke, as for Bacon and Hobbes, language is also a source of problems. While some of these are simply due to "*wilful Faults and Neglects*, which Men are guilty of," others are caused by "the Imperfection that is naturally in Language" (*Essay*, III.x.1). "The very nature of Words," Locke writes, "makes it almost unavoidable, for many of them to be doubtful and uncertain in their signification" (III.ix.1). The reasons for this uncertainty are, first, that "Sounds have no natural connexion with our *Ideas*, but have all their signification from the arbitrary imposition of Men," and, second, the inherent diversity of ideas that words can signify (III.ix.4). With words being tied to ideas only by human convention and the ideas themselves variable and unstable, the meaning of language itself is a source of instability.

This is true not only in the case of morality, where Locke believes human ideas are the most unstable, but also in the natural sciences. The sciences have the advantage that, unlike in morality, ideas of substances are based on a standard, namely repeating patterns of coexisting simple ideas. But these simple ideas that coexist in a pattern are "very numerous" (even "almost infinite") and all of them have an "equal right to go into the complex specifick *Idea*" that human beings construct on the basis of this pattern or "archetype." Accordingly, "the complex *Ideas* of Substances, in Men using the same Name for them, will be very various; and so the significations of those names, very uncertain" (*Essay*, III.ix.13; also III.vi.44–47).

Paying attention to the imperfections of language will not only help solve many philosophical, scientific, legal, moral, and theological disputes, but it will also improve humanity, Locke believes (*Essay*, III.ix.21). But Locke's admonition to pay attention to the imperfections of language does not confront the deep criticism Descartes raises against Hobbes. If language is conventional, and reasoning relies on language, does it not follow, in Descartes's words, that the earth is the sky, or anything else you wish?

Leibniz

As in logic, Leibniz synthesizes the competing trends in seventeenth-century philosophy of language. Leibniz reintroduces the logical perspective on human language and reunites the philosophical study of logic, language, and mind. The role of logic, as we will see below, is to deal with precisely the problem Descartes raised against the role of conventional language in human reasoning. But this comes at a cost: language is conventional, but not thoroughly so.

Leibniz prefaces the *New Essays* with the remark that his and Locke's "systems are very different" because Locke's "is closer to Aristotle and mine to Plato."[64] One expression of this is that

Leibniz rejects Locke's view that human language is wholly conventional and arbitrary.[65] He disagrees with "the Scholastics and everyone else" who hold "that the significations of words are arbitrary," adding that "perhaps there are some artificial languages which are wholly chosen and completely arbitrary," but "known languages involve a mixture of chosen features and natural and chance features" (*New Ess.*, III.ii.1).

He mentions with some approval the popular seventeenth-century doctrine that there is a primitive or Adamic language of nature that is at the root of all languages. He specifically cites Jakob Böhme (1575–1624), the best known proponent of this doctrine, and writes that his writings "actually do have something fine and grand about them" (*New Ess.*, IV.xix.16).[66] Böhme held that all objects have inner essences that are expressed by unique sounds that make up the "language of nature, with which everything speaks according to its properties, and reveals itself."[67] Leibniz rejects the suggestion that any current natural language is the Adamic language of nature, but he does believe that current spoken languages "considered in themselves have something primitive about them" (III.ii.1).

Leibniz goes on to describe sound symbolism or the onomatopoeic features of natural languages, which he illustrates with the Latin *coaxare* and the German *quaken* for the sound of frogs (*New Ess.*, III.ii.1).[68] But Leibniz also has a more subtle and more durable idea in mind, namely that natural languages, when properly analyzed, express a "natural order of ideas" that is "common to angels and men and to intelligences in general" (*New Ess.*, III.i.5). This natural order of ideas is a combinatorial structure in which complex ideas are built out of a set of simple ideas that Leibniz calls "a kind of alphabet of human thought" (L 222). Moreover, this order is not "instituted or voluntary" and it is not subject to human control: "it is not within our discretion to put our ideas together as we see fit" (*New Ess.*, II.xxviii.3; III.iii.15). Although in ordinary thinking and speaking, human beings depart from this structure because they must follow their contingent interests, proper reflection and analysis can uncover it.

Accordingly, Leibniz concurs with Locke "that languages are the best mirror of the human mind, and that a precise analysis of the signification of words would tell us more than anything else about the operations of the understanding" (*New Ess.*, III.vii.6).[69] But

Locke and Leibniz are looking at very different images in this mirror. Whereas Locke looks for the psychological clues language offers, Leibniz sees the structure of natural languages as a source of information about the deductive structure of the mind's ideas. For Leibniz, even though natural languages depart from the natural order of ideas, they remain tied in significant ways to the mind's universal underlying logical structure. Even the argumentation of an orator with all its ornamentation has a "logical form (*forme logique*)," namely, content that is relevant to validity and that can be exhibited with the principles of logic (IV.xvii.4).

Leibniz is careful to distinguish the natural and logical structure of human ideas from the contingent psychological processes of the human understanding. Leibniz captures this difference by distinguishing thoughts from ideas. Many of Locke's claims about ideas, for example, that some ideas are arbitrary while others are not, hold true, Leibniz argues, only of "actual thoughts" or "noticeable thoughts." If we turn to ideas as "the very form or possibility of those thoughts" or as the "objects of thoughts," Leibniz continues, then Locke's account of the limits of the human understanding is wrong. The realm of ideas is the realm of "possibilities and necessities," and what is possible and necessary is "independent of our thinking" (*New Ess.*, III.v.3; III.iii.14).

This distinction plays a role in Leibniz's discussion of the nature of propositions. For Locke, "the *joining* or *separating* of signs . . . is what by another name, we call Proposition" (*Essay*, IV.v.2), and these signs are occurrent psychological entities: either occurrent thoughts or declarations made by a person on a particular occasion. Consequently, for Locke, truth is a property of mental or verbal entities. For Leibniz, however, a proposition is a structure of ideas and truth is a property of such structures, which "we have in common with God and the angels." A dialogue Leibniz writes in Paris about Hobbes's conventionalism expresses the same point: a truth of geometry "is true even if you were never to think of it" and "even before the geometricians had proved it or men observed it." Leibniz goes on to maintain that truth is a property of propositions, but not "all propositions are being thought" and consequently propositions are "possible thoughts" (L 182–83).

Leibniz now stands face-to-face with the difficulty Descartes raised against Hobbes. On the one hand, Leibniz argues that ideas are not conventional, and the truth of propositions is independent of actual human thought. On the other hand, he agrees with Hobbes that some human thinking is "blind" or "symbolic" in that it relies on conventional symbols.[70] Reasoning in arithmetic and geometry "presupposes some signs or characters" (L 183), and in the *New Essays* Leibniz states baldly that *all* abstract thoughts require "something sensible" and that human beings "cannot reason without symbols" (I.i.5; II.xxii.73). But if human beings can think about, say, arithmetic only with the help of symbols, and symbols are conventional, does it not follow that "truths depend on the human will?" (L 183). The conventionality of language, the reliance of reasoning on language, and the objectivity or unconventionality of truth appear to be in serious conflict.

The solution Leibniz offers is crucial to understanding his contribution to the philosophy of language. Leibniz claims that although different languages and artificial symbol systems can be used to reason, "there is in them a kind of complex mutual relation or order which fits the things . . . in their combination and inflection" (L 184). He adds:

> Though it varies, this order somehow corresponds in all languages. This fact gives me hope of escaping the difficulty. For although characters are arbitrary, their use and connection have something which is not arbitrary, namely a definite analogy between characters and things, and the relations which different characters expressing the same thing have to each other. This analogy or relation is the basis of truth. For the result is that whether we apply one set of characters or another, the products will be the same or equivalent or correspond analogously.
>
> (L 184)

Leibniz illustrates this point with the fact that both the decimal and the binary systems of arithmetic preserve truths about the natural numbers.

For Leibniz, conventional symbol systems can have a structure that is not conventional, and this structure can be the same across different systems of signs. Moreover, the similarity of structure need not be explicit in the apparent structure, e.g. the surface grammar of a language. All that is needed is that there be an equivalence or correspondence. Two structures that appear to be distinct can in fact correspond to each other because there is a precise one-to-one mapping between them. For example, as Leibniz points out, there is a correspondence between a circle and an ellipse because "any point whatever on the ellipse corresponds to some point on the circle according to a definite law," and it is on account of this that the ellipse can represent a circle (L 208).[71] In the same manner, languages can correspond to each other and, more importantly, to the natural order of ideas. For example, a sentence in a natural language can correspond to a sentence of the universal characteristic, or any other logical calculus, because there is a precise mapping between the two sentences.

For this reason, Leibniz devotes some effort to showing how the diverse grammatical forms of natural languages can correspond to the forms of a more rational symbol system.[72] The form this sort of grammatical analysis takes is the substitution of certain characters for others that are equivalent in use to the former.[73] Leibniz's idea is that by an orderly sequence of well-defined substitutions, a sentence of natural language can be transformed into a sentence of a more precise characteristic or calculus that reveals the logical form of the sentence of natural language. Then again, using successive substitutions within the characteristic or logical calculus, the sentence can be subjected to various logical operations and used in logical demonstrations.

In this manner Leibniz reintroduces the logical perspective on human language that was lost during the Renaissance. As we saw, a major reason for this loss was the wide gap between the apparent grammatical structure of natural languages as used in ordinary discourse and the languages of traditional formal logic. Leibniz aimed to bridge this gap by rejecting the assumption that natural language's logical form is identical to its contingent surface grammatical structure.[74]

So while Locke found little or no room for logic in his account of mind and language, Leibniz locates logical order in the abstract structure common to mind and language. One might say that what Locke missed by taking into account only *actual* human thought and speech, Leibniz recognized by trying to capture all that *could* be said and thought. By looking for an account of all possible judgments, Leibniz added logic to the union Locke had already forged between philosophy, psychology, and the study of language. Leibniz's vision overcomes the disparities between formal logic and ordinary language and preserves the demands of both truth and the conventionality of human language and thought. This reconciliation of the strict demands of truth and logic with commonplace and conventional human practice bears witness to the grandeur and optimism of seventeenth-century philosophy.

NOTES

1 Kneale and Kneale 1962, p. 345; also p. 298.
2 Ibid., p. 320.
3 Kretzmann 1967, p. 379; also Kretzmann 1968.
4 Ashworth 1974, pp. 16–17; Freedman 1984, pp. 86–87; Risse 1964, vol. II, pp. 516–17; Nuchelmans 1998, p. 104.
5 Kneale and Kneale 1962, p. 234; Peter of Spain 1972; Ashworth 1974, p. 2.
6 Ashworth 1988, p. 143.
7 Ashworth 1974, pp. 19–20 and 1988, p. 163; Nuchelmans 1998, p. 103.
8 Kneale and Kneale 1962, p. 310.
9 Ashworth 1988, pp. 152–53; Jardine 1988, p. 181; Mundt 1994, pp. 108–17.
10 Agricola 1992, p. 212, also p. 228. Subsequent parenthetical numerals refer to pages in this text.
11 See Ong 1983, p. 102.
12 It also earned him a royal decree in 1544 forbidding him to teach. The decree was canceled in 1547, but he was murdered during the St. Bartholomew's Day Massacre of 1572, during which 3,000 Protestants were killed in Paris.
13 Ramus 1964, p. 61. Subsequent parenthetical numerals refer to pages in this text.
14 Ong 1983, pp. 232–39; Ashworth 1974, p. 14.
15 Ong 1983, pp. 227–28; Copenhaver and Schmitt 1992, p. 235.
16 Copenhaver and Schmitt 1992, p. 238.
17 Ramus also established and funded a chair in mathematics at the Collège Royal de France.
18 Mahoney 1975, p. 289.
19 Copenhaver and Schmitt 1992, p. 236.
20 There is some controversy about how much influence Ramus had on Bacon, who comments both favorably and unfavorably on Ramus. See Rossi 1960; Jardine 1974; Ong 1983, pp. 302–4; Pérez-Ramos 1988, p. 107; Zagorin 1998, pp. 54–57; Walton 1999, p. 294; Gaukroger 2001, p. 43.

21 Bacon 2000, p. 16.
22 Ibid., p. 28.
23 Gaukroger argues that Bacon aims to "transform the epistemological activity of the philosopher from something essentially individual to something essentially communal" (2001, p. 5). This is an important corrective to our understanding of Bacon and helps explain his interest in language, but it is also true that for Bacon, social interaction is a source of errors, and that human beings need forms of reasoning that adhere to nature, not convention.
24 Urbach 1987, p. 172.
25 Broad 1926, p. 57.
26 Gaukroger 2001, p. 153.
27 Broad 1926, pp. 1, 64; also Urbach 1987, p. 185.
28 L 471, n. 2.
29 Couturat 1901, pp. 73–74, n. 4; also Ashworth 1974, pp. 17–18; Krolzik 1990–92; Mates 1986, pp. 211–12.
30 Leibniz 1966, pp. 4–5.
31 Ibid., p. 26.
32 Ibid., pp. 122–44.
33 Ibid., p. 11; L 654, 221.
34 The seventeenth century was rife with projects for developing unambiguous universal characters or languages whose syntactic structure closely tracked semantic content. A paradigm example is John Wilkins's *Essay towards a Real Character, and a Philosophical Language* (1668), in which he builds his language out of forty basic categories, each assigned to a unique pair of consonants and vowels for speech and a unique inscription for writing. Others who contributed or promoted universal language projects include Cave Beck (1623–1706?), George Dalgarno (1626?–87), Jan Amos Komensky (1592–1670), Francis Lodwick (1619–94), and Marin Mersenne (1588–1648). See Rossi 1960; Knowlson 1975; Slaughter 1982; Poole 2003; Maat 2004.
35 Frege 1879, pp. v–vi.
36 See Rutherford 1995b, p. 231.
37 Hobbes 1839, vol. I, p. 3.
38 Frege 1980, p. 9.
39 Leibniz 1973, pp. 97–98; L 661; AG 71, 193; *Discourse*, §13 (AG 46); *New Ess.*, III.v.3. Also Lewis 1918; Carnap 1956, p. 10; Mates 1972 and 1986, pp. 69–73; Adams 1994, pp. 46–50.
40 Leibniz 1903, pp. 259; 1966, p. 122; also 1966, pp. 34, 53.
41 The theorem appears in both Frege's *Begriffsschrift* and Whitehead and Russell's *Principia Mathematica* (1997, p. 23).

42 Frege 1960, p. 64; Quine 1980, p. 27. See Ishiguro 1990, pp. 17–43, who argues that for Leibniz this was a principle defining the identity of concepts, not the synonymy of expressions.
43 See Couturat 1901; Keynes 1921; Carnap 1950; Hacking 1975; Daston 1988.
44 Copenhaver and Schmitt 1992, p. 351.
45 Valla 1962, vol. I, p. 679.
46 Vives 1782–90, vol. III, pp. 41, 53.
47 Bacon 2000, p. 16.
48 Ibid., pp. 17–18.
49 Bacon 1973, p. 134.
50 *De corpore*, I.ii.1 (1839, vol. I, p. 13)
51 This appears to be a departure from Hobbes's earlier position in *De corpore*, according to which there clearly is such a thing as reasoning "in our silent thoughts, without the use of words" (I.i.3) (Hobbes 1839, vol. I, p. 3). On this tension in Hobbes, see Losonsky 1993a.
52 Arnauld and Lancelot 1975, pp. 41, 65–68.
53 Arnauld and Nicole 1996, p. 23. Arnauld and Nicole go on to claim that because in communication we must associate ideas and words, "this habit is so strong that even when we think to ourselves, things are presented to the mind only in the words in which we usually clothe them in speaking to others" (pp. 23–24). This, however, is treated only as a habit, and the conclusion they draw is that they need to examine how ideas and words are joined, and not how words are presented to the mind and play a role in reasoning.
54 Ibid., p. 26.
55 Ibid., p. 28. Another Cartesian work that is devoted primarily to language is Géraud de Cordemoy's *Discours physique de la parole* (*A Philosophical Discourse concerning Speech*) (1668). Cordemoy aims to examine speech more closely in order to better understand which aspects of language use can be attributed to the body alone and which require a rational soul.
56 Kretzmann 1968, p. 379.
57 Jolley 1999, p. 14.
58 Wolterstorff 1996, p. 227.
59 See Losonsky 1989.
60 On the relation between Locke and Hobbes, see Rogers 1988.
61 Losonsky 2007.
62 Compare Jolley 1999, who writes: "Locke's major theses concerning the metaphysics and epistemology of classification can be understood independently of his teachings about language" (p. 162; also see p. 144).
63 See Guyer 1994, p. 116.

64 Leibniz 1981, p. 47.
65 Aarsleff 1982, p. 42.
66 On Leibniz and Böhme, see Aarsleff 1982, pp. 42–83; Losonsky 1992 and 1993b.
67 Böhme 1956, vol. VI, p. 4; also 1963, vol. I, pp. 58–59, 208. In *Academiarum Examen, or the Examination of the Academies* (1653), the 'Behemist' John Webster (1610–82) suggests that the language of nature is the universal characteristic that Wilkins and others were trying to construct. Wilkins and the mathematician Seth Ward (1617–89) responded in *Vindiciae academiarum* (1654), arguing against the possibility of a language of nature and defending artificial universal language projects. See Debus 1970; Aarsleff 1982, p. 262; Losonsky 2001, pp. 105–10.
68 Also see Leibniz 1903, pp. 151–52.
69 The mirror metaphor also opens Leibniz's posthumously published work *Unvorgreifliche Gedanken, betreffend die Aushebung und Verbesserung der teutschen Sprache* ("Unassuming Thoughts concerning the Practice and Improvement of the German Language"): "It is known that language is the mirror of the understanding," and when understanding flourishes, so does the use of language (Leibniz 1838–40, p. 449).
70 L 292; *New Ess.*, III.i.2. On the constitutive role of symbols in reasoning in Leibniz's philosophy, see Dascal 1987; Losonsky 2001, pp. 160–63, 171–73.
71 For Leibniz, "that is said to express a thing in which there are relations which correspond to the relations of the thing expressed" (L 207). Also see *Theod.*, §357 and *New Ess.*, II.viii.13.
72 Rutherford 1995b, pp. 249–50.
73 Leibniz 1903, p. 351.
74 On the distinction between surface and underlying form in Leibniz, see Brekle 1971 and Dascal 1987, pp. 125–44.

7 The passions and the good life

Introducing his *Essay on the Nature and Conduct of the Passions and Affections*, which was published in 1728, Francis Hutcheson remarked that the conclusions he was about to defend were none the worse for having been "taught and propagated by the best men of all ages."[1] Among the views that writers such as Hutcheson inherited were various images of the good life, some handed down from Roman antiquity,[2] some derived from Christianity, and some, such as Machiavelli's account of princely *virtù*,[3] forged in comparatively recent times. While the most general of these interpretations offer a picture of the good life for humanity, a blueprint of the patterns of feeling and action to which all men (and in some cases arguably all women) should aspire, others are explicitly adjusted to persons of a particular gender, class, or profession, and to individuals who occupy several roles at once. Handbooks such as Cicero's *De officiis* not only specify what is involved in being a good father, son, husband, or magistrate, but also indicate how the demands imposed by these relationships can be reconciled.[4] Living virtuously is therefore partly a matter of experiencing passions that are held to be appropriate to one's station and its duties, and ideally consists in possessing them to just the right degree. Furthermore, because any one role is defined in relation to others (that of a ruler in relation to that of a citizen, or that of a servant in relation to a master), the demands of a particular office are implicitly both social and political. With few exceptions, good lives are conceived as contributing to a cooperative existence within an organized community, and virtuous individuals are therefore expected to be emotionally capable of engaging in a range of common projects.

Although it was generally accepted that particular patterns of feeling help to define specific forms of the good life, the exact nature of these patterns was a much more contentious issue, and authority to pronounce on it was shared between a number of traditions, each with its own internal disputes and complexities. From classical times, medical specialists had been regarded as experts on the causes and control of the affects, and they retained this role throughout the early modern era. While novel accounts of human physiology and psychology emerged within this period, many of these innovations drew on long-established organizing principles such as the theory of the four humors, so that learned doctors retained much of their established power to explicate the bodily character of the passions and specify which are healthy, and which are pathological.[5]

At the same time, Christian theologians of various denominations were authorized to determine what affective dispositions characterize a truly religious existence. In this arena, the seventeenth century inherited a dispute bequeathed by the Reformation between Roman Catholic theologians who distinguished the religious offices of ordinary people from those of individuals who had dedicated themselves to religion, and some Protestants who argued that everyone should aspire to the more taxing standards formerly applied solely to priests and members of religious orders. The question of how far a good life must be dominated by affects such as humility and piety, and the manner in which these affects should be expressed, exercised both religious and political communities, and in some cases generated disagreements that contributed to war.

Finally, it was taken to be part of the office of the philosopher to explain what part the passions could play in the quest for virtue and wisdom. The idea that virtue depends on self-knowledge, which in turn includes an understanding of one's passions, had an ancient lineage. But the precise nature of the knowledge involved was hotly disputed, as was the kind of life it vindicated. One dimension of this disagreement, which became increasingly prominent in the course of the seventeenth century, concerned the relationship between ethical questions about virtue and natural philosophy. For a philosopher-scientist such as Descartes, it was important to show how a correct grasp of physics could yield insights into the operation and control of the passions, and could thus reveal how physics was relevant to an understanding of the good life.[6] However, some of his near contemporaries, among whom Locke is a good example, remained unconvinced by this approach.[7] We are far too ignorant, they claimed, about the workings of our own bodies and general physical principles to see how these bear on the project of living virtuously, but we are nevertheless capable of arriving at knowledge of ourselves and the good life by reflective means.

Although the ethical dimension of the passions continued to be explored in distinct ways within each of these traditions – medical, theological, and philosophical – they nevertheless drew on a shared bundle of classical and medieval theories, which gave rise to a common sense of the problems to be addressed. Foremost among these was the question of whether the passions are morally good or bad, and thus the extent to which virtuous people need to transcend or control them. While there was no generally agreed answer, it was widely accepted that the passions at least sometimes need to be modified or redirected, and this conviction gave rise to a second problem: how is this control to be achieved? Here various responses were offered. Perhaps the most influential was the view that the passions can be controlled by reason, but this answer in turn led people to ask how far reason is capable of modifying the affects. If its power is relatively limited, as many theorists maintained, perhaps it is more fruitful to use one passion to modify another. The opposition between reason and passion around which this debate was organized dominated discussion throughout the early modern period, but in the course of the seventeenth century it began to be comprehensively reexamined. As a result, the notion of a passion was progressively reconfigured, and accounts of the psychological conditions on which virtue depended acquired an even greater complexity.

States that we now describe as emotions, such as love, hatred, grief, or joy, were usually classified by seventeenth-century writers as passions (in Latin *passiones* or *perturbationes*) or as affects (in Latin *affectiones*), terms that were often treated as interchangeable.[8] In using the word 'passion,' authors alluded to a distinction between passion and action that had played a central part in Greek and Roman philosophy and continued to be debated. For example, Hobbes, Descartes, and Malebranche are among a large group of thinkers who engaged with Aristotle's view that, when one body brings about a change in a second, as when a stove warms someone's hand, the first is active and the second passive. The stove is said to act when it warms the hand, while the hand has something done to it when it is warmed.[9] To undergo a passion is therefore to be changed by an external object or state of affairs, and for early modern writers this remained a defining feature of a passion or affect. Whenever we experience joy, grief, or hope we are acted on by something external, and are in this sense passive. As a result, passions were understood, both etymologically and metaphysically, as responses to the way that things impinge upon us from outside, and this idea was taken up in a string of metaphors that represent us as blown about, moved, weighed down, or swept away by passion.[10]

The capacity to experience affects is therefore a capacity to respond to the world, above all those features of it that we can see, hear, smell, touch, or taste. It is true, as Locke in particular pointed out, that some passions do not seem to fall into these categories; for example, one might be disgusted or attracted by something abstract, such as a particular conception of the good life.[11] Nevertheless, it was generally agreed that the most powerful affects are responses to sensory experiences, and that these are usually stronger than those caused by recollections of such experiences, or fantasies about them. As Malebranche remarks, "the soul is more occupied by a simple pinprick than by lofty speculations, and the pleasures and ills of this world make far more of an impression on it than the dreadful pains or infinite pleasures of eternity."[12] This orientation to the sensible world enables the passions to fulfill their function, which is to help us survive. By prompting us to avoid situations that strike us as harmful, as when fear moves us to flee, and to seek out situations that we view as beneficial, as when hope encourages us to put up with hardship, the affects make us alive to the dangers and benefits that the world presents. Even before we are born, many early modern theorists believed, we are capable of experiencing certain primitive passions which may shape our subsequent development;[13] and these most basic forms of response are rapidly extended and modified by our postnatal experience, as we not only learn what to love and what to be afraid of, but also develop the ability to experience a wider repertoire of affects. Adults, unlike neonates or very small children, are capable of feeling the difference between benevolence and compassion, or shame and guilt, and will often experience complex blends of passions as they respond to multifaceted situations. Moreover, because an individual's affects are shaped by a range of factors such as their bodily constitution, history, and education, each person develops a passionate character of their own which is in a constant process of change. Although two individuals who have grown up in the same culture or family may have more passionate dispositions in common than a pair of strangers, and although early modern writers never tire of contrasting the passionate tempers of people of different nationalities, they nevertheless insist that each individual responds affectively to the world in their own particular way.

By enabling us to apprehend states of affairs as broadly beneficial or harmful, or as a mixture of both, our affects give normative color to our sensory experience and provide the basis of our capacity to make evaluative distinctions. This being so, should we not view them with admiration and gratitude? Some seventeenth-century writers do indeed praise them on these grounds, admiring their usefulness and wondering at a God who has devised such intricate survival mechanisms;[14] but most authors regard them with deep suspicion and ambivalence. While they acknowledge that we could not manage without affects or some comparable form of responsiveness, they nevertheless emphasize that they provide only a crude moral compass which often leads us astray.

The inaccuracy and unreliability of the evaluations contained in our passions is said to stem from three loosely connected aspects of the way they focus on the here and now. First, as we have already seen, they fix on the sensible properties of the world at the expense of its other features; for example, the fact that a man looks frightening to me is likely to be enough to make me fear him, even if he in fact poses no threat. At the same time, passions are held to be intrinsically forceful and impetuous, so that there is something commanding about my fear that prevents me from questioning it. Finally, our passions tend to be directed toward our present experiences, rather than to the past or future, so that the pleasures of the moment can obliterate prudent fears about the morrow, just as a present sadness can drive out the memory of past joys.[15] Commanding and inconstant as they are, our affects prompt us to act in ways that are far from judicious or virtuous, and our inability to control them places us at the mercy of a part of ourselves that is both morally and metaphysically doubtful. In extreme cases, people who act on their passions are self-destructive and dangerous to others, and even individuals whose affects are comparatively moderate will generally be prey to certain passionate impulses that threaten their virtue and disrupt the harmony of their social relationships.

Pessimism about the ethical value of the passions pervades many genres of early modern writing, and gains particularly strong support from Platonist and Stoic traditions, as well as from the Christian doctrine of the Fall. Malebranche, for instance, reiterates the Augustinian view that, before Adam and Eve were expelled from the Garden of Eden, their passions were forceful enough to protect them from harm but not so strong as to distract them from the one true good, namely God.[16] It is part of humanity's punishment for original sin that our passions are now much stronger and more compelling than they were, so that any attempt to lead a good life is an unremitting struggle, and the task of overcoming or counter-acting our affects is a central aspect of any good life. Underlying this view is the assumption that the capacity to live well rests on an ability to conform to certain norms, which in turn requires a considerable degree of self-discipline. The inconstancy of the passions, combined with their forcefulness and impetuousness, therefore makes them an obstacle to virtue by undermining the steadfastness that is one of its essential characteristics. Moreover, the ability to live virtuously is, ideally speaking, the ability consistently to do the right thing, not just for oneself but for everyone concerned. In deciding how to act, a virtuous person must therefore take account of a range of interests, claims, and circumstances, and where these are complicated, must be capable of adjudicating between them. Once again, the passions are held to stand in the way of this process by giving us a partial and misleading conception of the states of affairs we encounter. Because one's affective responses answer to one's own character and experience, they embody an individual viewpoint; and although this need not be narrowly self-interested, it lacks the distance that is often taken to characterize virtuous judgments. My passions tell me, for example, what I find lovable or admirable in a particular situation, rather than assessing it from the impersonal position that Adam Smith would later describe as that of the impartial spectator.[17] They thus lack an essential kind of insight on which a good life depends.

If the passions are ethically wanting, as this account suggests, they need to be controlled or manipulated. But how can this be done? What therapeutic techniques can be used to modify our passionate natures and bring them in line with virtue?[18] Taking up another classical commonplace, many writers based their answers, as we have seen, on the assumption that the most powerful means of modifying our affects is to make use of our capacity to reason. They then went on to explore the operations that purportedly enabled reason to keep the passions in check. Conceiving of it as a kind of force opposed to, and potentially stronger than, the passions, they tended to interpret reason's power as simultaneously physical, epistemological, and psychological. Descartes's *Passions of the Soul* contains an influential version of the first of these approaches. Reasoning, Descartes argues, gives rise to volitions, which have physical effects that are sometimes capable of countering the bodily motions that constitute passions. When one wills oneself to act in a particular way, one creates a flow of animal spirits within the body, and when these are forceful enough to repulse a contrary, passionate flow, the passion in question gives way to the volition.[19] Although passions can be too strong for the will to control, so that the technique is not always successful, volitions grounded on rational ethical judgments can contain the affects and play a part in enabling us to live virtuously.

If this mechanism is to work, rational judgments must produce strong volitions, and in explaining how they do so Descartes relies on the further and popular assumption that there is something uniquely epistemologically compelling about the fruits of reasoning. In his version of this argument, the step-by-step patterns of inference on which clear and distinct ideas are grounded endow them with certainty, and our grasp of their epistemological status in turn enables them to function as a counterweight to the judgments embodied in passions. When one possesses a clear and distinct idea, it is difficult to ignore it or fail to take it into account, and these qualities are often reflected in the strength of the volitions to which it gives rise. Once again, the process is not foolproof, and one can lose such rational insights as one has gained. But a person whose ethical judgments are rationally grounded is nevertheless relatively well equipped to control their deviant passions. Furthermore, according to a widespread psychological view, they will be assisted by the fact that reasoning in itself is exceptionally pleasurable.[20] Just as our perceptions of sensible objects are bound up with passion, so the processes of rational thought give rise to a kind of nonpassionate joy capable of offsetting and counteracting it. Reason is thus endowed with various kinds of force that help to explain how it can impose order on the unruly affects, either by opposing unvirtuous feelings and the actions they engender, or by endorsing and encouraging passions that are in tune with the good life.

This conception of the human soul as divided between reason and passion, the first indicative of the true self and the second of external invasion, continued to dominate much seventeenth-century philosophy. However, it was always embedded in a debate about how far such subjection was ethically desirable. At one end of the spectrum, writers indebted to Stoicism viewed the passions as erroneous judgments, and argued that reason ought in principle to transcend them completely. People who progressively overcome their passions by cultivating a rational and correct understanding of the world are gradually released from the emotional ups and downs of a passionate life, and come to experience a state of joyful tranquility or *ataraxia*. A taste of this kind of joy creates a desire to sustain it by extending one's understanding still further, and urged on by these two intellectual emotions, joy and desire, the individual gradually achieves a perspective from which the delights and sorrows of their previous existence appear insignificant. Virtue thus consists in understanding, and moral perfection lies in a kind of indifference or insensibility to events that might normally be expected to provoke such passions as grief, hope, or sadness.[21]

Even the most rigorous early modern neo-Stoics treated this ethical view as an ideal to be aspired to rather than a condition that can fully be achieved, and only claimed that we should try to transcend the passions as far as possible. Nevertheless, many of their opponents vehemently repudiated this position, on the grounds that a person who fails to feel sorrow, anger, or fear in the face of catastrophe is a monster rather than a sage, a block rather than a human being.[22] This powerful criticism was widely accepted; but a number of authors continued to be attracted by the Stoic view that reasoning generates a distinct form of emotional engagement which can modify and sometimes extinguish passion. Writers such as Descartes and Spinoza, who in different ways regard the passions as bodily phenomena that are an ineradicable and morally necessary part of human life,[23] write positively about the emotional satisfaction and control that reasoning generates. There are therefore traces of Stoicism in the Cartesian contention that the pleasure we derive from understanding encourages us to form rational judgments that reveal the theoretical and practical limitations of our passions. And the same is true of the Spinozistic claim that, although the passions are always with us, a philosophical understanding of ourselves and the world both transcends them and provides ways of controlling passions, so that reasoning reduces their power to monopolize our feelings and determine our actions.[24]

Unconvinced of the benefits of the drastic therapy recommended by the Stoics, many philosophers adhered to the broadly Aristotelian view that the passions form an integral part of a good life. A virtuous person will experience the whole range of passions, positive and negative, but the objects and intensity of their feelings will always be appropriate; their anger will always be righteous, their admiration will never shade over into adulation, their generosity will be at just the right pitch. Reasoning can help us to attain this condition by teaching us what virtue consists in and what we should be aiming for, and can also give us some critical distance on our passions. As we learn what the world is really like, we come to appreciate the shortsightedness and partiality inherent in the affects, and this itself can change us. To take a simple case, once I know that the species of spider that terrifies me is in fact harmless, I may feel less afraid. Since our passions are molded by our understanding of general truths, as well as by our individual, embodied experience, rationally grounded knowledge may alter our aspirations so that goals which used to attract us cease to do so, and feelings by which we used to set great store cease to be satisfying. Part of the attraction of this approach is that it represents good lives as continuous with less good ones, and makes virtue correspondingly easier to imagine. Moral improvement is held to consist in refining and redirecting the affects with which ordinary people are already acquainted, rather than in acquiring unfamiliar intellectual emotions, and this also preserves a diverse emotional landscape of sorrows as well as joys. This analysis consequently claimed a wide range of adherents, who continued to explore it in detail throughout the seventeenth and eighteenth centuries, and defended it against a variety of criticisms.

Some of the most straightforward objections to their stance emphasized the sheer difficulty of getting individuals and communities to bring their affects under rational control, and introduced a note of pessimism about the extent to which reason can in fact subdue the passions. In the first place, as some skeptical writers pointed out, it is useless to pretend that reasoning is especially pleasurable and contains its own affective source of motivation. The truth is that it is exceptionally arduous, and also grates on the imagination, so that most people are repelled by what Philip Sidney describes as its "thorny arguments" and "base rule."[25] It is therefore a mistake to think that the art of demonstration can provide a practical counterweight to antisocial passions, and can induce people of ordinary talents to cultivate the kind of understanding that promotes virtue.

One might feel, as many early modern philosophers did, that this account exaggerates the difficulty of learning to be rational. But even if reasoning is not as unattractive as it suggests, the objection points to a further issue about the extent to which the capacity to control the passions depends on education, and can therefore only be attained by a small and predominantly male elite. In the face of a general consensus that uneducated people are prone to antisocial passions (manifested, for example, in some of Spinoza's remarks about the *vulgus* or crowd)[26] and that part of the point of education is to correct a range of natural flaws (as explained, for instance, by Francis Bacon in his analysis of the idols),[27] it made sense to consider how far reasoning is in practice capable of preventing people's affects from disrupting social and political life.

Confronted by the claim that appeals to reason are largely useless, even authors who held a dark view of the passions sometimes protested that everyone possesses some ability to think critically about their affects. Hobbes, for example, takes humans to be ravenous for the kinds of power that will guarantee their security,[28] but nevertheless argues in *De cive* that everyone has calmer moments in which the process of using rational judgment to modify the passions can at least get started. As he emphasizes, the ability to grasp the laws or theorems that specify the nature of the good life "teaches good manners or virtues" by altering our desires and the affects associated with them.[29] To a great extent, this type of view dominated seventeenth-century debates about the efficacy of reasoning and marginalized the doubts of those who suspected that its practical impact would normally be negligible. However, it existed alongside theologically grounded forms of skepticism, which viewed reason as inefficacious, and recommended the use of some extra-rational source of knowledge as the sole means of arriving at a true understanding of the good. An enormously influential version of this stance had been articulated by Luther, who argued that, since reason cannot enlighten us as to how God wishes us to act, the only way to attain virtue is to cultivate a passive faith in the deity, who may then grace individuals with a kind of unmerited righteousness. Righteousness therefore replaces virtue as the ideal to be striven for, and a conception of the good life as the fruit of an active process of learning and self-discipline gives way to the idea that one must practice an unreasoning faith in the hope that God will instill in us the grace that enables us to be saved.[30]

This denigration of reason remained a central theme of early modern Protestantism, and also took hold among a group of French Catholic writers influenced by the work of Cornelius Jansen.[31] According to the greatest of the Jansenists, Blaise Pascal, the Fall has left human beings in a flawed condition. On the one hand, we are capable of reasoning and can comprehend the advantages of the certainty it promises to supply. On the other hand, it is a delusion to believe that reasoning can yield knowledge of the good. We therefore find ourselves torn between a yearning for a knowledge of virtue, and a recognition that it is beyond us. "We perceive an image of the truth and possess nothing but falsehood, being equally incapable of absolute ignorance and certain knowledge; so obvious is it that we once enjoyed a degree of perfection from which we have unhappily fallen."[32] The only means of escaping from this dilemma is to submit to faith, recognizing that God will help individuals who set themselves to believe the central truths of the Christian religion by giving them an overwhelming desire to love him and lead a pious life, and that this in turn will enable them to conform to the laws of Christian morality that constitute the true good. Pascal acknowledges that the passions are destructive of both reason and piety, but he interprets the conviction that we can use reason to quash them as one aspect of an undue pride and arrogance that is itself a consequence of original sin. Our busy attempts to reason our way to ethical truths and a moral way of life are self-defeating, because they divert us from the centrality of faith, and ensure that our efforts to conform to the good are frustrated.[33] Reason, then, does not help us to control the passions and live well; instead it distracts us from cultivating the piety and submissiveness that are the only means to virtue.

Pascal's suggestion that humans can move in the direction of virtue by fostering a particular set of affects draws on a further deeply entrenched view: that the best way to deal with the passions is to use one to control another. The very fact that we experience such a range of affects is, so some writers suggest, evidence of God's benevolent intention to help us toward virtue. As Jean-François Senault explains, "Thou employest fear to take off a covetous man from those perishable riches which possess him; thou makest a holy use of despair to withdraw from the world a courtier, whose youth has been misemployed in the service of some prince; thou makest an admirable use of disdain to extinguish therewith a lover's flames, who is enslaved by a proud beauty."[34] Whether or not they were persuaded by this interpretation of our affective constitutions, early modern authors working in a wide range of genres explored the techniques and principles that could be used to modify morally deviant passions. We see this at a theoretical level in a work such as Spinoza's *Ethics*, which sets out the central psychological principles around which the passions are purportedly organized, and charts the relations between the operations of sympathy (as when exposure to someone else's sadness makes me sad), of animosity (as when I compete with you for someone else's love), and of association (as when your resemblance to someone I love makes me feel love for you as well).[35] An understanding of these causal relationships can help us to manipulate our own and other's affects, and enable us to develop techniques for restraining or modifying them, for instance by formulating and appealing to maxims.[36] Descartes compares this approach with training dogs, thus reminding his readers that modifying a passion is a matter of creating a bodily change,[37] and goes on to describe some of the indirect ways in which soldiers, for example, can learn to suppress fear and replace it with determination and hope. While one cannot will oneself to feel brave, he points out, one can discover through experience that certain actions have the effect of bolstering one's courage, and can train oneself to perform them before a battle.[38] This example, interpolated in a theoretical treatise, focuses on one of a large number of types of disciplinary practice that made up the fabric of ordinary life, some of which were formalized in manuals of religious meditation,[39] in rules for giving sermons,[40] in books of advice to courtiers and gentlemen,[41] in instructions for educating children,[42] and so on. In all these *genres* we find more or less explicit analysis of bodily and psychological procedures by which the passions can be molded, and individuals with the virtuous dispositions required by specific offices created.[43]

Few commentators denied that this approach to the problem of controlling the passions was capable of bringing about moral improvement, and was sometimes sufficient to induce people to act well. For instance, although the soldiers of Descartes's example might fail to make themselves utterly proof against fear and cowardice, they might nevertheless generate enough courage to fight valiantly in all the battles they encountered. But in order to use disciplinary techniques in the service of virtue, one obviously had to know what passionate dispositions a good life requires, and here many theorists continued to appeal to reason. Only reasoning, they believed, could tell one what to aim for, though once this goal had been specified, practical experiment and training of the passions could help one to achieve it. This hybrid view remained extremely common, but in the course of the seventeenth century the fundamental opposition between reason and passion on which it rests was subjected to a profound challenge, which began to alter the terms of philosophical debate and to open up a series of fresh questions about the relation between virtue and the affects.

The initial steps in this innovative line of argument can be traced to the work of Thomas Hobbes, and particularly to *Leviathan* where, rather than conceding in traditional style that there are two sources of human motivation, passion and reason, Hobbes argues that there is only one. The passions, he claims, alone motivate us to act, since our ability to reason depends on the strength of our passionate desire for various forms of power, such as wealth, knowledge, or honor. A strong and steady desire for power motivates us to invest our energy in working out how to get it by making distinctions, formulating definitions, and carefully considering what follows from them. Taken together, these capacities produce what Hobbes calls judgment, so that a person's capacity for judgment rests ultimately on their passionate temperament.[44] This argument contains two crucial claims. First, the only force that moves us to reason is desire, and there is nothing special about the definitions and inferences of which reasoning consists that enables them to hold our attention. Secondly, since the process of reasoning does not induce a distinct kind of feeling, such as the intellectual pleasure to which some philosophers appealed, our interest in it varies with our passions. Our natural inclination to preserve ourselves by maintaining or increasing our power includes a disposition to find out about causes and effects, which manifests itself in the passion of curiosity, and this can be exercised with more or less sophistication.[45] While everyone is at least a little curious and possesses a degree of what Hobbes calls prudence, or the ability to learn about causes and effects from experience, certain individuals have a particularly strong desire for power which prompts them to develop a more extensive and reliable grasp of causal relations. Reasoning is thus an enhanced version of a universal inclination to cultivate prudence, and is rooted in the same passionate desire for power. Rather than standing over against the passions, it depends on them; and when the ends we desire to achieve are aggressive and antisocial, as Hobbes believes they often are, reason does not struggle against them, but fights, so to speak, on their side.

If reason is inert, in the sense that rational inferences do not themselves motivate us, it cannot be the most active and godlike of our capacities, or the ultimate means by which we acquire and exercise control over ourselves and the world. But by dispensing with these traditional views, Hobbes places himself in a position that many of his contemporaries found deeply troubling, above all because of its ethical implications. If reasoning only serves our passions, and if our passions are often tumultuous and misguided, how are we to live well? Hobbes's own answer again harks back to the affective elements in human nature. The strongest of human desires, he claims, is the desire to live in a condition where one is not plagued by fears of insecurity, and the force of this passion regularly prompts us to reason our way to the conclusion that the best way to gain safety is to try to live peacefully with others. Since this is in fact the greatest good for human beings, a good life must be one devoted to a cooperative quest for peace, and our passion-led inferences are likely to lead us to this conclusion. Unfortunately, this argument seemed to many of Hobbes's readers to contain a loophole. If our strongest passions lead us to pursue our own security, they objected, and if the way to attain security is (at least in some circumstances) to attack others, what stands in the way of the conclusion that unprovoked aggression may be an element of a good life?[46]

The problems posed by Hobbes's work gave fresh impetus to inquiries into the relation between the passions and virtue. His claim that our affects lead us to behave in ways that are competitive and antisocial, and that reason has no independent power to prevent this outcome, were subjected to a variety of criticisms. One way to deal with the first of these contentions was to deny the premise and insist that humans are not so bad after all. According to the Earl of Shaftesbury, for instance, there is no need to assume that passionate dispositions which emerge in desperate circumstances – "under monstrous visages of dragons, leviathans, and I know not what devouring entities" – are always dominant, and thus that human beings are invariably driven by aggressive desires.[47] One should also acknowledge the role of such affects as love and benevolence, which move us to take pleasure in the happiness of others, and to behave in the broadly cooperative fashion usually held to be virtuous.[48] This line of response helped to spark off a lively eighteenth-century debate as to whether or not humans are naturally sociable, in the course of which Shaftesbury's view was subjected to a number of refinements and criticisms. Among its most enthusiastic opponents was Bernard Mandeville, who regarded self-interest as the driving force behind all human action.[49] And among its most enthusiastic supporters was Francis Hutcheson, who developed an elaborate account of the mental capacities that incline and encourage us to live virtuously.

To understand human nature adequately, Hutcheson proposed, we need to recognize that, in addition to the feelings of pleasure and pain produced by the five external senses, humans also experience several further kinds of sensation. They take a specific form of pleasure in objects that combine variety and uniformity in such a way as to be beautiful; and they derive three additional types of pleasure from human characters and actions. A public sense causes us to gain satisfaction from other people's pleasure, and to feel dissatisfaction at their distress; a moral sense prompts us to take pleasure in states of mind intended to promote happiness or diminish pain; and a sense of honor inclines us to feel pleased when other people express their gratitude for our morally good actions.[50] Together, these three senses give rise to our conception of the good, and cause us to experience desires and aversions for the objects to which they are directed. Hutcheson further argues that benevolence, the inclination to increase the happiness of others that constitutes our moral sense, is an instinct "antecedent to all reason from interest."[51] Since it underpins a range of sociable affections, humans are naturally disposed to be concerned for one another's happiness, and to gain pleasure from satisfying each other's desires.

Although Hutcheson does not deny that people are subject to selfish or antisocial impulses, his remapping of the mind incorporates two features designed to minimize their impact. First, he separates the affections aroused by the various senses from passions, which, on his account, are accompanied by violent bodily motions that obstruct reflection.[52] This redefinition makes the passions intrinsically inimical to virtue as Hutcheson conceives it, and comparatively marginal to everyday life. The main thing people have to do in order to act well is therefore to control the weaker, selfish affections, and here they can rely on both reason and habituation, as well as on the promptings of moral and public sense. Secondly, Hutcheson abandons the widely held view that desire and aversion are species of passion; these two, he remarks, "lead directly to action and are wholly distinct from all sort of sensation."[53] This step prepares the way for the further claim that humans are equipped with calm desires, devoid of pleasant or unpleasant sensations, which enable them to respond to the benevolent promptings of moral sense.[54] Once again, the causes of wayward and potentially disruptive forms of behavior are distinguished from those of sociable actions, and priority is given to psychological resources that incline us to virtue. The task of combating excessive or inappropriate passions is no longer conceived as belonging principally to reason, to passion, or to a combination of the two, but is supported by a further pair of natural capacities, the moral sense and calm desire. Humans possess resources that purport to be relatively free from the inaccuracy and instability that had been associated with the passions since ancient times, and which attune them to sociability.

The strategies underlying Hutcheson's reconfiguration of the mind were taken up in a series of eighteenth-century attempts to explore the place of the passions in both self-interested and benevolent behavior. Among the most influential of these was the work of David Hume, who incorporated some of Hutcheson's insights into a novel, and on the face of things more threatening, analysis of the springs of action. In a striking opening move, Hume reverts to Hobbes's analysis of the impotence of reason and, reversing orthodoxy with a rhetorical flourish that Hobbes would have admired, pronounces reason to be the slave of the passions.[55] Rather than being our most active capacity, as generations of philosophers had claimed, reasoning does not move us, and is itself activated by passion; thus, if a man's passions were to make him more averse to the scratching of his finger than to the destruction of the world, reason would be powerless to intervene.[56] As this melodramatic example indicates, Hume was anxious to emphasize the startling implications of the view that there is a gulf between reason and action; but whereas Hobbes had combined this insight with a bleak analysis of the passionate dispositions that motivate us, Hume's gentler psychology owes a good deal to Hutcheson. Although he does not shrink from classifying phenomena such as pride, humility, love, or hatred as *passions*, his account of the manner in which they operate allows that they can just as easily move us to virtuous as to vicious behavior.

Hume's account of the principal mechanisms governing the passions is drawn from the work of Malebranche. Malebranche had offered a systematic interpretation of the working of comparison (our disposition to feel such passions as pride, humility, esteem, or contempt when we compare ourselves to others) and of sympathy (our inclination to respond to the passions and situations of others, as when someone else's happiness makes us glad, or their exploitation makes us angry).[57] His account had dwelt on the potentially competitive and destructive consequences of comparison, and although Hume takes over much of its structure, he is at pains to argue that these negative effects are limited and confined by our disposition to sympathize with the joy or sadness of those around us. He thus portrays individuals whose natural dispositions are already moderately sociable, and who, although they are not immune to passions such as contempt or envy, are nevertheless disposed to rejoice in the well-being of others and to share their suffering.[58] As a result, a morally commendable life does not have to be lived against the grain of human nature.

By analyzing the psychological resources with which human beings are endowed, the philosophers we have been considering strove to define the basis on which our capacity for virtuous action rests, and the limits above which it cannot rise. However, alongside the possibilities licensed by nature, there was a pervasive concern in the early modern period with the way that culture can mold the passions, a concern partly aroused by the encounters with distant and unfamiliar societies that were part and parcel of imperial expansion. The works of writers such as Michel de Montaigne[59] and Thomas More[60] attest to the way that reports of the unfamiliar practices and beliefs to be found in exotic cultures gave a new edge to debates about the good life, and prompted people to wonder how far the images of virtue associated with the offices of European communities were grounded in human nature, and how far they rested on patterns of feeling inculcated through education and convention. Furthermore, visions of radical difference were encouraged by the thought experiments of natural lawyers and social contract theorists, whose fantasies concentrated attention on the historical as well as the geographical diversity of cultural mores, and fed the suspicion that conceptions of virtue might be underdetermined by psychology. While one could to some extent fend off this possibility by naturalizing a range of virtuous affects, or by explicating the content of a moral sense, another way to deal with the problem was to acknowledge the cultural origins of certain morally valuable traits, together with the passionate dispositions on which they rested.

The idea that the members of a society can only fully realize their capacity to live virtuously in certain circumstances, and that these circumstances are themselves historically variable, came to be generally accepted among seventeenth-century philosophers. The idea is perhaps most memorably elaborated by Spinoza, who touches on the differences between the Hebrews, whose experience of slavery made them afraid of taking decisions for themselves, and the inhabitants of the Dutch republic, who have developed greater self-confidence.[61] While the latter group subscribe to images of virtue that revolve to some extent around notions of individual independence and creativity, the former would have been quite incapable of enacting these, and perhaps also incapable of recognizing them as virtuous. The project of devising images of virtue that people can live by is therefore a social and psychological experiment, a matter of finding out both how people react emotionally in different conditions, and what forms of social organization answer to their existing emotional capacities.

Among the assumptions implicit in Spinoza's discussion is the idea that the capacity to live virtuously develops progressively, a thought taken up in the works of a number of historians, who tried to give it empirical support by producing stadial narratives of human development. Influenced by Montesquieu's *Spirit of the Laws*, a number of Scottish writers, such as Adam Smith,[62] John Millar,[63] and Adam Ferguson,[64] defined the historical steps by which barbarism gave way to civilization, and charted some of the passions that predominated at different stages. A parallel philosophical project can be found in Hume's classification of natural and artificial virtues, which distinguishes between the pleasurable and unpleasurable feelings that are experienced by all peoples, regardless of their circumstances, and those that depend on culture and expectation. Among the passions in the latter category are "a pleasure from the view of such actions as tend to the peace of society, and an unease from such as are contrary to it," which can only arise in societies where rules determining what is just and unjust have been established.[65] As Hume presents the matter, the practice of assessing the justice of states of affairs, and the feelings of indignation, satisfaction, and so on that make it possible to maintain such a practice, develop together and sustain each other; and the virtue of responding positively to justice is consequently artificial in the sense that it presupposes the existence of a particular set of social conventions.

On the whole, eighteenth-century writers believed that humanity had progressed throughout the course of history, and that civilized peoples were in various ways superior to their predecessors. There were, however, some opponents of this view, one of the most outspoken being Jean-Jacques Rousseau, who articulated a deep but novel form of pessimism about the moral development of humankind. Rejecting the Christian conception of human beings as inherently sinful, while reworking the Christian dogma that they are morally wanting, he offered a picture of humanity as naturally peaceable and benevolent, but as corrupted by society.[66] Rather than improving us, the competitive mores of social life destroy virtue by inducing destructive passions and habituating us to a distorted conception of the good, so that the only way to cultivate virtue is to withdraw from these social pressures. The source of moral trouble, therefore, is not our nature, which is well adapted to a presocial existence, but culture, which creates the destructive traits that philosophers have mistakenly laid at nature's door.

The pervasive suspicion of the passions that runs through early modern philosophy, and the perceived difficulty of successfully defusing it, is fundamentally linked to the idea that self-control is a condition of virtue. Unless a person develops some capacity to control their affects and the behavior to which they lead, they will remain in an infantile condition, subject to bouts of rage, love, and envy that exceed the limits of their offices. But how much self-control does a virtuous person need? Must they be absolutely proof against passion, in the manner of a Stoic sage, or need they only remain within bounds that license it in certain circumstances? Throughout the early modern era, one prominent strand of thought continued to invest enormous value in images of self-control. At a social and political level, this emphasis yielded a means to condemn the tantrums of rulers or spouses and the violence of masters or mistresses, and stood firmly on the side of established order. At a more philosophical level, it sustained the idea that the exercise of reason or other resources enables the passions to be manipulated. By itself, it seems, control might or might not be a good thing – one can imagine a villain who suppresses his fear and compassion in order to commit horrible crimes. But for writers such as Descartes or Spinoza, reliable control over one's passions is the fruit of true understanding, and is therefore accompanied by knowledge of the nature of virtue. The achievement of the one enhances the achievement of the other, and vicious behavior is consequently best seen as a mark of ignorance. This conception of individual power is central, for example, to the Cartesian notion of *générosité*, itself the keystone of a morally good life, as well as Spinoza's conception of freedom as the ability to maintain one's power and joyfulness in the face of difficulties.

We can see from the case of Hobbes that this preoccupation with control can be a force for intellectual change. Hobbes is as anxious as any of his contemporaries to understand how societies can protect themselves from the destructive effects of the passions by finding a way to control them, and this concern seems to be one of the factors that prompted him to reassess the accepted view that reason and affect are distinct. But among early modern writers we also find a reaction against the assumption that control is the central issue. As we have seen, the eighteenth century brought with it an increasing emphasis on the sociability of our emotional dispositions, which come to be seen as more conducive to virtue than before. At the same time, this shift gave rise to a new conception of good character, no longer so focused on the careful control of passion, but hospitable to the spontaneous expression of sentiment. Divested of their more troublesome features, the affects moved center stage in the analysis of a good life.

NOTES

1 Hutcheson 2002, p. 3.
2 See Miller and Inwood 2003; Kraye 1988.
3 *The Prince*, in Machiavelli 1988.
4 See Coleman 2005.
5 On the debt of "new" physiological theories to long-established medical traditions, see Sutton 1998; Siraisi 1990, pp. 97–114.
6 Descartes, *Passions*. See also Clarke 2003, pp. 106–34; Talon-Hugon 2002, pp. 207–48.
7 Locke, *Essay*, II.xxiii.16 and IV.iv.1–9. On the view that the study of the passions falls within the domain of moral as opposed to natural philosophy see James 1997, p. 3.
8 The view that these are interchangeable can be traced to Augustine, *City of God*, bk. 9, ch. 4. On the transition from the use of the terms 'passion' and 'affection' to that of the term 'emotion,' see Dixon 2003; Rorty 1982.
9 Aristotle, *Metaphysics*, bk. II, 1046a27. See also James 1997, chs. 2 and 4.
10 See Kovecses 2000.
11 Locke, *Essay*, II.xxi.15.
12 Malebranche, *Search*, I.xviii.1.
13 See, for example, Charleton 1674, pp. 75–76; Descartes, *Passions*, art. 107; Daston and Park 1992.
14 See for example Senault 1649, sig. B 2r–v; Malebranche, *Search*, V.7.

15 See also James 1997, ch. 7.
16 Malebranche, *Search*, v.3; Harrison 1998.
17 *The Theory of Moral Sentiments*, III.3.iii, in Smith 1984.
18 On the control of the passions as a therapeutic exercise, see Nussbaum 1994.
19 Descartes, *Passions*, arts. 46–47.
20 Descartes, *Passions*, arts. 49, 147; Spinoza, *Ethics*, III, def. 2; prop. 1. See James 1997, ch. 8.
21 See Long 2003; Zanta 1914; Saunders 1955; Levi 1964.
22 See, for example, Nicolas Coeffeteau, *Tableau des passions humaines*, 1630, p. 133; Richard Burton, *The Anatomy of Melancholy*, in Burton 1989–94, vol. I, p. 249.
23 Lloyd 1998.
24 Lloyd 1996, chs. 1 and 4; James 1993; Long 2003; Rutherford 1999.
25 *The Defense of Poesie*, in Sidney 1962, vol. III, pp. 13–14. See James 1997, pp. 215–44.
26 See, for example, Spinoza, *Ethics*, I, appendix.
27 *The Advancement of Learning*, ch. 14, par. 9, in Bacon 1973.
28 *Lev.*, ch. 15.
29 *On the Citizen*, ch. 3, par. 31, in Hobbes 1998.
30 "Two Kinds of Righteousness," in Luther 1957. See Gerrish 1962.
31 Cornelius Jansenius, *Augustinus* (1640).
32 *Pensées*, 131, in Pascal 1958. For further discussion see James 1998, pp. 1384–91.
33 Moriarty 2003.
34 Senault 1649, sig. B 2.
35 Spinoza, *Ethics*, III.
36 Spinoza, *Ethics*, V, prop. 10.
37 Descartes, *Passions*, art. 50.
38 Descartes, *Passions*, art. 47
39 See, for example, Ignatius of Loyola, *The Spiritual Exercises*, in Ignatius of Loyola 1950.
40 Shuger 1988.
41 Skinner 1988, pp. 423–34; Hunter 2005.
42 See, for example, John Locke, *Some Thoughts concerning Education*, in Locke 1989.
43 Elias 1978; Schmitt 1989; Foucault 1977.
44 *Lev.*, chs. 6 and 8.
45 On the passion of curiosity see Kenny 2004, pp. 41–47; Daston 1995.
46 For example, Henry More, *An Account of Virtue* (1690). See also James 1998.
47 "The Moralists: A Philosophical Rhapsody," II.5, in Shaftesbury 1999.

48 "*Sensus Communis*: An Essay on the Freedom of Wit and Humor," in Shaftesbury 1999.
49 *The Fable of the Bees*, in Mandeville 1988.
50 *An Essay on the Nature and Conduct of the Passions and Affections*, sec. 1; see also the editor's introduction to Hutcheson 1999, pp. ix–xiv.
51 *An Inquiry into the Original of our Ideas of Beauty and Virtue*, "Treatise concerning Moral Good and Evil," sec. 2.10, in Hutcheson 1729.
52 *Essay*, sec. 2, in Hutcheson 1999.
53 Ibid., sec. 3.
54 Ibid., sec. 2.
55 *Treatise*, II.iii.3.
56 Ibid. See Baier 1991, ch. 6; Penelhum 1994; Jones 1982.
57 Malebranche, *Search*, V.7.
58 James 2005.
59 "Of Cannibals," in Montaigne 1965, pp. 150–59.
60 *Utopia*, in More 1989.
61 *Theological-Political Treatise*, chs. 17, 20, in Spinoza 1998.
62 *Lectures on Jurisprudence*, in Smith 1982.
63 *The Origins of the Distinction of Ranks*, in Lehmann 1960.
64 *An Essay on the History of Civil Society*, in Ferguson 1995. See also Pittock 2003.
65 *Treatise*, III.ii.6.
66 *Discourse on the Moral Effects of the Arts and Sciences* and *Discourse on the Origins of Inequality*, in Rousseau 1997.

STEPHEN DARWALL

8 The foundations of morality: virtue, law, and obligation

Historians commonly date the beginning of early modern epistemology and metaphysics from Descartes's attempt in the *Meditations* to find a foundation for knowledge that is immune to skeptical challenge for an individual self-critical mind. There is no comparable consensus about when early modern ethical philosophy begins, but, as J. B. Schneewind has argued, it makes sense to link it similarly to an engagement with forms of ethical skepticism in the writings of Montaigne in the late sixteenth century and Hugo Grotius in the early seventeenth.[1] If one were to seek a parallel canonical moment, one might do no better than a passage in Grotius's *On the Law of War and Peace* (1625), in which Grotius puts into the mouth of the ancient skeptic Carneades the challenge that "[T]here is no law of nature, because all creatures . . . are impelled by nature towards ends advantageous to themselves . . . [C]onsequently, there is no justice, or if such there be, it is supreme folly, since one does violence to his own interests if he consults the advantage of others."[2]

To appreciate the force of this challenge, we must know what Grotius and his contemporaries would have understood by a "law of nature." Natural laws (of the normative or ethical sort) were thought of as universal norms that impose obligations on anyone who is capable of following them, on all moral agents, rather than on citizens of a more specific jurisdiction. And, differently from positive law, they were thought to require no positing, legislative act, at least no human one. Hobbes wrote in the mid-seventeenth century that "all writers do agree, that the natural law is the same with the moral."[3] At the end of the eighteenth, Kant also would speak of the "moral law," but most early modern thinkers simply used the term 'morality' to refer to the same idea.

It is an important feature of this period that the ideas referred to by terms like 'morality,' 'moral law,' and 'moral agent' came to have a distinctive shape that we might call the "modern conception of morality." Together, they comprised a way of thinking about a significant part of ethics, at least, that still has currency today. The early modern natural law tradition of Grotius and his contemporaries, including Pufendorf, Hobbes, and Locke, played an especially important role in developing and defending these ideas. Properly to understand their contribution, however, we must see it against the background of the classical natural law tradition of Thomas Aquinas and his followers.

The idea that there are norms or laws to which all rational human beings are subject goes back as far as the Stoics. But it was not until Aquinas in the thirteenth century that it was developed systematically. For Thomas, natural law is a formulation of "eternal law," God's ideal or archetype for all of nature – "the exemplar of divine wisdom . . . moving all things to their due end."[4] This is Thomas's distinctive synthesis of Aristotelian teleology and the Christian idea of divine rule. Eternal law specifies the distinctive perfection or ideal state of every natural being, and so "rule[s] and measure[s]" them, but rational beings are subject to the law in a distinctive way. Having "a share of the eternal reason," they can act in the light of their awareness of eternal law. And this binds them to what Aquinas calls "natural law": eternal law made accessible to and applicable by rational creatures in practice.[5]

Since Thomas's theory of good was perfectionist, the good of each creature being its perfection, it followed that individual human beings realize their respective goods only within the overall scheme specified by eternal law.[6] Any genuine conflict between individuals' interests is thus ruled out – harmony is guaranteed by perfectionist-teleological metaphysics.[7] For Aquinas, natural law and individual benefit effectively provide the same normative standard. In the classical view, teleological metaphysics is what gives natural law its normative purchase. Inherent in every being's nature is an ideal end: what that being *should* be. Normativity is "built into" nature.

The Thomist classical natural law tradition was carried into the seventeenth century by such influential writers as Francisco Suárez. However, like most modern forms to come, Suárez's version gave greater stress to a conception of moral *obligation* premised on God's authoritative command. Suárez nevertheless accepted the main tenet of Aquinas's synthesis of Christianity and Aristotle that natural law is fixed by eternal law. Good and right are codetermined in such a way that doing what is right is the same thing as acting for one's own good.

By the seventeenth century, however, this position had begun to wear thin in Europe as a basis for public moral and political order. Antagonistic religious division, as in Montaigne's France, undermined consensus on a common good or on the idea even that one exists. At the same time, an emerging modern science seemed likelier to be mechanistic than teleological. And once metaphysical teleology was given up, it was guaranteed neither that human interests are necessarily harmonized nor that human nature has any intrinsic normative implications. When Grotius came to write his famous treatise on international law, therefore, he confronted what Schneewind calls the "Grotian problematic." Lacking hope of agreement on a common good rooted in a shared religious outlook, Grotius attempted to articulate a conception of moral and political order that could be convincing to people without a common vision of the good life or any reason to believe that outcomes that would be good for one must be good for all.

The skeptical challenge that Grotius considers – that there might be no reason to do what is right and just when this conflicts with the agent's own good – simply could not have arisen on the classical view. The point is not that the classical tradition asserted that acting rightly promotes the agent's interest also. There is a form of that doctrine in modern natural lawyers like Locke and Hobbes as well. It is rather that it claimed that acting rightly and acting for one's good are one and the same thing. With Grotius, on the other hand, we get the beginnings of the modern conception of morality as a body of universal norms whose claim on us is fundamentally independent of that of our own good, indeed, that can conflict with our good and bind us even so.

Disagreement about a common good or conflict between individuals' goods is the source of what we now call "collective action" problems: situations in which all do worse by acting for their individual benefit than they would if all were to follow an alternative collective strategy. This is the genus of which the famous "Prisoner's Dilemma" is a species.[8] And it was the most fundamental aspect of the problematic that Grotius and his contemporaries faced, to which they proposed the modern conception of natural law as solution. Lacking confidence that a sufficiently rich conception of common good could gain sufficiently wide acceptance among reasonable persons for unconstrained prudence to govern without significant conflict, they sought a conception of mutually advantageous, prudence-constraining norms (natural law or morality) to solve the otherwise inevitable problems of collective action. The nub of the problem was that, although mutual advantage could explain why everyone should want all to follow such norms (in general), it could not directly underwrite the normativity of the norms themselves, since collective action problems can be solved only by the *constraint* of self-interested conduct. As a consequence, early modern moralists faced the philosophical issue of defending and explicating the normativity of what Sidgwick called a "regulative and governing faculty" that is independent of self-interest: the moral faculty or conscience.[9]

An important aspect of Grotius's solution was an original distinction between perfect rights (of justice), which create *enforceable* obligations, and imperfect rights (of love), which do not.[10] Grotius argued that it was in the case of justice that Aristotle's theory of virtues breaks down most severely. Since justice involves publicly authorizable demands, it must be mediated by publicly accessible and enforceable rules rather than by an insight possessed only by the virtuous. The Grotian problematic, therefore, was how to account for prudence-constraining, though mutually advantageous, norms, along with the authority to enforce at least some of these.

This distinction between a part of morality, justice, which is essentially concerned with exactable conduct and requires formulation in publicly acceptable rules, on the one hand, and another having to do more with motive and character that neither can, nor need, have the same publicly available enforcement, on the other, became a central element of much of the moral philosophy of this period. It runs through Pufendorf, Samuel Clarke, Hume on natural and artificial virtues, and later, Adam Smith and, of course, Kant on perfect and imperfect obligations. It is a distinctively modern development; so far as we know, Grotius invented the distinction. Moreover, in doing so, he initiated, as we shall see, the modern preoccupation with the relation between *accountable* normative guidance and freedom of the will.

LAW, OBLIGATION, AND FREEDOM

Despite this, responsibility played no fundamental role in Grotius's account of the normativity of natural law, which he based on a hypothesized "impelling desire for society."[11] Grotius's followers did not find this strategy especially convincing, however, and after him, mainstream modern natural law doctrine took a more voluntarist turn. The notion of authoritative demand became utterly central to the accounts of moral obligation and natural law in the writings of Pufendorf, Locke, and Hobbes.

As I mentioned, this is prefigured in Suárez. Although mainly a classical natural lawyer, Suárez criticizes Aquinas for his inability to explain natural law's power to *obligate*.[12] By this Suárez does not mean that Aquinas cannot explain why there is reason to do what is right; he and Aquinas agree that we always benefit by acting rightly. Rather, Thomas's doctrine is impotent to explain why anyone, even God, has the authority to *demand* that we not violate natural law, and, therefore, why God may legitimately hold us accountable for wrongdoing. This leads Suárez to what will be the central tenet of theological voluntarist forms of modern natural law, namely, that morality's power to obligate follows from natural law's relation to God's authority to command.

Before we consider how this idea was developed by Pufendorf and Locke, we should note some general features.[13] First, it makes accountability and authoritative demand central to morality in a plausible way. Mill famously said that "we do not call anything wrong, unless we mean to imply that a person ought to be punished in some way or other for doing it; if not by law, by the opinion of his fellow creatures; if not by opinion, by the reproaches of his own conscience."[14] The very ideas of moral blameworthiness and guilt involve that of authoritative demand.[15] To blame someone for wrongdoing is to make a demand of him. Second, this connection to moral responsibility brings along with it issues about freedom. Holding someone responsible presupposes that the agent to whom the demand is addressed can comply with it by accepting its authority. This means, third, that morality (or at least that part having to do with exactable obligations) essentially involves a relation that is only possible between rational wills: the addressing of a demand from one free and rational will to another. It is true that according to early modern natural lawyers like Pufendorf and Locke, moral obligation ultimately involves a form of subjection. It is because we are God's subjects that God can create natural law by his command. But Pufendorf also thought that God can do this only if he (and we) presuppose that we can determine our conduct through our free acceptance of his authority.

Pufendorf makes a fundamental distinction between physical and moral "entities," between how things stand in nature without the address of a commanding will, on the one hand, and the "superadded" moral changes resulting from this form of address, on the other.[16] God produces moral entities by "*imposition*."[17] Without the imposition of God's authoritative will through command, all beings (including human beings) stand "physically complete," their respective physical natures fixing "their ability directly to produce any physical motion or change in any thing."[18] With God's command, however, "moral entities" are superadded to the physical realm – moral law and moral reasons are created. And this divine creation enables us to solve collective action problems that would otherwise be irresolvable. "Moral entities" make possible the "orderliness and decorum of civilized life."[19] Without the moral law, "men should spend their lives like beasts."[20]

When God addresses his will to free and rational beings, he makes us "moral causes," agents to whom actions and their effects can be *imputed* and for which we are therefore accountable. The formal nature of a moral action "consists of its 'imputativity'," "whereby the effect of a voluntary action can be imputed to an agent."[21] This is the "primary axiom in morals": "a man can be asked for a reckoning" for anything in his power; "any action controllable according to a moral law, the accomplishment or avoidance of which is within the power of a man, may be imputed to him."[22] According to Pufendorf, then, when God addresses his will to free and rational beings, he simultaneously creates the moral law and makes them "moral causes" who are accountable for complying with it.

We find essentially the same position in Locke.[23] In the *Essay*, the problem of collective action follows from Locke's hedonistic theory of individual good. If each pursues his own individual pleasure independently of divinely imposed natural law, then everyone is worse off. Locke had earlier asserted his belief in the unavoidability of rational human conflict without divine legislation in his *Essays on the Law of Nature*. And he held there that human beings can infer both the content and form of natural law from empirical observations. From the manifest design of the universe, we can infer the existence of a supremely wise and powerful Creator.[24] And since we need to live "in society with other men," it is evidently God's will that we do so. But how *can* we do so if there are collective action problems and if, as Locke also believes, self-interest is the only rational motive?[25] God does not will in vain, so since our only rational motive is self-interest, he must have created supernatural benefits for compliance and burdens for noncompliance, beyond their natural consequences, sufficient to make obedience invariably in each agent's interest, and, moreover, given us a way to determine ourselves by our knowledge of this very conclusion. This effectively gives Locke a deduction of the immortality of the soul, the availability of self-determination, and the doctrine of eternal sanctions as necessary conditions for the very possibility of morality and reasonable social unity.[26]

Pufendorf, however, believed that fear of punishment is a motive of the wrong kind for moral obligation. Locke and Pufendorf agreed that moral accountability presupposes that moral agents can freely determine themselves to act as they are obligated. But Locke believed that self-determination is simply the ability to discern the likelihood of sanctions and vividly consider them in a way that influences current desire. Pufendorf, by contrast, makes a fundamental distinction between motivation by sanctions, on the one hand, and being moved by respect for authoritative demands, on the other. Obligation "affects the will morally"; it "is forced of itself to weigh its own actions, and to judge itself worthy of some censure, unless it conforms to a prescribed rule."[27] Obligation thus "differs in a special way from coercion." Although "both ultimately point out some object of terror, the latter only shakes the will with an external force." "An obligation," however, "forces a man to acknowledge of himself that the evil, which has been pointed out to the person who deviates from an announced rule, falls upon him justly."[28] This is the difference between the fear of censure and internally acknowledged blame. Pufendorf's insight is pregnant with philosophical possibilities about the nature and deliberative role of respect, dignity, or authority, and reciprocal recognition. However, he did not develop these, and ultimately offered no alternative moral psychology that such a development would require.[29]

Although more famous (or infamous) for his political theory, Thomas Hobbes's moral philosophy is also within the modern natural law tradition. A materialist, Hobbes holds that judgments of value are ultimately projections of the judger's desires in something like the way Galileo had held that the ascription of color involves an objectifying projection of color experience. When we see that something is necessary to an end we desire, like self-preservation, we therefore think it is something we *should* do. The "laws of nature," Hobbes concludes, are really "theorems concerning what conduceth to the conservation and defense" of oneself.[30] Their normativity comes from instrumental rationality in the service of ends judged valuable. Considered only so far, however, they are "but improperly" called laws.[31] To be law proper, these generalizations must be connected to obligation and authoritative demand. The theological voluntarists accomplished this from God's assumed authority to command. Hobbes's alternative was to argue that agreements and contracts involve obligation as part of their definition and that acknowledging the validity and bindingness of agreements is necessary to avoiding the evils of a state of nature where unconstrained pursuit of advantage leads to a life that is "nasty, brutish, and short."[32] Reducing obligation to instrumental rationality and advantage in this way, however, seems to founder on a version of Pufendorf's point mentioned above. It seems to give a reason of the wrong kind to support the moral bindingness of agreements: a reason of self-interest for wanting to recognize these obligations is not a reason on the basis of which we might recognize them as obligating.[33]

RATIONALIST REACTIONS

Many aspects of the modern natural law tradition elicited criticism and inspired alternative ethical conceptions. Modeling morality on law seemed to some to overemphasize external conduct at the cost of motive and character, which they thought the center of the moral life. According to the Cambridge Platonist Ralph Cudworth, it made morality a "*dead Law of outward Works*, which . . . subjects us to a *State of Bondage*."[34] Voluntarism also faced a dilemma that its proponents never adequately confronted. What gives God the right to our obedience? Voluntarists had two possible responses. They could reduce God's authority to, say, his power to sanction or they could defend this authority as an irreducible moral proposition. Taking the former tack conflated Pufendorf's distinction between coercion and moral obligation. And taking the latter required at least one moral fact, indeed, apparently one moral obligation, that does not derive from God's command. As Cudworth put it, "it was never heard of that any one founded all his authority of commanding others . . . in a law of his own making, that men should be required, obliged, or bound to obey him."[35] Leibniz argued similarly that if God's goodness is a reason to obey him, then that must be so independently of his command. And then the question naturally arises, if there are reasons for God to benefit us that are independent of anyone's command, then why aren't these reasons good enough for us also?[36] Finally, grounding moral obligations in God's commands made them seem arbitrary and "factitious."[37] The most basic moral duties are "eternal and immutable," not the sort of thing that would need to be created by a command or that even could be.

The latter thought, especially, led a number of philosophers – Cambridge Platonists like Cudworth, their follower Shaftesbury, Leibniz, Spinoza, and Malebranche – to develop rationalist ethical approaches that stressed the necessity of fundamental ethical truths and focused on motive and character. With the possible exception of Grotius, the modern natural law tradition had been characterized by a broadly naturalist metaphysics and empiricist epistemology. Rationalists like Cudworth argued, however, that ethical truths have a kind of rational necessity that could not possibly be grasped empirically.

Seventeenth-century ethical rationalism was elaborated in very different ways by different philosophers. One important difference is between those, like Cudworth and later Shaftesbury and Leibniz, who took the Grotian problematic seriously and those, like Malebranche and Spinoza, who saw ethics as primarily concerned, not with how we should conduct ourselves toward one another given the possibility of plurality and conflict, but with our orientation toward a unified order of value. Against the latter, the former group agreed with the modern natural lawyers that morality is distinct in its nature from prudence (even when they also thought that the moral life is the most beneficial as well). However, they also believed that ethics is primarily an internal matter that cannot be externally imposed. But although their ethics focused primarily on virtue rather than duty, it was not in the Aristotelian sense of the excellent exercise of natural powers in which we flourish. Theirs was an ethics of *moral* virtue in the modern sense.

Known for their liberal theology and ethics, the Cambridge Platonists were a group of thinkers at Cambridge in the mid-seventeenth century who stressed independence of judgment and a loving character rather than any doctrine or creed, and who helped shape some of the major trends of late seventeenth-century and eighteenth-century British ethics, from moral sentimentalism, in Shaftesbury, Hutcheson, and Hume, to forms of rational intuitionism, like Samuel Clarke's, to Bishop Butler's ethics of autonomous conscience. Benjamin Whichcote was the spiritual leader of the group, but the most sophisticated philosopher by far was Ralph Cudworth, whose *Treatise concerning Eternal and Immutable Morality* appeared posthumously in 1731. Cudworth's ideas were nonetheless well known to his contemporaries, and he had substantial influence on Shaftesbury and, through his work on self-determination, on the thought of John Locke. In the *Treatise*, Cudworth mounts a systematic attack on voluntarism and empiricism in ethics. Ultimately, he argues, what ethical properties a thing has depend on its nature, not on anything external to it, like a command. And it is only through our "intellectual nature" or reason that moral agents can apprehend ethical truths.

This suggests the sort of rational intuitionism of later British intuitionists like Samuel Clarke or Richard Price, according to which reason apprehends "eternal and immutable" ethical truths that are independent of the mind. When, however, the *Treatise* is read in the light of Cudworth's extensive unpublished writings, a different position emerges, one that anticipates the sort of idealism of practical reason to be found in Kant.[38] The eternal essences that determine ethical truths do not exist in the "individuals without us"; but neither are they "somewhere else apart [from] the individual sensibles, and without the mind."[39] Forms are aspects of *forming substance*, that is, of mind. "[I]ntelligible forms by which things are understood or known," Cudworth writes, "are not stamps or impressions passively printed upon the soul from without, but ideas vitally protended or actively exerted from within itself."[40]

All universal natures or essences, including moral ones, are therefore modifications of mind and have reality, Cudworth believes, only so long as mind (specifically, God's archetypal mind) exists.[41] Thus, although he is no theological voluntarist, Cudworth is a theological moralist nonetheless. Were there no God, there would be no morality. But then, were there no God, there would be nothing. Nevertheless, ethical essences differ from merely theoretical or "intellectual" ideas, since they are essentially practical. The mind's "anticipations of morality" come from a "more inward and vital principle, in intellectual beings as such, whereby they have *a natural determination in them to do some things and to avoid others*."[42] As Kant will later, Cudworth believes that morality requires the possibility of pure *practical* reason. But Cudworth identifies pure practical reason with love, rather than, like Kant, a faculty of formal reasoning. God's perfect love is both perfect virtue and perfect mind. The "Law of Love" frees us "in a manner from all Law without us, because it maketh us become a *Law unto our selves*."[43] Although Cudworth's ethics focuses fundamentally on virtue rather than duty, he is nonetheless concerned, like Locke and Pufendorf, with issues of freedom and accountability. Cudworth left many volumes of unpublished manuscripts that are devoted to understanding the nature of moral blame and its presuppositions, including "self-comprehensive" self-command or autonomy, which Cudworth believes consists in being able to reflect on one's own desires and form new ones in light of critically formed moral judgments.[44]

Of special interest here is Cudworth's distinction between "animal" and "moral" forms of "obligation," which echoes Pufendorf's distinction between motivation by sanctions and motives that are distinctive of moral obligation. The former requires the sort of self-determination Locke defends in his *Essay* – the ability to step back and consider long-run interest in a way that can affect the strengths of current desires. But this is not yet, Cudworth insists, an "obligation truly moral." "Laws could no otherwise operate or seize upon them than by taking hold of their animal selfish passions . . . and that will allow of no other moral obligation than this utterly destroys all morality."[45] The motivation true moral obligation must draw on, Cudworth believes, is the same love or pure practical reason we find in God. The "candle of the Lord" within is not just a source of moral knowledge, but a moral motive as well.

These themes, that morality and moral obligation are internal to the moral agent and not externally imposed, and that sharing in the divine creative intelligence makes ethics possible, were central also to the thought of Shaftesbury two generations later. It was primarily through Shaftesbury, indeed, that the influence of Cambridge Platonism passed on to the eighteenth century. And Shaftesbury was even farther from the modern natural lawyers. He was so thoroughly a virtue ethicist that he did not even recognize evaluations of actions other than on the basis of motives. And his views about moral motivation develop the Cambridge Platonist identification between moral virtue and self-determination. Shaftesbury dismisses the picture of moral motivation he finds in Hobbes and Locke, whom he sees as giving the moral agent the "tame and gentle carriage" of a beast, cowed by "fear of his keeper."[46] Virtuous (or as Shaftesbury also calls them, "natural") motives have, unlike fear, an immediate beauty or amiability when we contemplate them. It is their pleasing appearance to "moral sense," a kind of cultivated disinterested taste, in fact, that makes them virtues.[47]

Shaftesbury also develops a distinctive version of the Cambridge Platonist doctrine of the dignity of rational persons, which he holds to derive from the human ability to shape and "author" lives. "Only good fortune or [a trainer's] right management" can control a savage beast, but moral agents can control themselves.[48] By self-reflection, we gain critical distance on our motives and, through moral sense, endorse or reject them, making the motives on which we subsequently act our own and not causes to which we are simply subject. Shaftesbury describes at some length a process of self-critical deliberation or "self-converse" through which a person can become her own master.[49]

This last, proto-Kantian theme combined in Shaftesbury's thought with another that anticipated Kant's doctrine that moral worth is realized only by actions undertaken for self-consciously moral motives. The "mere goodness" of motives such as pity or kindness, which "lies within the reach and capacity of all sensible creatures," contrasts with genuine "virtue or merit," which can be achieved only by beings who can determine themselves through moral sense. Talk of a "sense" is misleading here, since Shaftesbury's whole point is that, unlike the senses for which we have organs, moral sense depends upon how an agent critically "frames" its object in thought. A person cannot appropriately be held responsible for visual defects, but she can, he thinks, for failure adequately to determine herself through moral sense.[50]

Although Shaftesbury thought, like Cudworth, that voluntarism destroys morality, he did not think that moral properties need have metaphysical reality to support genuine moral distinctions. "If there be no real amiableness or deformity in moral acts, there is at least an imaginary one of full force. Though perhaps the thing itself should not be allowed in Nature, the imagination or fancy of it must be allowed to be from Nature alone."[51] Moral properties' "way of being" is through moral sense, and so long as disinterested reflection leads to a convergent response, this will adequately found judgments of vice and virtue. What assures convergence in Shaftesbury's scheme is Cambridge Platonism's confidence in rational order. For his empiricist followers, Hutcheson and Hume, however, convergence in moral judgment results from contingent universal aspects of the human condition.

Much of Shaftesbury's critique of voluntarism and his ethics of virtue is anticipated in Leibniz. However, Leibniz turned these ideas in the direction of what would come to be called utilitarianism. Moreover, within Leibniz's distinctive metaphysics, his virtue ethics lacked anything like Shaftesbury's doctrine of the moral sense. Leibniz agreed with the natural lawyers that obligation involves "moral necessity," but he thought that the requisite constraint operates *within* the will, not by external imposition. Even without recognizing a superior, a person can be constrained by necessity, since "the very nature of things and care for one's own happiness and safety . . . have their own requirements."[52] Moral necessity is thus a kind of natural necessity: "that which is 'natural' for a good man," where "a good man is one who loves everybody, in so far as reason permits."[53] What one ought to do is whatever act would be determined by good (benevolent) nature – what a good person would do or what one would do were one good.

Leibniz's position was like the classical natural law view, however, in requiring a metaphysical guarantee of various harmonies and coincidences, both within morality and between morality and self-interest. (There is a sense in which Leibniz's view, like Cudworth's "law of love," can be considered a kind of natural law view.) Within morality, Leibniz's perfectionism led him to identify all of justice, enlightened benevolence, wisdom, virtue, and happiness. Justice is "the charity of the wise," so whatever an informed love of all leads to is just.[54] And since every being's good is its perfection, wisdom and benevolence cannot come apart: intellectual perfection implies perfection of the will, and vice versa.

The good life is pleasurable, but that is due, not to pleasure's intrinsic goodness, but to pleasure's involving "a knowledge or feeling of perfection, not only in ourselves, but also in others."[55] Knowing (the prospect of) good (perfection) in anyone will lead to a desire for that for its own sake.

Leibniz's identifying moral goodness with universal benevolence led him to an early, perhaps the earliest, form of the greatest happiness principle: "To act in accordance with supreme reason, is to act in such a manner that the greatest quantity of good available is obtained for the greatest multitude possible and that as much felicity is diffused as the reason of things can bear."[56] Later utilitarians would reject Leibniz's perfectionist conception of happiness, but follow him in drawing similar maximizing conclusions from an equal concern for the good of all.[57]

The forms of ethical rationalism put forward by Malebranche and Spinoza were even farther from the Grotian problematic than Leibniz's. Both were notable for locating their ethical views within their distinctive metaphysics. Although certain aspects of their ethics – for example, their respective conceptions of freedom – were influential, neither provided a competing conception of morality that could be considered alongside the natural law view.

Malebranche's epistemology and metaphysics are thoroughly theocentric. Perception of external objects is possible only through ideas in God, and only God has genuine causal power, everything else being but an occasion for his causation. And Malebranche's ethics was no less theologically focused. Ethics concerns the correct orienting of love to forms of perfection, hence to God. Love of God is thus the central ethical attitude, and ethical knowledge concerns an order of perfection that can be found only in God.[58]

It is an expression of his perfection, Malebranche held, that God rules the universe by a general will rather than by particular volitions. Had the latter been the case, it would have been wrong for us ever to attempt to avoid natural evils. The idea that God's will must be general would later influence attempts, like those of Berkeley and Butler, to square rule-based conceptions of morality with God's benevolence, and, in political form, Rousseau's idea of the general will.[59] Perhaps most significant, however, was Malebranche's idea of freedom, which also played a prominent role in his theodicy. It is impossible for us not to love good in general, but our senses lead us astray with distorted seeming goods and evils. However, Malebranche argued that God also gives us the ability to "suspend" these appearances and decide whether to "consent" to them or to the more perfect goods with which they conflict. And this makes us responsible for our choices. This idea would resonate with Locke's account of freedom in the *Essay*, and, later, with Kant's idea that action always involves the implicit endorsement of a principle or "maxim."[60]

Spinoza's ethics and moral psychology provided an especially interesting foil for the early modern natural law tradition as well as a source of ideas for thinkers, like Hume and, much later, Nietzsche, who would seek to problematize conceptions of morality that are tied to accountability and autonomous agency. We can see the general thrust of Spinoza's thought in the final proposition of his *Ethics*: "Blessedness is not the reward of virtue, but virtue itself; nor do we enjoy it because we restrain our lusts; on the contrary, because we enjoy it, we are able to restrain them" (v, prop. 42). There are several major elements of Spinoza's ethical thought here: the blurring of a sharp distinction between the beneficial and the morally right; a conception of freedom that consists, not in any capacity to transcend appetites by autonomous choice that might be necessary for moral accountability and desert, but in something emergent within rightly ordered desires themselves; and, finally, a view of happiness as, not what the morally virtuous deserve, but that through which virtue and self-restraint are realized.

As Edwin Curley has observed, Spinoza's *Ethics* provide a "serene, but remorseless dissection of human nature,"[61] one that is profoundly naturalist in the modern sense of eschewing Aristotelian final causes (which Spinoza associates with self-congratulatory anthropomorphizing) but that might nonetheless ground an ethic that, like ancient Greek (and classical natural law) views, can unify virtue and happiness as following nature. Spinoza rejects a host of dualisms – between mind and body, God and nature, freedom and necessity, reason and passion, and morality and prudence – and argues against ethical conceptions that depend upon them. A religious thinker for whom love of God is central to the highest good, Spinoza was nonetheless seen as an atheist because he steadfastly rejected a supernaturalist view of the divine. God consists rather in the necessary order of nature. And human conduct is no less immanent in the necessary causal order than the divine. Freedom involves no exception to or intervention in a necessary causal order, but it is rather self-determination within it. Since God is the totality of nature's self-determination, He is necessarily free. But so also can human freedom coincide with natural necessity when the causes of human behavior are suitably internal to the self and related to self-understanding.

Many of Spinoza's critics who disdained his ideas as atheistic rejected them also for their denial of antinecessitarian freedom or, as some saw it, their fatalism. And thinkers who held the moral realm to involve an accountability that requires desire-transcending rational choice found Spinoza's conception of freedom too thin to support morality as they conceived it. This was Cudworth's reaction, and something like it was Berkeley's also.[62] But for philosophers like Hume and Nietzsche, Spinoza's moral psychology was liberating, a vision of human freedom without freedom of the will and of practical thought that didn't starkly oppose reason and inclination. And these thinkers found also in Spinoza a way of thinking about ethics that, although thoroughly modern (and lacking metaphysical teleology), did not assume a transcendent will, human or divine, or distinguish sharply between what is morally right or obligatory, on the one hand, and what is most useful and beneficial to the agent, on the other.

Spinoza held that our actions become freer and more properly our own as they involve greater self-understanding. Unfreedom is not determination by desire – every action results from desire – but being in the grip of passions that involve confused ideas.

"[A] passion ceases to be a passion as soon as we form a clear and distinct idea of it" (*Ethics*, v, prop. 3). As we understand our place in the natural order, moreover, we come to a clearer conception also of the interdependence of human good. This is owing, not to metaphysical teleology, as with Aristotle or Aquinas, but to the role of self-understanding in human freedom and good. For Spinoza, the sources of external conflict are internal. Only "insofar as men are torn by affects which are passions" are they "contrary to one another" (*Ethics*, IV, prop. 34). Self-understanding that harmonizes the self also produces external harmony. "Men most agree in nature, when they live according to the guidance of reason." And they are "most useful to one another, when each one most seeks his own advantage" in a calm, free, self-understanding way (*Ethics*, IV, prop. 35 and cor. 2).[63]

EGOIST CRITIQUE

A far more radical critique of mainstream moralizing was posed by Bernard Mandeville's *The Fable of the Bees* (1714).[64] Perhaps best known for its unmasking, egoistic psychology, the *Fable*'s subtitle, "Private Vices, Public Benefits," indicates its main theme: the effects of widespread virtue and vice, taken in the aggregate, can be the reverse of what agents intend. The actual, if unintended, effects of everyone's trying to help others at his own cost, Mandeville argued, can be significant public harm.

The centrality of benevolence was common to the ethics of the Cambridge Platonists, Shaftesbury, and Leibniz, as it would be to Shaftesbury's follower, Francis Hutcheson. But what if widespread altruism is actually socially costly? Mandeville's *Fable* sketched a story of how it might be, and argued that it actually would be in the conditions of eighteenth-century European life. A hive of vain, self-serving creatures, "endeavouring to supply each other's lust and vanity," creates great wealth, which all enjoy. When, however, they grumble about the wicked avarice, dishonesty, and luxury in their midst, God makes them all honest. The results are catastrophic. With no desire for luxuries, avarice, or vanity, the engine of their productive activity is stilled, and all are left in poverty.

The significance of Mandeville's thesis for modern economics, beginning with Adam Smith's *Wealth of Nations* (1776), is obvious.

But it also had a powerful influence on earlier eighteenth-century moral philosophy. Particularly significant was its role in the development of utilitarianism after Hutcheson. Once the possibility was taken seriously that the effects of widespread benevolence might diverge from those intended by the benevolent, the question of the relative importance for morality of motive and consequence was forced. And, increasingly, those attracted by utilitarian ideas would reject Leibniz's and Hutcheson's position in favor of one, like Bentham's, that made good consequences fundamental.

Mandeville's major lasting contribution was to make vivid how subtle and complex the relations between intended and actual effects can be. It lies behind, for example, Butler's, Berkeley's, and Hume's later insistence that rules of justice that strictly regulate the pursuit of overall good, as well as individual good, can lead to a greater good than could be achieved by individuals each trying to promote the good themselves.[65]

REASON VERSUS SENTIMENT AS THE FOUNDATION OF MORALS

Perhaps the most central issue of early eighteenth-century moral philosophy, however, concerned the very foundation of morals and whether that can be provided by reason or sentiment. There were several different issues under this general heading: (a) the epistemological question of whether we discern moral features through reason or feeling, (b) the moral psychological issue of the roles reason and affect play in moral motivation, and (c) the metaphysical, metaethical issue of whether relation to reason or sentiment can be what, say, an action's being morally right or wrong consists in.

Although Shaftesbury's idea of moral sense derived from a kind of rationalism, his major eighteenth-century influence was through philosophers like Francis Hutcheson and David Hume who developed his idea in a distinctly empiricist, antirationalist way. For Hutcheson, moral sense followed from the Lockean thesis that all ideas come from experience, together with Hutcheson's own claim that moral approbation and disapprobation involve distinctive, irreducible ideas, a claim that would be exploited by intuitionists like Richard Price for their own rationalist purposes. Hutcheson's doctrine of moral sense was the contingent psychological thesis that contemplating motive and character causes these distinctive ideas. Hutcheson believed, moreover, that moral sense follows a simple empirical law: we approve characters and motives in proportion to the degree of benevolence that is manifested in them. Like Leibniz, Hutcheson drew the proto-utilitarian conclusion that the action "which procures the greatest happiness for the greatest numbers" is always the morally best choice.[66] But whereas Leibniz thought this followed on metaphysical grounds, Hutcheson regarded it as part of an empirically confirmed theory of (contingent) human nature. This, together with Hutcheson's hedonism, brought his formulation far closer to the form the greatest happiness principle would take in the utilitarian tradition of Bentham and his followers.

Hutcheson also diverged from Shaftesbury in other ways. Despite extolling benevolence, Shaftesbury had held that self-interest is the primary source of rational motivation. Hutcheson argued, however, that universal benevolence is no less rational in the only sense that, by empiricist lights, a motive can be. Theoretical reasoning, informing ourselves perfectly in a way that allows us to respond equally to all we know, leads no less to benevolence than it does to self-love.[67] There is, then, an irresolvable dualism of rational motive, which God happily renders otiose by arranging the coincidence of the interests of the benevolent agent and the interests of all.[68]

Importantly, however, Hutcheson argued that reason is not *itself* a source of motivation, as the rationalists supposed: there is no such thing as pure practical reason. Reason is simply the faculty through which we discern truths and, while this can move us to *belief*, without other passions or "affects" it cannot move us to action.[69] Indeed, Hutcheson argued that moral sense itself cannot directly motivate, since it is a felt response to a motive rather than a motive itself. So whereas Shaftesbury had held that true virtue must involve self-conscious self-direction by moral sense, Hutcheson argued that this gives no further moral motive; worse, it is likelier to breed self-indulgent self-congratulation.

David Hume's critique of ethical rationalism is far better known these days than Hutcheson's, but Hume took many of the essentials from Hutcheson.[70] Still, it was Hume who most sharply focused arguments against the claim that "moral distinctions" derive from reason in either the epistemological or the metaphysical sense. The

Hume/Hutcheson claim that reason cannot motivate is a central premise in Hume's main argument for the former. Unlike "the calm and indolent judgments of the understanding," moral judgments standardly move us in some way.[71] So we must make moral distinctions through sentiment rather than reason. But neither can anything become moral or immoral – virtuous or vicious, right or wrong – *because* of its relation to reason. Strictly speaking, Hume argued, only beliefs can accord or conflict with reason. Actions, passions, and feelings lack the "representative quality" that makes beliefs fit for reasoning and apt for rational criticism. So actions and passions can't possibly have moral properties in virtue of their rational properties; strictly, they don't even have the latter.

Hume also followed Hutcheson in his positive thesis that moral properties derive from sentiment, but there were important differences of detail. Whereas Hutcheson thought in terms of a dedicated "moral sense," Hume held that the moral sentiment results from the workings of more basic psychological principles: human sympathy and the association of ideas. Roughly, we approve of whatever motives tend to lead to human happiness because our contemplation of these motives is associated psychically with these normally good consequences, which we then vicariously experience through sympathy, leading to a positive moral sentiment toward the motive. This departure from Hutcheson's psychology went together with a rejection of his identification of virtue with benevolence. Hume took seriously the lesson of Mandeville's *Fable*, and he agreed with Bishop Butler that on reflection we approve a variety of motives, prominently including justice, that cannot be reduced to benevolence.[72] Justice can require us to return property to a "seditious bigot" even when an alternative use of it would be more in the public interest.[73] Even so, Hume argued, "however single acts of justice may be contrary, either to public or private interest, it is certain that the whole plan or scheme is highly conducive, or indeed absolutely requisite, both to the support of society, and the well-being of every individual."[74] We all do better if we treat as "sacred and inviolable" certain artificial rules structuring property, contract, promise, and other practices of justice, and regulate ourselves by them. Justice is in this way an "artificial virtue," unlike natural virtues like benevolence.

With his theory of justice and of the obligation to be just, Hume took an important step away from the kind of virtue ethics, founded entirely on love, that had been advanced by Shaftesbury, Hutcheson, and Leibniz. Under the usual conditions of human life, Hume argued, love simply cannot provide an adequate basis for social order. A notion of justice that is distinct from any form of love is required: governance by mutually advantageous rules. This evidenced and helped stimulate a renewed interest in what had earlier energized the seventeenth-century tradition of natural law – the idea of a regime of norms or laws relating (and obligating) individuals who cannot expect to be loved by others as each loves himself, or even as each loves his family, neighbors, or those with whom he shares the same confession. An ethics of virtue, whether empiricist or rationalist, appeared ill suited to structure an acceptable conception of moral order, at least under the social and political conditions of life in eighteenth-century Europe.

Not surprisingly, therefore, eighteenth-century forms of ethical rationalism tended to be ethics of duty rather than virtue. Moreover, the rationalists turned against empiricist approaches a criticism that was very similar to one earlier virtue ethicists had made against voluntarist natural law. The voluntarists, these earlier critics complained, made morality an external rather than an internal matter, something like magnetism, with human beings playing iron filings to God's lodestone. Take away the magnet and there would be no morality. A similar criticism was made of empiricist virtue ethics by a number of writers who sought to defend a rationalist ethics of duty in the first half of the eighteenth century: John Balguy, Samuel Clarke, and William Wollaston, and, after them, Richard Price and Thomas Reid.[75] The doctrine of moral sense, they argued, grounded morality in a contingent and arbitrary sense in something like the way that earlier critics of early modern natural law claimed the voluntarists had based morality on posited will. And although they applauded Hutcheson's thesis that there is a motive to morality other than "the prospect of private happiness," they objected that empiricist virtue was "of an arbitrary and positive nature . . . entirely depending on instincts, that might originally have been otherwise."[76]

The rationalists thought morality to be necessary in several different senses. As against a contingent moral sense, the rationalists argued that morality is, in Cudworth's phrase, "eternal and immutable." Hutcheson and Hume were agreed that virtue and vice "may be compar'd to sounds, colours, heat and cold, which, according to modern philosophy, are not qualities in objects, but perceptions in the mind."[77] The rationalists objected that fundamental moral truths could not depend in this way on human sentiment.[78]

The empiricists held also that any motivation to be moral is likewise contingent. But Balguy objected that "moral goodness no more depends originally on affections and dispositions, than it does on [positive] laws."[79] Had "we found in our hearts no kind instinct towards our benefactors," we would nonetheless be able to recognize an obligation to gratitude and, in that recognition, have an adequate motive to do so.[80] For the rationalists, it is necessarily true that moral agents can be virtuous; what makes us subject to morality also ensures the capacity for moral virtue.

Empiricists thought also that nothing guarantees that moral considerations will have conclusive force in practical reasoning, that moral conduct is something we really should do. The rationalists, on the other hand, defended the view that to do wrong is to act contrary to reason.

The rationalists argued that all these aspects of the empiricist approach resulted from an impoverished conception of agency and a mistaken view of the relation between practical reason and the will. For the empiricists, agency emerges from the combination of belief and desire. A person desires a state of affairs, believes something within her power will achieve that, and is caused by those two internal states to act. Reason has a wholly theoretical role in this picture, informing agents of facts about means to satisfying desires and, perhaps, as Hutcheson held, of (nonethical) facts that can cause modifications of desires as well. The rationalists, however, distinguish between "mere" intelligent goal-seeking of this sort and genuine agency. Distinctively, agents act *for reasons*; they undertake conduct on account of considerations they regard as justifying what they do. While an intelligent goal-seeker need have no end in addition to the various goals he seeks, an agent has a defining aim: doing whatever the best reasons recommend. As Balguy put it: "The end of rational actions, and rational agents, consider'd as such, is reason and moral good."[81] Bishop Butler's famous thesis of the "authority of conscience" amounted to the same thing. Without a "principle of reflection" or "conscience" – in this context, a conception of what one *should* do – a being is not an agent capable of having reasons to act.[82]

The rationalists agreed with Shaftesbury's proto-Kantian thesis (as against Hutcheson and, to a considerable extent, Hume), that genuine virtue is realized only by moral agents who govern themselves by their own moral convictions. Only if "virtue consists in a rational determination, and not in a blind pursuit of the instinct," Balguy insisted, is it rightly attributed to a *person* as opposed to something in her. Although they often treated this issue as identical to the metaphysical problem of free will and determinism, the contrast the rationalists had in mind is better seen as that between autonomy and heteronomy, between self-determination and determination by something other than the self. A moral agent, Butler argued, must have the capacity to govern himself by normative convictions he accepts, thereby making the moral agent a "law to himself."[83]

The rational intuitionists shared the modern natural lawyers' contention that there are universal norms of conduct that obligate all rational persons. The problem, recall, was to show why these norms include obligating, interest-constraining, moral demands. Clarke and Balguy were united, however, in believing that we neither need nor can have any argument to convince us of the most fundamental moral norms; they are (and must be) self-evident. Nor is there any use for a theory that aims to say what normativity consists in; that notion is fundamental and irreducible. Attempts like the theological voluntarists' derive whatever plausibility they might be thought to have from simply assuming a fundamental, irreducible moral fact in the background. Otherwise, they just change the subject from ethics to psychology or theology.[84]

The intuitionists' preferred analogy was to another area where truths seem to hold necessarily and self-evidently: mathematics. Clarke thought it is no less evident that acts are related to situations as "fitting" or "unfitting" as "that one magnitude or number is greater, equal to, or smaller than another."[85]

Like Grotius, the rationalists made a fundamental distinction between a part of morality, rooted in love or benevolence, that cannot be demanded as our due, and a part, justice or equity, that can be. Even if we lack any concern for the good of others, Balguy wrote, we can see that it is "reasonable" to do unto them "as we would be done unto."[86] Love, Clarke added, leads us "to promote the welfare and happiness of all men," while equity requires that we "deal with every man, as in like circumstances we could reasonably expect he should deal with us."[87]

When we recall the problematic of modern natural law, we can see why equity or reciprocity might appear a more promising source of the normativity of moral norms than self-love or benevolence. But what obligates an agent to forgo either his own good or the good of all, when justice calls for that? If the norms are mutually advantageous, we might say that since the agent would want others to conform in their place, with roles reversed, it is reasonable for her to conform here. Such a rationale does not require that the agent be able to care about others for their own sakes. It depends rather on an ideal of reciprocal or reasonable treatment that is independent of fellow feeling, and so may be better suited to ground a conception of normative order among individuals (and groups) who cannot expect each other's love.

As promising as this idea is, however, it still left the rationalists with a number of unsolved problems. The most vexing from their critics' perspective was how to fit moral facts as the rational intuitionists conceived them into a plausible metaphysics. But Hume's challenge remained also. The rationalists generally agreed with Hume that moral convictions necessarily motivate, but it was unclear how on their account this could be. Finally, a problem that remained for both empirical sentimentalist and rational intuitionist accounts of morality is that, unlike the natural law tradition, neither had even the beginnings of an account of the essential connection between morality and moral *responsibility*, of why we are appropriately held accountable for violating moral norms. Without, however, some explanation of the authority to *demand* compliance with mandatory moral norms, we apparently have no satisfying explanation of moral *obligation*.

NOTES

1 Schneewind 1998. This is a monumental work that should be consulted by anyone interested in the history of modern moral philosophy. For a discussion of this work, see Darwall 1999, from which I here draw.

2 Grotius 1925, pp. 10–11. For a discussion of Grotius as responding to the skeptical challenges posed by Montaigne and Charron, see, in addition to Schneewind, Tuck 1983 and 1987. Tuck argues that Grotius's response foreshadows Hobbes. For a different view see Shaver 1996. There are obvious parallels between this passage and Hobbes's famous reply to "the Foole" in ch. 15, par. 4 of *Leviathan*.

3 *Philosophical Rudiments concerning Government and Society* (the English translation of *De cive*) (1651), ch. 3, par. 31, in Hobbes 1839, vol. II, p. 47.

4 *Summa theologiae*, IaIIae, q. 93, a. 1, in Aquinas 1945.

5 Ibid., q. 91, a. 2.

6 *Summa contra Gentiles*, bk. III, ch. 16, in Aquinas 1945.

7 For the question of human law and governance, Aquinas recognizes that important issues of conflict arise. See, e.g., *De regno*, ch. 1, in Aquinas 1945. Although these could be raised well enough in terms of conflicting *beliefs* about the good, consistently with the doctrines concerning the relation between eternal law and good already cited, Aquinas does speak here about conflicting interests.

8 For a discussion of the Prisoner's Dilemma, see Barry and Hardin 1982, pp. 11–12, 24–25. The classic discussion of collective action problems is Olson 1971.

9 Cf. Sidgwick's perceptive remark that "the most fundamental difference" between modern and ancient ethical thought is that, whereas the ancients believed that there is only one "regulative and governing faculty" to be "recognized under the name of Reason," "in the modern view, when it has worked itself clear, there are found to be two – Universal Reason and Egoistic Reason, or Conscience and Self-love" (Sidgwick 1954, pp. 197–98). In this respect, although Aquinas's idea of natural law encodes a conception of morality and moral obligation that is far from anything in Aristotle, it is nonetheless fully within the ancient framework, since it allows only one fundamental principle. Eternal law's teleological archetype simultaneously determines the agent's good and natural law, so that these necessarily prescribe the same actions. As befits his subject in that book, Sidgwick confines his remarks to modern English thought. For a discussion of this claim, see Frankena 1992.

10 See Schneewind's excellent discussion of Grotius in Schneewind 1998, esp. pp. 78–81.

11 Grotius 1925, p. 11.

12 *A Treatise on Laws and God the Lawgiver*, I.i.1, in Suárez 1944.

13 For an extended discussion of these elements in Suárez, Pufendorf, and Locke, see Darwall 2004, from which I draw here.

14 John Stuart Mill, *Utilitarianism*, ch. 5.
15 I argue for this claim in Darwall 2006.
16 *The Law of Nature and Nations*, I.i.2–6, in Pufendorf 1934.
17 Ibid., I.i.3.
18 Ibid., I.i.4.
19 Ibid., I.i.3.
20 Ibid.
21 Ibid., I.v.3.
22 Ibid., I.v.5.
23 Locke sketched this first in his *Essays on the Law of Nature* (Locke 1954) and then in *An Essay concerning Human Understanding*. For an extended discussion of these aspects of Locke's thought, see Darwall 1995, pp. 33–52, from which I draw here.
24 Locke 1954, pp. 151–55.
25 "Moral rectitude . . . considered barely in it self is not good or evill nor in any way moves the will" (entry in Locke's 1693 Commonplace Book titled "Voluntas." Bodleian Library, Oxford, Lovelace MS. C28, fol. 114).
26 It is interesting to compare here Kant's idea in the *Critique of Practical Reason* that immortality of the soul and God's existence are "postulates of pure practical reason."
27 *The Law of Nature and Nations*, I.vi.5.
28 Ibid.
29 In Darwall 2006, I argue that the theme is picked up in ideas we find in Kant on respect and equal dignity, Adam Smith on the role of empathy in moral judgment and, especially, judgments of justice and dignity, and Fichte on the role of reciprocal recognition in both realizing and recognizing a distinctive form of freedom that we presuppose in second-personal address.
30 *Lev.*, ch. 15, par. 41.
31 Ibid.
32 Hobbes himself, however, is sometimes interpreted as a theological voluntarist. See, for example, Martinich 1992.
33 Another important natural lawyer of the time who sought to provide an empirical naturalist account of the normativity of laws of nature was Richard Cumberland, whose *De legibus naturae disquisitio philosophica* (London, 1672), translated as *A Treatise of the Laws of Nature* (1727), was quite influential. Although he is much less well known these days, his ideas actually anticipate many important strains of contemporary ethical naturalism. Cumberland sought to show that the "whole of moral philosophy" can be "resolv'd into *natural* observations known by the experience of all men" (1727, p. 41), and to

understand the normativity of laws of nature in terms of instrumental rationality. He also defended a version of utilitarianism and argues, as Sidgwick will much later, that deliberation sets both the agent's own good *and* the good of all as rational ends. (In this, as in many other ways, Francis Hutcheson is a student of Cumberland's thought.) For a discussion of Cumberland, see Darwall 1995, ch. 4.

34 "A Sermon Preached before the House of Commons," in Cudworth 1970, p. 123.

35 *A Treatise concerning Eternal and Immutable Morality* (hereafter *Treatise*), I.ii.3, in Cudworth 1996.

36 "Opinion on the Principles of Pufendorf," in Leibniz 1988, pp. 64–75. Leibniz also criticized Pufendorf for failing to appreciate that motive and character, specifically benevolence, mattered much more than "external acts."

37 Cudworth, *Treatise*, I.i.1.

38 As I argue in Darwall 1995, ch. 5.

39 Cudworth, *Treatise*, IV.iv.4.

40 Ibid., IV.i.1.

41 See e.g. *The True Intellectual System of the Universe* (1678) in Cudworth 1978, p. 736.

42 Cudworth, *Treatise*, IV.vi.4 (emphasis added).

43 "Sermon," in Cudworth 1970, p. 124. The last phrase is a reference to Romans 2:1, which was frequently taken during the period as referring to a form of autonomy that morality presupposes.

44 BL Add. MS. 4980, p. 239.

45 BL Add. MS. 4980, p. 9.

46 "An Inquiry Concerning Virtue or Merit," I.ii.2, in *Characteristics of Men, Manners, Opinions, Times* (Shaftesbury 1999, originally published 1711).

47 Ibid., I.ii.3, I.iii.1.

48 Ibid., I.ii.2.

49 "Soliloquy, or Advice to an Author," in *Characteristics*. See also the selections from Shaftesbury's Stoic notebooks contained in Shaftesbury 1900. For a discussion of this as well as other aspects of Shaftesbury's ethics, see Darwall 1995, ch. 7.

50 "An Inquiry concerning Virtue or Merit," I.ii.3.

51 Ibid., I.ii.4.

52 "Opinion on Pufendorf," in Leibniz 1988, p. 73.

53 "Preface to *Codex Juris Gentium*," in Leibniz 1988, p. 171.

54 Ibid.

55 "Felicity," in Leibniz 1988, p. 83.

56 This comes from a review Leibniz published anonymously, "Observationes de principio juris," published in 1700 in *Monathlicher Auszug aus allerhand neu-herausgegebenen nützlichen und artigen Büchern* (Hanover, 1700), p. 378. It is quoted (and translated) in Hruschka 1991, p. 166. Hruschka argues that this is the first formulation of the greatest happiness principle.
57 Leibniz's major follower, however, was Christian Wolff, who provided the authoritative version of rational perfectionism for German philosophy of the first half of the eighteenth century. What might be called the Leibniz/Wolff view was virtual academic orthodoxy in Germany during this period. Echoing Leibniz, Wolff identified obligation with "whatever gives a motive" (*Reasonable Thoughts about the Actions of Men*, I.i, in Scheewind 2003, p. 335). And, like Leibniz, he assumed a harmony of goods (perfections) to be metaphysically guaranteed and concluded that each person is obligated to promote the greatest perfection of all. In so acting, each simultaneously promotes his own greatest good (perfection) and, so much as it is in his power, that of every other person as well.
58 *Traité de morale* (1684), in Malebranche 1993.
59 On the latter, see Riley 1986.
60 See Vienne 1991. See also Yaffe 2000.
61 Spinoza 1985, p. 402.
62 Cudworth, *True Intellectual System of the Universe* (1678); Berkeley, *Three Dialogues between Hylas and Philonous*, Second Dialogue, in Berkeley 1948–57, vol. II.
63 For a current version of a view that argues similarly that the motive of self-understanding is central to free agency and to human cooperation, see Velleman 2000 and "The Centered Self," in Velleman 2006.
64 Mandeville 1988.
65 Butler, *Fifteen Sermons Preached at the Rolls Chapel* (1726), sermon 12, par. 31, and *Dissertation upon the Nature of Virtue* (1751), par. 8, both in Butler 1950; Berkeley, *Passive Obedience* (1712), p. 21; Hume, *Treatise*, III.ii.
66 *An Inquiry into the Original of our Ideas of Beauty and Virtue*, "Treatise concerning Moral Good and Evil," sec. 3.8, in Hutcheson 1729.
67 *An Essay on the Nature and Conduct of the Passions and Affections*, sec. 2, in Hutcheson 2002.
68 Sidgwick is the most famous example of a philosopher who advances a "dualism of practical reason" (Sidgwick 1967, pp. 373–89, 507–9). Sidgwick claims Butler as the source of this idea, but Hutcheson is a much better example. A case could be made for Cumberland as the first philosopher implicitly to suggest it. On this point, see Darwall 1995.

69 This is the central theme of *Illustrations on the Moral Sense*, in Hutcheson 2002.
70 See Darwall 1997.
71 Hume, *Treatise*, III.i.1.
72 See, especially, Butler's *Dissertation upon the Nature of Virtue*, in Butler 1950.
73 Hume, *Treatise*, III.ii.2.
74 Ibid.
75 For most purposes, Bishop Butler might also be included within this group.
76 Balguy, *The Foundation of Moral Goodness* (1728), pp. 5, 8–9.
77 Hume, *Treatise*, III.iii.1; Hutcheson, *Illustrations on the Moral Sense*, sec. 4, in Hutcheson 2002.
78 Care is required here, since Hutcheson would also have held that it is no accident we have the moral sense we do, since that can be explained by God's benevolence, and it is no accident that he is benevolent.
79 *The Foundation of Moral Goodness* (1728), p. 11.
80 Ibid., p. 12.
81 Ibid., p. 48.
82 *Fifteen Sermons*, preface, pars. 14–29, sermon 1, par. 8, sermon 2, pars. 4–17, sermon 3, pars. 1–5, in Butler 1950.
83 Ibid., sermon 2, par. 8.
84 Clarke, *A Demonstration of the Being and Attributes of God* (1705), XII.
85 Clarke, *A Discourse concerning the Unchangeable Obligations of Natural Religion* (1706), I.
86 *The Foundation of Moral Goodness* (1728), p. 12.
87 *A Discourse concerning the Unchangeable Obligations of Natural Religion* (1706), I.

A. JOHN SIMMONS

9 Theories of the state

Great changes in the character and interrelations of western political societies were in progress during the sixteenth and seventeenth centuries. Early modern philosophers either directly witnessed these changes or were able to reflect upon them from no great distance, as crucial elements of their recent political history. Unsurprisingly, then, early modern political philosophy was in important respects preoccupied with the theoretical underpinnings of the emerging political order, with its new institutions and new expectations of citizens and public officials. The theories advanced by political philosophers of the period in turn played their own modest roles in influencing the development of the modern political institutions with which we are familiar today. Their questions and problems were thus importantly related to our own, which allows early modern political philosophy to speak to many of us in a way that is perhaps not fully possible for the political philosophies of earlier periods.

I will stress here two great "divides" or transitions within the period that can help us to understand some of the most salient features of early modern political philosophy. The first of these divides is the theoretical divide between what we can call "political naturalism" and "political antinaturalism." The second is the historical transition (mirrored by a corresponding transition in political theories) from political societies that existed as complex, hierarchical structures of overlapping religious and contractual relationships (such as those that characterized empire and the feudal order) to political societies that began to take the form of modern, sovereign, territorial states. These two transitions were, of course, related in important ways. Political naturalism was understandably suppressed as theorists began to think of political society in its modern form. But because there is no precise correspondence between the two – there were, for instance, many naturalistic defenses of the sovereign (particularly, monarchical) state – I will treat the two transitions independently.

POLITICAL NATURALISM AND ITS OPPONENTS

We can think of political naturalism as the view that it is part of the natural condition of humankind for persons to be politically organized, for some to be subject to the political authority of others. Government and subjection are simply part of the natural order of the world. The Aristotelian view that "every state exists by nature" and of man as "by nature a political animal"[1] – of human nature as essentially social and political, with some persons naturally suited to rule and others to be ruled – was a familiar (and enormously influential) ancient example of political naturalism; and modern "organic theories" of the state are similarly naturalistic in orientation. But the version of political naturalism that dominated the middle ages, that was still a powerful player during the early modern period, and that was the (stated or understood) adversary for many of the best-known early modern political philosophies, was a related, religious version of naturalism. The political authority of some (typically, monarchs, emperors, or pope) over others, or of communities over their members, is natural because naturally bestowed on those persons or communities by God.

Medieval political theorists like Aquinas and Marsilius, of course, used Aristotle's secular naturalism as the basis for their own religious political naturalism (though they differed concerning its implications on many points). Reformation theorists like Luther, despite their innovations, still generally took it to be essential to view political authority as instituted by God. Frequently, the justification offered for religious political naturalism consisted simply in an appeal to the doctrine of St. Paul: "there is no authority except from God, and those that exist have been instituted by God. Therefore he who resists the authorities resists what God has appointed, and those who resist will incur judgment."[2] Luther was, in fact, largely responsible for popularizing early modern appeals to this text (though others, like George Buchanan and John Milton, later challenged the naturalist reading of the Pauline text). According to the common understanding of the doctrine, not only is politics part of the order of nature, since it is ordained for man by God, but the precise structure of currently existing power relations is also taken to be divinely sanctioned. Established rulers were sometimes said to rule by "divine right," a right that correlates with subjects' obligations of passive obedience (obligations ultimately deriving from persons' obligations to respect their Creator's choices in his conferrals of authority on particular humans). Just as papal political power (or the unified political power of Christendom under emperor and pope) was taken to derive from God's authorization, so secular kings could be characterized as by divine will like "little Gods," to use James I's memorable phrase.[3] In James's view, monarchy (not just political society) is divinely ordained, and kings are accountable only to God. The quality of the governance that issues from earthly authorities is simply irrelevant to the argument's force. If government is natural and divinely ordained, the appropriate attitude toward it is acceptance; to rail against the natural or the divine is presumptuous and pointless. The prescribed remedy for bad government is prayer.[4]

Many of the most familiar defenses of religious political naturalism, of course, advanced more complicated arguments than have been suggested thus far. For instance, among the best-known versions of early modern religious naturalism is the "patriarchalist" naturalism of Robert Filmer, known to us chiefly through Locke's famous attack on Filmer's views in his *First Treatise of Government* (1689). For Filmer, political authority is natural, monarchical, and absolute, and Filmer identifies it with paternal power.[5] He attempts to derive the God-given authority of the Stuart monarchs from the natural authority over his offspring and the world originally granted by God to Adam. Filmer's derivation proceeds through (presumed) repeated instances of inheritance of this authority, descending from biblical times down through the ages to (among other places) Stuart England. This is plainly a more complicated argument than any simple, direct appeal to divine will. But the divide in early modern political thought to which I have referred was not motivated by opposition to any particular version of political naturalism, or even only to religious versions of naturalism (though the opposition to religious naturalism was particularly keen, tied as it was to important changes in many early modern philosophers' more general conception of the relationship between humanity and God). The opposition in question was principled and fundamental, an opposition to the very idea of politics as part of the natural order.

Political antinaturalism is the view that the natural condition of humankind is nonpolitical. Most early modern political philosophers (with the notable exception of Hobbes) believed, of course, that humans are naturally sociable, perhaps even best understood as naturally members of nonpolitical or prepolitical social groups (which groups might themselves, as Suárez maintained, have divinely granted authority over their members); and many held that among our most basic duties is the requirement that we enter into society with others. (Samuel Pufendorf, for instance, argued that developing and maintaining a peaceful sociality toward others is the fundamental law of nature.)[6] But while persons may be social by nature, it is still open to the philosopher to maintain that the specifically political order of the world is artificial (in Hume's sense of requiring human artifice), as is the particular form that a political society may take, neither being ordained by God nor otherwise natural. While it may be perfectly natural for humans to create political societies and to freely subject themselves to political authority, persons are naturally subject to no political authority: the existence of political authority derives from acts of human creation. Existing political powers receive their authority (if any) neither directly from God nor from the natural superiority of rulers or governors.

One familiar way of announcing this antinaturalism was to declare that the natural condition of humankind is a condition of freedom and equality.[7] In their commitment to antinaturalism, many of the early modern political philosophers we are taught to think of as rivals – for instance, Hobbes and Locke or Hobbes and Rousseau – are in fact staunch allies. For Hobbes, man's natural condition includes the "liberty . . . to use his own power, as he will himself, for the preservation of his own nature."[8] And for Locke, this condition is "a state of perfect freedom to order their actions, and dispose of their possessions and persons as they think fit, within the bounds of the Law of Nature . . . A state also of equality, wherein all the power and jurisdiction is reciprocal."[9] Pufendorf maintained that "man's natural state . . . also comes with the name of natural freedom";[10] and Rousseau's commitment to a similar position is apparent in the opening sentences of his *Social Contract*. Affirming in this way that God has not ordained any particular political order for humankind does not, of course, entail any diminution of God's role as creator and supreme lawgiver or of the authority of his will or commands to ground human morality.[11] It implies only that politics is one part of the business of humankind that God has chosen to leave to humans. Most antinaturalists during the sixteenth and seventeenth centuries were contractarians of one sort or another, arguing that legitimate political order arises from contract, pact, or covenant (either between individuals and rulers or, more commonly, between antecedently unified peoples and rulers). Antinaturalist appeals to utility, not contract, as the source of political obligation and authority became more common later in the early modern period, particularly after Hume's example; but many of the earlier contractarians (most notably, perhaps, Pufendorf) also stressed centrally the utility of political order (and have as a result occasionally been read by interpreters as proto-utilitarians).

Political antinaturalism was indicated within theories of the period in a variety of ways, most prominently by the use of state of nature stories, by defenses of natural rights, and by the insistence on contract or consent as the source of legitimate political authority. The idea of a (or the) state of nature (or the natural condition of mankind) was used in a variety of ways by early modern political philosophers. It had historical, descriptive, and normative senses, sometimes all within the same theory. Many theorists used it exclusively in its historical sense, to refer to the period in human history prior to the appearance of civil law, institutions of government, kings, or political society. So used it usually indicated an antinaturalist stance, since if humankind once lived without polities or rulers, politics could hardly be natural for man or ordained for man by God. Filmer's insistence that Adam wielded political power was precisely a naturalist denial that humankind ever existed in a nonpolitical state of nature.[12] Mankind's natural condition was political. The idea of a nonpolitical state of nature was, however, used by other conservative writers in a way broadly consistent with naturalism, when they used it to refer to the specific historical period before man's Fall (or before the Flood). Then political society could still be portrayed as natural to and ordained by God for fallen man.

The more familiar descriptive and normative senses of the state of nature correspond to those employed by Hobbes and Locke, respectively, and their uses were almost always antinaturalist in intent. For Hobbes, the state of nature was any condition of persons living together without a common power over them "to keep them in awe" (that is, to control by credible threat of punishment aggressive conduct). The state of nature was, in essence, the absence of effective government, and it not only characterized human prehistory, but was a condition that could reemerge at any time (as Hobbes believed had happened during the Civil War in England). Locke's normative idea of the state of nature was that of persons without a common legitimate government over them, a government legitimated by their mutual consent. People (or states) are in the state of nature with respect to one another, according to Locke, where they have not freely agreed to enter civil society together, by surrendering the individual rights necessary for effective government (including, importantly, the right to privately enforce the law of nature). On this account, all persons remain in the state of nature until they reach the age of consent, and mature persons can be in the state of nature even where they live together under effective government, if that government is illegitimate. On both the Hobbesian (descriptive) account and the Lockean (normative) account, then, the state of nature can be instantiated on those historical occasions (including human prehistory) that satisfy the conditions of the account; but it does not on either account, as it does on the historical account, refer essentially to any particular period in human history. And both the Hobbesian and Lockean uses of state of nature theories plainly signal their political antinaturalism, in their consideration of possible (and actual) nonpolitical or noncivil conditions of humankind (including, in Locke's case, nonpolitical conditions that are rationally preferable to at least some familiar cases of life under an effective ruler).

The defenses of natural rights that are so familiar from the late seventeenth and eighteenth centuries similarly were normally part of an antinaturalist program in political philosophy. Here it was crucial that what was being defended was natural rights, not merely natural duties to comply with the requirements of God's (natural) law. The emergence of natural rights theories from the long tradition of natural law moral theory was a slow and confused process.

But in the hands of philosophers like Grotius, Hobbes, Pufendorf, and Locke, these theories became an important component of the political antinaturalism that was to dominate the later modern political mindset. Natural rights were generally understood as individual moral prerogatives or as moral protections for certain spheres of individual choice or the pursuit of certain interests. Sometimes (as in Hobbes) these rights were taken to be mere moral liberties – that is, to entail only that the conduct in question was not wrongful. Other theorists (like Locke) defended natural rights as more strongly implying correlative duties on others to permit exercise of the right. But either way, the assertion of natural rights for persons directly implies a moral justification for acting contrary to the commands of political superiors. If we have a natural liberty-right to preserve ourselves (as Grotius and Hobbes believed), then we may without wrongdoing ignore the commands of our political superiors where they do not conduce to our preservation. We are not naturally subject to those superiors in all things. If we have a (stronger) natural right to "order our actions" as we choose (as Locke argued), correlating with others' natural duties to allow us to do so, then we cannot be legitimately subjected to the political power of others except by our choice. Natural subjection by (alleged) natural inferiority or by (alleged) divine grant is not possible.[13] Natural rights talk was thus almost always implicitly also antinaturalist discourse.

Still more obviously antinaturalist in its implications was the widespread early modern employment of the idea of contract, promise, or consent as the historical source of political power or as the sole ground of legitimate political authority. In one sense, as we have seen, contractarianism wears its antinaturalism on its face, since if political authority requires human creation through contract, that authority can hardly be portrayed as natural or divinely ordained. On the other hand, an observation of that sort seems in certain ways simplistic or insensitive to the actual variety of contractarian thought of the period. Some early appeals to contract or consent in explaining political authority (such as those of Hooker and Suárez) were not entirely or unambiguously antinaturalist in tone, still relying as they did on the idea of God's grant as the ultimate source of such authority. And, more generally, appeals to contract were certainly not routinely indicative of a revolutionary or even a nonconservative political spirit. On the contrary, use of the idea of the contract came quite naturally to philosophers of many orientations. Even Augustine had referred to a general contract by human societies to obey their kings. Feudal political order had largely consisted in a complex network of overlapping contracts, exchanging protection for various services, with both lord and vassal consequently possessing both rights and obligations. So there was nothing particularly revolutionary about early modern uses of the idea of contract to explain political order.

Further, most of the early employments of the idea of covenant or contract as the foundation of political society were quite distant from the more familiar and individualist uses of them in the work of philosophers like Hobbes, Locke, or Rousseau. For normally the early contractarians referred to political contracts that were neither individual nor contemporary – that is, contracts that were neither made by individual, free persons nor made by the persons alleged to be bound by the contracts (or their contemporaries). Instead, the relevant contracts were generally supposed to be between already constituted or incorporated peoples and their rulers (or governments) and to have taken place at the historical founding of each political society. Contemporary political life was not itself constituted by consent or contract, but was seen rather in terms of a continuation of the original, founding contract (or contracts: typically the founding was conceived of in terms of a series of contracts). The justification of a historical people's authority to act for its contemporary constituent members and the authority of a historical political contract with respect to subsequent generations of subjects in that political society were often left somewhat vague, with frequent (and relatively uncompelling) recourse to historical tradition, implicit acceptance through nonrebellion, and the like. The contract theories of Buchanan, Hooker, and Althusius were of this sort, and those of Grotius and Pufendorf certainly leaned in that direction. English justifications of contemporary political arrangements by reference to the terms of their "ancient constitution" (or to ancient customs, or to the Magna Carta as their confirmation, or to the unwritten rules of historical common law) – which were especially frequent during Stuart rule – displayed a similar theoretical bent. Appeals to ancient, hazy, founding contracts of existing societies, while certainly technically antinaturalist – since political authority is still a human artifact and peoples retain the right to resist violations of the contract – nonetheless often manage to have much of the feel of the political naturalist's appeal to the divinely ordained, time-honored inevitability of the existing political order. For the temporal and emotional distance of founding contracts from the lives and concerns of contemporary subjects remains potentially enormous, and the opportunity to interpret ancient contracts as authorizing tyranny is omnipresent.

Similarly, even nonhistorical contract theories of political authority seldom were taken by their early proponents to have the liberal, antiabsolutist, anticonservative (and possibly revolutionary) implications that later contractarians attempted to derive from their theories. Their unwillingness on these scores generally flowed from one or more of three sources: a theory of presumed, tacit, or implicit consent (together with certain factual assumptions); a theory of the unlimited alienability of rights; or an acceptance of the binding force of coerced consent.

Many early modern contractarians denied that political resistance (as opposed to passive, conscientious refusal to obey) could ever be justified, or affirmed that such active resistance could be justified only when one's own preservation was directly put in jeopardy. The standard argument was that it was in every free person's best interests to live in an enduring, peaceful society and thus to grant to a ruler or government all the rights one possesses whose transfer might be necessary to preserving stability and peace. These powers in fact include all the rights one has, perhaps excepting the right to defend one's life from immediate threats. Since it is in each person's best interest to (virtually) absolutely empower a sovereign in this way, we can presume that each person implicitly or tacitly consents to such an arrangement. Further, the argument proceeded, a serious theory of contracts must hold that the contractor's will should determine the content of the agreement. Contractors may transfer to others (virtually) any rights that they wish to transfer, meaning that even voluntary enslavement or political absolutism (the collective, political equivalent of slavery) is perfectly possible morally and a perfectly possible legitimate consequence of contractual relationships. That contractors made what in retrospect seems a bad bargain is neither here nor there; bargains must be kept. Thus, even if we ignore the possible binding force of an ancient, original (founding) contract, a contractarian argument was available that appeared to demonstrate that by way of a perfectly contemporary (if presumed or implicit) contract, political superiors can and routinely do enjoy absolute authority, and political inferiors possess no right to resist a lawful sovereign's rule. Each in his own way, Suárez, Grotius, John Selden, Hobbes, Spinoza, and Pufendorf all employed variants of this argument.

In addition, illiberal conclusions seemed bound to flow from belief in the binding force of contracts or promises produced by intimidation, coercion, or radically unequal bargaining power. And, again, many of the early modern contractarians subscribed to such a view. It was a view that could seem perfectly natural and plausible, of course, given that familiar feudal contractual relations were regularly tainted by such defects, as were the common military and diplomatic treaties and agreements of that age (and every other age). But if coerced agreements are morally binding, then conquest and intimidation can be perfectly legitimate sources of political authority, again tending to confirm conservative and absolutist conclusions about the legitimacy of existing political power structures. Hobbes went so far as to argue that all political covenants are equally made from the motive of fear, so that all such covenants (including those made with conquerors at swordpoint) must be equally binding.[14] This Hobbesian position has often been equated with the idea that "might makes right," though it is more accurately the view that the power to destroy reliably produces willing submission, which in turn makes the actions of the mighty rightful.

Ultimately it was left to later contractarian philosophers like Locke to utilize the idea of the political contract in its purest antinaturalist form, making political authority rest on individual, contemporary consent (or, depending on one's interpretative leaning, on what it would be rational for individual, contemporary persons to consent to) – thus rejecting the idea of historical, founding contracts as binding on subsequent generations – and drawing broadly liberal conclusions from this antipolitical naturalism. Even purely antinaturalist contractarian thought, of course, remained perfectly consistent with conservative political views (as Hobbes showed), just as purely antinaturalist utilitarian political thought did (as Hume demonstrated). And it remained consistent with the defense of political absolutism as well (as we have seen), until the Levellers and Locke made prominent the arguments that there are limits on the power of even a free adult to contractually transfer to others certain personal individual rights and that consent produced by coercion or intimidation is not binding, failing as it does to express the will of the agent. Once such limits were established, absolute government simply could not be a legitimate outcome of a contract – hence, it could not be a legitimate form of polity at all – and the path was clear for the development of the more explicit, eighteenth-century defenses of inalienable natural rights and the necessary limits to political power that they establish. Of the sources of antinaturalist, contractarian illiberality, only the theory of tacit consent remained in Locke's political philosophy; and it is that theory of tacit consent which is most often challenged by liberal philosophical commentary on Locke.

While the defense of or opposition to political naturalism thus characterizes much of the substance of early modern political philosophy, it must be reemphasized that the contrast between the two views, while very important, was not especially sharp. For instance, a common position of the period was that while political life was a direct gift from God, political life was not fully natural for man, since the first humans had existed in a nonpolitical condition. Whether or not this counted as political naturalism seems a fine point. Similarly, it was regularly maintained that all persons were born free with respect to other individual persons (but perhaps not with respect to groups with quasi-political status), that political society is perfectly natural but not any particular ruler or form of government, that nonpolitical (but fully incorporated) societies are natural to man, or that God commands the human creation of polities. All of these positions, all perfectly familiar in early modern political philosophy, lie close to the border between naturalism and antinaturalism. So we should not assume that the debate over political naturalism was one in which philosophers simply lined up on one of two clearly defined sides.

But why did they care which side they were on, or try so hard not to take a side at all? Here the answers are as varied as the positions on the question, and were sometimes as simple as the antinaturalist's desire to make the study of politics more scientific by clearly delineating it from the discipline of theology (a desire made clear by theorists like Althusius and Buchanan, for instance). But two very general answers from among the many seem the most important.

First, early modern political philosophers had clearly before them a virtually unparalleled display of theoretical and practical conflict over the nature of Christian religion and its relation to politics, a bloody and unsettling recent history of passionate debate, schism, and religious war. They wrote while the French Huguenots were massacred, during the religious wars that consumed France for most of the rest of that century, while the Thirty Years War raged, and during the Puritan rising against royal power in England. Or they wrote with the memory of these bloody and unsettling events clearly fixed before their minds. The available positions were many, and precisely where one stood on the role of God and church in the practical life of the polity obviously mattered deeply in that context, stances sometimes costing philosophers their careers, their freedom, or even their lives (Grotius, for instance, wrote his most important work while imprisoned and in exile, due to his involvement in a political controversy that ultimately rested on differences over issues of religious toleration).

Second, the early modern period witnessed the birth of several traditions of thought committed to the possibility of justified political resistance, along with countertraditions determined to undermine this conclusion. The standing of rulers or governments – as naturally superior or as ordained by God, say – makes a plain difference to the plausibility of conclusions about resistance and revolution. If government is made by human beings, not by God or nature, then it is an artifact that can without impropriety be altered and improved by human beings. It is not, simply by existing, what it ought to be. Some government is better, some is worse, and many are capable of obvious improvement. As a human creation, made to serve human needs, official refusals to permit such improvements begin to look themselves like refusals to be guided by the end or point of political society. The unjust and unresponsive ruler breaches a trust, reneges on an implicit agreement, is himself more the rebel than those who oppose or attempt to remove him (as Locke famously argued). While there was, of course, some Catholic resistance theory in the period, it was principally Calvinist theorists in France, Scotland, and England who advanced this line of argument. In the *Vindiciae contra tyrannos*,[15] in Buchanan and in Althusius, the doctrine of popular sovereignty received its first influential defenses, paving the way for the culmination of Calvinist resistance theory in Locke's *Second Treatise*. None of this is to say, as we have seen, that conservative philosophers all lined up on the naturalist side of this divide; the period was rife with antinaturalist defenses of doctrines of passive submission and nonresistance. But it was the rise of antinaturalism in early modern political philosophy that made justified political resistance seem a possible conclusion in the debate. No issues are more central to political philosophy than the duties of subjects, the nature and source of political authority, and the limits on the political relationship; and it was through the debate about political naturalism that these issues were approached in early modern political philosophy.

OLD AND NEW FORMS OF POLITICAL SOCIETY

I turn now to the second of the divides or transitions of early modern political philosophy to which I referred above: the transition from earlier forms of political life to the modern state (along with the corresponding conceptual changes this historical transition facilitated). Much of the most influential political philosophy of the period was written at the dawn of the modern nation-state. Indeed, many historians date the beginning of the modern state system well into the early modern period, at the Peace of Westphalia that closed the Thirty Years War in 1648. Prior to the sixteenth century, the term 'state' was seldom even used to refer to an independent political society. Machiavelli's writings helped to change this (though Machiavelli himself rarely used 'state' in the modern sense, he did clearly work with the idea of independent, territorial polities). But the political order of Europe on which Machiavelli could look back was very different from that which existed during the lives of Hume or Rousseau; and the concept of the modern state that developed in early modern political philosophy developed along with the ideas of territorial exclusivity and political sovereignty, emerging features of the new political order.

The political organization of the middle ages lacked several of the distinctive features of modern political society, the most striking of which were the absence of clear territorial jurisdictions and the absence of clear hierarchical structures of authority. The familiar modern tendency of politics to aid in the convergence of national and political identities was also largely missing. Christendom was structured by a complicated and decentralized system of power relations, in which the claims to obedience made by localities (towns and cities), feudal lords and kings, church leaders (popes and bishops), and quasi-religious leaders (the Holy Roman emperors) cut across one another and overlapped, often without clear priority. The claims in question were (with the exception of some localities' claims) claims over persons, not claims over geographical territories (and over persons only insofar as they were in those territories). Feudal society was a network of quasi-contractual relationships, in which some promised protection or support to others in exchange for promises of various other goods or services. One's rights and obligations depended on the nature of these agreements, not on one's geographical location in the world, and particular individuals were regularly subject to claims from a variety of superiors. Feudal barons might hold fiefs from different kings in different territories, for instance, and military support might be promised to different kings for different kinds of occasions. While the church claimed a more universal authority, its authority too was over persons – specifically, over believers – and not over territory. Nor, of course, was its authority clearly located in any uncontroversial hierarchy of authority. The Holy Roman emperors claimed authority over precisely the same body of persons (the inevitable rivalry between church and empire eventually seriously weakened both); and they claimed superiority over all other rulers, a claim widely denied by rival kings. But while the emperors ruled over specific parts of Europe, like the earlier Roman emperors, they claimed no bounded territory as their own. The empire was meant eventually to have universal jurisdiction, not territorially limited jurisdiction.

From this morass of interrelated power structures, the modern state gradually emerged – more rapidly in France, Spain, and England, and more slowly in areas (Germany, Italy) controlled by the Holy Roman empire. Where states grew slowly, they were preceded by other alternatives to the old order, such as city leagues (e.g. the Hanseatic League) and the independent, territorial (but internally factional) city states of northern Italy, all of which themselves were eventually replaced by modern states. Why these changes occurred is a matter of some controversy among historians (though efficiencies of scale and the changing nature of warfare seem to be at least part of the story). More important for our purposes is that these were the political changes witnessed by early modern political philosophers, changes that helped to set the philosophical agenda for the period.

The emerging order of modern states consisted of multiple independent polities, each claiming jurisdiction over a distinct portion of the earth (and over the persons in that territory), each claiming the right of external sovereignty – that is, autonomy or independence from the authority of other states, persons, or organizations – and each displaying an internal hierarchy of political and legal authority, with the shared understanding that some office or body must hold supreme (or sovereign) authority relative to others within the polity. In addition, the new order tended to bring about the convergence of polities and nations (think here of the aforementioned theoretical conception of polities as based in an original, founding contract between a preexisting people and a ruler). Church and empire were political organizing systems that reached across myriad nations, while feudal relationships cut freely across the lines of nationality. Modern states, by contrast, tended both, on the one hand, to correspond to preexisting, historical communities connected to particular territories and, on the other, to foster new, more political kinds of nationality, premised not only on cultural and territorial continuity, but on mutual subjection to a common set of (relatively) fixed laws and participation in a common civic life.

Early modern political philosophy, appropriately, concerned itself principally with understanding the nature of the new political entities of this kind and of the claims they made (e.g. to sovereignty and territory) – focusing on questions about the justifications (or lack thereof) available for these claims, on questions about the specific ways in which states needed to be organized or limited in order for these claims to be defensible, and on questions about the best forms such states could take.

SOVEREIGNTY, TERRITORY, GOVERNMENT

Internal sovereignty is supremacy of authority (right, power) within the territories of the state. External sovereignty is the independence of the state from authorities external to it. Early modern political philosophy was preoccupied with both ideas, concern with the former yielding competing theories of the nature, location, and ground of sovereignty within the state, while concern with the latter yielded competing theories of international relations and war and peace. I begin with internal sovereignty.

Jean Bodin focused attention on the problem of sovereignty, and the account he gave of the notion was a significant event in the development of Western political thought. In every state, Bodin argued, there must be a single person or group in which the entire authority of the state is concentrated. This authority must be supreme and final, the last legal and political word in the state; so law can simply be understood as the command of the sovereign. Without such finality, there is not one state, one clear source of law. For there to be such finality and supremacy, this authority must be completely unlimited: by temporal limits, by the constraints of civil law, by other governing bodies (as in a mixed constitution), or by anything else. Sovereignty must be perpetual, absolute, and undivided.[16] Hobbes presented virtually identical arguments.

Most early modern political philosophers agreed that there must be a final, supreme, legal authority in every civil society, properly conceived (though not all used the term 'sovereign,' and there was disagreement about whether finality of legislative or executive authority was the more basic requirement). The most serious debates about sovereignty concerned not its necessity for political society, but rather its ground, its location, and the possibility of limits on state sovereignty. Disputes about the ground of state sovereignty we have already considered – whether it is grounded in divine will, in the power to compel submission, or in consent or contract (historical or personal); and conclusions about the ground of sovereignty had clear implications for debates concerning the location and extent of sovereignty. Disputes about the location of sovereignty tended to be of two sorts. The first, more philosophical, dispute concerned whether sovereignty rested ultimately and inalienably in the people as a whole, who merely delegate or entrust (rather than transfer) their authority to government (as e.g. Buchanan, Althusius, the Levellers, and Locke maintained),[17] or whether sovereignty was located in a government or ruler who was the rightful holder of that supreme authority (as e.g. Bodin, Grotius, Hobbes, and Pufendorf held). The second, often related (but usually more historical and empirical) kinds of debate about the location of sovereignty concerned the question of where sovereignty lay in particular states – typically those with mixed constitutions, and most prominently England.

By far the most interesting aspect of the early modern discussion of sovereignty, however, was the disagreement about the possibility of limits on sovereignty. As we have seen, Bodin and Hobbes held that sovereignty was necessarily unlimited and absolute; limited sovereignty was simply not sovereignty, being inferior to that which limited it. The opponents of absolutism replied with the powerful argument that, in effect, supremacy within a domain and absoluteness are simply different notions, not necessarily connected. An authority can be the supreme, final authority within a realm – and so be sovereign – without necessarily possessing the absolute authority to do anything at will. A government can be the sole, final, legislative and executive authority in a polity while empowered only to make and enforce laws within certain limits. Defenders of absoluteness, in response, remained suspicious that proponents of limited sovereignty were in fact with such claims only disguising their true belief in absolute, but popular, sovereignty or in a divided sovereignty that unintelligibly lacked an authority to specify the terms of the division. But since proponents of popular sovereignty almost never maintained that the people's authority to act on behalf of its members was absolute, limited as it was by moral law, the first charge, at least, seems unsustainable.

The apparent logical possibility of limited sovereignty immediately raised the question of the ways in which sovereignty should be understood to be limited. This question was typically addressed by considering the proper task, sphere, or end of civil government, an approach which was itself related to the question of what powers rational contractors would in fact delegate to government. Assuming that such contractors want government chiefly to bring about and continually secure civil peace and prosperity, we must ask what authority governments need to accomplish these ends. Here the proponents of limited sovereignty argued on empirical grounds that absolute authority is simply not necessary to the task. Governments do not need the authority to invade certain basic personal rights – to innocent personal liberties, to property, to religious freedom. Many of these rights would later come to be regarded as in principle inalienable and imprescriptible, thus setting necessary limits to sovereign authority; and some, such as rights to religious liberty, came to be regarded as belonging in a special class of rights. But it was at first sufficient for the argument that such rights were not necessary to government's proper task, so that persons could not be simply assumed to have implicitly surrendered these rights in creating a sovereign. The course of Locke's writings on religious toleration serves as an excellent illustration of the argumentative transition from (in his early writings) regarding the power to legislate in religious matters as necessary to the preservation of civil peace, to his final view of "the care of souls" as simply none of "the business of civil government."[18] Hand in hand with this defense of limited sovereignty grew doctrines of justified political resistance against sovereigns that act beyond their limited authority – expanding from the idea of justified resistance in the name of God (i.e. to uphold the true faith), through the idea of justified resistance by inferior magistrates or representatives of the people, to the more radical doctrine of justified popular resistance (either by the people collectively, or even more radically, by wronged individuals).

About the early modern discussion of external sovereignty I will say little (though much of modern thought about the nature and authority of states was in fact prompted by prior concerns about international morality and policy). The medieval international order rested primarily on overarching ecclesiastical and imperial authority. The modern order of independent states, equal in authority (if not in power), required a very different model for political philosophy. The emerging political antinaturalism (discussed above), with its emphasis on the natural freedom and equality of persons, possessed just the model required for the job. In the same way that individual persons could be conceived of as existing in a state of nature, so could the free and equal (i.e. sovereign) nation states of the world be thought of as corporate individuals existing in an international state of nature. For the single most salient feature of the new order was the absence of any higher authority with the right to make law for, adjudicate disputes between, or punish the sovereign states. And the absence of (effective or legitimate) higher authority with such rights was, as we have seen, for most philosophers the defining characteristic of the state of nature. Understanding legitimacy or right and wrong in the international sphere, then – including, for instance, the laws of war and the rights of various nations to portions of the earth or sea – was simply a matter of seeing how the characteristics of the state of nature applied to nations in that state.

Grotius and Pufendorf produced extensive and detailed theories on this subject. Hobbes and Locke produced equally important, though far less detailed, accounts. The primary division in such theories depended on the moral condition that was taken to characterize the state of nature. On the one hand, there were theories like that of Hobbes, according to which the state of nature is essentially a moral vacuum, such that "the notions of right and wrong, justice and injustice have there no place"; and political societies in such a condition are "in the state and posture of gladiators," prepared at all times to use force to promote their rational advantage and utterly unconstrained morally from doing so whenever they judge it best.[19] On the other hand, more moralized conceptions of the state of nature (like Locke's), where that state was seen as governed by a law of nature that binds persons (and, by analogy, states) even without a common superior to keep all in awe, permitted as a conclusion in this context a significant body of rules for international conduct (corresponding to the natural law rules for individual conduct), including nonaggression, the keeping of pacts, and so on.

The claims of modern states to enduring geographical territories – claims to territorial exclusivity and sovereignty – were issues in the theories of both internal and external sovereignty. For just as the claims of states to have exclusive jurisdiction over particular territories needed to be justified against rival claimants within the state (e.g. individual landowners or groups desiring territorial autonomy), they needed to be justified against the claims of rival states wishing to control or use that same territory. On the subject of territorial sovereignty, however, early modern political philosophers (like their successors) had surprisingly little to say, seeming simply to accept that the division of the earth by occupation and conquest was legitimate. Insofar as they displayed interest in justifying this acceptance, they by and large appeared to assume that if they had explained the authority or sovereignty of the state over persons within a particular territory, then they had ipso facto explained the right of the state to control the territory itself (by e.g. regulating border crossings, preventing secession, controlling resources within it, etc.). But this assumption, of course, is false. It is not enough to show that persons within the state's dominion can be understood to have tacitly or implicitly consented to its authority (as most of the contractarians believed). Unless the individuals rightly subject to sovereign authority themselves have rights over the relevant portions of the earth, then those territories appear only to be within the reach of the state's power (and often not even that), not within its sphere of rightful authority.

Grotius and Locke seem to have been alone among the early modern political philosophers in appreciating this problem. Grotius, largely in passing, suggests that the boundaries of states must be the same kinds of things as the boundaries of private estates. Locke, in considerably more detail, argues that the consent that makes a person a member of any legitimate political society must be understood as an agreement to join permanently to that state as well the land in which that person has private property. Since Locke (following Grotius) famously argues as well that persons can by labor (and subsequent free exchange) enjoy morally binding rights to property even in a state of nature, he can present the picture of a state's legitimate territories as cobbled together from the preexisting property rights of its constituent members. (Common, unowned land surrounded by the private property incorporated into the state, Locke supposes, is regulated by international consent to local state control.)[20] While Locke's theory faces obvious problems, it alone among early modern theories of the state at least has the proper form to explain the claims over territory (rather than over persons) made by modern states.

Finally, even supposing that we understand the nature of, limits on, and justification for political societies exercising the kind of territorial sovereignty that modern states claimed for themselves, there still remains the ancient question of the best form of government for such states to employ. In one respect, most early modern political philosophers followed the lead of the ancients (particularly, Aristotle) by considering the question in terms of the options of rule by one (monarchy), rule by the few (aristocracy or oligarchy), and rule by the many (democracy). The standard line of political antinaturalists (and even many naturalists) was that because God had ordained no particular form of government, the people founding a political society were simply free to choose their preferred form. Legitimate territorial sovereignty could in principle be exercised by any of these forms of government.

There remained the question of which form of government was most likely to achieve those ends for which the people erected government over them. On this question, early modern political philosophers seem to have introduced relatively few novel or interesting arguments to take the debate beyond its ancient and medieval forms. Acceptance of monarchy as an appropriate form of government was very widespread, despite the bitter disagreement over whether or not such monarchs' sovereign authority should (or must of necessity) be absolute. Defenders of democracy were few. Republican authors of the period clearly cared more about the people's right to choose their government (and about its being nonabsolute) than they did about government's form. The Levellers, Locke, and Rousseau (to mention likely candidates) were not defenders of democracy, though Rousseau did believe that democracy might be most suitable for certain kinds of very small states (and Spinoza also had kind words for democracy). And with the exception of Rousseau's case for "natural aristocracy" (i.e. rule by the wisest),[21] even rule by the few received relatively little in the way of original support.

There are two chief qualifications to the claims made above that merit mention in closing: the first concerning the idea of mixed government, the second concerning representation. Political philosophers, in large numbers beginning during the seventeenth century, started to mention "mixed" ("balanced," or "federal") forms of government as preferable alternatives to the three pure forms, no doubt using as their models the actual governments of some existing nation states. This move was opposed by others, not just as a mistaken claim about the best form of government, but as a confused claim about possible forms of government. Bodin and Hobbes, as we have seen, thought that political sovereignty was necessarily indivisible. And both concluded from this that mixed government was not so much a bad form of government as it was no government at all. There is no sovereignty exercised by a mixed government, hence a society so governed is not in a political condition at all.

Given our contemporary acceptance of mixed constitutions and divided sovereignty (which we take to be exemplified with particular clarity, for example, in the United States), the rejection of mixed government may seem plainly confused (as contemporary philosophers regularly conclude). But it is worth considering briefly the actual form of Hobbes's argument (the more sophisticated of the two), before we leap to this comforting conclusion. Hobbes's principal point was that where sovereignty is genuinely divided between two governing bodies (or persons), it will always be impossible to determine what the law is (and hence to predict that for which one will be punished). There is always the possibility that at any moment the two bodies will disagree in their declarations or interpretations of the law. If their competencies are governed by a written constitution, then whatever body has authority to interpret that written document is in fact sovereign over all others; and if no body has such authority, then the law remains uncertain. A single, undivided sovereign body (by contrast) is always the indisputable source of the law. The force of this argument for practical politics seems to be that nonsovereign mixed governments can only make clear law (and so govern effectively) where subjects and governors are in steady agreement about the division of powers specified by the constitution; disagreement, without a single indisputable source of law to correct it, will produce uncertainty, conflict, and possible civil war. There seems to be much to be said for this empirical political hypothesis.

The second qualification is this: Some theorists of the period, particularly among supporters of Parliament during the years surrounding the Civil War in England, defended the view that in order to be legitimate, government needed to be representative. Representative government was often presented by them as the middle ground between unwieldy, chaotic, democratic governments and monarchies that tended to tyranny. Not only was it thus the best form of government, avoiding the ills of its competitors; but it was legitimate in a way that monarchy could not be, since monarchs could not pretend to be representing the diverse population of a nation-state in the way that a multiplicity of elected officials could. This was not simply a defense of rule by the few. It was a defense of rule by a particular few who maintained an ongoing connection with the will of the people, long beyond the original, founding contract that authorized government of that form. Defenders of monarchy (like Hobbes) tended to respond that monarchs could perfectly well represent their subjects, since in consenting to their rule people authorized them to act on their behalfs – in short, to represent them; all legitimate governments were representative in the relevant sense. But as the idea of a founding contract began to be regarded more and more as a myth, the contemporary consent (allegedly) given by citizens in electing their representatives came more and more to be regarded as a necessary condition for governmental legitimacy. Defenses of pure monarchical rule as a result became increasingly infrequent, and political discourse about legitimate forms of government began to display the focus on the idea of representation so familiar from later modern political philosophy and practice.

NOTES

1 Aristotle, *Politics*, I.2.
2 Romans 13:1–2. See also 1 Peter 2:13–14.
3 The "divine right of kings" doctrine is best understood as a Reformation doctrine (like its rival, the natural rights theory), being essentially a Protestant defense of divinely ordained secular political authority, mounted to rival the Catholic defense of divinely ordained papal political authority.
4 Alternatively, for philosophers like Montaigne, the appropriate response is stoic endurance, patience, and submission.
5 See e.g. *Patriarcha*, I.3–4, in Filmer 1991.
6 *The Law of Nature and Nations*, II.iii.15, in Pufendorf 1934.
7 There were prominent philosophers who, on this point, appeared to straddle the naturalist divide. Suárez, for instance, held both that politics is natural, that political authority is naturally bestowed on human communities by God, and that persons are naturally free, with legitimate political rule resting on consent. The appearance of simultaneous naturalism and antinaturalism is explained by uncertainty as to whether for Suárez a community holding political power, but without familiar political institutions or rulers, counts as a kind of political society or only as a nonpolitical social organization. Richard Hooker similarly (and slightly earlier) held that persons are naturally free and equal, that (most) political authority derives from consent, and that political authority ultimately derives from God. For Hooker's peculiar consent theory, see *Of the Laws of Ecclesiastical Polity*, I.x.4, 8, in Hooker 1989.
8 *Lev.*, ch. 14, par. 1.
9 *Second Treatise of Government*, par. 4, in Locke 1993.
10 *The Law of Nature and Nations*, II.ii.3.
11 Grotius, notoriously, denied the necessity of God's will to the binding force of natural law (*Of the Law of War and Peace*, prolegomena §11, in

Grotius 1925), as did Hobbes (less explicitly). Philosophers like Pufendorf and Locke were emphatic in reaffirming this necessity.

12 Even antinaturalists like Pufendorf denied, on the basis of the condition of Adam and Eve, that mankind ever existed all at once in the state of nature (*The Law of Nature and Nations*, II.ii.4). Locke's later efforts to clearly distinguish conjugal and paternal power (of the sort wielded immediately by Adam) from properly political power were thus crucial to the effort to characterize mankind's natural condition as genuinely nonpolitical.

13 Antinaturalists, of course, often had to walk a fine line on this point, accepting that divine grants of political authority to some could in principle produce for others legitimate subjection, but denying that there is any reason to suppose that such grants have actually taken place (or that a wise God would choose to intervene in such ways). Thus, for example, Locke follows his assertion of mankind's natural freedom and equality with the caveat, "unless the Lord and Master of them all should by any manifest declaration of his will set one above another" (*Second Treatise of Government*, par. 4). Locke's argument that our right to freedom is natural to mature persons, of course, clearly implies that no such divine act has occurred (or will occur).

14 *Lev.*, ch. 20, pars. 1–2. Hobbes, of course, ignores in this argument the apparently quite significant difference between acting from fear of a harm threatened by another agent (in order to induce compliance with his will) and acting from fear of consequences that will only predictably flow from the joint behavior of other persons, without direct coercive threats.

15 The *Vindiciae* was an anonymous Huguenot tract published in 1579, generally credited to Philippe Duplessis Mornay, Herbert Languet, or both. For a modern edition see *Vindiciae contra tyrannos* 1969.

16 *Les six livres de la république*, I, 8, par. 1; I, 10, in Bodin 1992.

17 See e.g. Althusius, *Politica methodice digesta*, IX, 18–19, in Althusius 1995.

18 *A Letter concerning Toleration*, pars. 4–10, in Locke 1993. See also Simmons 1993, pp. 123–36. In his *Theological-Political Treatise*, Spinoza argued that toleration of diversity of opinion and freedom of speech were in fact not just consistent with, but necessary to the preservation of civil stability (Spinoza 1958).

19 *Lev.*, ch. 13, pars. 12–13.

20 See *Second Treatise of Government*, pars. 120, 45.

21 *Social Contract*, III.5, in Rousseau 1978.

THOMAS M. LENNON

10 Theology and the God of the philosophers

The God that philosophers in the early modern period intended to refer to was the God of the Judeo-Christian tradition, which is to say, the being who created the world, who spoke to Moses from the burning bush, and who, through Jesus Christ, saved mankind from the consequences of sin. But who that being is, and what he means for human existence, was a matter of serious and sometimes mortal debate, even, and especially, within this tradition. This controversy is rather ironic because it was agreed that God had explicitly revealed himself through the texts that had come to be known as the Bible ("the book").

Outside this tradition, there was not much of relevance. Islam was regarded as the paradigmatic religion of the infidel, and was summarily dismissed, especially insofar as it was thought to embrace a fatalism incompatible with human freedom and responsibility. Even so, it had a few important, if unacknowledged, influences. There is a connection, for example, between David Hume's famous analysis of causation in terms of constant conjunction (via Nicolas Malebranche and Francisco Suárez) and the Arab occasionalist al-Farabi. Second, largely because of Jesuit missionaries, there was a certain interest in the Far East which at least shaped some philosophical thinking. When Malebranche produced the single best short exposition of his system, he framed it as a dialogue between a Christian and a Chinese philosopher. Benedict de Spinoza's relation to Chinese thought also has been the object of study. Finally, Judaism itself, the target of perennial persecution, was nonetheless viewed as being of interest in three ways: as the ur-religion containing the original and uncontaminated roots of Christianity, as the bearer still of a pure revealed religion (a view held today by some

Christian fundamentalists), or, finally, as an example (applied to Christianity, tacitly or otherwise) of religion as a purely human invention based on fear and ignorance (this view emerging sometimes from within Judaism, as in the case of Spinoza).[1]

THE GOD OF THE PHILOSOPHERS

The book of Genesis tells us that on the sixth day of creation God said, "let us make man in our image, after our likeness . . . So God made man in his own image" (1:25–26). In the eighteenth century, at the very end of the period covered here, Voltaire said, hardly less famously, "if God did not exist, it would be necessary to invent him."[2] This dramatic shift to man creating God, presumably in his own image, expresses two important developments in thinking about God in the early modern period.

One is that in discussing God, philosophers of the period seem to reveal less about God than about themselves, or at least about the world as they see it. They all pretty much agree on what attributes God must have, but certain of these attributes come in for greater emphasis, depending on the philosopher. Thus G. W. Leibniz, for example, repeatedly insists upon wisdom as an essential attribute of God, as would befit the creator of the well-regulated world that he experiences. Pierre Bayle, on the other hand, emphasizes divine goodness, without which the world would be nothing more than the irremediable nightmare of crime and suffering that he experiences it to be. René Descartes, as will be seen below, for reasons of his own emphasizes divine power, or omnipotence.

This development should come as no surprise, because God was generally invoked in philosophical contexts to explain the world, typically as its cause. What attributes God is thought to have, therefore, will depend on what attributes the world is thought to have. Even in the case of Descartes, which is complicated because his notion of cause is complicated, God still plays a central theoretical role. In early correspondence, Descartes announces that he has discovered the foundations of his physics, which is to say his metaphysics, in theology. He does not say explicitly what he got from theology, but he immediately turns, with great excitement, to his belief that all truth, including the eternal truths of mathematics, depends on God. Descartes goes on to explain that God is the total and efficient cause of truth, that the essence of things no less than their existence depends on his will, and that had he willed otherwise, all truth would have been otherwise.[3] This notion of an utterly omnipotent God, who acts with an unconstrained freedom of indifference, later generates and overcomes for Descartes the ultimate doubt of skepticism. Because truth depends entirely on divine power, the being exercising that power must be shown to be reliable before we can accept as true what appears to us to be true. But once that reliability has been established, the road to certain knowledge is opened to us.

To some extent, this explanatory relation between the God of the philosophers and the world is to be found earlier – consider Aquinas's five ways, for example – but in the early modern period the explanatory role of God came to dominate because of the dominance of natural theology. We can distinguish two kinds of theology: first, revealed theology, wherein faith provides premises about God and related matters, to which reason is applied, and second, natural theology, wherein only reason is employed in understanding the same matters. The first adopted the "handmaiden view" of philosophy, found as early as the fourth century with Augustine, according to which reason is the helpmate of faith, explaining and defending it as far as is possible. On the second view, theology is just a part of philosophy. In the seventeenth century, natural theology became increasingly important. Despite many efforts to preserve a place for faith, it was decidedly on the wane, with reason ultimately usurping its place altogether. This reversal is related to the second development, expressed by Voltaire's quip.

In the early modern period, the world, including man as a part of it, increasingly came to be understood as no longer needing God as an explanation. This was due primarily, though not exclusively, to the development in physics of a mechanical account of the world. The world was thought to be a machine, not unlike a clock, that could be explained on the basis of the motion of material parts of matter influencing each other by their contact according to fixed laws. On such a view, the role of God would be restricted to that of a creator and winder-up of the clock, who could then retire gracefully from the scene. The two notions, that God is an absent clockmaker and that everything that can be known about his clock can be known by reason unaided by faith, are the two tenets of deism, the characteristic doctrine that emerged at the turn of the eighteenth century. From deism to outright atheism was but a short step, both logically and historically. Now, if it was necessary to invoke God, it would be not as part of a theoretical inquiry, but as a more or less cynical means of social and political control. This control is the reason why God would have to be invented.

At the outset of the early modern period, however, and even throughout much of it, outright atheism was not an option, certainly not a public option. Lucien Febvre has argued that in the sixteenth century, atheism was literally "unthinkable" – not just in the sense that that no one could with impunity hold or express the thought that God does not exist, but that no one could have held the thought at all. The arguments and concepts for such a thought just did not exist. Even the scholarly language was inappropriate to such a revolutionary view. According to Febvre, Latin was at that point suitable only for codifying and preserving already extant views. It was a "medium of ossification."[4]

Although Febvre's thesis has been challenged and modified, it remains largely applicable, not only to the sixteenth century, but to the seventeenth as well. To be sure, the term 'atheist' is to be found, and frequently, but it was used as a term of abuse for those thought to have a heterodox conception of God. To talk about the divinity, it was thought necessary to have an appropriate conception of God. It was not enough merely to say, "I believe in God." Someone who talked about "God," but worshipped and somehow thought of him as an onion, for example (as Malebranche reports the ancient Egyptians to have done), really was not talking about *God*. Whatever he might say, such a person would be described as an atheist. Even less obvious, barely discernible deviations from the perceived orthodoxy were described as atheistic.

Bayle at the end of the seventeenth century reports three degrees of atheism according to what is being claimed: first, there is no God; second, the world is not the work of God; third, God created the world by the necessity of his nature, not by his free will.[5] Even at this point, it is not clear that atheism in the first degree involves an outright denial of the existence of God rather than a misrepresentation of God. It might well be that the first atheist of the first degree was Jean Meslier, a French country priest who when he died in 1729 left behind a heterodox testament that most naturally would lead him to be interpreted as such.[6]

Previous to Meslier, the figure most notoriously despised as an atheist, certainly the one most universally condemned as such, was Spinoza, who was expelled from his Jewish community in Amsterdam. He held the pantheistic view that everything is either God or some aspect of God. This view, that there is but one substance comprising the entire universe, which Spinoza called "God or Nature," was denounced by Bayle as "the hideous hypothesis." (He also called it "extravagant," "absurd and monstrous.") But however much Spinoza's view might have been contrary to orthodox views of God, and however much he might have contributed to the overthrow of the notion (those who criticized him were right about the threat he posed), Spinoza was not a first-degree atheist. He might have had a "horrid notion" of God, as Bayle also put it, but it seems still to be a concept of God.

DISSIMULATION

How, then, did Meslier emerge when and where he did? How to account for Meslier's apparently pure vein of atheism? He is not known in the history of thought as a great creative genius, capable of such a momentous redirection of the course of intellectual history. The Athena of atheism cannot have emerged full-blown from the head of such a Zeus. One alternative explanation is that in fact atheism is already to be found in the previous century, even in the work of some of its leading figures, who, because of the political and social unacceptability of their views, dissimulated. They are supposed to have conveyed their real views only indirectly, as suggestions or inferences to be understood only by the intelligent, who were their real audience. Their explicit professions of religious belief are explained as mere irony, as expressions made with a wink to indicate they are not to be taken seriously, or, more precisely, not at their face value.

This sort of dissimulation was alleged in the period, and continues to be alleged today, although, with a single exception, it has never been anything more than a minority position. In any case, it does not fully answer the question just raised about Meslier, because one still wants to know how these seventeenth-century figures arrived at their views.

The most spectacular case is that of Descartes, who, following the publication of the *Meditations*, almost immediately was accused by the theology faculty at the University of Utrecht of disseminating the very skepticism that he claimed to overcome. More recently, Descartes has been taken to have realized that his new mechanical, and allegedly materialistic, worldview did not require the existence of God. His *Meditations*, with its proofs of the existence of God of various sorts, and of the immortality of the soul based on mind–body dualism, are in fact part of a metaphysical burlesque. His intention was to ridicule and parody the very arguments and positions that have been misinterpreted as his real view, which is, rather, that any such attempt to prove the existence of God, for example, must fail.[7]

Evidence for this interpretation, presented early in such critics as Bishop Pierre-Daniel Huet and in the recent literature, is that Descartes's arguments are so transparently lacking in cogency that he could not have intended them to be taken seriously. Descartes was too intelligent not to see that his proofs for the existence of God, which are central to the argument of the *Meditations*, fail. Indeed, it was pointed out to him by Arnauld that the overall argument of the work itself is circular: Descartes overcomes skepticism only if he proves the existence of God, but the truth of the premises he needs to do so is secured only if he knows that God exists.

But this interpretation faces a dilemma. If Descartes's argument is so transparently bad as to be an explanation of why he could not really have meant it, then the appeal to irony as a ploy to disguise the argument must fail; on the other hand, if there is no transparency, then the real, hidden argument remains hidden, and Descartes's ploy would be pointless.[8] Moreover, as more than three centuries of serious and sustained debate over their merits suggests, Descartes's arguments are not transparently bad. Finally, there is the additional complication that Descartes had many followers, far more than any other figure in the period. Although they were sometimes disparaged by their opponents as mere sectarians, many of them were very bright people. They would have been too intelligent not to have seen through Descartes's ruse; they therefore would have needed to be party to it, thus making its secrecy impossible to keep. In any event, no one has ever alleged such a widespread conspiracy.

A second major figure charged with dissimulation with respect to the existence of God is Hobbes. Although the charge both early and late has been more widespread than in the case of Descartes (only Spinoza was more vilified in the period as an atheist), its plausibility is questionable. One sort of evidence for it is metaphysical.[9] Hobbes was a materialist; "that which is not Body," he said, "is no part of the Universe." Since antiquity, certainly, the view that all that exists is body or matter has been seen as a premise for atheism. But not every materialist had been an atheist, and what Hobbes meant by his claim about body is not altogether clear. He might have meant to claim only that everything that exists is in space (and time), which was a view subscribed to by other English philosophers of the century whose theism is more or less beyond reproach, such as Locke, More, Cudworth, and Newton. God would have to be material in this sense in order to be an individual, which would be a necessary, though not sufficient, condition for his entering into the sort of dialogue he had with Moses and other prophets. The difference between him and other such individuals would be that he is present in all space and all time.

Epistemological problems have also been found in reading Hobbes as a theist. If there is a single epithet for God, according to Hobbes, it is divine incomprehensibility. Now, there are two ways to interpret this view. One is that God is incomprehensible in the way that a square circle is incomprehensible, or inconceivable, i.e. there does not exist anything to be comprehended. On Hobbes's ontology, God's presence everywhere would be the analogue of the square circle. But another interpretation, found repeatedly among the orthodox, is simply that we cannot understand God, whose inscrutable ways are beyond comprehension. On this reading of Hobbes, all we can know of God is that he exists.[10] The inscrutability of God is emphasized by Hobbes's unwillingness to admit the credibility of revelation. There might have been prophets who truly reported the word revealed to them by God, but, in a way that anticipated Hume, Hobbes argued that there can never be any justified reason to believe them. To be sure, this incipient deism might later have greased the skids of atheism, but by itself it does not does make Hobbes a dissimulator.

The undeniable fact is that Hobbes produced arguments for the existence of God, most notably as the cause of the world as a whole. Some readers, again both early and late, have read his argument as an ironic parody, but to do so the argument must be antecedently problematic. All other things being equal, it would be hard to read some author's narration of the proof of the Pythagorean theorem, for example, as a parody. Hobbes's cosmological argument has been found problematic on several grounds. For one thing, he does not take it to show that the world has a beginning in time, or even to show that God exists, only "what men call God." But consider Aquinas, whom no one has accused of dissimulation. He also held, without impugning God's status as cause of the world, that its beginning in time is not rationally demonstrable, and his *via prima* concludes by commenting on the unmoved mover just demonstrated, "and this everyone understands to be God."

A third major figure who was read as dissimulating in his statements about God is Bayle. In his case, it has been the minority view to accept more or less at face value his professions of Calvinist religious belief. He came to be known as the "Arsenal of the Enlightenment" for his arguments favorable to toleration, skepticism, and, it would seem, atheism. Recently, a very strong case has been made that the whole logic of Bayle's very complicated work leads to "Stratonian atheism" (so called without any real connection to the ancient follower of Aristotle). Although Bayle might have castigated Spinoza's "hideous hypothesis," a close reading reveals that the condemnation is not wholesale, but is restricted to Spinoza's assertion of a single substance and of strict necessitarianism (nothing is contingent). The alleged atheism is not condemned as such.[11]

The most cogent, and poignant, if the least original, feature of Bayle's thought that insinuates atheism is found not in metaphysics, but in the moral domain. Most notable is the problem of evil, which Epicurus had introduced in antiquity as an argument for atheism: if God is good, he is willing to prevent evil; if God is almighty, he is able to prevent evil; there is evil in the world; therefore, any being we take to be God, who is both good and almighty, is not God. Partly because of the circumstances of his own miserable life, Bayle was near obsessed with this problem. His view is that the problem has no rational solution. The Manichean solution in terms of two equal principles of good and evil is, because simplest, the best that reason can provide, but nonetheless fails. Instead, the problem remains a paradox; for its conclusion, while following logically, is known to be false on the basis of faith. As in the case of Hobbes, there are two ways of reading the claim that religious belief is irrational: either it should not be held at all, or it should be held contrary to reason.

Those who take Bayle to be a theist regard him as a fideist of the most extreme sort, and take at face value his profession of belief. Those who reject his profession as insincere, or misguided, or inappropriate, on the other hand, read at face value what he says about the virtue of atheists. For Bayle, the three domains of religion, morality, and salvation are conceptually distinct. Religion has to do with ceremony, morality with conscience, and salvation with grace. Theoretically, then, an atheist is capable of right action, and this is what the Huguenot Bayle suggests in a thinly disguised polemical work in which he argues that atheists are no worse than idolaters, which is what he takes Catholics to be on account of their reverence of the Eucharist as the real presence of Christ.[12] The argument proceeds by way of a refutation of the objection that atheists are in fact worse than idolaters. The objection is based on the fact that God permits idolatry in order that fear of false gods should at least regulate passion and make society possible among pagans. Bayle rebuts this on empirical grounds, which amount to a criticism of Catholic persecution of the Huguenots in France. While this criticism appears to be his main point, the defense of a moral atheistic society is the more obvious point. As an argument for atheism, however, this reasoning fails, because of the trinary distinction on which it is based: the atheist might be moral, but, lacking grace, does not have true belief (and a fortiori does not participate in the true religion). The atheist might be capable of morality, but is still mistaken about the existence of God.

However weak the case for dissimulation, the fact is that a transition took place in this period. A view less extreme than dissimulation would be that these early modern figures unwittingly laid the grounds for atheism by providing the concepts and even the premises for arguments whose conclusions they themselves were either unwilling or unable to draw. A report from Bayle is again helpful. "According to the opinion of many, the same [Cartesians] who have in our age removed the darkness which the Schoolmen had spread over Europe, have increased the number of freethinkers, and made way for Atheism, or skepticism, or the disbelief of the greatest mysteries of Christianity."[13] Whether or not Bayle subscribes exactly to this opinion, he clearly thinks that philosophy, "sometimes serviceable against error, is sometimes prejudicial to truth."[14] This is an expression of Bayle's frequently expressed view that reason is better suited for tearing down than for building things up. The fact is that, however sincere the Cartesians' intentions to prove by reason the existence of God and emphasize its centrality in their experience of the world, the opposite was the perhaps inevitable result.

One mechanism for the introduction, or at least the expression, of atheism might have been a recasting of *reductio ad absurdum* arguments, which seem to have enjoyed special prominence in the period. I try to convince you of some position on the basis that its denial leads to some consequence that we both know to be false (strictly speaking, a contradiction). So, the argument might be that if God did not exist, then morality would be a human invention, or the world would be without design, or whatever. But morality is not a human invention, the world does have design, and so forth; therefore God exists. But at the turn of the eighteenth century, morality, cosmic design, and other relevant concepts were independently questioned in such a way as to falsify the relevant premises of the *reductio* arguments, thus providing an argument for the opposite conclusion.

Nor was the *reductio* the only sort of argument to be reversed in this way. Huet tried to argue the truth of theism, and of Christianity in particular, on the basis of the argument called *consensus gentium*: what all peoples assent to must be true. He carried this argument so far as to prove the virgin birth of Christ on the basis of beliefs such as the birth of Athena from the head of Zeus. But the latter is of course a myth, and so the argument was easily reversed while preserving the premise that the two beliefs are of the same status.[15]

THE FATHER OF MODERN PHILOSOPHY

In the conception of God, as in so much of early modern philosophy, Descartes is the seminal figure. Descartes has four arguments for the existence of God. More precisely, he has four different ways of "guiding the natural light in such a way as to enable us to have a clear awareness"[16] of what he takes to be obvious to an unclouded mind, namely that God exists. (He takes this to be more obvious than anything else, even his own existence.) These heuristic approaches to the existence of God suggest four related ways of conceiving of God. Some have thought that they are not all compatible, but they in fact converge on a single conception, namely omnipotence, which is the basis for the other three. Descartes also holds, however, that the difference among divine attributes is not a real one, but only a distinction of reason from our limited perspective; so the conception of God as almighty is only the best way we humans have of conceiving God.

Given the nature of its object, our conception of God must be less than perfect. On the other hand, Descartes also holds that to be aware of anything at all we must grasp its essence. He attempts to reconcile these apparently incompatible positions by saying that while we do grasp the essence of God, we do not comprehend it because of its immensity. He thinks of it as rather like coming in contact with a mountain by touching it, but without thereby being able to get our arms around it because of its literal size.

The first three arguments are found in the Third Meditation, where to show that we are not being deceived in some way about the things we take to be most obviously true, Descartes attempts to prove the existence of a God who creates us in such a way that, if we exercise proper caution, such deception is impossible. All three arguments appeal to the notion of God as a cause, and differ by invoking different notions of cause. The first argument is that he could not think of God as he does, that is, have his idea of God, unless an existent God caused the idea as its object. In Descartes's technical language, the cause of any idea must have at least as much formal reality, outside the mind, as the thing thought about has objective reality, in the mind. The kind of causation involved results in the idea being of one thing, in this case God, rather than of some other thing, a tree, let's say.

Descartes thinks that he could give himself all his ideas other than the idea of God. (While he could do so, he in fact does not. He thinks that there are ideas other than the idea of God that are not made by him, and that do not come from the senses.) What is it about the idea of God that requires an object as a cause other than himself? As opposed to the idea he has of himself, this idea is uniquely of something that is "immense, incomprehensible and infinite." Only such an existent object could cause such an idea. The merits of the argument aside, it is worth noting that the spatial metaphor at the root of all three of these terms is power. Although God might be ubiquitous, i.e. in some sense present everywhere, his immensity refers not literally to some size, as in the case of a mountain, but to his power, which has no restriction (CSM II 79).

A second argument appeals to the notion of efficient causation, which requires a real distinction between cause and effect – i.e. cause and effect are different things (CSM II 167). This is the kind of distinction thought to hold between God and anything he creates – here, Descartes himself. Not only does God bring Descartes into existence, God sustains him in existence by the same power by which he created him, and without which Descartes would cease to exist. It is as if God is constantly recreating Descartes – and whatever else exists as long as it exists.

The notion of God as cause is also mobilized by the third argument, in this case as cause of himself. Among many previous philosophers, Aquinas for example, God was thought to be the *uncaused* cause of everything else. In departing from this tradition, Descartes is careful to insist that God is not the *efficient* cause of himself, with the impossible requirement that as cause he be really different from himself as effect. Instead, Descartes opts for a middle way, which he says is only "analogous to an efficient cause," between efficient cause and no cause at all (CSM II 167). The issue is whether an existent thing has existence in, by, or through itself, or else in, through, or by something else. The various prepositions express a relation of dependence, so to say that God is the only existent in the first category is to express the negative thesis that God's existence does not depend on anything else. In taking God to be cause of himself, Descartes departs from this tradition by construing the concept in a positive sense. The inexhaustible power or immensity of the divine essence is the *formal* cause of God's existing, as well as the reason why, unlike everything else, he does not depend on anything else or need to be preserved by anything else (CSM II 78, 165).

In introducing this argument in the Third Meditation, and developing it in his Replies to Objections, Descartes repeatedly refers to the essence of God, which he takes to be the unrestricted power of existing. This power enables God to be the cause of himself, as well as the cause and preserver in existence of everything else, and as such to be the explanation of our idea of God, which would otherwise be inexplicable.

Descartes's fourth argument, which is found in the Fifth Meditation, is widely taken to be a mere restatement of Anselm's so-called ontological argument, that God necessarily exists because existence is contained in the idea of God or in his very essence, such that a nonexistent God would be a contradiction. To be sure, much of what Descartes says can be read in this way, but in his correspondence there is the suggestion that he did not read Anselm before publishing the *Meditations*. Descartes's sincerity about this claim was later questioned by his critic Huet, but there is in any case a way of reading the argument other than as a restatement of Anselm's argument. Not incidentally, it makes better sense of Descartes's return to proving the existence of God after having already given three arguments to establish it.

Key to the previous three arguments is the appeal to the essence of God as unrestricted power. What is key to the argument of the Fifth Meditation is that God's existence follows from his essence as the equality of its interior angles to a straight angle follows from the essence of a triangle. Descartes might have intended his later argument as nothing more than a summary of at least what is key to the previous three, the truth of whose conclusion can be definitively accepted only in the Fifth Meditation, after all impediment to appreciation of the truth of God's existence has been removed in the Fourth Meditation. [17] There is, in any case, an important difference in what motivated the arguments of Anselm and Descartes. At the turn of the twelfth century, Anselm was concerned to refute the view of Peter Damian, who, like Descartes later, thought God to be omnipotent without restriction. So powerful was God, in his view, that all truth depended on him; God could even alter the past, or put himself out of existence. Such a God, who could self-annihilate, would be less than omnipotent, according to Anselm, as his argument attempts to show. To be sure, Descartes agrees with this view of Anselm, and thus we find him offering a version of the ontological argument; yet he also accepts Peter Damian's view that all truth depends on God. But does the truth of God's existence depend on God's will? Descartes would answer in the affirmative for the very reason that distinguishes his version of the ontological argument, namely, that God is by his very nature the cause of himself and thus must exist. Anything that could self-annihilate would not have this nature and thus would not be God.

THEOLOGICAL DEBATES

There was a drift among the followers of Descartes, and certainly among those rationalists influenced by him, toward pantheism, the view that the world just is God, or is somehow a part of God. The most obvious case of this drift was, of course, Spinoza, who is most often associated with the notion of the "God of the philosophers." He held that there exists but one substance, which he called *Deus sive Natura* (God or Nature). In holding this view, he was only taking literally, and without qualification, Descartes's view that a substance is that which needs nothing other than itself in order to exist. Such a view was certain to be found theologically unacceptable, and Spinoza suffered accordingly, for he held, or seemed to hold, that everything true of the world followed from the definition of God with the same necessity whereby the theorems of geometry followed from its axioms, postulates, and definitions. The result was the denial not just of any real distinction between God and the world, and thus creation out of nothing, but also of human freedom and thus responsibility. Such apparent consequences of his view were bound to cause him problems.

The challenge for rationalists was to show how their own principles did not lead to just these consequences. Malebranche attempted to do so by insisting that while God, if he creates, must do so according to a rational necessity, the actual fact of his creating depends entirely on his utterly free and indifferent will. Leibniz drew a similar distinction, in his case between two kinds of necessity, absolute and hypothetical. In his view, all truth has a sufficient reason, but not everything is absolutely necessary (true in all possible worlds). Some truths obtain only in certain worlds, and depend on the creation of those worlds rather than others. How well either of these rationalists avoided the objectionable results of Spinoza's system was debated in the period and continues to be debated.

Here, the details of Spinoza's metaphysics are of less importance than the support his epistemology gave to deism, for this was an issue that transcended the problems of rationalism and involved the major theological debates of the period. In particular, Spinoza's application of Descartes's philosophy to the new science of Bible criticism gave deism a great boost. He followed the lead of Isaac La Peyrère (1596–1676), who had been led by his rationalist principles to deny the Mosaic authorship of the Pentateuch (wherein the death of Moses himself is recounted – inexplicably if he was the author), the authenticity of the existing biblical text (which La Peyrère took to be a "heap of copie upon copie"), and the Bible as the framework of human history (in his view, it is the history only of the Jewish people).[18] Indeed, it might well be that accepting such views from La Peyrère led, at least in part, to Spinoza's expulsion from the Jewish community. Spinoza was quoted as saying that "God exists, but only philosophically," which says it all.[19]

There were a number of responses to the new "historical and critical" method of Bible criticism, and to the deism that it helped to foster. Beyond outright condemnation without response or alternative, which of course occurred, one response was to accept the validity of the method, but to contain its significance by finding a place for revelation based on faith. Such was the response of Locke, for example, although historically, as will be seen below, it proved to be an untenable position. Another response was a mysticism that avoids the problem altogether in favor of a direct communication with God. On the face of it, this alternative seems the exact opposite to Spinoza's approach, as indeed it is to most of his *Ethics*. But in its fifth and last part, Spinoza, not unlike other great monists including Parmenides himself, talks of intellectual perfection in mystical terms. Consider proposition 36: "the intellectual Love of God [which arises from the third and highest form of knowledge (prop. 33)] is the very Love of God by which God loves himself." From this knowledge "the greatest satisfaction of Mind there can be arises" (prop. 27), and, so satisfying is the resulting love of God, that whoever loves God in this way "cannot strive that God should love him in return" (prop. 19). As will be seen below, these propositions that negate individual selves and their interests could well have been accepted by the most notorious mystical movement at the end of the seventeenth century.

Before any investigation of these historical alternatives, the context for Spinoza's deism must be set. A good place to begin for the period as a whole is with Socinianism. The eponymous source of the doctrine was Fausto Sozzini, born in Siena in 1539. Largely because of his unorthodox theological views, he had a colorful career, fleeing Italy for Switzerland and then France, Transylvania, and finally Poland, where he became the effective leader of the group known as the Polish Brethren. He died in Poland in 1604 (having almost died earlier at the hands of angry students).

Sozzini denied original sin as contrary to reason, his only criterion of religious faith. (In arriving at his wholesale revision of traditional theology, Sozzini relied constantly on what he took to be principles of reason.) With no original sin, he reasoned, there is no need to regard Christ as other than figuratively divine. The role of Christ is not to atone for sin, but to set an example of how to be saved. He has special knowledge, immortality, and power, but not omnipotence, which belongs to God alone. In addition, the Holy Spirit is not a person but the power of God, and thus Sozzini denied Trinitarianism (according to which there are three persons in one God: Father, Son, i.e. Christ, and Holy Spirit), which he took to be at odds with monotheism. He also denied divine omniscience, including knowledge of future contingents, on rational grounds. If God knew the future evils committed by human kind, then he would have prevented them. Instead of concluding in Epicurean fashion that God does not exist, he denied that God knew of such evils. Since Christ is not the Redeemer as in traditional theology, divine grace ceases to be of much significance, and free will emerges as paramount. People save themselves. Those who are not saved are not damned, but simply perish. Eternal damnation of the reprobate would be contrary to reason: God would make mortal man immortal only to punish him.

Throughout the seventeenth century, Socinianism was taken to be a term of abuse. Regardless of the views that one might have held, no one admitted to being a Socinian. Rather, the response to being considered one was to find some respect in which the label did not apply (and often then to apply the label to the accuser). It was not until the eighteenth century that this species of deism became respectable, and then only under the name of Unitarianism. Still, there were many to whom the label was applied with a certain plausibility before the acceptance of the view, perhaps most notably, John Locke.

In his *Essay concerning Human Understanding* (first edition, 1690), Locke tried to place rational limits on what could be accepted on the basis of faith. At a minimum, nothing contrary to reason was acceptable. But the way in which he articulated such limits suggested that faith is unnecessary. In his *Reasonableness of Christianity* (1695), he set out views that led in the following year to an explicit charge of Socinianism from John Edwards. Locke's attempt to reply in his *Vindication* of that work only aggravated the charge, which Edwards repeated in *Socinianism Unmask'd* and other works. Even as a practicing Anglican, Locke had claimed that the only dogma essential to Christianity is that Christ is the Messiah. The claim by itself would have been enough to raise orthodox hackles, but even worse perhaps was what Locke meant by the Messiah. For he, like Sozzini, called into question the notion of redemption by denying the doctrine of an imputed original sin as incompatible with the notion of God. He also denied eternal damnation; as on the Socinian view, he held that the reprobate simply perish. Moreover, although he never explicitly denied the divinity of Christ, there is evidence in his notebooks showing that he took it to be unlikely. So, although Locke could never have agreed to his description as Socinian, his views certainly approximated much of what was condemned as such.

Although it did not emerge specifically as an alternative to deistic Bible criticism, mysticism might be understood in connection with these questions because it obviated the problems associated with this new approach to the Bible. Mysticism in the west has had a long history of acceptance, even adulation, on the one hand, and mistrust, even condemnation, on the other. In the strain of it most relevant to these questions, mysticism, despite its potential as a block against deism, was received in negative fashion.

It seems that the fourteenth-century monks of Mount Athos became convinced that divine communication was best facilitated by the absolute repose of mind and body. One technique employed by these "hesychasts" (after the Greek word for quiet) for achieving such repose was to keep their eyes fixed on their own umbilical regions, whence they were derided by a critic as "omphalopsychi" (navel-gazers). In the seventeenth-century version of this navel-gazing, the techniques of repose were rather different, the scene shifted from monastery to high society, and the movement was called, more politely, "Quietism." Still, the phenomenon came to be regarded as a dangerous form of salon shenanigans, and it was condemned by the church, though not before some of the biggest names in French theology and philosophy were involved in the dispute over it.

Early modern mysticism originated with Miguel de Molinos (1628–96), a Spanish cleric whose works were censured, and for which he died in prison. His views were nonetheless taken up by others with claims to orthodoxy, most notably by Jeanne Bouvière de la Motte, Madame Guyon (1648–1717), and her protector François de Salignac de la Mothe Fénelon (1651–1715), a prominent literary figure who became archbishop of Cambrai. Guyon was for various periods confined to a convent and even to the Bastille. Fénelon, his work censured by the Sorbonne, appealed to Rome, but lost his case in 1699. Their implacable opponent was the most important churchman in France, Bishop Jacques-Benigne Bossuet (1627–1704). The story has it that Fénelon learned of the decision against him as he was about to ascend the pulpit to preach, whereupon he abandoned his prepared text and instead dramatically announced his submission on the Quietism issue.

It is difficult to describe the views, or precisely what it was about them, that caused such hostilities, especially since views similar to those of the Quietists are to be found in such mystics as Teresa of Avila and John of the Cross, who had been canonized by the church. At a minimum, the Quietists rejected petitionary prayer, which asks God for something in what they took to be a violation of the absolute divine will. Instead, they advocated a disinterested, pure love of God. Their prayer was Christ's own: not mine but thy will be done. They advocated an acceptance of divine will beyond interest even in one's own salvation. With such an attitude, considerations of personal morality begin to evaporate in theory, and in practice led to suspicions about how pure the actual love of the Quietists was. Guyon, known for her outspokenness, did not help the cause in this regard. "Don't speak to me of humility," she said; "the virtues are not for me."[20]

They also rejected meditation, especially of the sort instituted by St. Ignatius of Loyola, whereby one imagined scenes of the passion of Christ, for example, in an effort to morally perfect oneself. Instead, they advocated contemplation, a sort of imageless thought about God alone, without reference to oneself. Such an activity raises the unresolved problem of the legitimacy of ecstasy, of distinguishing genuine inspiration from lunacy or even diabolical possession. This problem goes back to the second-century Montanists, who like the Quietists were condemned, and even to St. Paul.[21]

The Quietist controversy was observed with interest by philosophers of the time, notably by Leibniz, and of course Bayle, but it was Malebranche who found himself implicated in it through the unwelcome efforts of his disciple, François Lamy (1636–1711). This Benedictine was one of the first to teach Cartesianism in the schools, and was strongly attached to the views of Malebranche, whom he defended against Arnauld in their dispute over the nature of ideas. While composing the third volume of his *De la connaissance de soi-même* (1694–98), Lamy became convinced of the Quietist position, which he defended by citing previously published texts from Malebranche.

That Lamy should have deployed the Oratorian's work in this way was far from implausible. After all, Malebranche very obviously taught that truth is apprehended by pure thought, in the absence of the commotion generated by the senses and the imagination; that what we really know in apparently knowing the world is an idea in the mind of God (a theory he called "the vision of all things in God"); that we can be free from error by restraining the will such that we accept as true only that whose truth forces itself upon us; that this passive acceptance of the truth is in every case, whether we realize it or not, a matter of listening to the voice of Christ. All of this obviously smacked of Quietist mysticism. Nonetheless, Malebranche thought himself ill served by Lamy, and wrote his *Traité de l'amour de Dieu* (1697) in an effort to distance himself from Lamy. There ensued an exchange of published letters that typified the bewildering exchange taking place around them between the Quietists and their opponents; as the great Malebranche editor André Robinet puts it, the Malebranche–Lamy debate was part of "one of the most indecipherable imbroglios in bibliographical history" (OC XIV ix).

For what it is worth, here is how the issue is expressed in the foreword to Malebranche's *Traité*: Malebranche believes "that the will, in so far as it is capable of loving, is but the desire for the unshakable happiness that God constantly impresses upon us in order to love him as our end. The Benedictine Lamy claims, to the contrary, that disinterested love is possible, that the will is different from the desire to be happy" (OC XIV 3). This way of putting the issue might in fact be worth a great deal, for it might shed light on the philosophical debate, reintroduced by Thomas Hobbes and continued by Joseph Butler, over psychological and ethical egoism, namely, whether and in what sense we can act contrary to perceived self-interest.

The major theological debate in the Western church occurred in the sixteenth century, during the Reformation. There were three issues of enduring importance: the significance of grace for human salvation; the real presence of Christ in the sacrament of the Eucharist; and (most importantly, because on it depended the resolution of these and all other differences) the proper authority for the interpretation of scripture. The differences that distinguished Catholic and Protestant positions constituted one of the great scandals of Christianity: not just the enmity between sects, all of which acknowledged the duty to turn the other cheek and love their enemies, but the fact of there being different sects at all. A serious attempt was made to begin the reunification Christendom when Leibniz on behalf of the Lutherans entered into negotiations with Bossuet; but through ill will and misunderstanding, no productive or even interesting discussion took place.

During the seventeenth century, remnants of the previous controversies continued to be debated, intramurally, within the various sects. Jansenism, for example, was a continuation within Catholicism of the debate over grace. The movement attracted some of the best minds of the period, most notably Pascal, Arnauld, and Nicole, and was so called because its view on grace was derived from the book *Augustinus* (1640) of Cornelius Jansen, bishop of Ypres.

Because the view came to be condemned by Rome and was repeatedly condemned, with ever greater severity, it is important to be clear on what that view was. Because the Jansenists insisted on remaining within the church, they could accept only that the pope had condemned something, and had done so infallibly, but that he had not condemned anything that they held. (This tactic was based on their famous distinction between questions of right and questions of fact.) Indeed, they insisted throughout that there was no such thing as Jansenism. Everyone else, however, took the view to be defined by the five propositions at the core of the successive condemnations. Roughly, they amount to the view that grace is necessary and sufficient for salvation, that God saves those and only those whom he wills to save. To assign any efficacious role to those saved would smack of the Pelagian heresy that was a perceived failing of their Jesuit opponents (hilariously sent up in Pascal's *Provincial Letters*, a classic of French literature).

The so-called Jansenists tried to defend themselves by pointing, plausibly enough, to St. Paul and St. Augustine as the source of their view. But exactly how their articulation of it differed from the strict predestinationism of Calvin was never clear. For it appeared that God not only saved gratuitously, i.e. without any justification on the part of the saved, but also damned gratuitously, without any guilt on the part of the damned. Moreover, the number of the latter far surpassed the former, according to the Jansenists, so their picture of God was of an altogether angry and vengeful deity, represented by their typical crucifix, with Christ's hands close together above his head to indicate how few he had died for. Amidst all this fire and brimstone, both theological and political, one finds a great deal of sophisticated thought that is applicable to the freedom–determinism issue then being independently raised in the context of the mechanical picture of the world.

FIDEISM

In his classic *History of Skepticism*, Richard H. Popkin advanced the thesis that in the late Renaissance and early modern period, philosophical skepticism was often the ally of religious belief. In particular, the *libertins érudits* argued that reason was sufficient for knowledge in none of the three domains of philosophy: not in logic, nor in physics, nor in ethics. The skeptics' arguments were taken by them to be invincible, with the result that only faith can overcome uncertainty, thus confirming 1 Corinthians 1: "it is necessary to be foolish and ignorant according to the world, in order to be wise and learned before God." In the homely analogy of one of them, La Mothe le Vayer (1588–1672), the human mind is like a field that must be stripped of its weeds, i.e. its pretence to certain knowledge, before being sown with the seeds of faith. Whether, contrary to Popkin, such fideism is only a veneer for heterodox views, expressed ironically with tongue in cheek, has always been a matter of debate. The view itself, however, is clear enough: religion is independent of natural reason and perhaps even contrary to it.

Many have attributed such fideism to Blaise Pascal (1623–62). Certainly, there are many statements in his *Pensées* ("Thoughts," a posthumous collection of rather brief remarks on religion) that denigrate reason in favor of faith: "humble yourself, impotent reason; be silent, dull-witted nature, and learn from your master your true condition which you do not know. Listen to God."[22] Indeed, reason's role is precisely to acknowledge its own limitation: "Reason's last step is the recognition that there are an infinite number of things that are beyond it" (373). The most reasonable thing we can do is to reject reason: "There is nothing so much in conformity with reason as the rejection of reason" (367). And it is faith that makes up for the deficiency of reason. One of the most famous of all the *pensées* reads: "The heart has its reasons that reason knows not" (224), which can be read in just these terms.

Pascal's fideism is not, however, an exact instance of Popkin's thesis. The total elimination of reason, except perhaps as an instrument of its own demise, is not to be found in Pascal, who warns against "two forms of excess: to exclude reason, and not to admit anything but reason" (368). In another posthumous work, *Conversation with Saci*, Pascal compares the relative value of Epictetus's Stoicism and Montaigne's Pyrrhonism. Both have advantages and disadvantages. Stoicism leads us to focus on God, accepting our lot without complaint. But it also leads us to the vain belief that we can know and serve God by our own effort alone. Skepticism, at least as deployed in Montaigne's *Apology for Raymond Sebond*, has proved to be the scourge of heretics. But it too leads to an impenetrable tangle of ignorance and error, especially among those with a penchant for impiety and vice. The failings of both philosophies are traced to ignorance of original sin: Stoicism fails to see our present corruption, skepticism our previous dignity.

Pascal transcends both skepticism and Stoicism. It is he in the period who most explicitly identifies and rejects the God of the philosophers, who fails to be a God of love and consolation. Indeed, even the God of Abraham, Isaac, and Jacob fails in this respect. "It is not only impossible, but useless to know God without the intermediacy of Jesus Christ" (382). For Pascal, God is less an object of the understanding than of the will. With such a conception, Pascal places himself in the more respectable tradition of French mysticism from earlier in the century, before the appearance of Quietism. François de Sales (1567–1622), for example, had emphasized the incomprehensible transcendence of God that can be approached only by the will's act of love. In this voluntarism, there is, ironically, something of a rapprochement with Descartes, whom Pascal otherwise takes to be "useless and unreliable" (297). The doctrine of the Fourth Meditation is that by contrast to the intellect, the human will is essentially as great as the divine will, "so much so that it is above all in virtue of the will that I understand myself to bear in some way the image and likeness of God" (CSM II 40).

The clearest statement of fideism is found in Bayle. His *Historical and Critical Dictionary* (1697) became the philosophical best-seller of the period, which only insured that the accusations against it by his irascible coreligionist, Pierre Jurieu, would be investigated by the Huguenot authorities. Living in exile, Bayle was summoned by the Consistory of the Walloon church of Rotterdam, and was led to publish with the second edition his *Eclaircissements* (elucidations or explanations) on four topics. The third dealt with the perceived threat to religion posed by Bayle's apparently favorable treatment of skepticism. His response was to emphasize the message of Paul in Corinthians and elsewhere, that the wisdom of the world is but foolishness according to the Gospel, and conversely, with the result that faith is impervious to skeptical argument. The basis for this dismissal of skepticism is his conception of Christianity itself, which "is of a supernatural order, and centers in the supreme authority of God proposing mysteries to us, not that we may comprehend them, but that we may believe them with all the humility that is due to the infinite being, who can neither deceive nor be deceived."[23]

Several times in this text, Bayle sets reason and faith at odds, to the point that faith concerns things not only beyond reason, but even "repugnant" to it. Indeed, the more faith is contradicted by reason, the more valuable it is, such that the contradictions of reason can even be accorded an instrumental role in bringing the philosophically innocent to an appreciation of God's goodness in providing the grace of faith. Lest reason be presumed victorious over faith for having provided unanswerable objections to it, no solution to them is forthcoming from reason, either. Bayle would seem, therefore, to be a corroborating case of Popkin's thesis, were it not for his condemnation of the Pyrrhonists, who, rejecting every certain sign of truth and falsehood, would be unable to recognize the truth should they encounter it. They are thus least worthy of all philosophers of "being allowed to dispute concerning the mysteries of Christianity."[24] As for Pascal, so for Bayle, God seems to be beyond all philosophy.

NOTES

1 See Popkin 2001.
2 Letter to Frederick William, Prince of Prussia (1770), in Brinton 1956, p. 367.
3 To Mersenne, 15 April, 27 May 1630 (CSM III 22–23, 25).
4 Febvre's thesis is discussed by Kors 1990, pp. 6–9.
5 Pierre Bayle, *Dictionary*, art. Thales, rem. D.
6 Kors 1990, pp. 4–6.
7 For a version of this interpretation, see Caton 1971 and 1973.
8 Leo Strauss's (implausible) explanation is that "a careful writer of normal intelligence is more intelligent than the most intelligent censor, as such." Moreover, what is true of writers is true of readers: "thoughtless men are careless readers, and only thoughtful men are careful readers" (1988, pp. 25–26).
9 For the dissimulation reading of Hobbes, see Jesseph 2002, pp. 140–66.
10 Watkins 1973, p. 45.
11 See Mori 1999, who does not charge Bayle with dissimulation, but who nonetheless makes out the best case for why, if Bayle knew what he was doing, he ought to have been dissimulating and likely was. For the best defense of Bayle as a theist, albeit a tepid one, see Labrousse 1964 and 1983, which is also a wonderful introduction to Bayle.
12 *Pensées diverses sur la comète* (1683), translated as *Miscellaneous Reflections, occasion'd by the Comet* (Bayle 1708).
13 *Dictionary*, art. Takiddin, rem. A.
14 Ibid.
15 Lennon (2006).
16 Fourth set of Replies (CSM II 168).
17 I am grateful to Alan Nelson for discussion of this point.
18 Popkin 1982, pp. 64–65.

19 Popkin 1982, p. 66; and Nadler 1999, p. 134.

20 Knox 1950, p. 279.

21 See what John Locke has to say about this case in the *Essay concerning Human Understanding* (IV.xviii.3). A version of the difficulty persists today in Pope John Paul II's concerns about Buddhist techniques of detaching oneself from the world. "For Christians, the world is God's creation, redeemed by Christ. It is in the world that man meets God. Therefore he does not need to attain such an absolute detachment in order to find himself in the mystery of his deepest self" (1994, p. 89). Not unlike the Quietist repose, the Buddhist nirvana is a passive state, which the pope sees as indifference to the world, where alone God is to be found (p. 86).

22 *Pensées*, 246. This and subsequent parenthetical references are to numbered passages in the Lafuma edition (Pascal 1958), as translated in Pascal 1962.

23 Bayle 1991, p. 421.

24 Ibid., p. 422.

M. W. F. STONE

11 Scholastic schools and early modern philosophy

Few students of philosophy recognize that ideas and doctrines advanced by scholastic thinkers made a distinctive contribution to philosophical inquiry in the seventeenth and eighteenth centuries.[1] For most, scholasticism is believed to have been eclipsed and subsequently displaced by self-styled "modern" movements in philosophy and science associated with Galileo, Bacon, Descartes, Hobbes, Locke, Spinoza, Leibniz, and Newton.[2] Due to the enduring perception that it is premodern, and thus by assumption ill at ease with or else hostile to the predilections of modern philosophy, scholasticism is dismissed as recondite or rebarbative, and viewed as largely irrelevant to the study of early modern thought.[3]

And yet, even though the ideas of the scholastic schools undoubtedly challenge the contemporary reader in ways that surpass the act of engaging with the thought of canonical thinkers, their general neglect by historians of philosophy and absence from standard textbooks is perverse. For on any objective assessment, the schools of early modern scholasticism constituted a very large part of the philosophical activity in continental Europe, as well as in North and South America, from the sixteenth century up to the time of Immanuel Kant.[4] Since so many confections of scholastic thought were present in early modern universities and academies, and the works of certain authors were actively discussed and widely disseminated, it should be beyond doubt that "philosophy" in this period embraced not just the established figures who now dominate our analysis of seventeenth- and eighteenth-century thought, but a much wider group of thinkers who looked to different intellectual traditions and resources of argument. Even if we leave open the question whether or not any scholastic philosopher ever attained the dizzying heights of "originality" achieved by Descartes, Hobbes, Leibniz, or Spinoza, the fact remains that by dint of their publications, and by virtue of their prominence in institutions of higher education, scholastic thinkers were a significant and conspicuous presence in the philosophy of the era.

Such considerations, however, have yet to be embraced by historians of early modern philosophy, most of whom still maintain that all things "scholastic" are contrary to the spirit and practice of "modern" philosophy.[5] Why is this so? This question invites neither a quick nor a facile response since it takes us to the heart of a host of difficult issues connected with the historiography of "modern philosophy," and many deep-seated assumptions about how seventeenth- and eighteenth-century figures continue to shape philosophical inquiry to the present day. That said, the question can be partially illuminated by highlighting a widespread proclivity among philosophers (here English-language thinkers are no different from their French, German, or Italian counterparts) to classify the history of their subject in terms of mutually exclusive chronological divisions (e.g. "ancient," "medieval," "Renaissance," and "modern"), divisions that preclude any worthwhile investigation of the ways in which seemingly different eras of philosophy inform and condition one another. This last remark helps to explain, if only partially, why scholasticism has been disenfranchised from the story of early modern philosophy. Held to be the offspring of a distant and alien medieval civilization, it is supposed to exemplify the interests of a form of thought at odds with modernity. Seen thus, scholasticism and its practitioners are assumed to represent the dying embers of a philosophical culture still clinging to the last remains of its tawdry life by means of a recalcitrant opposition to all things modern.[6]

Slowly but surely, historians of philosophy are beginning to reject the above caricature and are now minded to accept, albeit with certain qualifications, that the scholastic schools are deserving of study. In the last thirty years or so, greater time and conceptual generosity, as well as a modicum of historical sympathy, have all been extended to specific authors by scholars eager to assess and clarify the intellectual context inhabited by the canonical authors of modern thought.[7] As such, these more ecumenical efforts have helped to bring aspects of the philosophy of the schools within the purview of mainstream research, and much has been learned about the relationship between the influential figures of seventeenth- and eighteenth-century philosophy and the scholastic ideas and preoccupations of their day.[8]

Despite these welcome developments, there is still a sense in which the schools are not studied for their own sake but are rather viewed instrumentally: namely, to facilitate a vivid depiction of how and why canonical thinkers advanced the positions they did. While it would be silly and ungracious to disparage the efforts of those scholars who have promoted the importance of analyzing canonical figures in their appropriate setting, it remains the case that our existing grasp of the industry and sophistication of the schools is enervated by a resistance on the part of these same scholars to viewing scholastic thinkers as objects of intrinsic interest. Our understanding of the schools will be ameliorated only when sufficient justice is done to the methods that individual scholastics used to broach the philosophical problems *they* deemed to be significant. This requires that we rid ourselves of all antecedent judgments concerning the merit or relevance of their work, and instead focus upon those questions that were believed to be salient, and the resources by way of argument and appeal to tradition that were used in their clarification and resolution. The scholastic schools are one of the few remaining subjects of early modern philosophy yet to be studied *in extenso*. One might conjecture that the continuing progress and future good order of the discipline is dependent upon their systematic analysis.

In what follows, I shall endeavor to provide a provisional cartography of the most prominent scholastic schools and thinkers of the early modern period. Throughout this survey, my aim will be to show that while individual scholastic thinkers looked to the luminaries of the medieval past for inspiration, and were further guided by ideas of authority and tradition, their approach to philosophical questions was fashioned by the needs and exigencies of their own times.[9] In my assessment of the contribution made by the schools, I shall have cause to note two points of significance: first, that early modern scholastics made an important bequest to their own philosophical traditions, and second, that the relationship between the self-styled "schoolmen" and the so-called "moderns" was one of mutual involvement rather than an association characterized by cursory influence, utter dependence, or irrevocable hostility. Gauging the precise nature of this relationship – a task which lies beyond the remit of this essay – will have important implications for our general understanding of early modern philosophy.

SCHOLASTIC SCHOOLS

The scholastic schools (*sectae scholasticae*) that enjoyed some standing in the years from the end of the Reformation to the outbreak of the French Revolution were numerous. Created by the fragmentation of late medieval philosophy into competing movements,[10] and heavily conditioned by overt theological allegiances, the schools exhibited considerable flexibility in philosophical orientation and were composed of disparate elements. Two of the greatest in terms of numbers and influence were the Thomist and Scotist schools. Promoted by two prominent orders of friars, the Dominicans and Franciscans – although by no means their exclusive preserve – both traditions proved themselves adept at withstanding the intellectual pressures of the early modern period. Other major schools were also sponsored by friars such as the Carmelites and the Augustinians, as well by new religious orders such as the Jesuits. Secular priests and laymen also contributed to scholastic philosophy, as did thinkers in traditional monastic orders such as the Benedictines and Cistercians.

Across the newly instituted confessional divide of Europe, scholastic movements graced the Lutheran, Reformed, and Anglican denominations. Neither as robust nor as enduring as the schools of the Roman Catholic church, a fact witnessed by their slow decline in the late seventeenth century, "Protestant scholasticism" made an important contribution to the theology and philosophy of the period. Not only did its members help to fashion the institutional conditions in which figures such as Leibniz, Locke, Berkeley, and even the young Kant were first exposed to philosophy – an achievement not without consequence, since many canonical figures would complain about the deficiencies of their "scholastic education" – but they produced many well-known textbooks in logic, metaphysics, and ethics that became staple fixtures of a philosophical education in Northern Europe and North America down to the last decades of the eighteenth century.[11] In the Netherlands,

Protestant scholastics were among the very first to engage systematically with the new approach to philosophy and science of Descartes,[12] while in German-speaking countries a tradition of scholastic metaphysics remained influential even as late as the last decades of the eighteenth century and was closely associated with the work of Christian Wolff (1679–1754).[13]

It is important to stress that the schools were neither monolithic nor closed intellectual systems. When one reviews the central features of philosophical practice among the Thomists, Scotists, or Jesuits, or peruses the theories of Lutheran, Reformed, and Anglican thinkers, one is immediately struck by the absence of any strict or overbearing "party line," and the extent to which considerable disagreement on issues in metaphysics, ethics, and philosophical theology was permitted in every school. For this reason, it is hazardous to arrive at general definitions of 'Thomism,' 'Scotism,' 'Jesuit Scholasticism,' and 'Protestant Scholasticism,' since at this time uniformity in method is not always in evidence when one compares writers of the same school, but resident in different universities and national philosophical cultures. Such flexibility in outlook could have surprising results. Throughout the period it was quite common for a Thomist in one part of Europe, reading the very same texts as a colleague in another part of the Continent, to arrive at entirely different views. Similar differences of opinion can be found among members of the Scotist school, and are recognizable in the ranks of Jesuit philosophers – one has only to recall the bitter disputes between Gabriel Vázquez (1549–1604) and Francisco Suárez – as well as among Lutherans, Calvinists, and Anglicans.[14]

Scholasticism in the early modern period exhibited a mature tolerance of incongruity (although this did admit of degrees), as well as an appetite for genuine debate. Given the texts and questions that scholastic thinkers struggled to understand, these traits are unsurprising. The bases of their detailed discussions were the seminal books of Aristotle, Thomas Aquinas, John Duns Scotus, and their Renaissance commentators – texts which occasioned multiple interpretations and encouraged different points of view.[15] As many of the important arguments of these same works gave rise to equivocal readings, it became incumbent upon interpreters to try to find coherent explanations of disputed passages, even when these passages did not lend themselves to simple or conclusive renderings. Hence the existence of disagreement among thinkers of the same school, and extensive disputes among members of different schools.[16]

THOMISM

The writings of Thomas Aquinas (1225–74) proved the most enduring source of inspiration to scholastic philosophers in early modern times, and for this reason Thomism is worthy of our greatest attention. Bequeathed to the period by a renewed and systematic interest in Thomas's corpus coincident with the great sixteenth-century commentaries of the Dominicans Sylvester Mazzolini (1456–1523), Francesco Silvestro di Ferrara (ca. 1474–1528), Cardinal Thomas de Vio Cajetan (1468–1534), Conrad Koellin (d. 1536), and Chrysostom Javelli (1470–1538),[17] its triumphal march led to the coronation of Thomas Aquinas as the "Prince of Theologians" when his *Summa theologiae* was laid beside the sacred scriptures at the Council of Trent (1545–62). In 1567, Pope Pius V proclaimed him a Doctor of the Universal Church, and the publication of the famous "Piana" edition of his works in 1570 ushered in several editions of his *Opera omnia*, a great many of which graced the libraries of the learned world. Most aspects of Thomist thought were refreshed and further developed, especially in the fields of moral and political philosophy, by leading thinkers of the so-called "school of Salamanca." Of these Francisco de Vitoria (1486–1546), Dominic Soto (1495–1560), Melehior Cano (1509–60), Peter Soto (1494–1563), Bartholomé de Medina (1528–80), and Domingo Bañez (1528–1604) stand out as capable exponents of Thomist philosophy and theology.[18]

Apart from the Dominican order, the decision of the Jesuits to adopt Thomas as the official philosopher of their order provided additional impetus and direction to Thomist philosophy,[19] although as we shall see, many Jesuit writers arrived at doctrines quite at variance with those of more "orthodox" Dominican exegetes. Thomism was embraced and valorized by the Carmelite theologians of Salamanca, the Salmanticenses, whose voluminous *Cursus theologicus* (1631–72) was widely cited and respected.[20] Protestant thinkers, in turn, appropriated Thomistic ideas and in countries such as England, Aquinas's natural theology, with its emphasis on the importance of a posteriori proofs for the existence of God, proved an enduring resource for savants as diverse as Richard Hooker (1554–1600), Henry More (1614–87), and John Norris of Bemerton (1657–1717).[21]

Among the noteworthy examples of seventeenth-century Thomism were the writings of Johannes Wiggers (1571–1639) and François Du Bois (1581–1649). Wiggers, a contemporary of Cornelius Jansen (1585–1638), was a theologian of Louvain whose main work, the posthumously published *Commentaria in totam D. Thomae summam* (Louvain, 1641), contained a wealth of interesting arguments and suggestions on topics such as philosophical theology and the philosophy of mind. A curious and agile thinker, Wiggers's commentary was alive to the tensions and ambiguities in Thomas's great work.[22] The Douai-based theologian François Du Bois wrote the *Commentaria in summam theologiae S. Thomae* (Douai, 1620–35, 1622–48), which also made a genuine contribution to the Thomist exegesis of his time. Less sagacious than Wiggers, Du Bois provided balanced and thorough comment on most aspects of the Thomistic system.[23]

Considered together, these commentaries are representative of a genre of Thomism peculiar to those parts of the Low Countries that had remained loyal to Rome. In these lands, scholastic thought had come under concerted attack not just from Protestant divines, but also from Catholic thinkers who wished to replace the rationalism of traditional scholasticism with a biblically based theology augmented by Patristic tradition. This position emphasized the importance of individual faith in God over a demonstration of his existence, and an account of human nature that drew sustenance from the antipelagian writings of Augustine. Supporters of these opinions, who ranged from figures as different as Michael Baius (1513–89) and Libertus Fromondus (1585–1653) on to Jansenius himself, argued that a nonscholastic form of theological discourse would serve more effectively the verities of the Christian tradition, and help to address the grievances of the Protestants.[24]

Fighting a rearguard action in this situation, scholastic thinkers sought to promote even more stringently the arguments of Thomas, since they held them to be indispensable to the project of proving doctrines such as the immortality of the soul, the existence of God, and the grounding of an account of human agency uncompromised by fulsome descriptions of divine providence. This context gave birth to one of the better-known scholastic figures of early modern philosophy, Johannes Caterus (1590–1655), who composed the first set of Objections to Descartes's *Meditations*. Caterus had been a pupil of Wiggers at Louvain, and most certainly carried forward his old master's commitment to a version of Thomist natural theology. He was clearly unimpressed by what he believed to be Descartes's disregard of traditional forms of scholastic argument.[25]

Beyond these writers, a highly capable quartet of French Dominican friars based at convents in Toulouse and Bordeaux took up the challenge of setting down an account of morality and human action inspired by the teaching of Thomas. The first of these was Vincent Baron (1604–74), whose pristine moral theology sought to flay the hide of "that dangerous innovation," this being the doctrine of probabilism then championed by Jesuit casuists.[26] The second was Pierre Labat (d. 1670), who wrote a seven-volume *Theologia scholastica secundum illibatam D. Thomae doctrinam sive cursus theologicus* (Toulouse, 1658–61) which fired a dual broadside at Jansenism and Molinism.[27] In addition to these authors, the *Theologia mentis et cordis seu speculationes universae sacrae* (Lyons, 1668–69) of Vincent Contenson (1641–74), combined a sophisticated blend of metaphysics, biblical exegesis, and dogmatic theology, while the *Clypeus thomistica contra novos eius impugnatores* (Bordeaux, 1659–69) of Jean-Baptiste Gonet (1615–81) took up the task of defending Thomist moral teaching against the Jesuits.[28]

Prominent Dominicans based in Paris struggled to match the contribution of their southern colleagues. One of the best-known Thomists of the French capital was Nicolas Ysambert (1569–1642). Professor of Theology at the Sorbonne, Ysambert held the first chair in "controversy," an institution created in imitation of the highly successful Jesuit practice perfected by the likes of Robert Bellarmine (1547–1621) and Martin Becanus (1563–1624), in which a professor discussed topical arguments. From 1616 to just before his death in 1642, the indefatigable Dominican lectured on the *Summa theologiae* of Thomas, the results of which were posthumously published as *Disputationes* from 1643 to 1648. An unoriginal mind, Ysambert attempted to create a doctrinal synthesis of the teaching of Bonaventure, Aquinas, and Scotus, and convinced very few that a union of these minds was in fact possible.

One of the more interesting French Dominicans was the historian and moralist Alexander Natalis (1639–1724). He published in ten octavo volumes a commentary on the *Catechismus romanus* entitled *Theologia dogmatica et moralis* (Paris, 1693), a work which provides a clear statement of Thomist moral thought against the Jesuit casuistry of the day. A prominent figure in intellectual circles, Natalis was no stranger to controversy, and his heated spat with the Jesuit Gabriel Daniel (1649–1728) on probabilism and Molinist ideas of grace and predestination aroused such acrimony that the parties were eventually silenced by King Louis XIV. Like other Dominicans, Natalis's polemical case was clear: there was no basis for these Jesuit theories in the texts of Thomas. While writing his moral works he also published several historical dissertations in which he attempted to prove that Thomas was the author of the entire *Summa theologiae*. In addition to this historical midwifery, he wrote an engaging short dialogue between a Franciscan and a Dominican on the subject of the originality of Thomas. Natalis's double conclusion was that Thomas was not a disciple of Alexander of Hales (d. 1245) – a medieval Franciscan professor of theology – and that the *Secunda secundae* of the *Summa theologiae* was not borrowed from the latter, as had been claimed by "scurrilous" Franciscans.

Moral debates aside, other Thomists were moved to defend the following theses. First was the idea that angels and human souls are without matter, but that every material composite being (*compositum*) has two parts, prime matter and substantial form. The thought here is that in a composite being which has substantial unity, and is not merely an aggregate of distinct units, there can be but one substantial form. For Thomists, the substantial form of man is his soul (*anima rationalis*), to the exclusion of any other soul and of any other substantial form. The principle of individuation, for material composites, is matter with its dimensions: without this there can be no merely numerical multiplication; distinction in the form makes specific distinction, hence there cannot be two angels of the same species.[29]

Another distinctive commitment of the Thomists was their detailed defense of the Angelic Doctor's moral psychology. At *Summa theologiae*, Ia, qq. 82–86, and *De malo*, q. 6, Thomas had argued against then contemporary forms of voluntarism which held that the will moves the intellect *quoad exercitium*, i.e. in its actual operation; rather, the intellect moves the will *quoad specificationem*, i.e. by presenting objects to it: *nil volitum nisi praecognitum*. In the early modern period, Thomists were concerned to counter more recent voluntarist ideas derived either from late medieval philosophy or from the theological debates of the Reformation.[30] The origin of all human action, for the Thomists, resided in the apprehension and desire of good in general (*bonum in communi*). Human beings desire happiness naturally and necessarily, not by a free deliberate act. Particular goods (*bona particularia*) are chosen freely. Thus, the will (*voluntas*), though a proactive force in human action, is not the superior partner in the composite known as *liberum arbitrium* (freedom of decision); as a faculty it always follows the last judgment of the practical intellect (*ratio practica*).[31]

Another widely supported thesis was that the senses and the intellect are passive, i.e. recipient, faculties; they do not create, but receive (i.e. perceive) their objects.[32] There was also extensive discussion of the theory that the direct and primary object of the intellect is the universal, which is prepared and presented to the passive intellect (*intellectus possibilis*) by the active intellect (*intellectus agens*) which illuminates the phantasmata, or mental images, received through the senses, and divests them of all individuating conditions. For the Thomists, this was called "abstracting" the universal idea from the phantasmata, and there was a lively debate among them as to how such abstraction was to be understood. The general consensus they formed was that abstraction is not a transferring of something from one place to another; the illumination causes all material and individuating conditions to disappear, then the universal alone "shines" out and is perceived by the action of the intellect. Because this process was believed to be vital, and elevated far above material conditions and modes of action, the nature of the acts and of the objects apprehended was thought to show that the soul was immaterial and spiritual. Thus, the soul was by its very nature held to be immortal. Not only was it thought to be true that God will not annihilate the soul, but from its very nature the soul was held to continue to exist, there being in it no principle of disintegration. This last thought formed the basis of Aquinas's much-disputed doctrine – one supported by most of his early modern enthusiasts – that human reason can prove the incorruptibility (i.e. immortality) of the soul.[33]

While it is always invidious to elevate one individual above all others, a case could be made that the most important Thomist thinker of the seventeenth century was John of St. Thomas, this being the religious name of the Portuguese Dominican João Poinsot (1589–1644). His major philosophical works were collected and published during his lifetime under the title *Cursus philosophicus thomisticus* (Madrid and Rome, 1637; Cologne, 1638; and after his death, Lyons, 1663). This collection is composed of detailed tracts on logic and natural philosophy. His theological writings, named the *Cursus theologicus*, were originally prepared in the form of a commentary on the *Summa theologiae*, and published at Alcalá, Madrid, and Lyons from 1637 onwards.[34]

Though in every sense a dedicated disciple of Thomas, Poinsot was by no means an unthinking follower of his master's ideas. In one of the more methodologically reflective passages written by an early modern Thomist (see *Cursus theologicus, tractatus de approbatione et auctoritate doctrinae D. Thomae*, disp. II, a. 5), Poinsot provides five marks (*signa*) which he believes ought to guide the reading of Thomas. These are: (i) when there is doubt about what Thomas means one should defer to authoritative commentators; (ii) the faithful reader of Thomas should aim to "energetically" defend and explain Thomas's teaching rather than "disagreeing captiously"; (iii) the commentator should stress the "glory and brilliance" of the master's teaching rather than parade his own talent; (iv) the commentator should endeavor to explain Thomas's reasons in his own terms; and (v) the test of fidelity is to be observed in the agreement of the commentator with earlier disciples of Thomas.[35] Faithfulness meant everything to Poinsot; yet his was a critical fealty that aimed to tease out ambiguities and resolve textual problems in order to make the mind of Thomas tractable and appealing.

A noteworthy but rarely explored feature of Thomism in the late seventeenth century was the manner in which it became increasingly fixated with historical treatments of its own portfolio of arguments. Several Dominican works written at this time sought to recreate the "timeless teaching" of Thomas himself, in order to juxtapose the verities of his ideas with those of other contemporary "Thomists" – usually the hapless Jesuits – who claimed a warrant for their views in the *corpus thomisticum*. Powerful examples of this type of work were tomes of moral theology by the aforementioned Alexander Natalis, as well as by Daniel Concina (1687–1759), and the studies on grace and nature by Jacques Hyacintha Serry (d. 1738), who penned the influential *Historia congregationis de auxiliis* (Louvain, 1700).[36] While the advent of this more belligerent style of writing did not signal a total decline in more speculative Thomist thought – the theoretical writings of Charles-René Billuart (d. 1757),[37] especially his voluminous if arid *Summa S. Thomae hodiernis academiarum moribus accommodata, sive cursus theologiae* (Paris, 1746–51), reveal that aspect to be in reasonable order – it does show that by the end of the eighteenth century many Thomists were much less critical of their tradition than in preceding decades, and more concerned with the enterprise of sketching a definitive picture *ad mentem Thomae*. This tendency would become commonplace in the so-called "neo-Thomist" movement of the nineteenth and twentieth centuries, and testifies to the fact that several of the more decadent aspects of early modern Thomism have been adopted, albeit without acknowledgment and reflection, by modern-day "Thomist" writers.[38]

SCOTISM

The next great school of early modern scholasticism was Scotism.[39] Based on the teaching of the *Doctor Subtilis*, John Duns Scotus (ca. 1265/66–1308), as that had been passed down from the medieval period, it was only at the beginning of the sixteenth century that a "Scotist School" became an identifiable presence in European philosophy. The works of Scotus were then collected, published in many editions, and systematically commentated upon. From 1501 we also find regulations of general chapters of the Franciscans recommending or directly prescribing "Scotism" as the teaching of the order, although the writings of Bonaventure (ca. 1217–74) were also promoted in some quarters.

Scotism reached its zenith in the first half of the seventeenth century, with the establishment some years before of specialist chairs at the universities of Paris, Rome, Coimbra, Salamanca, Alcalá, Padua, and Pavia. One observer, the Cistercian polymath Juan Caramuel y Lobkowitz (1606–82), was moved to remark: "the school of Scotus is more numerous than all the other schools taken together."[40] In the eighteenth century, the movement still had an important following, but subsequently fell into decline, a state of affairs explicable by the repeated suppressions endured by Franciscan communities in many countries,[41] and by the increasing tendency of several popes from the late eighteenth century onward to recommend the teaching of Aquinas as normative for Roman Catholic intellectuals.

Among the main personalities of sixteenth-century Scotism, Paul Scriptoris (d. 1505), professor at the University of Tübingen, proved an influential figurehead for the movement in German-speaking countries, while the commentaries of Francis Lichetus, General of the Order (d. 1520), were greatly admired. Anthony Trombetta (1436–1517), the Paduan opponent of the Dominican Cajetan, wrote and edited many able works of Scotist philosophy, [42] as did James Almainus (d.ca. 1515), a Paris-based theologian who was not a Franciscan. His legacy in the theology faculty would help to establish a tradition of scholastic thought which, though highly eclectic, drew on many aspects of Scotist metaphysics. In the following century, this trend would find expression in the textbooks of Eustachius a Sancto Paulo (1573–1640) and the writings of Yves of Paris (ca. 1590–1678).[43] At the close of the sixteenth century, José Anglés (d. 1588), a celebrated moralist, wrote the much cited *Flores theologicae*, while Damian Giner (fl. 1605) produced an edition of the *Opus oxoniense Scoti* which was to become a template for the later critical edition of Luke Wadding (1588–1657).[44]

In the seventeenth century, Scotism came into its own. The crowning achievement of the school at this time was the publication by Wadding and other Irish Franciscans working at the College of St. Isidore in Rome of the complete works of Scotus (12 volumes, Lyons, 1639).[45] The work included detailed commentaries by Pitigianus of Arezzo (d. 1616), John Pounce (Poncius) (ca. 1599 or 1603–1672/3), Hugh Mac Caughwell (Cavellus) (d. 1626), and Anthony Hickey (1586–1641).[46] The very clever Bonaventuri Belluti (1600–1676) edited with Bartolomeo Mastri (1602–73) the most widely regarded Scotist manual of the century, *Cursus integer philosophiae ad mentem Scoti* (Venice, 1678, 1688, and many other editions),[47] while Mastri himself wrote a celebrated *Disputationes theologiae* (many editions) and *Theologia ad mentem Scoti* (1671), a work which probably represents the high water mark of Scotist thinking in the period.[48]

Mastri was by no means the most original of the Scotist philosophers of his day – maybe Belluti deserves that garland – but he was among the most learned. His knowledge of the medieval and Renaissance scholastic tradition was probably unsurpassed, and he was nicknamed *Dottore Ubertoso* by his biographer Franchini in virtue of the plethora of authorities (*auctoritates*) he cited. Mastri's development of a philosophical opinion was a remarkable feat of synthesis and conceptual engineering, whereby different aspects of medieval Scotism would be fused, compared, or even gainsaid by opinions drawn from contemporary debate.[49] This method enabled Mastri to demonstrate the diversity of arguments available to Scotist thinkers. His studies displayed the subtlety and rigor traditionally associated with Duns Scotus himself.[50]

After Mastri, Scotist philosophers continued to labor to some point and purpose. The Croatian Matthaeus Ferchius (Mate Frkic) (1583–1666) wrote the *Vita et apologia Scoti*,[51] while the Frenchman Jean Gabriel Boyvin (1605–81) wrote the esteemed *Theologia Scoti a prolixitate et subtilitas eius ab obsuritate libera et vindicata* (4 volumes, Caen, 1665–71).[52] Another valuable work, the product of an eclectic as opposed to a purely Scotist mind, was the *Collationes* by a Portuguese professor at Padua, Francisco a Santo Augustini Macedo (1596–1681). This work set itself the unenviable task of assessing the respective merits and compatibility of Thomist and Scotist doctrines, and as such it throws a great deal of light on the disputes (at least at Padua) conducted by these competing schools.[53]

As we move to the eighteenth century, Scotist philosophy continued to hold its own in some parts of the Catholic world, although elsewhere it went into a swift decline. Many Enlightenment writers found its metaphysics anachronistic or prolix, while Catholic thinkers looked increasingly to Thomas. By the end of the eighteenth century, individual Scotists can be said to manifest an unwillingness to engage critically with their pluriform tradition. It is instructive to compare, in this regard, the erudition of Mastri or the intelligence of Belluti with writers such as Du Randus (d. 1720). His popular *Clypeus scotisticus* (many editions) merely aimed to expound the kernel of Scotist teaching without much thought to its truth or plausibility. There were, however, some good examples of Scotist writing in the period, as can be observed in the profound and lucid work of Hieronymus a Montefortino (1632–1738), *Duns Scoti summa theologiae ex universis operibus ejus concinnata, juxta ordinem et dispositionem summae Angelici Doctoris* (6 volumes, 1728–34), and the *Theologiae scholasticae morali-polemicae liber IV sententiarum iuxta verum sensum, et mentem doctoris subtilis Joannis Duns Scoti* (Augsburg, 1732), of the German moralist Marin Panger (d. 1732).[54] These accomplished texts represent the swan song of a once vibrant tradition of philosophy.

THE JESUITS

Just as it made an enduring contribution to the arts, sciences, politics, and religious life of its day, so the Society of Jesus, or the Jesuits, provided a home to original philosophical achievement.[55] Deferential though never wholly compliant to their *auctoritates maiores* such as Aristotle and Thomas Aquinas,[56] and highly respectful of *auctoritates minores* such as Scotus and other Renaissance luminaries such as Cajetan, Jesuit authors from the foundation of the society in 1540 to its suppression in 1773 were responsible for innovations in logic, natural philosophy (including psychology), metaphysics, ethics (including casuistry), jurisprudence, political philosophy, and philosophical theology.

Some of the best-known figures in the annals of early modern scholasticism were Jesuits. First and foremost was Suárez, whose magisterial *Disputationes metaphysicae* (1597) and *Tractatus de legibus, ac Deo legislatore* (Coimbra, 1612) were read throughout Europe by Catholics and Protestants alike. Following Suárez in intellectual stature is Luis de Molina (1536–1600), author of the *Concordia* (Lisbon, 1588). This work instituted one of the most enduring debates of early modern scholasticism, the *De auxiliis* dispute, a theological quarrel concerning the compatibility of human freedom and divine providence, which commanded the attention of (among others) Bañez, Arnauld, Leibniz, and Malebranche. The debate even influenced the Dutch Calvinist censure of the thought of Jacob Arminius (1550–1609). Molina's other great work, *De iustitia et iure* (Cuenca, 1593–1600), proved to be one of the most durable books of *philosophia practica* or "practical philosophy" of the period, making many novel contributions to ethics, politics, and economics. Finally, the Conimbricenses (1592–1606), a collection of Jesuits writers based at Coimbra, rose to eminence. This group, which included Emmanuel de Goes (1542–97), Cosmas de Magalhães (1551–1624), Balthasar Alvarez (1561–97), and Sebastian do Couto (1567–1639), were responsible for a highly successful series of commentaries on Aristotle's *Physics*, *De caelo*, *Meteorologica*, *Parva naturalia*, *Ethics, De generatione et corruptione*, *De anima*, and *Dialectica* (commentaries on the logical treatises). Combining scholastic argument with a humanist attention to philology, these works had been reprinted a staggering 112 times by 1633 in Catholic territories such as Portugal, France, Italy, and Rhineland Germany.

Less well known in our time but highly regarded in their own day were another group of Jesuit philosophers. These included the aforementioned Gabriel Vázquez, Pedro da Fonseca (1528–99),[57] Gregory de Valencia (1550–1603),[58] Leonardus Lessius (1554–1623),[59] Adam Tanner (1572–1632),[60] Antonio Perez (1599–1648),[61] Juan De Lugo (1583–1660),[62] Thomas Carleton Compton (1591–1666),[63] Pietro Sforza Pallavicino (1607–67),[64] and Sebastián Izquierdo (1601–81).[65] This pool of talent was supplemented by writers of important textbooks such as Francisco Toletus (1534–96),[66] Rodrigo de Arriaga (1592–1667),[67] and Pedro Hurtado de Mendoza (1578–1641),[68] all of whom advanced the scope and cause of scholastic philosophy by making its ideas tractable. The Jesuits played a further part in the dissemination of scholastic thought through their elaborate network of schools and colleges in Europe and the New World, of which the Collegio Romano was the most influential. Many intellectuals of the period, including clerics and laymen and notable minds like Descartes and Voltaire, were educated in Jesuit schools and university colleges.[69]

When compared with the far from homogeneous schools of Dominican Thomism and Scotism, it is significant that Jesuit scholastics were less motivated to construct a binding philosophical consensus, especially in subjects such as metaphysics and ethics, even though various generals of the order had endorsed the teaching of Thomas.[70] In the case of metaphysics, nowhere is this more apparent than in the great *Disputationes metaphysicae* of Suárez.[71] Such is the originality of this work – a book whose arguments are prosecuted by means of a sustained reflection on the debates of medieval thought – that Suárez's final opinion was neither beholden to Thomism nor Scotism. Whenever he was minded to side with either Thomas or Scotus, he was led to endorse their respective positions by means of an impartial scrutiny of the claims at issue. This approach led him to modify aspects of their teaching for his own purposes. For example, he accepted the doctrine of analogical predication, siding with Thomas, but thought that a concept of being (*esse*) can be found which is strictly unitary, thereby supporting the *communis opinio* defended by Scotus and his disciples.[72] Conversely, he embraced the Scotist doctrine of matter's existing without form by divine power, but sided with Thomas on the issue of the plurality of forms.[73] The extent of Suárez's distance from classical Thomism is most forcefully paraded in his discussion of the so-called "real distinction," whereby the "essence" of things is distinguished from their "existence."[74] Against Thomas, he argued that there is a third distinction other than the "real and rational." Skeptical of the traditional Thomist dichotomy between essence and existence, Suárez posited a distinction of reason with a basis in things, and a distinction between substance and accidents.[75] In matters of philosophical controversy, the *Doctor Exigimus* kept his own counsel.

In ethics, many Jesuits endeavored to defend versions of an Aristotelian–Thomist practical philosophy, a plural tradition which also nourished their distinctive approach to applied ethics or "casuistry."[76] Here again there were profound differences of opinion among Jesuits, as well as a propensity on the part of individual authors to think beyond the texts of Aristotle and Thomas on a range of controversial issues.[77] If there is a common tendency among Jesuit writers in practical philosophy, it is best illustrated by their penchant to defend an account of morality that emphasizes the importance of human freedom. Jesuit writers often cited the account of freedom set down by Molina's *Concordia* (see IV, esp. q. 14, a. 13, disp. 2, §3), whose practical implications were subsequently worked out by the same author in his later *De iure et iustitia*.[78]

For Molina, what helps to define a human being as a rational creature is the power to act freely. The faculty of *liberum arbitrium*, or the ability to make reasoned choices, distinguishes human beings from other animals and living things. Under the doctrine of "middle knowledge" (*scientia media*), the *liberum arbitrium* of human beings is not affected by divine causality or by God's foreknowledge of future contingent events; free actions shape and mold the direction of any human life because they are undertaken in conditions exempt from all coercion and constraint. It is against the background of this account of human action that Molina outlined his own distinctive view of the natural law.[79]

Few would deny the influence of Thomas and his Salamancan interpreters on Molina's *De iure et iustitia*, but his strong emphasis on the mutability of the principles of the natural law, a flexibility he deemed to be indispensable for their subsequent application to the varied contexts of human action, is indicative of a distinctive Jesuit perspective. Molina first began to discuss this question in his 1570 lectures on *Summa theologiae*, Ia–IIae, qq. 98–108. There, he adopted a position familiar to earlier thinkers such as Vitoria and Soto that while the principles of the Decalogue and other valid universal principles do not admit of exceptions, judgment is required to determine how and when they apply to a particular case.[80] Molina developed this opinion a stage further, however, by arguing that certain principles, especially those that express general moral norms, do not always oblige in recalcitrant cases. The point here was not that such cases constitute exceptions to these principles, but rather that no appropriate specification of the general principles was possible. Such ideas, so often misunderstood by rigoristic critics such as Blaise Pascal and Pierre Nicole, were an important component of Jesuit casuistry.[81]

It is commonplace among historians to declare that later Jesuit writers, be they metaphysicians, moralists, or contributors to debates in natural philosophy and psychology, did not maintain the high intellectual standards of their late sixteenth-century forebears.[82] This of course may be true, since at first glance the decades following the publication of Pascal's *Les provinciales* in 1656 appear bereft of thinkers of any great originality. Still, this verdict, like so many others imposed upon the study of early modern scholasticism, is at best unfair and at worst derisory. The fact of the matter is that even after many years of historical study of eighteenth-century philosophy, vast quantities of scholastic works and textbooks, especially those by Jesuit authors in the years up to their suppression in 1773, are unread and unstudied.[83] It is premature to assume that there are neither interesting texts nor palpable conceptual achievements in the twilight years of the scholastic tradition.

Something of the intellectual energy of eighteenth-century Jesuit scholastics can be learned by glancing at those figures who were actively involved in the debates of the day. The writings of Claude Buffier (1661–1737), especially his *Traité des premières veritéz et de source de nos jugements* (Paris, 1724), are known to have influenced Thomas Reid, and were widely discussed outside scholastic circles.[84] Bertold Hauser (1713–62), a professor of mathematics at Dillingen, wrote the *Elementa philosophiae ad rationis et experientiae ductum conscripta atque usibus scholasticis accommodata* (Augsburg, 1755–58), which drew heavily on the thought of Christian Wolff. Despite diverging from Wolff on questions regarding truth and mind–body union, Hauser was motivated to use him as a suasive authority on many questions; hence the occurrence of phrases like *Wolfio ipso fatente et docente.*[85] Many of the preoccupations of Wolffian metaphysics, such as a developed interest in the principle of sufficient reason, were adopted by other Jesuit authors working in German-speaking lands.[86] These writers provide some modest evidence that scholastics were applying themselves to the topical concerns of their day.

PROTESTANT SCHOLASTICS AND OTHERS

Hitherto, Protestant philosophy and theology between the deaths of the magisterial reformers and the advent of the Enlightenment has been viewed as a period of intellectual decline. This assessment, the creation of twentieth-century theologians who had little understanding or sympathy for scholasticism, such as Karl Barth (1886–1968), is no longer the accepted wisdom among historians of the period.[87] In the last two decades, several sophisticated studies have set the concepts and issues confronted by Lutheran and Reformed scholastics in context, with the consequence that it is now possible to appreciate their palpable contribution to the philosophical and theological debates of their time.[88]

On reading the Protestant scholastics one is immediately struck by the extent to which they appropriated and preserved important vestiges of the medieval philosophical tradition. While leading reformers such as Martin Luther (1483–1546)[89] and John Calvin

(1509–64)[90] kept their distance from more abstract philosophical topics, their immediate followers, especially Philip Melanchthon (1497–1560),[91] Andreas Hyperius (1511–64),[92] and Theodore Beza (1519–1605),[93] proved more congenial to the methods of scholasticism. Among Reformed thinkers, various Thomist themes and allegiances are on display in authors such as Girolamo Zanchi (1516–90)[94] and Peter Martyr Vermigli (1500–1562). Vermigli also adopted an Augustinian position on grace and predestination which is closely associated with the work of Gregory of Rimini (d. 1354).[95]

Other Protestant scholastics willingly threw themselves into the debates of the time, especially after they came to dominate those universities and academies in northern European lands that had parted company from Rome. The acute and encyclopedic mind of Johan Alsted (1588–1638), despite its millenarian preoccupations, made a number of important contributions to metaphysics and natural philosophy.[96] The scientist and philosopher Rudolf Goclenius (1547–1628), who was well known for his philosophical dictionary, *Lexicon philosophicum* (Frankfurt, 1613), presented a synthesis of scholastic metaphysics in his *Isagoge in peripateticorum et scholasticorum primam philosophiam* (Frankfurt, 1598). This tome reveals similar ontological preoccupations, especially on the subject of the *ens reale*, to then contemporary Catholic writers such as Suárez.[97]

Given the role and influence of Gisbertus Voetius (1589–1676) at the Synod of Dort's (1618–19) condemnation of Arminius, one might expect that he, like fellow members of the *Nadere Reformatie*, or the Dutch Second Reformation, would have little enthusiasm for scholasticism. This proves to be far from the case, however, since Voetius believed there to be no tension between an account of religious faith which stressed its experiential efficacy and a form of scholastic theology. While insisting on the ultimate superiority of faith over reason, he considered a more streamlined form of scholasticism to be a profitable methodology which could be employed in the conceptual clarification of both the intellectual and emotional aspects of faith.[98] Voetius is well known for crossing swords with Cartesianism, a system he believed to have placed reason on a par with the assumed verities of scripture. What was so ghastly about Descartes's thought, he believed, was its unwarranted elevation of human beings above their natural station as sinful wretches to the very zenith of creation. For a pious Calvinist like Voetius, it was abhorrent that humans could free themselves from subservience to the divine will by the use of reason.[99]

Among Anglicans, two English divines who became Irish bishops, John Bramhall (1594–1663), archbishop of Armagh, and Jeremy Taylor (1613–67), bishop of Down and Connor, proved astute custodians of certain aspects of scholastic thought. Bramhall tends to be disparaged by modern critics in virtue of his tenacious attempt to refute Hobbes's discussion of human freedom.[100] The good bishop, however, does make several salient points at Hobbes's expense, and is particularly adroit at drawing attention to his opponent's somewhat parsimonious and highly reductive description of human psychology. For Bramhall, any rejection of a traditional scholastic account of *liberum arbitrium* will have real consequences for the study of ethics. Of course, many modern interpreters, like Hobbes himself, are simply unimpressed with Bramhall's reiteration of scholastic teaching. This is to be regretted, since it denies the latter's argument the attention it deserves.[101]

Jeremy Taylor was a theologian who built upon numerous scholastic discussions, using them to effect in his natural theology, account of the Eucharist, and moral theology. More judicious, if still vehement, in his criticism of the "Romish errors" of Catholic casuistry, his *Ductor dubitantium* (London, 1660) was one of the few English works of the period to advance a method of moral reasoning which bore some similarity to the approach of the continental casuists. An inveterate reader of the Christian past – his knowledge of the Fathers is just as impressive as his command of the teaching of the schoolmen – Taylor's work bears testimony to a sympathetic engagement with medieval and more recent scholastic thought.[102] Through his efforts, and those of other divines such as James Ussher (1581–1656) and Edward Stillingfleet (1635–99), vestiges of scholasticism remained a live presence in late seventeenth-century English philosophy and theology.[103]

Leaving the Protestants, it is perhaps fitting to complete our far from conclusive survey of the scholastic schools by drawing attention to an intellectual colossus, a figure whose reputation would surely be secured if scholastic thought became a more topical subject of scholarly research. The Spanish Cistercian, Juan Caramuel y Lobkowitz, left an extensive body of writing that contrives to say something sensible on just about every topic it considered, ranging from logic, mathematics, metaphysics, and natural science to theology, moral philosophy, casuistry, and music.[104] It reveals a myriad of influences ranging from Plato and Ramón Lull (ca. 1235–1315) to more established scholastic sources such as Aristotle, Thomas, and Scotus.[105] In a time of considerable ferment in the arts, sciences, and politics of Catholic Europe, Caramuel was on hand to witness these intellectual shifts by virtue of his prolonged residencies in Spain, Portugal, the Low Countries, Bohemia, and Italy.[106] His philosophical writings from 1660 onward are especially important in that they display a detailed appreciation of the work of Descartes and other innovators in the natural sciences.[107] Willing to acknowledge the force of a good argument, Caramuel reveals himself open to the claims of the new learning and tries to appropriate many of its insights within the accepted parameters of scholastic discourse. Of particular interest is his discussion of the Cartesian method of hyperbolic doubt and his thoughts on the nature of logic.[108] Anyone interested in philosophy will gain something from reading Caramuel, and the same remark could be made about other figures, especially those whose work has been surveyed above. It is high time for the scholastics to be brought in from the cold; the prospect of a more inclusive and historically reliable portrait of early modern philosophy must surely depend upon our assigning them a place nearer the hearth.[109]

NOTES

1 This is so despite the efforts of successive generations of European scholars to display the vitality of early modern scholasticism, a movement that found expression in several schools each of which claimed a measure of fidelity to the ideas and intellectual methods of the middle ages. There is no complete or authoritative survey of early modern scholasticism presently available in any language, a fact which is explicable more in terms of the profusion of sources rather than the indolence or disinterest of scholars. The best general account can be found in Schmutz 2000a, while an older but still useful study is available in Giacon 1944–50. Full treatments of early modern scholasticism as it impinged upon national philosophical cultures can be found in Lewalter 1935, Wundt 1939, and Blum 1999 for German-speaking countries; Brockliss 1987 for France; Poppi 2001, Burgio 1998 and 2000, and

Forlivesi 2002 for Italy and Sicily; Stegmüller 1959, Belda Plans 2000, and Calafate 2001 for the Iberian peninsula; Krook 1993 and Southgate 1993 for English-speaking countries; and Knuutilla 2001 and Ogonowski 2001 for Scandinavia and Eastern Europe. For an instructive essay on the changing attitudes to scholasticism see Quinto 2001. See also Trentmann 1982, Stone 2002, and Fitzpatrick and Haldane 2003 for English-language commentary on aspects of scholasticism. For those unfazed by new technology, much can be learned from the excellent website, *Scholasticon* (http://www.ulb.ac.be/philo/scholasticon/), maintained by Jacob Schmutz of the Sorbonne (Paris-IV).

2 See Sorell 1993, and Garber and Ayers 1998.

3 For examples of traditional disdain of scholasticism by well-known early modern writers, see Pierre Bayle's entry on Arriaga in the *Dictionnaire* (1697). For more recent assessments that concur with Bayle's general judgment, see Williams 1978, Cottingham 1988, Scruton 1994, and Bennett 2001.

4 This becomes apparent in any survey of university teaching at this time. For England, see Costello 1958 and Tyacke 1997; for France, see Brockliss 1987; for German-speaking lands, see Bauer 1928 and Boehm 1978; for Central Europe, see Freedman 1997; and for the colonies of North and Latin America, see Miller 1939 and Beuchot 1996.

5 While many contemporary scholars are motivated to explore the relationships that are said to exist between early modern thinkers and ancient traditions of philosophical thought, e.g. Stoicism, Epicureanism, and skepticism (see the recent collection by Miller and Inwood 2003), few are moved to investigate the debt that seventeenth-century philosophy may or may not owe to medieval thought. For recent attempts to restore this imbalance in subjects such as logic, metaphysics, psychology, ethics, and philosophical theology, see the collections by Brown 1998, Lagerlund and Yrjönsuuri 2002, Boulnois et al. 2002, Bardout and Boulnois 2002, Friedman and Nielsen 2003, Pink and Stone 2004, Ebbesen and Friedman 2004, and Kraye and Saarinen 2004.

6 It is revealing that in a major recent study of the contribution made by seventeenth-century philosophy to the making of "modernity," the scholastic schools are totally ignored; see Israel 2001.

7 For recent examples, see Garber and Ayers 1998 and the trilogy by Des Chene 1996, 2000, and 2001.

8 Examples of this approach can be found in the writings of (among others): Grene 1991, Garber 1992, Biard and Rashed 1997, Rozemond 1998, Ariew 1999, and Secada 2000 on Descartes; Leijenhorst 1998 on Hobbes; Brown 1984 and Mercer 2001 on Leibniz; Milton 1984 on

Locke; Coppens 2003 on Spinoza; and Connell 1967 and Pyle 2003 on Malebranche.

9 This last point can also be observed in the decision of early modern scholastics to write philosophy in a different way. They ceased to use the older medieval practices of the *quaestio disputata* and *quaestio quodlibetilis*, and no longer wrote commentaries on the *Sentences* of Peter Lombard. For further discussion of these developments, see Lawn 1993 and Quinto 2001.

10 On late medieval schools of philosophy and the problems inherent in their assessment, see the articles by Hoenen 1997, 1998, and 2003.

11 Among the best-known writers of scholastic manuals in the Protestant tradition are Bartolomeus Keckermann (1572–1609) and Franco Burgesdijk (1590–1635). For discussions of Keckermann's work and career, see Freedman 1997 and Stone 2000, while Burgesdijk's contribution is covered by Bos and Krop 1993 and Blom 1995, pp. 67–100.

12 See Verbeek 1992 and Goudriaan 1999.

13 On the origins of this school, see Wundt 1939 and Beck 1969. On Wolff and scholasticism, see Ruello 1963 and Carboncini 1991.

14 On the disputes between the two Jesuits as they pertained to morals, metaphysics, and theology, see Vereecke 1957, Castro 1974, and Schmutz 2002d.

15 This point is discussed by Giacon 1944 and Schmutz 2000a.

16 Two of the most heated disputes were on the subjects of grace and nature, topics considered in the *De auxiliis* controversy, and the discussion of moral reasoning concerning probabilism. On divine foreknowledge as it was discussed by scholastics and nonscholastic authors, especially Leibniz and Arnauld, see Sleigh 1990 and 1996, Murray 1995 and 2002, Knebel 1991 and 1996b, Ramelow 1997, and Kremer 1994. On probabilism, see Deman 1936 and Stone 2004e.

17 On the figures and issues of "Renaissance Thomism," see Kristeller 1992, Pinchard and Ricci 1993, and Tavuzzi 1997.

18 For general discussion of the Thomism of these authors, see Belda Plans 2000 and Stone 2004c; and Carro 1944, Brett 1997, and Stone 2005b for different assessments of their moral and political philosophy.

19 On the adoption of Thomas by the Jesuits, see the *Constitutions of the Society of Jesus*, no. 464, and the definitive version of their *Ratio studiorum* (1599): "Rules for professors of scholastic theology" (*Regulae professoris scholasticae theologiae*); see Rule 2: " S. Thomas sequendus."

20 See Merl 1947, Corazón 1955, and Borde 2001.

21 See Ryan 1948 for general discussion of Thomism among the English. On Hooker, see Voak 2003; on More and the Cambridge Platonists, see Dockrill 1997; and for Norris, see Acworth 1979.

22 On Wiggers, see Marcus-Leus 1995.
23 See Amann 1939.
24 For further discussion of these issues as they pertain to the Low Countries, see Lamberigts 1994 and Stone 2005b. For corresponding debates as they were conducted in Catholic circles in France, see Quantin 1999.
25 On Caterus and his formation in this intellectual tradition, see Verbeek 1995 and Armogathe 1995. The arguments of Thomist natural theology were also used by Protestant theologians in the Netherlands, especially at the University of Leiden. On these figures, see Platt 1982.
26 On the heated debates on probabilism and Jesuit casuistry, see Schüßler 2002 and Stone 2004e.
27 See Chenu 1925.
28 On Gonet, see Peyrous 1974.
29 For a full discussion of all these issues, see Beuchot 1996, Schmutz 2002b, and Pasnau 2004.
30 For late medieval and early modern scholastic discussion of the freedom of the will, see Stone 2004a and Pink 2004. Schneewind 1998, pp. 17–36, 95–100, 138–40, 159–61, 184–89, and 250–60 contains an extensive discussion of the debate about voluntarism in early modern philosophy.
31 See Leahy 1963 for discussion on how early modern Thomist writers dealt with these issues.
32 Thomas Aquinas, *Summa theologiae*, Ia, q. 78, a. 3; q. 79, a. 2.
33 *Summa theologiae*, Ia, q. 84, a. 4; and q. 85, a. 1, ad lum, 3um, 4um. For further discussion of how these passages were discussed by early modern scholastics, see Des Chene 2000, and Fowler 1999 who is instructive in charting the relationship between this discussion and the attempts of Descartes to demonstrate the immortality of the soul.
34 For two of the few more general studies of Poinsot, see Deely 1985, pp. 394–514, and Forlivesi 1993.
35 See John of St. Thomas, *Cursus theologicus* (1931–53), vol. 1, pp. 297–301.
36 On Concina and Serry, see Cessario 1998.
37 On Biluart, see Cessario 1998.
38 For a study of nineteenth-century Thomism, see McCool 1977, and for more recent versions, see Shanley 2002 and Kerr 2002.
39 The best available survey is by Schmutz 2002c; see also Hoenen 1998. For a discussion of the relationship between Cartesianism and Scotism, see Ariew 1999, pp. 39–57.
40 Caramuel, *Theologia moralis fundamentalis* (Lyons, 1657), bk. II, disp. 10: " Scoti schola numerosior est omnibus aliis simul sumptis." On the quotation, see the study by Bak 1956.

41 During the early modern period, the Franciscans were divided into three main congregations: Friars Major, Friars Minor, and the Capuchins, all of whom strongly supported Scotist philosophy.

42 On Trombetta and Scotism at Padua, see Poppi 1962 and 1966, and Mahoney 1976 and 1978.

43 On the early modern Parisian theological faculty, see Garcia Villoslada 1938, Brockliss 1987, and Ariew 1999.

44 On Wadding, see Cleary 1925 and Mooney 1958.

45 On the Irish Franciscans, see Millet 1964.

46 On Ponius and his colleagues, see Grajewski 1946 and Sousedik 1996. Further coverage is given by Cleary 1925.

47 On Belluti, see the older but still useful study by Scaramuzzi 1927.

48 See Schmutz 2002c, and Forlivesi 2002 for a very full account of Mastrius's life and career.

49 On this aspect of his work, see Poppi 1989 and Coombs 1993.

50 For further discussion, see Hoffmann 2002, Forlivesi 2002, pp. 202–4, and Schmutz 2002c.

51 On the Croatian friar, see Roscic 1971 and Forlivesi 2002.

52 See Smeets 1942, §215 and §545.

53 For discussion of the *Collationes* and other aspects of Macedo's work, see De Sousa Ribeiro 1951 and Ceyssens 1956.

54 See De Armellada 1997.

55 On the impact of the Jesuits on culture, society, and politics, see O'Malley 1999 and Höpfl 2004. On Jesuit science, see Feingold 2003a and 2003b. For a major treatment of Jesuit philosophers, see Knebel 2000.

56 It is interesting that many early Jesuits wanted to create a synthesis of scholastic teaching rather than rely upon the work of Thomas. On these debates, see O'Malley 1993, pp. 244–53.

57 For commentary on Fonseca's logic, metaphysics, and Aristotelian commentaries, see Pereira 1967, Martins 1994, and Menn 1997.

58 See von Hentrich 1928 and Asensio 1998.

59 For Lessius's philosophical theology, see Le Bachelet 1931, and Stone and Van Houdt 1999 for his ethics.

60 See Lurz 1932.

61 See Ramelow 1997, Knebel 1998 and 2000, pp. 79–86, 131–42, and Schmutz 2003.

62 On his practical philosophy, see Brinkman 1957, and for his metaphysics and theology, see Olivares 1984.

63 On Carleton Compton's interesting metaphysics, see Doyle 1988 and 1995, and Knebel 2000, pp. 12–15, 310–16, 421.

64 See Knebel 1996a and 2001.

65 See Di Vona 1994, Knebel 2000, pp. 79–84, 128–34, 331–43, and Schmutz 2002e.

66 See Hellin 1940, Baldini 1992, and Des Chene 1996 and 2000.

67 See Thorndike 1951, Leinsle 1985, pp. 317–20, and Sousedik 1981 and 1998.

68 See Caruso 1979 and Forlivesi 2000.

69 See Garcia Villoslada 1954 on the Roman College, and O'Malley 1993 on Jesuit education.

70 For the diversity of metaphysical views among early modern Jesuits, see Lohr 1988 and 1999, Schmutz 2002d and 2004, and Ariew 1999. Menn 1997 contains some interesting philosophical commentary, although he exaggerates the importance of what he calls "liberal Jesuit scholasticism," a term of his own invention rather than one with a basis in historical fact.

71 Recent monographs on Suárezian metaphysics are by Courtine 1990 and Darge 2004. Suárez's psychology has also been the subject of important articles by South 2001 and 2002. A full list of publications on Suárez can be found in the *Bibliographica suareciana* which is now available on line at *Scholasticon* (http://www.ulb.ac.be/philo/scholasticon/).

72 Francisco Suárez, *Disp. met.*, disp. 28, §3, nn. 2–7; and §1, n. 9.

73 *Disp. met.*, disp. 34, §5, n. 36; and disp. 15, §10, n. 61.

74 On the real distinction in Thomas Aquinas, see Wippel 1984.

75 *Disp. met.*, disp. 7, §1, n. 16; and disp. 31, §1, n. 3.

76 On Jesuit approaches to ethics and casuistry see Jonsen and Toulmin 1988, Courtine 1999, Knebel 2000, Höpfl 2004, and Stone 2004d.

77 For examples, see the debate among Jesuit scholastics on taxes described by Gómez Camacho 1998a and 1998b, and lying described by Somerville 1988.

78 Apart from the *Concordia*, Molina addresses the theme of human liberty in his polemical writings against the Protestants: see *Summa haeresium maior*, written against the Lutherans, Stegmüller 1935, pp. 394–438, and *Summa haeresium minor*, written against the Calvinists, Stegmüller 1935, pp. 439–50. Central to Molina's case in these tracts is his argument that by diminishing the scope of human liberty the Protestants make God into a tyrant.

79 See Díez-Alegría 1951 and Stone 2005b.

80 See Vitoria, *Commentaria in summam theologiae IIa–IIae*, v, p. 210, and Soto, *De iure et iustitia*, I, 2, q. 3.

81 On Molina's thought about these issues, see Díez-Alegría 1951. For the case against Jesuit casuistry advanced by Pascal's *Les provinciales* (Paris, 1656), see Baudin 1946–47, vol. III, pp. 33–254; and Stone 2004e.

82 See Jansen 1938.
83 For an attempt to open up some of the unstudied aspects of eighteenth-century scholastics, see Northeast 1991.
84 In 1780 an anonymous author attacked Reid and accused him of plagiarizing Buffier's treatment of common sense. For a full discussion of the grounds, or otherwise, of this charge, see Marcil-Lacoste 1982. Reid's more general relationship to the work of the scholastic tradition, in the form of Aquinas and Scotus, is assessed by Haldane 1989 and Broadie 2000.
85 On Hauser and his milieu, see Gurr 1959.
86 See Benedict Stattler (1728–97), *Philosophia methodo scientiis propria explanata* (Augsburg, 1769–72); and Sigsmund Storcheneau (1731–97/8), *Institutionum metaphysicarum libri IV* (Venice, 1772).
87 See Muller 2003 for the theological obstacles that thwarted a more objective and historical study of Protestant scholasticism.
88 Among these are the anthologies by Trueman and Clark 1999 and Van Asselt and Dekker 2001, and the magisterial study by Muller 2003.
89 On Luther and scholasticism, see Steinmetz 1995.
90 Calvin's complicated relationship to philosophy is discussed by Helm 2004.
91 For detailed discussions of Melanchthon's use of the Aristotelian and scholastic traditions in philosophy and science, see Frank 1995 and Kusukawa 1985.
92 See Sinnema 1999.
93 See Muller 1999.
94 On Zanchi, see Donnelly 1976.
95 On Vermigli, see James 1999 and 2001.
96 See Hotson 2000a and 2000b.
97 See Leinsle 1985.
98 On Voetius, see Van Ruler 1995 and Beeke 1999. Similar views to Voetius were also abroad among English Puritans such as John Owen (1616–83).
99 See Verbeek 1992.
100 For Bramhall's attack on Hobbes, see *Castigations of Mr. Hobbes* (London, 1655) and *The Catching of Leviathan or the Great Whale* (London, 1658).
101 A clear and interesting interpretation of the differences on moral agency between the scholastic tradition and Hobbes can be found in Pink 2004.
102 On Taylor, see Wood 1952.
103 For a discussion of Ussher's considerable erudition, see Knox 1950 and Trevor-Roper 1989, and Carroll 1975 for Stillingfleet.

104 For synoptic commentary on Caramuel, see Schmutz 2000b and Franklin 2001.
105 On Caramuel's eclectic brand of scholasticism, see Pastine 1975.
106 On his life and times, see Velarde Lombraña 1989.
107 See Ceñal 1953 and Fartos Martinez 1997.
108 See Pastine 1972. For a complete list of writings about Caramuel and his works, see the *Bibliographia caramueliana* at *Scholasticon* (http://www.ulb.ac.be/philo/scholasticon/).
109 I am grateful to Jacob Schmutz and to Donald Rutherford for their assistance with this essay.

J. B. SCHNEEWIND

12 Toward enlightenment: Kant and the sources of darkness

The title page of Christian Wolff's *Vernünftige Gedancken von Gott, der Welt und der Seele des Menschen* of 1720, the so-called "German Metaphysics," shows a brilliant sun beaming through dark clouds above a peaceful rural landscape. A Latin phrase over the sun explains the picture: "light restored after clouds." Many other philosophy books published in Germany during the first part of the eighteenth century carried similar pictures. In at least two the word *Dispellam* is shown at the top.[1] Enlightenment or *Aufklärung* was the sun dispelling the clouds. The sun was reason; the clouds were ignorance and false belief. The darkness they caused was favorable to despotic government, overbearing priests, misguided religiosity, abusive nobility, repressive laws backed by ferocious punishments, unjust taxation, and stultifying economic practices. Enlighteners opposed these by trying to reform legislation, government, and penal systems, to increase religious toleration and the freedom to think and publish, to spread scientific knowledge, to improve education, and to rationalize economic policies. Success, they thought, depended on removing the dark clouds inherited from the past. Reason was the tool for the job. And philosophers were taken to be among those best equipped to show what reason could do and how it could help.

Kant's essay "An Answer to the Question: What Is Enlightenment?" is widely taken to be a classic statement of enlightened thinking, and he himself to be one of its great advocates.[2] While this is broadly speaking correct, Kant's stance toward *Aufklärung*, as toward almost everything else, is very much his own. One way of seeing how he differs from his enlightening predecessors is to compare his view of the sources of darkness with theirs. I begin with a few general comments about Enlightenment. In the second section, I review briefly some of the thinkers who express views on the sources of darkness – not all of them do. In the last part, I look at Kant's complex position.

ENLIGHTENMENTS

The reforming outlook toward which I gestured above was consciously shared by many thinkers and activists whom we classify as enlightened. It is, however, a matter of scholarly debate whether they should all be thought of as participating in a single movement of Enlightenment.[3] Expressing a now common view, one scholar argues that if enlighteners were reformers, the national differences in the institutions to be reformed must have made a significant difference to the ideas they used to question established beliefs. He is defending the claim that there was a uniquely Scottish Enlightenment: "Since there is demonstrably something distinctively Scottish about the large institutions . . . which informs the experience that supports and motivates the thinkers' reflections, there will also be something distinctively Scottish about those reflections about the concepts . . . and values" involved in the institutions.[4]

There is much to be said for this view. German philosophers, for instance, lived under a wide variety of political regimes, with several religions permitted and sometimes backed by the different governments.[5] In France, by contrast, a central government imposed one religion, while in England a central government more or less tolerated a number of them. Nonetheless, there were commonalities that crossed political boundaries. Jonathan Israel has argued powerfully that we should take Enlightenment to be "a single highly integrated intellectual and cultural movement" occurring all over Europe, coming at various times but centered on the same problems and often stimulated by the same books.[6]

Israel also argues that what he calls the early radical Enlightenment, which developed in the latter part of the seventeenth century, was decisive in shaping European and eventually world thought thereafter. Nationality, for him, is not deeply significant. What does matter is that some groups of thinkers advocated far more sweeping changes in thought and action than others. The radical enlighteners were atheistic, materialistic, and naturalistic. They advocated governments that would be much more liberal and democratic than any under which they lived. For Israel, their most influential philosopher was Spinoza. Because he rejected all the main points of Jewish and Christian conceptions of God, he was seen as an atheist, even though he called the basic substance of the universe "God or Nature." His views were spread by innumerable pamphlets, books, letters, discussion circles, and clandestine manuscripts.

More moderate enlighteners were appalled by the radical Spinozistic program, seeing it as a threat to the religion many of them still accepted as well as to morality and public order. But even moderates found much darkness in the practices of religion. Their aim was to bring light to drive away what they saw as harmful excrescences on much-needed belief rather than to eliminate it altogether. Kant himself was neither atheistic nor materialistic nor naturalistic. He devoted much of his work to arguing that these views were not supportable. He has consequently been thought by some scholars not to belong to the *Aufklärung* at all.[7] But metaphysically based antireligious claims are not the only markers of Enlightenment.

Whether radical or moderate, enlighteners used a common vocabulary to identify what they rejected. Ignorance was not the only enemy. It simply opened the way for mistaken beliefs that were more directly the causes of the practices the enlighteners opposed. In religious matters, they tended to think of these beliefs as falling into two main categories: superstition and enthusiasm. By "superstition," the enlighteners sometimes meant any religious belief, but often they meant belief in the value of the worship of saints, the use of relics and images, and the necessity of priestly intercession to obtain salvation – all of which they took to be distinctively Roman Catholic. By "enthusiasm," they might mean any sort of religious fanaticism, but often they meant the largely Protestant belief that individuals could receive inspiration – and political instruction – directly from God.[8]

Superstition and enthusiasm were tied to what the enlighteners called "prejudice." By this they meant, not negative and hostile attitudes toward "other" people, but inherited beliefs and practices with the authority of long acceptance behind them. The term had a wide application. In the *Ethics*, published in 1677, Spinoza said that the belief that everything in nature acts for an end, as humans do, is foremost among the prejudices he wishes to remove.[9] D'Alembert spoke of prejudices in favor of Aristotle opening the way to benighted scholasticism.[10] Some students at Jena, inspired by the French Revolution, formed a group "to set Reason on the legislative throne that she deserves." They proclaimed that "Reason tolerates no prejudices, which mock her. Dueling is such a prejudice."[11] In the *Critique of the Power of Judgment*, Kant identified prejudice with the passivity and hence the heteronomy of reason. He added that "the greatest prejudice of all is . . . **superstition**."[12] Later I present more evidence of the importance of these Enlightenment concepts in Kant's thinking.

THE SOURCES OF DARKNESS

Why do the religious prejudices that form the dark clouds have such a strong hold? After all, most of these beliefs impose severe regimens, call for sacrifice, interfere with one's life. Why do people hold to them with such tenacity? Why is the struggle for Enlightenment so difficult? Does the answer lie in our psychology? Kant says that while it is permissible to represent the corrupter of mankind as external to us, that is, as a devil, the ultimate source of corruption is within: after all, "we would not be tempted by [the devil] were we not in secret agreement with him" (*RR*, 6.60). What attracts us to superstition and enthusiasm, and makes us cling to our prejudices? What are the sources of darkness?

Spinoza opens the preface to his *Theological-Political Treatise* (1670) with some suggestions of an answer. Men would not be held by superstition (*superstitione*), he says, if they could control their own lives and had rules by which to govern their actions. But they often have no idea about how to cope with the difficulties fortune puts in their way. They fluctuate between hope and fear, and grasp at any belief that offers help. They wonder at anything unexpected, and take it as a sign or a portent of the will of the gods requiring sacrifice. But if greed and fear are the main source and sustainer of superstition, they are aided by statecraft. It profits despotic rulers to keep their subjects in thrall by religion. Spinoza's aim in the book is to show that only freedom of thought, fostered by freedom in society, can lead to true piety and to civil peace and order. To do so he must convince the masses of the truth of these views.[13]

Later, he explains why the task is so difficult. The best way to convince people of the truth of anything is to prove it, deducing it rigorously from self-evident principles. But most people find arguments of this kind too hard to follow. They prefer to take their beliefs from experience. The main points of true religion can be brought to the masses, whose minds cannot perceive ideas clearly and distinctly, only by embodying the ideas in stories. And while the masses need stories that move them to obedience, they cannot themselves judge which are best for this purpose. Hence they always need "pastors or ministers of the church" as their guides. Otherwise they attend to trivial narrative details and not to the lessons to be learned.[14]

Even with such guides, men's minds are easily led astray. In the *Treatise on the Emendation of the Intellect* and the *Ethics*, Spinoza says the masses have at best perceptions of kinds that allow for error.[15] In the *Ethics*, he adds that falsity "consists in the privation of knowledge which inadequate, or mutilated and confused, ideas involve."[16] Confused ideas constitute the passions and desires that drive most people. The masses think God made everything for their benefit. They develop their own ways of trying to influence God to direct all of nature to satisfy their own "insatiable greed." Thus the prejudice that everything in nature works for an end "was changed into superstition" and lodged firmly in men's minds. We would all have remained in this sorry state had not mathematics, which is not concerned with ends, "shown men another standard of truth."[17] It will take a clear deductive demonstration of the truth, such as his own *Ethics*, to free men from their superstitions; but this is exactly the kind of thinking most people cannot follow.

Locke discusses the sources of darkness in religious matters in many places.[18] Here I can consider only a little of what he says. Unlike Spinoza, he believes that we have been given a genuine divine revelation and he defends a version of Christianity. The domain of faith begins where reason cannot deliver knowledge, but faith cannot require us to believe anything that goes against clear reason. Moreover, our acceptance of claims as divinely revealed must rest on our having reasons for believing that the revelation does indeed come from God. A proper understanding of the relations between reason and faith, and due reliance on reason, is essential if we are to avoid superstition.[19] But few men care to reason or to seek truth for its own sake. Their passions and interests all too often dictate their beliefs; and in religious matters, this leads to enthusiasm. Having disregarded both reason and Christian revelation in imposing beliefs on themselves, they proceed to impose them on others. They set up the "ungrounded fancies" of their own brains as "a Foundation both of opinion and Conduct." Becoming an authority for others without going to any trouble "flatters many Men's Laziness, Ignorance, and Vanity": hence the great appeal of being an enthusiast and claiming immediate divine inspiration.[20]

Locke thinks that failure to reason is in general a major source of error. Men hold many beliefs without grounds, even when grounds are available. Many people are unable to think well enough to assess evidence and follow arguments. There is "a difference of degrees in Men's Understandings . . . to so great a latitude . . . that there is a greater distance between some Men, and others . . . than between some Men and some Beasts." Some just refuse to consider reasons for and against various claims. And many are content to give up their own ability to reason. They simply accept the "current Opinions, and licensed Guides" of their country.[21] Many do not have time and energy to think after their exhausting work. But the truths about God and morality needed for right living are so easily accessible that most people could think their way to them. And those who cannot – farm hands and dairy maids – can learn them from the preacher.[22]

It is not just ignorance or confusion that is the source of darkness for Locke. It is mainly the inability or unwillingness to think clearly. In his writings on education and the conduct of the understanding, he repeatedly says that most people can reason, that it is lack of desire or practice that leads them to fail to seek grounds for their beliefs, and that sound education can do much to remedy the defect. Spinoza does not seem to share his optimism on this point. Nonetheless, both he and Locke are rejecting strong Calvinist views about the inability of sinful humans to reason clearly or to improve their faculties.[23] Neither attributes the darkness to the depravity that Calvinists thought we inherited from Adam. They are offering not a supernatural view of the tendency to accept corrupt forms of religion, but naturalistic accounts. Contingent facts about human energy and ability, not divinely imposed punishment, explain the darkness. Something can be done about it.

Whether Hume himself was or was not wholly without religious belief – a much-discussed question – he seems to have allowed that there is some reason to accept a minimal single deity, the first cause of the universe, but otherwise barely describable. The rich variety of religious belief beyond this is caused by ignorance, hope, and fear. With almost no knowledge of a causal order in nature, surrounded on all sides by threats to life and happiness, and with "a universal tendency . . . to conceive all things like themselves,"[24] humans first invented a variety of deities whom they could blame for misfortune and supplicate for aid. Monotheism emerged only slowly. And "whoever thinks it has owed its success to the . . . reasons, on which it is undoubtedly founded, would show himself little acquainted with the ignorance and stupidity of the people, and their incurable prejudice in favor of their particular superstitions."[25] Nor do irrational forces cease to work once monotheism is reached. Religious belief is unstable: it tends "to rise from idolatry to theism, and to sink again from theism into idolatry."[26]

The consequences are not trivial. On the whole, polytheists are tolerant of other religions, and monotheists are not. Human sacrifice was practiced in "barbarous nations" but it nowhere equaled the horrors of the Inquisition. And the proclivity of monotheists to attribute infinite superiority of every kind to their deity leads them into a submissiveness and passivity that takes them far from the virtues displayed by the heroes of antiquity. Moreover, as theism is more in accordance with sound reason than polytheism is, it more easily coopts philosophy. But theology insists on limiting the scope of reason. Religion – or the clergy – must have "Amazement . . . Mystery . . . Darkness" in order to keep the masses in awe.[27] Hume delights in pointing out absurdities in the beliefs and practices of monotheistic religions, especially Roman Catholicism. He also argues that every religion tends to corrupt its adherents. Votaries, he says, "will still seek the divine favor, not by virtue and good morals, which alone can be acceptable to a perfect being, but either by frivolous observances, . . . by rapturous extasies, or by the belief of mysterious and absurd opinions."[28] Were there to be so unlikely a thing as a religion insisting that only pure morals can be pleasing to God, "the people's prejudices" are so strong that they would find ways to make even attendance at moral instruction into a superstitious means of ingratiating themselves with their deity.[29]

There is no way we can escape religious controversies except to leave the different superstitions to quarrel among themselves, while we turn to "the calm, though obscure, regions of philosophy."[30] But in fact on Hume's view there is more room for hope than this remark suggests. Ignorance, combined with fear and desire, creates religion. If Newtonian accounts of natural events become widely known, they will dry up the sources of superstition. Whatever his skeptical doubts in the obscure regions of philosophy, Hume holds to the Enlightenment belief that scientific knowledge will dispel the darkness.[31]

"Man is unhappy only because he mistrusts Nature," declaims Baron d'Holbach at the opening of his *System of Nature* (1770). "His mind is so pervaded with prejudices that one might believe him forever condemned to error . . . It is time to seek in Nature the remedy for the ills that enthusiasm has made for us."[32] The *System* is perhaps the fullest Enlightenment account of the sources of darkness. In it Holbach makes a comprehensive effort "to scatter the clouds that prevent man from walking with a sure foot on the path of life."

His undefended starting point is empiricism. All knowledge comes from sensory experience, Holbach holds, and so do all ideas. We should strip the language of words with no determinate ideas attached to them. If we do, we will get rid of beliefs in a mind distinct from the body, free will, and purely spiritual beings – all of them props for religion. Holbach has no interest in tracing the experiential pedigrees of ideas he takes to be sound. His main effort is to show how we came to have the harmful ideas and beliefs that enable princes and priests to tyrannize over us. And he has no doubt about where the trouble lies: "It cannot be too often repeated, it is in error that we find the true source of the ills by which the human race is afflicted . . . not Nature; not an irritable God; not hereditary depravity; it is only error."[33]

Holbach vehemently denies that religion does any good. Religion and theology, "far from being useful to mankind, are the true sources of the ills that afflict the earth, of the errors that blind it, the prejudices that benumb it."[34] There is no rationale for religious belief: Holbach examines the arguments of Clarke, Descartes, Newton, and Malebranche and proclaims them worthless. Hence a causal, naturalistic account of religious belief is needed.

The account Holbach gives is close to Hume's. Mankind begins with almost total ignorance of nature's ways. And "it is solely ignorance of natural causes and the forces of nature that gives birth to the gods."[35] Our sufferings, our fears and needs, and our tendency to model everything on our own feelings lead us to attribute extraordinary powers to natural objects and events that we do not understand. Religion is "always a system of conduct invented by imagination and ignorance to win favor from the unknown powers to which Nature is supposed to be submitted . . . [T]hese crude foundations support all religious systems."[36] Priesthood originated when old men started supervising offerings to the deities. Eventually they told stories about the gods, and then developed elaborate theories to explain their contradictory ways. They "enveloped [the gods] in clouds . . . and became the masters of explaining as they pleased the enigmatic being they made to adore."[37] In all this they were aided by the regrettable fact that men love mysteries and marvels, and so are complicit in spreading the system that oppresses them. Men "need mystery to move their imaginations," Holbach says, and once they have the mysteries they spend their time praying, rather than investigating nature.[38]

To improve matters, education is clearly needed. But we cannot easily get rid of the error and ignorance that are the sources of the harmful beliefs. The abstract arguments that would clarify our thinking cannot be understood by the masses. "It is not . . . for the multitude that a philosopher should propose to himself either to write or to meditate; the principles of atheism or the system of Nature are not made . . . for a large number of people." Still, the advance of science, exemplified especially by Newton's work, can give us hope. For science always drives out superstition: thus astronomy has put the alchemists out of business and science more generally has destroyed the credibility of magicians. A wise sovereign will be needed as well, to spread the light and drive away the clouds. But advanced ideas come to be accepted only slowly. The most we can hope for now is that people will lose interest in religious and theological controversies. "It is this indifference, so just, so reasonable, so advantageous to states, that healthy philosophy can propose to introduce little by little on earth."[39]

Nearly a quarter of a century after Holbach's *System* appeared, the Marquis de Condorcet wrote a classic Enlightenment account of the progress of knowledge and its effects in dispelling the clouds of prejudice and superstition. He holds that the history of error is an important part of the history of the progress of knowledge. And much more than his predecessors, he attributes both progress and opposition to it to structural features of social life, particularly to struggles for power. Individual psychology plays only a small part in the formation of the clouds that knowledge will eventually drive away.

There are two points on which individual psychology matters. Our faculties develop only slowly, and some prejudices served a useful purpose in their time. But "they have extended their seductions . . . beyond their season because men retain the prejudices of their childhood, their country and their age" even when enough is known to reject them.[40] To mental inertia Condorcet adds a feature of early thought that he does not explain. When some men came to know enough to be the leaders and teachers of others, two classes were formed, one trying to place itself above reason, "the other humbly renouncing its own reason and abasing itself to less than human stature."[41] This self-abasement helped in the rise of the priesthood. Since then that class has clung to power, terrifying the masses with superstitious fears of penalties in an afterlife for disobedience and fiercely opposing the progress of knowledge that would disabuse subjects of their belief in clerical superiority.

The priestly class sometimes sought to increase knowledge, but its aim was "not to dispel ignorance but to dominate men."[42] The death of Socrates, Condorcet says, "was the first crime that marked the beginning of the war between philosophy and superstition," a war still continuing.[43] Aristotle discovered the principle of empiricism, but did not take it very far. Under the Roman empire, the claims of reason were swamped by the triumph of Christianity, "to which the great mass of enthusiasts gradually attached themselves." Condorcet says the converts were the slaves and the poor, but offers no further account of why they adhered to the new faith.[44]

To sustain their power, the medieval priests exalted religious virtues above natural ones and kept the populace in ignorance. Their only achievement was "theological daydreaming and superstitious imposture." The Arab revival of science offered some hope, but was defeated by "tyranny and superstition": there was no way to defend it from "the prejudices of men who had already been degraded by slavery."[45] It was only with the invention of printing and the consequent wide dissemination of the advances of the new science that knowledge began what Condorcet considers a now irreversible advance. "There is not a religious system nor a supernatural extravagance," he says, "that is not founded on ignorance of the laws of nature." Science will end the reign of darkness.[46]

KANT

Kant begins to offer a view about the sources of darkness in the opening paragraph of his "Enlightenment" essay. To be enlightened is to have left the condition he calls self-incurred minority or tutelage (*selbst verschuldete Unmündigkeit*). "This minority is *self-incurred*," he continues, "when its cause is not in lack of understanding but in lack of resolution and courage to use it without direction from another" (*PracP*, 8.35). The imperative, "Have the courage to use your own reason!" is the motto of *Aufklärung*. If Enlightenment is thinking for oneself, the source of darkness would be the "laziness and cowardice" which hinder us from doing so. At least, that would be the source within individuals. Freedom to make public use of reason seems to be what it takes for a whole society to be enlightened. Here the sources of darkness would be efforts of rulers and clergy to prevent open critical discussion of their policies and decisions.

Kant devotes much of the essay to distinguishing between public and private uses of reason, and the critical literature has accordingly examined the distinction in detail. But the opening paragraphs raise questions about the inner source of darkness that Kant does not answer in the essay, and it is these that I shall explore.

When we think for ourselves, what are we to think *about*?[47] Religious beliefs are Kant's main concern in the essay. But he does not explain why it takes courage to think about them for oneself. It is also unclear what Kant means by saying that our being in a condition of minority or tutelage is self-incurred. Shortly after the "Enlightenment" essay was published, J. G. Hamann wrote a letter criticizing it and especially "that accursed adjective *self-incurred*."[48] Though Kant uses the adjective two more times in the essay (at *PracP*, 8.40 and 8.41) and plainly thinks it important, the essay itself does not offer much help in understanding it. Irresolution and cowardice may keep most people under tutelage, but are they also self-incurred?

The imperative of Enlightenment seems to be addressed to individuals.[49] Yet Kant also says that "it is hard for any single individual to work himself out of the life under tutelage." What is needed is a society in which citizens have the freedom to make public use of their reason (*PracP*, 8.36). If I do not live in such a society, is my tutelage still self-incurred? Do I personally bear the responsibility for it? We do not yet live in an enlightened age, Kant allows, but only in one going through the process of *Aufklärung*.[50] We still lack much that would be required for men to use their own reason in religious matters. The obstacles to escape from self-incurred minority are being removed, but not all at once. In what way then is our remaining in the condition of tutelage self-incurred? Kant does not here say.

A similar juxtaposition of individual and community responsibility occurs in Kant's "Conjectural Beginning of Human History." He there sketches a history of the awakening and gradual development of moral reasoning. In the course of this development, "man . . . has cause to ascribe to himself the guilt (*Schuld*) for all the evil that he suffers and for the bad that he perpetrates." Yet the suffering is unavoidable. It is part of nature's way of teaching the human race the moral lessons it needs to learn. Kant thinks we must "admire and praise" it.[51] Perhaps; but it is still hard to see how the individual can be responsible for all these evils.

An endnote to the final page of the "Orientation in Thinking" essay gives us vital help with Kant's view in "Enlightenment." I quote it in full here:

> *Thinking for oneself* means seeking the supreme touchstone of truth in oneself (i.e. in one's own reason); and the maxim of always thinking for oneself is **enlightenment**. Now there is less to this than people imagine when they place enlightenment in the acquisition of *information*; for it is rather a negative principle for the use of one's faculty of cognition, and often he who is richest in information is the least enlightened in the use he makes of it. To make use of one's own reason means no more than to ask oneself, for everything that one should assume, whether one could find it feasible [*wohl thunlich finde* = find it doable] to make the reason why one assumes something, or the rule from which there follows what one assumes, into a universal principle for the use of one's reason. This test is

one that everyone can apply to himself; and with this examination he will see superstition and enthusiasm disappear, even if he falls far short of having information to refute them on objective grounds. For he is using merely the maxim of reason's *self-preservation*. Thus it is quite easy to ground enlightenment in *individual subjects* through their education; one must only begin early to accustom young minds to this reflection; for there are external obstacles which in part forbid this manner of education and in part make it more difficult.

(*RR*, 8.146n.)[52]

Kant is here saying that Enlightenment consists in or requires the adoption of a maxim. Maxims, for Kant, are our most general practical principles. Enlightenment thus belongs within the domain of practical rather than theoretical reason. More specifically, Enlightenment is not a matter of getting more information. We do not need detailed information to accept or reject a proposed maxim. As Kant's whole ethical theory shows, there is an a priori test for such maxims. By identifying *Aufklärung* with adopting a maxim, Kant rejects all views holding that the clouds are dispelled simply by the removal of factual or scientific ignorance.

The Enlightenment maxim is "a negative principle in the use of one's faculty of cognition." By this Kant means that the Enlightenment maxim will lead us to reject certain cognitive claims – those made by the advocate of superstition or enthusiasm. The maxim directs one to use a test for whatever one is asked to assume (*was man annehmen soll*), and Kant says that everyone can use this test. Kant's phrasing suggests a possible procedure for applying the Enlightenment maxim: formulate a principle that would lead one to assume whatever it is that the advocate of superstition or enthusiasm says one should assume. Then ask if one could will that the principle be a universal principle of one's reason. Could the principle guide all of one's thinking? If not, reject it; and since it is this principle that would lead to acceptance of the advocate's claim, reject his claim as well.

By way of example, Kant says only that if one uses the test, superstition and enthusiasm will disappear. He does not tell us what reasons or rules would ground one's acceptance of the advice their advocates give us. He does however say that we do not need to bring "information" (*die Kenntnisse* = pieces of knowledge) to bear in order to reject the claims of the advocate of superstition or enthusiasm. We reject these claims not because we can prove them false on empirical grounds, but because the self-preservation of reason requires their rejection. Reason would contradict itself in some way were we to accept the principle that would lead us to accept what the advocate urges upon us. What exactly this means will become clear later, when I identify the sort of principle that the Enlightenment maxim tells us to reject.

Kant ends the note with a distinction between individual enlightenment and the enlightenment of an age, indicating the possibility of one and the difficulty of the other – but not in quite the same way he does in the "Enlightenment" essay itself.

An equally packed passage in the third *Critique* reinforces these points. Enlightenment, Kant there says, is thinking for oneself, which is "the maxim of a reason that is never passive." Superstition demands passivity of mind as an obligation. Hence it is the preeminent case of prejudice, and liberation from it is at the core of Enlightenment. In the note to this passage, Kant says that Enlightenment is in one way easy, in another way hard. "Always being legislative," i.e. active, is easy for someone who does not want to go beyond his essential end and seeks no knowledge which is beyond understanding. For Kant, our essential end is a moral end: that happiness should be distributed in accordance with virtue. Belief in God and immortality have no theoretical basis, but we can accept the beliefs on practical grounds. If we ask for knowledge beyond that, there are many who will promise it. Kant says that we will find their promises tempting. Hence we find it hard to stay enlightened, i.e. to maintain the critical stance, toward what they offer us for belief. And this will be especially difficult for a whole public (*CJ*, 5.294–95).

In both passages Kant treats being enlightened as having adopted a maxim, or as a matter of practical reason. In both he distinguishes between achieving enlightenment as an individual and achieving it as or for a whole public. In neither does he help us to understand just how our persistent condition of minority or tutelage can be self-incurred. But now that we know that we are considering matters within the domain of practical reason, we can see a parallel between the struggle for Enlightenment and the struggle for virtue. Virtue is strength of maxims in doing our duty. The opposition to doing so comes from within us, from our inclinations; and, Kant adds, "it is the human being *himself* who puts these obstacles in the way of his maxims" (*PracP*, 6.394). Moral difficulties, like the condition of tutelage, are self-incurred. But so far we do not see Kant explaining why we put these inclinations in the way of virtue, or why we are tempted by the thought of extra-moral knowledge of God, or why it is so hard to adopt the Enlightenment maxim. Thus in these passages he does not fully explain the source of darkness.

To find Kant's account of it we must look at his *Religion within the Boundaries of Mere Reason*. In part one, Kant presents his view of the radical evil that dwells in each of us. This resuscitation of what looks like the doctrine of original sin shocked many contemporaries. Kant, wrote Goethe in a frequently quoted passage, "after spending a long life cleansing his philosophical mantle of various grubby prejudices, has wantonly besmirched it with the infamous stain of Radical Evil so that Christians too can after all be lured up to kiss its hem."[53] Even his critics should admit, however, that Kant's radical evil is not St. Augustine's original sin. Kantian evil leaves us with our ability to see our duty and choose it, which strong views of Christian depravity did not. Kant says nothing of predestination, and he rejects prevenient grace. Even so, it is a surprising view for a philosopher of *Aufklärung* to hold.

That Kant is nonetheless a philosopher of *Aufklärung* is, however, nowhere clearer than in part four of the *Religion*. He there gives his fullest account of why we should reject the aspects of religion that enlighteners attacked. In doing so he puts the doctrine of radical evil to a surprising use. My suggestion is that radical evil is for Kant the ultimate source of the superstition, enthusiasm, and priestcraft which constitute so large a part of the darkness to be dispelled by *Aufklärung*. In what follows I try to support this suggestion.

I give only a brief reminder of Kant's view of radical evil. That we are evil is not a strict necessity of our nature, but a contingent fact, although it holds of all of us (*RR*, 6.32). Our being evil is not a matter of our having impulses to preserve and benefit ourselves which are often stronger than the impulse derived from our awareness of the moral law. This is simply human frailty. The inclinations themselves are not evil, but good (*RR*, 6.58). Nor is our being evil constituted by our complying with the requirements of the moral law out of incentives other than the law itself. This is merely impurity. Our depravity or corruption is rather "the propensity of the power of choice to maxims that subordinate the incentives of the moral law to others . . . it reverses the ethical order as regards the incentives of a *free* power of choice" (*RR*, 6.29–30). The good agent makes compliance with morality the *condition* for action from a nonmoral incentive. The evil agent makes compliance with a nonmoral incentive the condition for doing what morality requires (*RR*, 6.36).[54]

We need not retrace the qualifications and explanations with which Kant surrounds the claim that we are all inherently evil. It is important, however, to note that he is not talking of specific individuals when he makes this claim. He rules out the thought that some people might be inherently good, and only some evil. He is speaking of "the whole species" (*RR*, 6.25). And although he holds that we all start in corruption, he also insists that "[t]he human being (even the worst) does not repudiate the moral law . . . The law rather imposes itself on him irresistibly" (*RR*, 6.36). Awareness of the moral law is bound up with our freedom and "through no cause in the world" can anyone lose that freedom. Kant puts the point quite strongly:

> However evil a human being has been right up to the moment of an impending free action (evil even habitually, as a second nature), his duty to better himself was not just in the past: it still is his duty *now*; he must therefore be capable of it.
>
> (*RR*, 6.41; cf. 6.45)

The question of the proper order of moral and other maxims as related to faith recurs frequently in the rest of *Religion*.[55] Kant repeatedly contrasts rational religion as a pure moral position with statutory faiths which try to ignore or bypass or downgrade morality in favor of other means of appealing for the favor of the deity. He distinguishes "*religion of rogation* (of mere cult)" from "*moral religion,* i.e. the religion of *good life-conduct*" (*RR*, 6.51); ecclesiastical faith from the pure faith of religion (*RR*, 6.109); and faith as commanded from religion as compliance with morality understood as God's commands (*RR*, 6.163–64). Kant is eager to show that historical faith, transmitted by learned scholars, can be of assistance to moral religion. He accepts the claim that rituals and prayers in a limited community may help realize the moral religion that must ultimately be common to all. But whenever we think we can become well pleasing to God by something other than pure morality – when we think that living according to ancient prescriptions transmitted in a book, or carrying out rituals demanded by an ecclesiastical authority, will replace morality as a means to divine favor – we are getting things in the wrong order. The language is revealing: "to deem this statutory faith . . . essential to the service of God in general, and to make it the *supreme condition* of divine good pleasure toward humans" is itself what Kant calls "a delusion of religion" (*RR*, 6.168, my emphasis; cf. 6.170–71). It is the root error that leads to the darknesses of superstition and enthusiasm, and opens the way to priestly tyranny.

A noted authority on Kant's religious thought says that "The general subjective ground of religious delusion lies in the human tendency to anthropomorphism."[56] Kant does indeed say that we tend to think that God can be swayed as we can by entreaties and gifts. And his explanation of the strength of this tendency is tied to his accounts of superstition, enthusiasm, and priestcraft. All of them display the pattern characteristic of radical evil. Good life-conduct, Kant reminds us, is the only thing well pleasing to God. We know that in this life we cannot bring ourselves into complete compliance with the demands of morality. Hence we hope for some sort of aid beyond ourselves that will enable us to make progress in a task we cannot morally escape. Reason shows us, Kant says, that God will count sincere effort as sufficient to entitle us to divine grace. But because morality requires hard work and we are greedy for assurance of salvation, we look for other ways of obtaining it. We know that people can be bought off. So we think that we might obtain grace by some less arduous service to the divinity, and that then moral virtue will be added to it. We grant that grace might come in a mysterious way. We offer sacrifices which, however costly, are less demanding than morality. And we persuade ourselves that we can tell that we are feeling the effects of the grace our sacrifices and prayers have won us.

"The delusion that through acts of cult we can achieve anything in the way of justification before God is religious *superstition*," Kant says, "just as the delusion of wanting to bring this about by striving for a supposed contact with God is religious *enthusiasm*" (*RR*, 6.174). Superstition is using natural means, themselves not tied to morality, to bring about nonnatural, moral, effects. Enthusiasm calls on something not within human powers – immediate contact with the divinity – to effect nonnatural goals (*RR*, 6.174–75). Superstition at least offers many people the ability to try for grace, since it uses natural means. Enthusiasm, by contrast, is more irrational: because it ends as an appeal to inner feeling (*RR*, 6.114), it is "the moral death of reason without which there can be no religion" (*RR*, 6.175).

Priests simply formalize and reinforce the delusions at work in superstition and enthusiasm. There is no difference in principle between the refined priest of Europe and the primitive shaman of Asia. What they both want is "to steer to their advantage the invisible power which presides over human destiny" (*RR*, 6.176). As I noted, Kant thinks that morality can benefit from churches, rituals, and prayers. But when they, and the revelation that prescribes them, are made necessary to the inner life and not treated as mere means to enhance morality, the result is what Kant calls fetishism. The priest takes just this step. He turns what should be merely means into an end, and thus tells us to join means and true end in the wrong order.

Priestcraft is the constitution of a church devoted to fetishism. In such organizations the clergy rules, dispensing with reason and claiming authority over all the laity, including the secular ruler. Everyone must pretend to receive benefits from clerical rule, so unconditional obedience to priests undermines "the very *thinking* of the people." The hypocrisy necessary under such a regime even undermines the loyalty of subjects. Instead of bringing peace and order, it brings about their opposite (*RR*, 6.179–80). Ritualized service and moral effort may indeed be joined. They are both good things, but, Kant warns, "[s]o much depends, when we wish to join two good things, on the order in which we combine them!" "It is in this distinction," Kant significantly adds, "that true *Aufklärung* consists" (*RR*, 6.179).

Wherever Kant notes the temptation to treat aspects of religion which are at best means to morality as more important than morality, in the hope of currying divine favor, he indicates that this is the wrong ordering: it subordinates morality to desire for one's own happiness. Everywhere the pattern is that of radical evil. Then, at the end of the book, Kant characterizes the delusions of religion as "self-deceptions" (*RR*, 6.200). The self-incurred tutelage of the essay on Enlightenment may, I suggest, be understood in the same way.

The failure of courage to use our own reason is a moral failure. Radical evil is the ultimate source of the darkness resulting from the failure so far of all our efforts at *Aufklärung.*

What will the enlightened agent think when confronted by a superstitious or enthusiastic person? The enthusiast claims to have direct divine inspiration about a nonmoral way to become well pleasing to God. The superstitious person claims to know that attention to certain rituals or relics or saints will enable one to become well pleasing to God. To accept what they urge upon us, we must accept the principle that there is some nonmoral way of pleasing God. This is what enlightened agents reject. When thinking for themselves, they will always reject any claim grounded on the belief that there are nonmoral means to God's approval. In this application, the Enlightenment maxim has a negative outcome for the use of our faculty of cognition, as Kant says it has: we conclude that we do not know what the religious advocates claim to know. In this way the maxim leads, as Kant also says, to the death of both aberrant forms of divine service.

Can this point be broadened to take in other aspects of *Aufklärung,* as Kant suggests in the "Enlightenment" essay? To make this out, we have to think that the book or spiritual adviser that does our thinking for us, or the ruler, or the physician (*PracP,* 8.35), all urge us to courses of action that require placing our own interest ahead of morality. Perhaps our pastor directs us to persecute members of a group he thinks ungodly and despicable; perhaps our commanding officer tells us to kill the wives and daughters of the enemy as well as their soldiers; perhaps our physician urges us to bribe the pharmacist to give us priority for some important medicine in very short supply. To see that they should reject such directives, enlightened agents need not question any factual or quasi-factual claims that the priest or ruler or physician may make. They can see that the reasons underlying advice of the kinds I have imagined always involve placing self-interest, or special group interest, above moral principle. Mature agents cannot accept the basic reasons given for this sort of advice as rules for their own practical reasoning. Since practical reason gives morality precedence over other kinds of directive, to do so would be to use practical reason to destroy itself. Enlightenment thus ensures the self-preservation of reason. Enlightened agents can, however, accept church ceremonies or political directives or medical advice as long as these do not require overruling morality. The agent is free to decide by using prudential reason whether to accept or reject directions from any authority, insofar as their directives concern the use of means that lie within the bounds of morality. And he can decide simply to take the authority's advice without trying to think for himself about it any further than to see that it is morally permissible.

For Kant, the ultimate source of darkness – of our persistence in the unenlightened condition of tutelage – is, I have argued, the radical evil that besets all human beings. Emergence from radical evil is up to us. If we decide to reject it, we do so in a realm beyond experience. Nothing can be known of how the choice is made. The same is true if we decide not to emerge from radical evil. Our ignorance here spreads to other aspects of Kant's philosophy. Moral improvement requires steady refusal to place self-interest ahead of morality. *Aufklärung* requires steady adherence to the maxim of thinking for oneself, refusing to obey any authority that directs us to place morality in second place. Both moral improvement and Enlightenment must essentially be freely chosen. But if the choice of the right course is free, so is the choice of the wrong. And in that case, are we not always in the condition of thinking in practical terms for ourselves – of being not under tutelage but enlightened?[57] No theoretical answer to these difficulties is possible, on Kant's view. We cannot have a theoretical understanding of why the condition of tutelage is self-imposed. Kant can only say that we are morally required to think it is, because we are morally required to think that improvement is always possible.

The contrast between Kant's account of the source of darkness and the accounts of the other enlighteners whom I have discussed is striking. For them, darkness comes from cognitive failure of one sort or another. Enlightenment requires improvement in our theoretical grasp of the world. They therefore offer clarification of ideas, or improvement of reasoning, or increase of scientific knowledge as ways to dispel the darkness. And even those who, like Holbach, ardently defend the rights of man, preserve the idea that an intellectual elite of some sort must lead the rest of us toward the light. For Kant, the source of darkness is a moral failure of will. In moral matters we are all equally failures; but we all have essentially the same ability to get things right.

Kant advocates a republican form of government as best suited to express our essential moral freedom. He thinks we all have a duty to work toward a world federation of republics as most likely to preserve peace. But however enlightened Kant's goals may sound, he nowhere suggests practical steps anyone might take toward reaching them, except for improvement of moral education. He thinks that political revolution is never morally permissible. He praises Frederick the Great in the "Enlightenment" essay, but says nothing to challenge the ruler's authoritarian regime. It is his view of the source of darkness that provides the rationale for this quite minimal program of *Aufklärung*. What is essential is individual moral improvement. Political action cannot improve matters. Kant can offer only the morally necessary hope that we are moving ourselves through history toward Enlightenment.[58]

NOTES

1 Schneiders 1990, Wolff on p. 87, the others on pp. 84, 85, from books by Gundling, 1715, and Thomasius, 1726.

2 The "Enlightenment" essay is in *Ges. Schr.*, 8.33–42, translation in Kant 1996a, pp. 17–22, cited hereafter as *PracP*. With one exception, references to Kant are to volume and page numbers of the Akademie edition of the *Ges. Schr.*; the one reference to the *Critique of Pure Reason* follows the standard practice of using A and B page numbers for first and second edition references.

Allen Wood says that Kant was "perhaps the greatest philosophical proponent" of the Enlightenment (Kant 1996a, p. xxiii).

3 For a most illuminating look at the whole category, see Schmidt 2003. Schmidt shows that the Germans had in *Aufklärung* a word that long preceded the English *Enlightenment* as the name of a historical period.

4 Broadie 2003, pp. 2–3. For a more specific contrast between Enlightenments in Scotland and Germany, see Oz-Sulzberger 2002.

5 For an older but still useful view of the peculiarities of *Aufklärung* in Germany, see Beck 1969, pp. 244–47. Schneiders 1990, pp. 45–48, distinguishes four stages in the *Aufklärung*: an early stage from 1690 to 1720, stimulated largely by Thomasius; high *Aufklärung*, centered on Wolff, from 1720 to 1750; a popularizing *Aufklärung*, from 1750 to 1780, in which ideas were spread by less rigorous thinkers; and late *Aufklärung*, from 1780 to 1800.

Hunter argues for differentiation of Enlightenments *within* Germany, distinguishing between a movement aiming at making government wholly nonreligious and indifferent to the private beliefs of its citizens, and another trying to preserve an older view in which the state must protect religion and concern itself with the spiritual welfare of its citizens. He sees Pufendorf and Thomasius as the main thinkers favoring the civil enlightenment, Leibniz and Kant as theorists of the metaphysical Enlightenment. See Hunter 2001.

6 Israel 2001, p. v.

7 See Kondylis 2002, pp. 639–42.

8 In an early work, Kant distinguishes fanaticism from enthusiasm, reserving the first term for the feeling of immediate contact with a higher being and the second for an abnormally high degree of attachment to any principle whatsoever. He ties superstition especially to Spain, and thinks it more pernicious than fanaticism (*Observations on the Feeling of the Beautiful and Sublime, Ges. Schr.*, 2.250–51 and n.). In *Religion within the Boundaries of Mere Reason*, Kant ties enthusiasm to "supposed inner experience (effects of grace)" (*Ges. Schr.*, 6.53; cf. 6.174). I use the translations of Kant's writings on religion by Allen Wood and George di Giovanni in Kant 1996b. Future references to *Religion within the Boundaries* will be given in the text, indicated as *RR*.

9 The remark about prejudice occurs at the beginning of the appendix to part I of the *Ethics* in Spinoza 1985, p. 439.

10 Alembert 1963, p. 71.

11 Quoted in Boyle 2000, p. 112.

12 *Critique of the Power of Judgment* (*Ges. Schr.*, 5.294), as translated in Kant 2000. Cited hereafter as *CJ*.

13 Spinoza 1989, pp. 5–11.

14 *TTP*, ch. 5, in Spinoza 1989, pp. 179–85; also in Spinoza 1958, pp. 99–105.

15 Spinoza 1985, pp. 12–16; *Ethics*, II, prop. 40, schol. 2.

16 *Ethics*, II, prop. 35.

17 *Ethics*, I, appendix (Spinoza 1985, pp. 440–41), and bk. III generally.

18 He discusses these matters in his *Conduct of the Understanding*, in *Thoughts concerning Education*, and in *The Reasonableness of Christianity*, as well as in the *Essay concerning Human Understanding*, which I cite from Locke 1975.

19 *Essay*, IV.xviii.

20 *Essay*, IV.xix.3.

21 *Essay*, IV.xx.3–5.

22 *The Reasonableness of Christianity* (1695), in Locke 1958, p. 66.

23 See Spellman 1988, and Marshall 1994, whose criticisms of Spellman I follow.

24 *The Natural History of Religion*, III, in Hume 1993, p. 140. Referred to hereafter as Hume.
25 Hume, p. 153.
26 Hume, pp. 159–60.
27 Hume, p. 166.
28 Hume, p. 179.
29 Hume, p. 180.
30 Hume, p. 185.
31 See Buckle 2001 for strong development of this point.
32 Holbach 1990, vol. I, pp. 11–12; referred to hereafter as Holbach. The English translation by Samuel Wilkerson, 1820, is not fully reliable.
33 Holbach, vol. I, p. 360; cf. vol. I, p. 12.
34 Holbach, vol. II, p. 280.
35 Holbach, vol. II, p. 24.
36 Holbach, vol. II, p. 21.
37 Holbach, vol. II, p. 61.
38 Holbach, vol. II, pp. 178–82.
39 Holbach, vol. II, pp. 372–75.
40 Condorcet 1955, p. 11; referred to hereafter as Cordorcet.
41 Cordorcet, pp. 17–18.
42 Cordorcet, p. 36.
43 Cordorcet, p. 45.
44 Cordorcet, p. 71.
45 Cordorcet, pp. 77–87.
46 Condorcet, 163.
47 Rüdiger Bittner raises important questions on this point in "What is Enlightenment?" reprinted in Schmidt 1996, pp. 345–58. Bittner's criticisms of Kant helped me to reach the interpretation offered here.
48 The letter, dated 18 December 1784, is translated with annotations by Garrett Green in Schmidt 1996, pp. 145–53. The German text is reprinted and given detailed commentary in Bayer 1976. I am grateful to James Schmidt for pointing out the significance of Hamann's letter and for other advice. Bittner has a sharp paragraph criticizing Kant on this point in Schmidt 1996, p. 346.
49 And is so taken by e.g. Gordon Michalson in his valuable study *Fallen Freedom* (1990), p. 15.
50 On *Aufklärung* as process rather than as historical period, see the essay by Schmidt referred to in n. 3 above.
51 *Ges. Schr.*, 8.116, in Kant 1983, p. 54.
52 I have slightly modified Allen Wood's translation, in Kant 1996b, to make it conform more literally to the text.
53 Quoted in Boyle 2000, vol. II, p. 162; also in Michalson 1990, p. 17.

54 In the first *Critique*, Kant says that "the moral disposition, as a condition, first makes partaking in happiness possible, rather than the prospect of happiness first making possible the moral disposition" (A813–14/B841–42, Guyer–Wood translation).

55 See e.g. *RR*, 6.118–19; 6.174–75; 6.185 and n.

56 Bohatec 1966, p. 507.

57 Rüdiger Bittner raised this question in correspondence.

58 My thanks to Eckart Förster, Sean Greenberg, Don Rutherford, and Rüdiger Bittner for helpful suggestions and comments.

SHORT BIOGRAPHIES OF MAJOR EARLY MODERN PHILOSOPHERS

The biographies that follow are arranged in chronological order. For a more comprehensive survey of authors and works, the reader is encouraged to consult the biobibliographical appendix to the *Cambridge History of Seventeenth-Century Philosophy* (Garber and Ayers 1998), and the *Routledge Encyclopedia of Philosophy* (available online at http://www.rep.routledge.com).

MICHEL DE MONTAIGNE (1533–1592), French essayist, was born in Montaigne, near Bordeaux. He was educated at home in Latin (his first language) and later studied law at the University of Bordeaux. He served as a counselor to the Bordeaux parliament and as a royal courtier, before retiring to his country estate in 1571. There, during a period of intense reflection stimulated by his study of ancient skepticism, he began to record the thoughts that would become his famous *Essays* (first two volumes, 1580; third volume, 1588). He later served as mayor of Bordeaux (1581–85) and was instrumental in maintaining peace between Catholics and Protestants during the French wars of religion.

LUIS MOLINA (1536–1600), Jesuit philosopher and theologian, was born in Cuenca, Spain. He studied at Salamanca and Alcalá, before entering the Society of Jesus in 1553. He is best known for his attempt to reconcile the accounts of divine grace and free will in Catholic theology. He outlined this solution in *Concordia liberi arbitrii cum gratiae donis, divina præscientia, providentia, prædestinatione et reprobatione* ("The Harmony of Free Choice with the Gifts of Grace, Divine Foreknowledge, Providence, Predestination and Reprobation") (1588).

PIERRE CHARRON (1541–1603), philosopher, lawyer, and priest, was born in Paris and educated at the Sorbonne. He was a close aquaintance of Montaigne, who made him his adopted son and heir. His most important works are *Les trois véritez* ("The Three Truths") (1593) and *De la sagesse* ("On Wisdom") (1601; 2nd ed. 1604), which reflect the combined influence on him of Christian Pyrrhonism and Stoicism.

JUSTUS LIPSIUS (1547–1606), humanist scholar and Christian neo-Stoic, was born in modern-day Belgium and educated at Cologne and Louvain. He is best known for his efforts to revive the philosophy of the ancient Stoics and to adapt it to the conditions of his day, which he did beginning with *De constantia* ("On Constancy") (1584) and *Politicorum sive civilis doctrinae libri sex* ("Six Books of Politics or Civil Doctrine") (1589). These were followed by two summaries of Stoic teachings, *Manuductio ad stoicam philosophiam* ("Guide to Stoic Philosophy") and *Physiologia stoicorum* ("Physical Theory of the Stoics") (both 1604), and an edition of Seneca's philosophical works (1605).

FRANCISCO SUÁREZ (1548–1617), Jesuit theologian, philosopher, and jurist, was born in Granada, Spain and entered the Society of Jesus in 1564. He taught at a number of Spanish universities as well as at the Jesuit Collegio Romano. His *Disputationes metaphysicae* ("Metaphysical Disputations") (1597) are often seen as the last great flowering of scholastic philosophy. He also made important contributions to the development of natural law theory in his *Tractatus de legibus, ac Deo legislatore* ("A Treatise on Laws and God the Lawgiver") (1612).

FRANCIS BACON (1561–1626), English lawyer, politician, and philosopher, was born in London and educated at Trinity College, Cambridge. He entered parliament in 1584 and held a series of increasingly powerful government positions, culminating in his appointment as Lord Chancellor in 1618. Three years later he was forced from office following his conviction for bribery. In philosophy he was a tireless advocate for the advance of knowledge through empirical research guided by a new scientific method. His views are laid out most fully in *New Organon* (1620). Other works include *Essays* (1597; 3rd ed. 1625), *The Advancement of Learning* (1605), *De sapientia veterum* ("On the Wisdom of the Ancients") (1609), and *New Atlantis* (1624).

GALILEO GALILEI (1564–1642), the foremost scientist of the first half of the seventeenth century, was born and educated in Pisa,

Italy. He taught mathematics there and at Padua before his appointment as chief philosopher and mathematician to the court of Tuscany in 1610. His telescopic observations were the basis of his *Siderius nuncius* ("The Starry Messenger") (1610); other works include *The Assayer* (1623), *Dialogue concerning the Two Chief World Systems, Ptolemaic and Copernican* (1632), and *Discourses and Mathematical Demonstrations relating to Two New Sciences* (1638). In 1633 he was called to Rome and forced to retract his views, after which he was confined under house arrest for the rest of his life.

HUGO GROTIUS (1583–1645), usually recognized as the founder of modern natural law theory, was born in Delft, Holland. Educated in Leiden and in France, he was active as a jurist, historian, theologian, and diplomat. His first major work, *Mare liberum* ("The Free Sea") (1609), defended his country's right of maritime free trade. He was involved in republican politics, narrowly escaping a sentence of life imprisonment in 1621, and in efforts to reunite the Protestant and Catholic churches. His most famous works are *De iure belli ac pacis* ("On the Law of War and Peace") (1625) and *De veritate religionis christianae* ("On the Truth of the Christian Religion") (1627).

THOMAS HOBBES (1588–1679), English philosopher and political theorist, was born in Malmesbury, Wiltshire and educated at Oxford. During the English Civil War he lived in Paris where he was a member of the circle of Mersenne, who commissioned from him the third Objections to Descartes's *Meditations* (1641). His most influential work is *Leviathan* (1651), in which he argues for an ideal of undivided sovereignty and the subjection of religion to civil authority. He attempted to give a comprehensive account of his philosophy in the books *De cive* ("On the Citizen") (1642), *De corpore* ("On Body") (1655), and *De homine* ("On Man") (1658). Late in life he was involved in acrimonious disputes with John Bramhall (on free will) and John Wallis (on geometry).

MARIN MERSENNE (1588–1648), French cleric, mathematician, and natural philosopher, was born in Oizé, Maine and educated at La Flèche and the Sorbonne. Through his Paris circle and extensive correspondence, he played a critical role in facilitating communication among philosophers during the first half of the seventeenth century. He was also instrumental in securing the publication of Descartes's works, and contributed to the Objections appended to the latter's *Meditations*. His most important works include *L'imé des déistes* ("The Impiety of Deists") (1624), *La vérité des sciences* ("The Truth of the Sciences") (1625), and *Harmonie universelle* ("Universal Harmony") (1636–37).

PIERRE GASSENDI (1592–1655), French astronomer, philosopher, and humanist, was born in Provence and educated at Digne and Aix. His first book was a skeptical attack on Aristotelian philosophy, *Exercitationes paradoxicae adversus Aristoteleos* ("Paradoxical Exercises against Aristotle") (1624). Soon thereafter he embarked on his life's project of rehabilitating Epicureanism in a form compatible with Christianity. The results were published in the posthumous *Syntagma philosophicum* ("Philosophical System") (1658). Among his other writings are the Fifth Objections to Descartes's *Meditations* (1641), which were later published with Descartes's replies and Gasssendi's further criticisms in *Disquisitio metaphysica* ("Metaphysical Disquisition") (1644).

RENÉ DESCARTES (1596–1650), one of the most influential philosophers of the early modern period, was born in La Haye, France and educated at La Flèche and Poitier. Following a period of travel in the army of Prince Maurice of Nassau, he settled in Paris where he joined the circle of Mersenne. In 1630 he moved to Holland, where he remained until 1649, when he traveled to Sweden at the invitation of Queen Christina. His principal works are *Discourse on the Method* (1637), *Meditations on First Philosophy* (1641), *Principles of Philosophy* (1644), and *The Passions of the Soul* (1649). Important parts of his philosophy were also developed in correspondences with Mersenne, Princess Elisabeth of Bohemia, and Henry More.

ANTOINE ARNAULD (1612–1694), Cartesian philosopher and a leader of the Catholic Jansenist movement, was born in Paris and received his doctorate in theology in 1641, the same year that his Fourth Objections to Descartes's *Meditations* were published. He was persecuted by the church and the French government for his theological views, which led to his expulsion from the Sorbonne in 1656 and subsequent exile in the Low Countries. His best-known works are (with Claude Lancelot) *Grammaire générale et raisonnée* ("General and Rational Grammar") (1660), (with Pierre Nicole) *La logique, ou l'art de penser* ("Logic, or the Art of Thinking") (1662), and a series of critiques of Malebranche's philosophy, beginning with *Des vraies et des fausses idées* ("On True and False Ideas")

(1683). He also exchanged an important set of letters with Leibniz on the latter's *Discourse on Metaphysics*.

HENRY MORE (1614–1687), English philosopher and theologian, was born in Grantham, Lincolnshire, and educated at Eton and Christ's College, Cambridge, where he succeeded to a fellowship in 1641. He was one of the founders of the philosophical school known as Cambridge Platonism, which aimed to unite the theoretical insights of the new science with Platonist and neo-Platonist doctrines. His works include *Democritus platonissans* (1646), *An Antidote against Atheisme* (1653), *Conjectura cabbalistica* (1653), *The Immortality of the Soul* (1659), and *Enchiridion metaphysicum* (1671).

RALPH CUDWORTH (1617–1688), English philosopher, theologian, and classical scholar, was born in Somerset and spent his entire academic career at Cambridge. With Henry More, he was one of the principal architects of Cambridge Platonism. His masterwork, *The True Intellectual System of the Universe, wherein All the Reason and Philosophy of Atheism are Confuted*, appeared in 1678. Two other important works were published posthumously: *A Treatise concerning Eternal and Immutable Morality* (1731), and *A Treatise of Free Will* (1838).

ELISABETH OF BOHEMIA (1618–1680), eldest daughter of the Elector Palatine and King of Bohemia, Frederick V ("the Winter King") and Elizabeth Stuart, daughter of James I of England, was raised in Silesia and Holland, following her father's loss of his throne at the Battle of White Mountain (1620). Although she did not author a philosophical work of her own, in 1643 she began an extensive correspondence with Descartes on a range of topics, and was the stimulus for his composition of *The Passions of the Soul* and the fuller development of his ethical doctrines. In later life, as abbess of the Protestant convent of Herford in Westphalia, she was visited by Protestant reformers such as William Penn and exchanged letters with Malebranche and possibly Leibniz. In her philosophical interests, she was followed by her sister Sophie and her niece Sophie Charlotte, wife and daughter respectively of the Elector of Hanover, Ernst August, both of whom carried on long correspondences with Leibniz.

BLAISE PASCAL (1623–1662), French mathematician, natural philosopher, and spiritual writer, was born in Clermont-Ferrand and educated at home. Early in his career, he met Descartes and composed several scientific works, including *A Treatise on the Void* (1651). In 1654, a mystical experience intensified his faith, leading him to retire to the Jansenist community of Port-Royal in 1655. There he composed his famous *Provincial Letters* (1656–57) and the *Pensées*, begun in 1658 but published only after his death.

MARGARET CAVENDISH (1623–1673), English philosopher and literary figure, was born in Essex to a prominent Royalist family. Following her marriage to William Cavendish, first Duke of Newcastle, in 1645, she made the acquaintance of many of the leading intellectual figures of the day, including Descartes, Mersenne, Gassendi, and Hobbes, who himself served in the employ of the Cavendish family. Through these contacts she was led to a variety of critical reflections on the new science, which she published in *Philosophical and Physical Opinions* (1655), *Philosophical Letters: Or, Modest Reflections upon Some Opinions in Natural Philosophy* (1664), *Observations upon Experimental Philosophy* (1666), and *Grounds of Natural Philosophy* (1668).

ROBERT BOYLE (1627–1691), natural philosopher and theologian, was born in Lismore, Ireland, and educated at Eton. He is best known for his anti-Aristotelian mechanism and corpuscularianism, and for his skill as an experimentalist. A founding member of the Royal Society, his most significant works are *New Experiments Physico-Mechanicall, Touching the Spring of the Air* (1660), *The Sceptical Chymist* (1661), *Origine of Formes and Qualities* (1666), and *Experiments, Notes &c. about the Mechanical Origine or Production of Divers Particular Qualities* (1675). His writings in natural theology include *Some Considerations about the Reconcileableness of Reason and Religion* (1675) and *The Christian Virtuoso* (1690).

ANNE CONWAY (1631–1679), English metaphysician, was an autodidact in Latin, Greek, philosophy, and theology. She was close to many of the Cambridge Platonists, especially Henry More, who had been tutor to her half-brother, John. She articulated a metaphysical system in several notebooks, published posthumously as *Principles of the Most Ancient and Modern Philosophy, concerning God, Christ, and the Creatures, viz. of Spirit and Matter in General* (1692), and her ideas were cited approvingly by Leibniz, among others.

JOHN LOCKE (1632–1704), the leading English philosopher of the second half of the seventeenth century, was born in Somerset and educated at Westminster and Christ Church, Oxford, where he studied medicine with Thomas Sydenham. In philosophy he was a proponent of empiricism, religious toleration, and representative government. During the 1670s and 1680s he became active in Whig politics through his association with Anthony Ashley Cooper, the third Earl of Shaftesbury. In 1683 he left England for exile in Holland. Returning after the Glorious Revolution, he published in quick succession in 1690 *A Letter concerning Toleration*, *Two Treatises of Government*, and his masterpiece *Essay concerning Human Understanding* (2nd revised ed. 1694). These were followed by *Some Thoughts concerning Education* (1693), and *The Reasonableness of Christianity* (1695).

SAMUEL PUFENDORF (1632–1694), philosopher, legal scholar, and historian, was born in Saxony and educated at Leipzig and Jena, where he studied with Erhard Weigel, who also taught Leibniz. In philosophy, he is best known as an original exponent of natural law theory. His first work on this topic was *Elementorum jurisprudentiae universalis libri duo* ("Two Books on the Elements of Universal Jurisprudence") (1660). His magnum opus is *De jure naturae et gentium* ("On the Law of Nature and Nations") (1672), of which an abridgment appeared as *De officio hominis et civis juxta legem naturalem* ("On the Duty of Man and Citizen according to Natural Law") (1673).

BENEDICT DE SPINOZA (1632–1677), Dutch philosopher, was born in Amsterdam; he received a traditional Jewish education but later sought outside instruction in natural philosophy, including the philosophy of Descartes. He was expelled by the Jewish community in 1656, and thereafter supported himself as a lens grinder, while living in several Dutch towns, ultimately settling in The Hague. His first publication was a commentary on Descartes's *Principles* in 1663. His groundbreaking *Theological-Political Treatise* appeared anonymously in 1670; the *Ethics*, *Political Treatise,* and *Treatise on the Emendation of the Intellect* were published immediately following his death.

NICOLAS MALEBRANCHE (1638–1715), French philosopher and priest, was born in Paris and educated at the Sorbonne. He entered the Congregation of the Oratory in 1660 and was ordained in 1664. He was strongly attracted by the philosophies of Augustine and Descartes, from which he developed his theory of "vision in God" and his influential version of the doctrine of occasionalism (that God is the only true cause of change in the created world). He engaged in debates with, among others, Simon Foucher, Arnauld, Leibniz, and Pierre Régis. His most famous book is *The Search after Truth* (1674–75, plus five further editions expanded by many "Elucidations" through 1712). Other works include *Treatise on Nature and Grace* (1680), *Treatise on Ethics* (1683), and *Dialogues on Metaphysics and Religion* (1688).

ISAAC NEWTON (1642–1727), the foremost mathematician and natural philosopher of the early modern period, was born in Lincolnshire and educated at Trinity College, Cambridge, where he was appointed Lucasian Professor of Mathematics in 1669. In 1696 he became warden of the Royal Mint. He was active in the affairs of the Royal Society, through which as president he prosecuted his protracted quarrel with Leibniz over their respective claims to priority in the invention of the calculus. His most famous work is *Philosophiae naturalis principia mathematica* ("Mathematical Principles of Natural Philosophy") (1687; 2nd ed. 1713); other notable works include *Opticks* (1704) and *Universal Arithmetic* (1707). On his death he also left a voluminous collection of unpublished manuscripts on theology, scriptural interpretation, and alchemy.

GOTTFRIED WILHELM LEIBNIZ (1646–1716), renowned as a philosopher, mathematician, legal scholar, and historian, was born in Leipzig, and studied law and philosophy there and at Altdorf. During a four-year stay in Paris (1672–75) he discovered the principles of the differential and integral calculus, which he published in 1684. Through correspondence and personal contacts, he was acquainted with almost all the leading intellectual figures of the period. In philosophy, he is best known for the hypothesis of preestablished harmony, the metaphysics of monads, and the doctrine of divine justice he called 'theodicy,' which included the assertion that this is the best of all possible worlds. His major works include *Discourse on Metaphysics* (1686; pub. 1846), *New System of the Nature and Communication of Substances* (1695), *New Essays on Human Understanding* (1704; pub. 1765), *Essays on Theodicy* (1710), and *Monadology* (1714; pub. 1721).

PIERRE BAYLE (1647–1706) was born in Le Carla, France, and though a Calvinist, was educated at a Jesuit college in Toulouse until 1670, during which time he briefly converted to Catholicism. He taught in Geneva, Paris, and Sedan before becoming a professor at the Ecole Illustre in Rotterdam in 1681. He is best known for his application of Pyrrhonian skepticism and his advocacy of religious toleration. His most famous work is the massive *Historical and Critical Dictionary* (1697; 2nd ed., 1702); other notable works include *Pensées diverses sur la comète* ("Diverse Thoughts on the Comet") (1683) and *Commentaire philosophique sur ces paroles de Jésus-Christ 'Contrains-les d'entrer'* ("A Philosophical Commentary on the Words of Jesus Christ, 'Compel them to come in'") (1686).

DAMARIS MASHAM (1658–1708), English moralist, was the daughter of Ralph Cudworth and a disciple of John Locke, who resided at her home in Oates, Essex from 1691 until his death in 1704. Her published works are *Discourse concerning the Love of God* (1696) and *Occasional Thoughts in Reference to a Vertuous or Christian Life* (1705). She also conducted an extensive correspondence with Leibniz on metaphysical topics.

SAMUEL CLARKE (1675–1729), theologian and divine, was born in Norwich, England and educated at Cambridge University. He is best known for his advocacy of Newton's natural philosophy, which he defended in his famous exchange with Leibniz in 1715–16 (pub. 1717). He also was involved in various theological disputes (one with Anthony Collins), in which he criticized deviations from orthodoxy. Two sets of sermons delivered as the Boyle lectures in 1703–4 were published as *A Demonstration of the Being and Attributes of God* (1705) and *A Discourse concerning the Unchangeable Obligations of Natural Religion, and the Truth and Certainty of the Christian Religion* (1706).

CHRISTIAN WOLFF (1679–1754), German philosopher and professor, was born in Breslau in modern-day Poland, and educated at the universities of Breslau, Jena, and Leipzig. In his philosophical outlook he was strongly influenced by Leibniz, whose thought he attempted to systematize and develop. His first appointment at Halle in Prussia ended with his banishment in 1723 as the result of a conflict with Pietist theologians. During this time he published the *Vernünftige Gedanken* ("Rational Thoughts"), a series of treatises covering almost every major area of philosophy (1712–25). He later taught at Marburg, where he reframed his philosophy in a set of

Latin texts, before returning in 1741 to Halle, where he remained until his death.

GEORGE BERKELEY (1685–1753), philosopher and divine, was born in Kilkenny, Ireland and educated at Trinity College Dublin from 1700 to 1707. He was introduced by Jonathan Swift to London society, where he met such notables as Joseph Addison and Alexander Pope. During 1729–31 he resided in Newport, Rhode Island, where he attempted to advance the project of founding a college in Bermuda. He is best known for the doctrine of immaterialism (that matter has no mind-independent existence), which he defended in *A Treatise concerning the Principles of Human Knowledge* (1710) and *Three Dialogues between Hylas and Philonous* (1713); other notable works include *An Essay towards a New Theory of Vision* (1709), *De motu* (1721), *Alciphron, or the Minute Philosopher* (1732), and *Siris* (1744).

JOSEPH BUTLER (1692–1752), English philosopher, theologian, and divine, was educated at Oxford and ordained in the Church of England in 1718. His publications include *Fifteen Sermons Preached at the Rolls Chapel* (1726) and *The Analogy of Religion, Natural and Revealed, to the Constitution and Course of Nature* (1736), which attacked deist interpretations of religion. To the latter was appended a treatise on moral philosophy, *Of the Nature of Virtue*, in which he defended the role of conscience as the authoritative basis of moral judgment.

FRANCIS HUTCHESON (1694–1746), known for his contributions to ethics and aesthetics, was born in Ireland and educated at Glasgow University, where he held the chair of moral philosophy from 1730 until his death. He was a leading figure of the Scottish Enlightenment, along with Reid, Hume, and Smith. His most important works are *An Inquiry into the Original of our Ideas of Beauty and Virtue* (1725) and *Essay on the Nature and Conduct of the Passions with Illustrations on the Moral Sense* (1728), in which he explained morality in terms of benevolence, or a natural inclination to promote the happiness of others. A compilation of his lectures appeared posthumously as *A System of Moral Philosophy* (1755).

THOMAS REID (1710–1796), the leading member of the Scottish "common sense" school of philosophy, was educated at the University of Aberdeen and became a professor there in 1752. He is best known for his defenses (against Descartes, Locke, and Berkeley) of perceptual realism, and (against Hume) of free will as a causal power proper to human beings. His major works are *An Inquiry into the Human Mind on the Principles of Common Sense* (1764), *Essays on the Intellectual Powers of Man* (1785), and *Essays on the Active Powers of Man* (1788).

DAVID HUME (1711–1776), a preeminent philosopher of the eighteenth century, was born in Edinburgh and educated at the university there. Although he twice applied for professorships, at Edinburgh and Glasgow, he never held an academic position, being dogged by his reputation as an atheist and a skeptic. During 1734–37 he resided in France, where he composed *A Treatise of Human Nature* (1739–40), which he famously described as "falling dead-born from the press." He later recast his philosophy in the more successful *Enquiry concerning Human Understanding* (1748) and *Enquiry concerning the Principles of Morals* (1751); other notable works include *Essays, Moral and Political* (1741–42), *A Natural History of Religion* (1757), and *Dialogues concerning Natural Religion* (published posthumously in 1779).

JEAN-JACQUES ROUSSEAU (1712–1778), a leading figure among the French Enlightenment *philosophes*, was born in Geneva and was largely self-educated. His first major works were *Discourse on the Arts and Sciences* (1751) and *Discourse on Inequality* (1755), in which he argued for the corruption of human nature by society. In *The Social Contract* (1762), he defended an influential model of the state in which laws bind through the "general will," assented to by all citizens. Other important works include *Emile* (1762) and *Reveries of the Solitary Walker* (1776–78).

ADAM SMITH (1723–1790), Scottish political economist and moral philosopher, studied at Glasgow under Hutcheson and later briefly at Oxford. He was a close friend of Hume and later in life met many of the leading figures of the French Enlightenment. In 1751 he was appointed professor of logic at Glasgow, obtaining the chair of moral philosophy there the following year. His lectures became the basis for his influential *Theory of Moral Sentiments* (1759), which argued for the role of imaginative sympathy in moral judgment. He is best known for his landmark contribution to economic theory, *An Inquiry into the Nature and Causes of the Wealth of Nations* (1776).

IMMANUEL KANT (1724–1804), with Hume, the most distinguished philosopher of the eighteenth century, was born in Königsberg, Prussia, where he spent his entire life. He was strongly influenced by Leibniz and Newton, and is best known for his attempts to ascertain the conditions and limits of human knowledge, and to demonstrate the validity of a universal moral law dictated by reason alone. His most important works are *Critique of Pure Reason* (1781; 2nd ed. 1787), *Critique of Practical Reason* (1788), and *Critique of the Power of Judgment* (1790); other notable works include *Groundwork of a Metaphysics of Morals* (1785), *Religion within the Limits of Reason Alone* (1793), and *Towards Perpetual Peace* (1795).

BIBLIOGRAPHY

PRIMARY SOURCES

Agricola, Rudolph (1992). *De inventione dialectica libri tres*, ed. Lothar Mundt. Tübingen: Niemeyer.

Alembert, Jean Le Rond d' (1963). *Preliminary Discourse to the Encyclopedia of Diderot*, trans. Richard N. Schwab and Walter E. Rex. Indianapolis: Bobbs-Merrill.

Althusius, Johannes (1995). *Politica*, trans. Frederick S. Carney. Indianapolis: Liberty Fund.

Aquinas, Thomas (1945). *Basic Writings of Saint Thomas Aquinas*, ed. Anton C. Pegis. New York: Random House.

Arnauld, Antoine, and Lancelot, Claude (1975). *General and Rational Grammar: The Port-Royal Grammar*, trans. Jacques Rieux and Bernard E. Rollin. The Hague: Mouton.

Arnauld, Antoine, and Nicole, Pierre (1996). *Logic, or the Art of Thinking*, ed. and trans. J. V. Buroker. Cambridge: Cambridge University Press.

Aubrey, John (1972). *Aubrey's Brief Lives*, ed. Oliver Lawson Dick. Harmondsworth: Penguin.

Bacon, Francis (1857–74). *The Works of Francis Bacon*, ed. J. Spedding, R. L. Ellis, and D. D. Heath (14 vols.). London: Longmans.

(1973). *The Advancement of Learning*, ed. G. W. Kitchin. London: Dent.

(2000). *The New Organon*, ed. Lisa Jardine and Michael Silverthorne. Cambridge: Cambridge University Press.

Balguy, John (1728). *The Foundation of Moral Goodness*. London.

Bayle, Pierre (1708). *Miscellaneous Reflections, Occasion'd by the Comet*. London.

(1738). *Dictionary Historical and Critical*, trans. Pierre Desmaizeaux. London. Repr. New York: Garland, 1984.

(1991). *Historical and Critical Dictionary: Selections*, trans. Richard H. Popkin. Indianapolis: Hackett.

Beeckman, Isaac (1939). *Journal tenu par Isaac Beeckman de 1604 à 1634*, ed. Cornelis de Waard. The Hague: Nijhoff.

Berkeley, George (1712). *Passive Obedience*. London.

(1948–57). *The Works of George Berkeley, Bishop of Cloyne*, ed. A. A. Luce and T. E. Jessop (9 vols.). London: Nelson.

(1975). *Philosophical Works*, ed. M. R. Ayers. London: Dent.

Bodin, Jean (1992). *On Sovereignty*, trans. J. H. Franklin. Cambridge: Cambridge University Press.

Böhme, Jakob (1956). *Sämtliche Schrifte*, ed. Will-Erich Peuckert (11 vols.). Stuttgart: Frommann.

(1963). *Die Urschriften*, ed. Werner Buddecke (2 vols.). Stuttgart: Frommann.

Boyle, Robert (1991). *Selected Philosophical Papers*, ed. M. A. Stewart. Indianapolis: Hackett.

Buchanan, George (1964). *The Art and Science of Government among the Scots*, trans. D. H. MacNeill. Glasgow: MacLellan.

Burton, Robert (1989–94). *The Anatomy of Melancholy*, ed. Thomas C. Faulkner, Nicolas K. Kiessling, and Rhonda L. Blair (6 vols.). Oxford: Oxford University Press.

Butler, Joseph (1950). *Five Sermons Preached at the Rolls Chapel and A Dissertation upon the Nature of Virtue*, ed. Stuart M. Brown. Indianapolis: Library of Living Arts.

Cavendish, Margaret (2001). *Observations upon Experimental Philosophy*, ed. Eileen O'Neill. Cambridge: Cambridge University Press.

Charleton, Walter (1674). *A Natural History of the Passions*. London.

Clarke, Samuel (1705). *A Demonstration of the Being and Attributes of God*. London.

(1706). *A Discourse concerning the Unchangeable Obligations of Natural Religion and the Truth and Certainty of the Christian Revelation*. London.

(1738). *The Works of Samuel Clarke* (4 vols.). London: Knapton. Repr. New York: Garland, 1978.

Coeffeteau, Nicolas (1630). *Tableau des passions humaines*. Paris.

Coimbra [Collegium Conimbricensis] (1594). *Commentarii collegii conimbricensis . . . in octo libros physicorum Aristotelis* (2 vols. in 1). Coimbra. Repr. Hildesheim: Olms, 1984.

Condorcet, Jean-Antoine-Nicolas de Caritat, Marquis de (1955). *Sketch for a Historical Picture of the Progress of the Human Mind*, trans. June Barraclough. London: Weidenfeld and Nicolson.

Conway, Anne (1996). *The Principles of the Most Ancient and Modern Philosophy*, ed. Allison P. Coudert. Cambridge: Cambridge University Press.

Cudworth, Ralph (1678). *The True Intellectual System of the Universe* (2 vols.). London. Repr. in Cudworth 1978.

(1970). "A Sermon Preached before the House of Commons," in C. A. Patrides (ed.), *The Cambridge Platonists*. Cambridge, MA: Harvard University Press.

(1978). *The Collected Works of Ralph Cudworth*. New York: Garland.

(1996). *A Treatise concerning Eternal and Immutable Morality, with A Treatise of Freedom*, ed. Sarah Hutton. Cambridge: Cambridge University Press.

Cumberland, Richard (1727). *A Treatise of the Laws of Nature*, trans. John Maxwell. London.

Descartes, René (1974–86). *œuvres de Descartes*, ed. Charles Adam and Paul Tannery (11 vols.). 2nd ed. Paris: Vrin.

(1984–91). *The Philosophical Writings of Descartes*, trans. John Cottingham, Robert Stoothoff, Dugald Murdoch, and Anthony Kenny (3 vols.). Cambridge: Cambridge University Press.

Ferguson, Adam (1995). *An Essay on the History of Civil Society*, ed. Fania Oz-Salzburger. Cambridge: Cambridge University Press.

Filmer, Robert (1991). *Patriarcha and Other Writings*, ed. J. P. Sommerville. Cambridge: Cambridge University Press.

Fonseca, Petrus (1615). *Commentarium Petri Fonsecae Lusitani . . . in libros metaphysicorum Aristotelis* (4 vols. in 2). Cologne: Lazarus Zetzner. Repr. Hildesheim: Olms, 1964.

Galilei, Galileo (1952). *Dialogues concerning Two New Sciences: Discorsi e dimostrazioni matematiche, intorno à due nuove scienze*, trans. Henry Crew and Alfonso de Salvio. New York: Dover.

(1953). *Dialogue concerning the Two Chief World Systems, Ptolemaic and Copernican*, trans. Stillman Drake. Berkeley: University of California Press.

(1957). *Discoveries and Opinions of Galileo*, trans. Stillman Drake. Garden City, NJ: Anchor Doubleday.

(1974). *Two New Sciences*, trans. Stillman Drake. Madison: University of Wisconsin Press.

Grotius, Hugo (1925). *Of the Law of War and Peace in Three Books*, trans. W. Kelsey. Oxford: Oxford University Press.

Hobbes, Thomas (1839). *The English Works of Thomas Hobbes*, ed. William Molesworth (11 vols.). London. Repr. Aalen: Scientia Verlag, 1966.

(1968). *Leviathan*, ed. C. B. Macpherson. London: Penguin.

(1994). *Leviathan: With Selected Variants from the Latin Edition of 1668*, ed. Edwin Curley. Indianapolis: Hackett.

(1996). *Leviathan*, ed. Richard Tuck. Cambridge: Cambridge University Press.

(1998). *On the Citizen*, ed. Richard Tuck and Michael Silverthorne. Cambridge: Cambridge University Press.

Hobbes, Thomas, and Bramhall, John (1999). *Hobbes and Bramhall on Liberty and Necessity*, ed. Vere Chappell. Cambridge: Cambridge University Press.

Holbach, Paul Henri Thiery, Baron d' (1820). *System of Nature*, trans. Samuel Wilkerson. London. Repr. New York: Garland, 1984.

(1990). *Système de la nature* (2 vols.). Paris: Fayard.

Hooker, Richard (1989). *Of the Laws of Ecclesiastical Polity*, ed. A. S. McGrade. Cambridge: Cambridge University Press.

Hume, David (1948). *Moral and Political Philosophy*, ed. H. D. Aiken. New York: Hafner.

(1975). *Enquiries concerning Human Understanding and concerning the Principles of Morals*, ed. L. A. Selby-Bigge, rev. P. H. Nidditch. 3rd ed. Oxford: Oxford University Press.

(1993). *The Natural History of Religion*, ed. J. C. A. Gaskin. Oxford: Oxford University Press.

(2000). *A Treatise of Human Nature*, ed. David Fate Norton and Mary J. Norton. Oxford: Oxford University Press.

Hutcheson, Francis (1729). *An Inquiry into the Original of Our Ideas of Beauty and Virtue, in Two Treatises*. 3rd corrected ed. London: Knapton.

(1999). *On the Nature and Conduct of the Passions with Illustrations on the Moral Sense* (1728), ed. Andrew Ward. Manchester: Clinamen.

(2002). *An Essay on the Nature and Conduct of the Passions and Affections, with Illustrations on the Moral Sense*, ed. Aaron Garrett. Indianapolis: Liberty Fund.

Ignatius of Loyola (1950). *The Spiritual Exercises of Saint Ignatius of Loyola*, trans. W. H. Longbridge. London: Mowbray.

James I (1918). *The Political Works of James I*, ed. Charles Howard McIlwain. Cambridge, MA: Harvard University Press.

Jansenius, Cornelius (1640). *Augustinus* (3 vols.). Louvain. Repr. Frankfurt: Minerva, 1964.

John of St. Thomas (1931–53). *Cursus theologicus* (5 vols.). Paris: Desclée, 1931, 1934, 1937, 1946; Mâcon: Protat, 1953.

Kant, Immanuel (1910–). *Gesammelte Schriften*, ed. Akademie der Wissenschaften (29 vols.). Berlin: Reimer, later De Gruyter.

(1983). *Perpetual Peace and Other Essays*, trans. Ted Humphrey. Indianapolis: Hackett.

(1996a). *Practical Philosophy*, trans. Mary Gregor. Cambridge: Cambridge University Press.

(1996b). *Religion and Rational Theology*, trans. Allen Wood and George di Giovanni. Cambridge: Cambridge University Press.
(1997). *Critique of Pure Reason*, trans. Paul Guyer and Allen Wood. Cambridge: Cambridge University Press.
(2000). *Critique of the Power of Judgment*, trans. Paul Guyer. Cambridge: Cambridge University Press.
Leibniz, Gottfried Wilhelm (1838–40). *Deutsche Schriften*, ed. G. E. Guhrauer (2 vols.). Berlin. Repr. Hildesheim: Olms, 1966.
(1875–90). *Die Philosophischen Schriften von Gottfried Wilhelm Leibniz*, ed. C. I. Gerhardt (7 vols.). Berlin: Weidmannsche Buchhandlung. Repr. Hildesheim: Olms, 1960.
(1903). *Opuscles et fragments inédits*, ed. L. Couturat. Paris: Alcan. Repr. Hildesheim: Olms, 1988.
(1923–). *Sämtliche Schriften und Briefe*, ed. Deutsche [before 1945: Preussische] Akademie der Wissenschaften (multiple vols. in 7 series). Berlin: Akademie Verlag.
(1952). *Theodicy: Essays on the Goodness of God, the Freedom of Man and the Origin of Evil*, ed. Austin Farrer, trans. E. M. Huggard. New Haven: Yale University Press. Repr. La Salle, IL: Open Court, 1985.
(1966). *Logical Papers*, ed. and trans. G. H. R. Parkinson. Oxford: Clarendon Press.
(1967). *The Leibniz–Arnauld Correspondence*, ed. and trans. H. T. Mason. Manchester: Manchester University Press. Repr. New York: Garland, 1985.
(1969). *Philosophical Papers and Letters*, ed. and trans. Leroy E. Loemker. 2nd ed. Dordrecht: Reidel.
(1973). *Philosophical Writings*, ed. G. H. R. Parkinson, trans. Mary Morris and G. H. R. Parkinson. London: Dent.
(1981). *New Essays on Human Understanding*, trans. Peter Remnant and Jonathan Bennett. Cambridge: Cambridge University Press.
(1988). *Political Writings*, ed. and trans. Patrick Riley. 2nd ed. Cambridge: Cambridge University Press.
(1989). *Philosophical Essays*, ed. and trans. Roger Ariew and Daniel Garber. Indianapolis: Hackett.
(1994). *Writings on China*, trans. Daniel J. Cook and Henry Rosemont, Jr. Chicago: Open Court.
Lipsius, Justus (1939). *Two Books of Constancie*, trans. John Stradling, ed. Rudolf Kirk. New Brunswick, NJ: Rutgers University Press.
Locke, John (1722). *The Works of John Locke Esq.* (3 vols.). 2nd ed. London.
(1954). *Essays on the Law of Nature*, ed. Wolfgang von Leyden. Oxford: Oxford University Press.

(1958). *The Reasonableness of Christianity*, ed. I. T. Ramsey. Stanford, CA: Stanford University Press.

(1967). *Two Treatises of Government*, ed. Peter Laslett. 2nd ed. Cambridge: Cambridge University Press.

(1975). *An Essay concerning Human Understanding*, ed. Peter H. Nidditch. Oxford: Oxford University Press.

(1976–92). *The Correspondence of John Locke*, ed. E. S. de Beer (9 vols.). Oxford: Oxford University Press.

(1989). *Some Thoughts concerning Education*, ed. John W. Yolton and Jean S. Yolton. Oxford: Oxford University Press.

(1993). *Political Writings of John Locke*, ed. David Wootton. New York: Mentor.

Luther, Martin (1955–86). *Luther's Works*, ed. Jaroslav Pelikan et al. (55 vols.). Philadelphia: Fortress Press.

(1957). "Two Kinds of Righteousness," trans. Lowell J. Satre, in Luther 1955–86, vol. XXXI, pp. 293–306.

Machiavelli, Niccolò (1950). *The Discourses of Niccolò Machiavelli*, trans. Leslie J. Walker. London: Routledge and Kegan Paul.

(1988). *The Prince*, ed. Russell Price and Quentin Skinner. Cambridge: Cambridge University Press.

Malebranche, Nicolas (1958–84). *Œuvres complètes de Malebranche*, ed. André Robinet (20 vols.). Paris: Vrin.

(1992). *Treatise on Nature and Grace*, trans. Patrick Riley. Oxford: Clarendon Press.

(1993). *Treatise on Ethics*, trans. Craig Walton. Boston: Kluwer.

(1997a). *Dialogues on Metaphysics and on Religion*, ed. Nicholas Jolley, trans. David Scott. Cambridge: Cambridge University Press.

(1997b). *The Search after Truth*, trans. Thomas M. Lennon and Paul J. Olscamp. Cambridge: Cambridge University Press.

Mandeville, Bernard (1988). *The Fable of the Bees: or, Private Vices, Publick Benefits*, ed. F. B. Kaye (2 vols.). Indianapolis: Liberty Fund.

Mill, John Stuart (1974). *Utilitarianism and Other Writings*, ed. Mary Warnock. New York: New American Library.

Milton, John (1991). *Political Writings*, ed. Martin Dzelzainis, trans. Claire Gruzelier. Cambridge: Cambridge University Press.

Montaigne, Michel de (1965). *The Complete Essays of Montaigne*, trans. Donald M. Frame. Stanford, CA: Stanford University Press.

More, Henry (1690). *An Account of Virtue*. London.

More, Thomas (1989). *Utopia*, ed. George Logan and Robert Adams. Cambridge: Cambridge University Press.

Newton, Isaac (1999). *The Principia: Mathematical Principles of Natural Philosophy*, trans. I. Bernard Cohen and Anne Whitman. Berkeley: University of California Press.

Oresme, Nicole (1968). *Nicole Oresme and the Medieval Geometry of Qualities and Motions* (*Tractatus de configurationibus qualitatum et motuum*), ed. Marshall Clagett. Madison: University of Wisconsin Press.

Pascal, Blaise (1958). *Pensées*, ed. Louis Lafuma (2 vols.). Paris: Editions du Seuil.

(1962). *Pensées*, trans. Martin Turnell. London: Harvill.

(1964). *Lettres provinciales*, ed. Clémont Rosset. Paris: Pauvert.

(1966). *Pensées*, trans. A. J. Krailsheimer. Harmonsworth: Penguin.

Peter of Spain (1972). *Tractatus: Called afterwards Summulae Logicales*, ed. L. M. De Rijk. Assen: Van Gorcum.

Pufendorf, Samuel (1934). *The Law of Nature and Nations*, in *De jure naturae et gentium libri octo*, vol. II, trans. C. H. and W. A. Oldfather. Oxford: Oxford University Press.

Ramus, Peter (1964). *Dialectique* (1555), ed. Michel Dassonville. Geneva: Droz.

Rousseau, Jean-Jacques (1978). *On the Social Contract*, trans. J. R. Masters. New York: St. Martin's Press.

(1997). *The Discourses and Other Political Writings*, ed. Victor Gourevich. Cambridge: Cambridge University Press.

Selden, John (1726). *Opera omnia*, ed. D. Watkins (3 vols.). London.

Senault, Jean-François (1649). *The Use of the Passions*, trans. Henry, Earl of Monmouth. London.

Shaftesbury, Anthony Ashley Cooper, Earl of (1900). *The Life, Unpublished Letters, and Philosophical Regimen of Anthony, Earl of Shaftesbury*, ed. Benjamin Rand. London: Swan Sonnenschein.

(1999). *Characteristics of Men, Manners, Opinions, Times*, ed. Lawrence E. Klein. Cambridge: Cambridge University Press.

Sidney, Philip (1962). *The Prose Works*, ed. Albert Feuillerat (4 vols.). Cambridge: Cambridge University Press.

Smith, Adam (1982). *Lectures on Jurisprudence*, ed. R. L. Meek, D. D. Raphael, and P. G. Stein. Indianapolis: Liberty Fund.

(1984). *The Theory of Moral Sentiments*, ed. A. L. Macfie and D. D. Raphael. Indianapolis: Liberty Fund.

Spinoza, Benedict de (1925). *Opera*, ed. Carl Gebhardt (4 vols.). Heidelberg: C. Winter.

(1958). *The Political Works*, trans. A. G. Wernham. Oxford: Clarendon Press.

(1985). *The Collected Works of Spinoza*, vol. I, ed. and trans. Edwin Curley. Princeton: Princeton University Press.

(1989). *Tractatus theologico-politicus*, ed. and trans. Günter Gawlick and Friedrich Niewöhner (German translation with facing Latin text). Darmstadt: Wissenschaftliche Buchgesellschaft.

(1998). *Theological-Political Treatise*, trans. Samuel Shirley. Indianapolis: Hackett.

Suárez, Francisco (1856–78). *Opera omnia*, ed. D. M. André (28 vols.). Paris: L. Vivès. *Disputationes metaphysicae* (vols. xxv–xxvi), repr. Hildesheim: Olms, 1965.

(1944). *A Treatise on Laws and God the Lawgiver*, trans. Gwladys L. Williams, Ammi Brown, and John Waldron, in *Selections from Three Works of Francisco Suárez, S.J.*, vol. ii. Oxford: Oxford University Press.

(1971–81). *Tractatus de legibus, ac Deo legislatore*, ed. L. Perena, V. Abril, and P. Suner (8 vols.). Madrid: Consejo Superior de Investigaciones Científicas.

Valla, Lorenzo (1962). *Opera omnia*, ed. Eugenio Garin. Turin: Bottega d'Erasmo.

Vindiciae contra tyrannos (1969). In J. H. Franklin (ed.), *Constitutionalism and Resistance in the Sixteenth Century: Three Treatises by Hotman, Beza, and Mornay*. New York: Pegasus.

Vives, Juan Luis (1782–90). *Opera omnia*, ed. Gregorio Mayans (8 vols.). Valencia: Monfort. Repr. London: Gregg, 1964.

Wolff, Christian (1983). *Vernünftige Gedanken von Gott, der Welt und der Seele des Menschen auch allen Dingen überhaupt*, ed. Charles A. Corr. Hildesheim: Olms.

SECONDARY SOURCES

Aarsleff, Hans (1982). *From Locke to Saussure: Essay on the Study of Language and Intellectual History*. Minneapolis: University of Minnesota Press.

Acworth, Richard (1979). *The Philosophy of John Norris of Bemerton (1657–1712)*. Hildesheim: Olms.

Adams, Robert M. (1994). *Leibniz: Determinist, Theist, Idealist*. New York: Oxford University Press.

Alanen, Lili (2003). *Descartes's Concept of Mind*. Cambridge, MA: Harvard University Press.

Amann, Emile (1939). "Du Bois, François," in Vacant and Mangenot 1923–50, vol. xiv/2, cols. 2, 923–25.

Anderson, F. H. (1971). *The Philosophy of Francis Bacon*. New York: Octagon Books.

Arens, Hans (1984). *Aristotle's Theory of Language and its Tradition*. Amsterdam: Benjamins.

Ariew, Roger (1999). *Descartes and the Last Scholastics*. Ithaca, NY: Cornell University Press.

Ariew, Roger, Cottingham, John, and Sorell, Tom (eds.) (1998). *Descartes'* Meditations: *Background Source Materials*. Cambridge: Cambridge University Press.

Ariew, Roger, and Grene, Marjorie (eds.) (1995). *Descartes and his Contemporaries: Meditations, Objections and Replies*. Chicago: University of Chicago Press.

Armogathe, Jean-Robert (1995). "Caterus' Objections to God," in Ariew and Grene 1995, pp. 34–43.

Asensio, José Arturo Domínguez (1998). "'De efficacia sacramentorum novae legis': La causalidad sacramental en la obra polémica de Gregorio de Valencia," *Archivo teológico granadino* 61: 5–40.

Ashworth, E. J. (1974). *Language and Logic in the Post-Medieval Period*. Dordrecht: Reidel.

(1988). "Traditional Logic," in Schmitt, Skinner, and Kessler 1988, pp. 143–72.

Atherton, Margaret (1990). *Berkeley's Revolution in Vision*. Ithaca, NY: Cornell University Press.

(ed.) (1994). *Women Philosophers of the Early Modern Period*. Indianapolis: Hackett.

Ayers, Michael (1981). "Mechanism, Superaddition, and the Proof of God's Existence in Locke's *Essay*," *Philosophical Review* 90: 210–51.

(1991). *Locke* (2 vols.). London: Routledge.

Baier, Annette (1991). *A Progress of Sentiments*. Cambridge, MA: Harvard University Press.

Bak, Felix (1956). "Scoti schola numerosior est omnibus aliis simul sumptis," *Franciscan Studies* 16: 143–64.

Baldini, Ugo (1992). *Legem impone subactis: Studi su filosofia e scienza dei Gesuiti in Italia, 1540–1632*. Rome: Bulzoni.

Bardout, Jean-Christophe, and Boulnois, Olivier (eds.) (2002). *Sur la science divine*. Paris: Presses Universitaires de France.

Barker, Peter, and Ariew, Roger (eds.) (1991). *Revolution and Continuity: Essays in the History and Philosophy of Early Modern Science*. Washington, DC: Catholic University Press, 1991.

Barnes, Jonathan (1975). "Aristotle's Theory of Demonstration," in Jonathan Barnes, Martin Schofield, and Richard Sorabji (eds.), *Articles on Aristotle*, vol. 1: *Science*. London: Duckworth, pp. 65–87.

Barry, Brian, and Hardin, Russell (eds.) (1982). *Rational Man and Irrational Society?* Beverly Hills, CA: Sage.

Baudin, Emile (1946–47). *La philosophie de Pascal* (3 vols.). Neuchâtel: Editions de la Baconnière.

Bauer, Karl (1928). *Die Wittenberger Universitätstheologie und die Anfänge der deutschen Reformation*. Tübingen: Mohr.

Bayer, Oswald (1976). "Selbstverschuldete Vormundschaft," in Dieter Henke, Günther Kehrer, and Gunda Schneider-Flume (eds.), *Der Wirklichkeitsanspruch von Theologie und Religion*. Tübingen: Mohr, pp. 3–34.

Beck, Lewis White (1969). *Early German Philosophy*. Cambridge, MA: Harvard University Press.

Beeke, Joel R. (1999). "Gisbertus Voetius: Toward a Reformed Marriage of Knowledge and Piety," in Trueman and Clark 1999, pp. 227–44.

Belda Plans, Juan (2000). *La Escuela de Salamanca y la renovación de la teología en el siglo XVI*. Madrid: Biblioteca de Autores Cristianos.

Bennett, Jonathan (1983). "Teleology and Spinoza's Conatus," *Midwest Studies in Philosophy* 8: 143–60.

(1984). *A Study of Spinoza's* Ethics. Indianapolis: Hackett.

(1987). "Substratum," *History of Philosophy Quarterly* 4: 197–215.

(2001). *Learning from Six Philosophers: Descartes, Spinoza, Leibniz, Locke, Berkeley, Hume* (2 vols.). Oxford: Oxford University Press.

Beuchot, Mauricio (1996). *Historia de la filosofia en el Mexico colonial*. Barcelona: Herder.

Biagioli, Mario (1993). *Galileo, Courtier: The Practice of Science in the Culture of Absolutism*. Chicago: University of Chicago Press.

Biard, Joel, and Rashed, Roshdi (eds.) (1997). *Descartes et le moyen âge*. Paris: Vrin.

Biener, Zvi (2004). "Galileo's First Science: The Science of Matter," *Perspectives on Science* 12: 262–87.

Blackwell, Richard J. (1991). *Galileo, Bellarmine, and the Bible*. Notre Dame: University of Notre Dame Press.

Blay, Michel (1992). *La naissance de la mécanique analytique*. Paris: Presses Universitaires de France.

Blom, Hans W. (1995). "Morality and Causality in Politics: The Rise of Naturalism in Dutch Seventeenth-Century Political Thought." Diss. University of Utrecht.

Blum, Paul Richard (1999). *Philosophenphilosophie und Schulphilosophie: Typen des Philosophierens in der Neuzeit*. Stuttgart: Franz Steiner.

Boehm, Laetitia (1978). "Humanistische Bildungswegungen und mittelalterliche Universitätsverfassung: Aspekte zur frühneuzeitlichen Reformgeschichte der deutschen Universitäten," in Jozef Ijsewijn and Jacques Paquet (eds.), *The Universities in the Late Middle Ages*. Louvain: Leuven University Press.

Bohatec, Josef (1966). *Die Religionsphilosphie Kants in der "Religion innerhalb der Grenzen der reinen Vernunft"*. Repr. Hildesheim: Olms. First Published Hamburg, 1938.

Borde, Bruno-Marie (2001). "Le désir naturel de voir Dieu chez les salmanticenses," *Revue thomiste* 101: 265–84.

Bos, Egbert P., and Krop, Henri A. (eds.) (1993). *Franco Burgersdijk 1590–1635*. Amsterdam: Rodopi.

Boulnois, Olivier, Schmutz, Jacob, and Solère, Jean-Luc (eds.) (2002). *Le contemplateur et les idées: Modèles de la science divine du néoplatonisme au XVIIIe siècle*. Paris: Vrin.

Boyle, Nicholas (2000). *Goethe: The Poet and the Age* (2 vols.). Oxford: Oxford University Press.

Brekle, H. E. (1971). "Die Idee einer Generativen Grammatik in Leibnizens Fragmente zur Logik," *Studia leibnitiana* 3: 141–49.

Brender, Natalie, and Krasnoff, Larry (eds.) (2004). *New Essays on the History of Autonomy*. Cambridge: Cambridge University Press.

Brett, Anabel (1997). *Liberty, Right and Nature*. Cambridge: Cambridge University Press.

Brinkman, Gabriel (1957). *The Social Thought of Juan de Lugo*. Washington, DC: Catholic University of America Press.

Brinton, Crane (ed.) (1956). *The Portable Age of Reason Reader*. New York: Viking Press.

Broad, C. D. (1926). *The Philosophy of Francis Bacon: An Address Delivered at Cambridge on the Occasion of the Bacon Tercentenary, 5 October 1926*. Cambridge: Cambridge University Press.

(1981). "Leibniz's Last Controversy with the Newtonians," in R. S. Woolhouse (ed.), *Leibniz: Metaphysics and the Philosophy of Science*. Oxford: Oxford University Press, pp. 157–74.

Broadie, Alexander (2000). "The Scotist Thomas Reid," *American Catholic Philosophical Quarterly* 74: 385–407.

(ed.) (2003). *The Cambridge Companion to the Scottish Enlightenment*. Cambridge: Cambridge University Press.

Brockliss, Laurence (1987). *French Higher Education in the Seventeenth and Eighteenth Centuries: A Cultural History*. Oxford: Oxford University Press.

Brown, Stephen F. (ed.) (1998). *Meeting of the Minds: The Relations between Medieval and Classical Modern European Philosophy*. Turnhout: Brepols.

Brown, Stuart (1984). *Leibniz*. Manchester: Manchester University Press.

Buckle, Stephen (2001). *Hume's Enlightenment Tract*. Oxford: Oxford University Press.

Burgio, Santo (1998). *Teologia Barocca: Il probabilismo in Sicilia nell'epoca di Filippo IV*. Catania: Biblioteca della Società di Storia Patria.

(2000). *Filosofia e controriforma*. Catania: Dipartimento di Scienze Umane.

Burns, J. H. (ed.) (1991). *The Cambridge History of Political Thought, 1450–1700*. Cambridge: Cambridge University Press.

Calafate, Pedro (ed.) (2001). *História do pensamento filosófico português*, vol. II: *Renascimento e contra-reforma*. Lisbon: Caminho.

Carboncini, Sonia (1991). *Transzendentale Wahrheit und Traum: Christian Wolffs Antwort auf die Herausforderung durch den Cartesianischen Zweifel*. Stuttgart–Bad Cannstatt: Frommann-Holzboog.

Carnap, Rudolf (1950). *Logical Foundations of Probability*. Chicago: University of Chicago Press.

(1956). *Meaning and Necessity: A Study in Semantics and Modal Logic*. 2nd ed. Chicago: University of Chicago Press.

Carro, Venancio D. (1944). *Domingo de Soto y su doctrina juridica*. Salamanca: Biblioteca de Teologos Españoles.

Carrol, Robert T. (1975). *The Common-Sense Philosophy of Religion of Bishop Edward Stillingfleet 1635–1699*. The Hague: Nijhoff.

Caruso, Ester (1979). *Pedro Hurtado de Mendoza e la rinascita del nominalismo nella scolastica del seicento*. Florence: La Nuova Italia Editrice.

Castro, Cristobal de (1974). "Vida del P. Gabriel Vazquez," *Archivo teológico granadino* 37: 227–44.

Caton, Hiram (1971). "The Problem of Descartes's Sincerity," *The Philosophical Forum* 12: 273–94.

(1973). *The Origins of Subjectivity: An Essay on Descartes*. New Haven: Yale University Press.

Ceñal, Ramón (1953). "Juan Caramuel: Su epistolario con Atanasio Kircher, S.J.," *Revista de filosofía* 12: 101–47.

Cessario, Romanus (1998). *Le thomisme et les thomistes*. Paris: Cerf.

Ceyssens, L. (1956). "François de Saint-Augustin de Macedo: Son attitude au début du jansénisme," *Archivum franciscanum historicum* 49: 1–14.

Chenu, Marie-Dominique (1925). "Labat, Pierre," in Vacant and Mangenot 1923–50, vol. VIII, col. 2386.

Clarke, Desmond M. (1982). *Descartes' Philosophy of Science*. Manchester: Manchester University Press.

(1989). *Occult Powers and Hypotheses*. Oxford: Oxford University Press.

(2003). *Descartes's Theory of Mind*. Oxford: Oxford University Press.

Clatterbaugh, Kenneth (1999). *The Causation Debate in Modern Philosophy, 1637–1739*. London: Routledge.

Clavelin, Maurice (1974). *The Natural Philosophy of Galileo*. Cambridge, MA: MIT Press.

Cleary, Gregory (1925). *Father Luke Wadding and St. Isidore's College in Rome*. Rome: Bardi.

Coleman, Janet (2005). "Scholastic Treatments of Maintaining One's *Fama* . . . and the Correction of Private 'Passions' for the Public Good and Public Legitimacy," *Cultural and Social History* 2: 23–48.
Connell, Desmond (1967). *The Vision in God: Malebranche's Scholastic Sources*. Louvain–Paris: Nauwelaerts.
Coombs, Jeffrey (1993). "The Possibility of Created Entities in Seventeenth-Century Scotism," *Philosophical Quarterly* 43: 447–59.
Copenhaver, Brian P., and Schmitt, Charles B. (1992). *Renaissance Philosophy*. Oxford: Oxford University Press.
Coppens, Gunther (ed.) (2003). *Spinoza en de Scholastiek*. Leuven: Acco.
Corazón, Enrique del Sagrado (1955). *Los salmanticenses: Su vida y su obra*. Madrid: Ed. de Espiritualidad.
Costello, William (1958). *The Scholastic Curriculum in Early Seventeenth Century Cambridge*. Cambridge, MA: Harvard University Press.
Cottingham, John (1986). *Descartes*. Oxford: Oxford University Press.
(1988). *The Rationalists*. Oxford: Oxford University Press.
(1993). "A New Start? Cartesian Metaphysics and the Emergence of Modern Philosophy," in Sorell 1993, pp. 145–66.
Courtine, Jean-François (1990). *Suarez et le système de la métaphysique*. Paris: Presses Universitaires de France.
(1999). *Nature et empire de la loi: Études suaréziennes*. Paris: Vrin.
Couturat, Louis (1901). *La logique de Leibniz d'après documents inédits*. Paris: Felix Alcan. Repr. Hildesheim: Olms, 1985.
Craig, Edward (1987). *The Mind of God and the Works of Man*. Oxford: Clarendon Press.
Curley, Edwin (1969). *Spinoza's Metaphysics*. Cambridge, MA: Harvard University Press.
(1986) "Analysis in the *Meditations*," in Amelie O. Rorty (ed.), *Essays on Descartes's* Meditations. Berkeley: University of California Press, pp. 157–76.
(1990). "On Bennett's Spinoza: The Issue of Teleology," in Edwin Curley and Pierre-François Moreau (eds.), *Spinoza: Issues and Directions*. Leiden: Brill, pp. 39–52.
Darge, Rolf (2004). *Suarez' transzendentale Seinsauslegung und die Metaphysiktradition*. Leiden: Brill.
Darwall, Stephen (1995). *The British Moralists and the Internal 'Ought': 1640–1740*. Cambridge: Cambridge University Press.
(1997). "Hutcheson on Practical Reason," *Hume Studies* 23: 73–89.
(1999). "The Inventions of Autonomy," *European Journal of Philosophy* 7: 339–50.
(2004). "Autonomy in Modern Natural Law," in Brender and Krasnoff 2004.

(2006). *The Second-Person Standpoint: Morality, Respect, and Accountability*. Cambridge, MA: Harvard University Press.

Dascal, Marcelo (1987). *Leibniz: Language, Signs and Thought*. Amsterdam: Benjamins.

(1990). "Leibniz on Particles: Linguistic Form and Comparatism," in Tullio de Mauro and Lia Formigari (eds.), *Leibniz, Humboldt, and the Origins of Comparativism*. Philadelphia: Benjamins

Daston, Lorraine (1988). *Classical Probability in the Enlightenment*. Princeton: Princeton University Press.

(1995). "Curiosity in Early-Modern Society," *Words and Image* 11: 391–404.

Daston, Lorraine, and Park, Katherine (1992). *Wonders and the Order of Nature, 1150–1750*. New York: Zone.

Dear, Peter (1988). *Mersenne and the Learning of the Schools*. Ithaca, NY: Cornell University Press.

(1995). *Discipline and Experience: The Mathematical Way in the Scientific Revolution*. Chicago: University of Chicago Press.

De Armellada, Bernardino (1997). *La gracia misterio de libertad: El "sobrenatural" en el Beato Escoto y en la escuela franciscana*. Rome: Istituto Storico dei Cappuccini.

Debus, Allen G. (1970). *Science and Education in the Seventeenth Century: The Webster–Ward Debate*. New York: American Elsevier.

Deely, John (ed.) (1985). *Tractatus de signis: The Semiotic of John Poinsot*. Berkeley: University of California Press.

Delahunty, R. J. (1985). *Spinoza*. London: Routledge.

Della Rocca, Michael (1996). *Representation and the Mind–Body Problem in Spinoza*. Oxford: Oxford University Press.

Deman, Thomas (1936). "Probabilisme," in Vacant and Mangenot 1923–50, vol. XIII, cols. 416–619.

Des Chene, Dennis (1996). *Physiologia: Natural Philosophy in Late Aristotelian and Cartesian Thought*. Ithaca, NY: Cornell University Press.

(2000). *Life's Form: Late Aristotelian Conceptions of the Soul*. Ithaca, NY: Cornell University Press.

(2001). *Spirits and Clocks: Machine and Organism in Descartes*. Ithaca, NY: Cornell University Press.

De Sousa Ribeiro, Ilidio (1951). *Fr. Francisco de Santo Agostinho de Macedo: Um filósofo escotista português e um paladino da Restauração*. Coimbra: Universidade de Coimbra.

Díez-Alegría, José María (1951). *El desarrollo de la doctrina de la ley naturale en Luis de Molina y en los maestros de la universidad de Évora de 1565 a 1591: Estudio histórico y textos inéditos*. Barcelona: Consejo Superior de Investigaciones Científicas.

Di Liscia, Daniel A., Kessler, Eckhard, and Methuen, Charlotte (eds.) (1997). *Method and Order in Renaissance Philosophy of Nature*. Aldershot: Ashgate.

Di Vona, Piero (1994). *I concetti trascendenti in Sebastián Izquierdo e nella scolastica del seicento*. Naples: Loffredo.

Dixon, Thomas (2003). *From Passions to Emotions*. Cambridge: Cambridge University Press.

Dockrill, David W. (1997). "The Heritage of Patristic Platonism in Seventeenth-Century English Philosophical Theology," in G. A. J. Rogers, J. M. Vienne, and Y. C. Zarka (eds.), *The Cambridge Platonists in Philosophical Context: Politics, Metaphysics and Religion*. Dordrecht: Reidel, pp. 55–78.

Donelly, John Patrick (1976). *Calvinism and Scholasticism in Vermigli's Doctrine of Man and Grace*. Leiden: Brill.

Doyle, John P. (1988). "Thomas Compton Carleton SJ: On Words Signifying More than their Speakers or Makers Know or Intend," *The Modern Schoolman* 66: 1–28.

(1995). "Another God, Goat-Stags, Men-Lions: A Seventeenth-Century Debate about Impossible Objects," *The Review of Metaphysics* 48: 771–808.

Ebbesen, Sten, and Friedman, Russell (eds.) (2004). *John Buridan and Beyond: Topics in the Language Sciences 1300–1700*. Copenhagen: Royal Danish Academy of Science and Letters.

Elias, Norbert (1978). *The Civilizing Process: The History of Manners*, trans. Edmund Jephcott. New York: Urizen Books.

Fartos Martinez, M. (1997). "La teoría de la elipsis en la *Minerva* del Brocense y su influencia en la *Grammatica audax* de Juan Caramuel," in Ricardo Escavy Zamora et al. (eds.), *Homenaje al Profesor A. Roldán Pérez* (2 vols.). Murcia: Universidad de Murcia, vol. 1, pp. 341–58.

Feingold, Mordechai (1991). "Tradition versus Novelty: Universities and Scientific Societies in the Early Modern Period," in Barker and Ariew 1991, pp. 45–59.

(2003a). *Jesuit Science and the Republic of Letters*. Cambridge, MA: MIT Press.

(2003b). *The New Science and Jesuit Science: Seventeenth Century Perspectives*. Dordrecht: Reidel.

Fitzpatrick, P. J., and Haldane, John (2003). "Medieval Philosophy in Later Thought," in McGrade 2003, pp. 300–27.

Force, James E., and Popkin, Richard H. (eds.) (1998). *Newton and Religion: Context, Nature, and Influence*. Dordrecht: Kluwer.

Forlivesi, Marco (1993). *Conoscenza e affettività: L'incontro con l'essere secondo Giovanni di San Tommaso*. Bologna: Studio Domenicano.

"Materiali per una descrizione della disputa e dell'esame di laurea in età moderna," in A. Ghisalbesti (ed.), *Della prima alla seconda scolastica paradigini percorsi storiografici*. Bologna: Studio Domenicano, pp. 252–79.

(2002). *Scotistarum princeps: Bartolomeo Mastri (1602–1673) e il suo tempo*. Padua: Centro Studi Antoniani.

Foucault, Michel (1977). *Discipline and Punish: The Birth of the Prison*, trans. Alan Sheridan. London: Allen Lane.

Fowler, C. F. (1999). *Descartes on the Human Soul: Philosophy and the Demands of Christian Doctrine*. Dordrecht: Kluwer.

Frank, Günther (1995). *Die theologische Philosophie Philipp Melanchthons (1497–1560)*. Leipzig: St Benno Buch und Zeitschriften Verlagsgesellschaft.

Frankena, William (1992). "Sidgwick and the History of Ethical Dualism," in Bart Schultz (ed.), *Essays on Henry Sidgwick*. Cambridge: Cambridge University Press, pp. 175–98.

Franklin, James (2001). *The Science of Conjectures: Evidence and Probability before Pascal*. Baltimore: Johns Hopkins University Press.

Franklin, Julian H. (1963). *Jean Bodin and the Sixteenth Century Revolution in the Methodology of Law and History*. New York: Columbia University Press.

Frasca-Spada, Marina, and Kail, Peter (eds.) (2005). *Impressions of Hume*. Oxford: Oxford University Press.

Freedman, Joseph S. (1984). *Deutsche Schulphilosophie im Reformationszeitalter*. Münster: MAKS Publikationen.

(1997). "The Career and Writings of Bartholomew Keckermann," *Proceedings of the American Philosophical Society* 141: 307–64.

Frege, Gottlob (1879). *Begriffsschrift: Eine der arithmetischen nachgebildete Formelsprache des reinen Denkens*. Halle. Repr. Hildesheim: Olms, 1964.

(1960). *Translations from the Philosophical Writings of Gottlob Frege*, trans. Peter Geach and Max Black. 2nd ed. Oxford: Blackwell.

(1980). *Translations from the Philosophical Writings of Gottlob Frege*, trans. Peter Geach and Max Black. 3rd ed. Oxford: Blackwell.

Friedman, Russell, and Nielsen, Lauge (eds.) (2003). *The Medieval Heritage in Early Modern Metaphysics and Modal Theory, 1400–1700*. Dordrecht: Reidel.

Funkenstein, Amos (1986). *Theology and the Scientific Imagination: From the Middle Ages to the Seventeenth Century*. Princeton: Princeton University Press.

Garber, Daniel (1992). *Descartes' Metaphysical Physics*. Chicago: University of Chicago Press.

Garber, Daniel, and Ayers, Michael (eds.) (1998). *The Cambridge History of Seventeenth-Century Philosophy*. Cambridge: Cambridge University Press.

Garcia Villoslada, Ricardo (1938). *La universidad de Paris durante los estudios de Francisco de Vitoria O.P. (1507–1522)*. Rome: Universitatis Gregorianae.

(1954). *Storia del Collegio Romano dal suo inizio (1551) alla soppressione della Compagnia di Gesù (1773)*. Rome: Universitatis Gregorianae.

Garrett, Don (1999). "Teleology in Spinoza and Early Modern Rationalism," in Gennaro and Huenemann 1999, pp. 210–35.

Gaukroger, Stephen (1978). *Explanatory Structures*. Hassocks: Harvester.

(1989). *Cartesian Logic*. Oxford: Oxford University Press.

(1995). *Descartes: An Intellectual Biography*. Oxford: Oxford University Press.

(ed.) (1998). *The Soft Underbelly of Reason: The Passions in the Seventeenth Century*. London: Routledge.

(2001). *Francis Bacon and the Transformation of Early Modern Philosophy*. Cambridge: Cambridge University Press.

(2002). *Descartes' System of Natural Philosophy*. Cambridge: Cambridge University Press.

Gaukroger, Stephen, and Schuster, John (2002). "The Hydrostatic Paradox and the Origins of Cartesian Dynamics," *Studies in History and Philosophy of Science Part A* 33: 535–72.

Gennaro, Rocco J., and Huenemann, Charles (eds.) (1999). *New Essays on the Rationalists*. New York: Oxford University Press.

Gerrish, B. A. (1962). *Grace and Reason: A Study in the Theology of Luther*. Oxford: Clarendon Press.

Giacon, Carlo (1944). *La secunda scolastica*. Milan: Fratelli Bocca.

Gilbert, Neil W. (1960). *Renaissance Concepts of Method*. New York: Columbia University Press.

Gómez Camacho, Francisco (1998a). *Economia y filosofia moral: La formacion del pensamiento economico europeo en la escolastica española*. Madrid: Síntesis.

(1998b). "Later Scholastics: Spanish Economic Thought in the XVIth and XVIIth Centuries," in S. Todd Lowry and Barry Gordon (eds.), *Ancient and Medieval Economic Ideas and Concepts of Social Justice*. Leiden: Brill, pp. 503–61.

Gotthelf, Allan (ed.) (1985). *Aristotle on Nature and Living Things: Philosophical and Historical Studies*. Pittsburgh: Mathesis.

Goudriaan, Aza (1999). *Philosophische Gotteserkenntnis bei Suárez und Descartes: Im Zusammenhang mit der niederländischen reformierten Theologie und Philosophie des 17. Jahrhunderts*. Leiden: Brill.

Grajewski, Maurice (1946). "John Ponce: Franciscan Scotist of the Seventeenth Century," *Franciscan Studies* 6: 54–92.

Grene, Marjorie (1991). *Descartes among the Scholastics*. Milwaukee: Marquette University Press.

Gurr, John Edwin (1959). *The Principle of Sufficient Reason in Some Scholastic Systems 1750–1900*. Milwaukee: Marquette University Press.

Guyer, Paul (1994). "Locke's Philosophy of Language," in Vere Chappell (ed.), *The Cambridge Companion to Locke*. Cambridge: Cambridge University Press, pp. 115–45.

Haakonssen, Knud (1996). *Natural Law and Moral Philosophy*. Cambridge: Cambridge University Press.

Hacking, Ian (1971). "The Leibniz–Carnap Program for Inductive Logic," *Journal of Philosophy* 68: 597–610.

(1975). *The Emergence of Probability*. Cambridge: Cambridge University Press.

Haldane, John (1989). "Reid, Scholasticism, and Current Philosophy of Mind," in Melvin Dalgarno and Eric Matthews (eds.), *The Philosophy of Thomas Reid*. Dordrecht: Kluwer, pp. 285–304.

Harrison, Peter (1998). "The Fall, the Passions and Dominion over Nature," in Gaukroger 1998, pp. 49–78.

Hazard, Paul (1990). *The European Mind: The Critical Years, 1685–1715*. New York: Fordham University Press.

Hellin, L. Gomez (1940). "Toledo lector de filosofía y teología en el colegio romano," *Archivo teológico granadino* 3: 1–18.

Helm, Paul (2004). *John Calvin's Ideas*. Oxford: Oxford University Press.

Hentrich, Wilhelm von (1928). *Gregorius von Valencia und der Molinismus*. Innsbruck: Rauch.

Hill, Christopher (1965). *Intellectual Origins of the English Revolution*. Oxford: Clarendon Press.

Hoenen, Maarten (1997). "Thomismus, Skotismus und Albertismus: Das Entstehen und die Bedeutung von philosophischen Schulen im späten Mittelalter," *Bochumer philosophisches Jahrbuch für Antike und Mittelalter* 2: 81–103.

(1998). "Scotus and the Scotist School: The Tradition of Scotist Thought in the Medieval and Early Modern Period," in E. P. Bos (ed.), *John Duns Scotus: Renewal of Philosophy*. Amsterdam: Rodopi

(2003). "Via Antiqua and Via Moderna in the Fifteenth Century: Doctrinal, Institutional, and Church Political Factors in the Wegestriet," in Friedman and Nielsen 2003, pp. 9–36.

Hoffman, Paul (1986). "The Unity of Descartes' Man," *Philosophical Review* 95: 339–70.

Hoffmann, Tobias (2002). *Creatura intellecta: Die Ideen und Possibilien bei Duns Scotus mit Ausblick auf Franz von Mayronis, Poncius und Mastrius*. Münster: Aschendorff.

Höpfl, Harro (2004). *Jesuit Political Thought: The Society of Jesus and the State, c. 1540–1630*. Cambridge: Cambridge University Press.

Hotson, Howard (2000a). *Johann Heinrich Alsted (1588–1638): Between Renaissance, Reformation and Universal Reform*. Oxford: Oxford University Press.

(2000b). *Paradise Postponed: Johann Heinrich Alsted and the Birth of Calvinist Millenarianism*. Dordrecht: Reidel.

Hruschka, Joachim (1991). "The Greatest Happiness Principle and Other Early German Anticipations of Utilitarian Theory," *Utilitas* 3: 165–77.

Hunter, Ian (2001). *Rival Enlightenments*. Cambridge: Cambridge University Press.

(2005). "The Passions of the Prince: Moral Philosophy and *Staatskirchenrecht* in Thomasius's Conception of Sovereignty," *Cultural and Social History* 2: 113–29.

Ishiguro, Hide (1990). *Leibniz's Philosophy of Logic and Language*, 2nd ed. Cambridge: Cambridge University Press.

Israel, Jonathan (2001). *Radical Enlightenment*. Oxford: Oxford University Press.

James, Frank (1999). "Peter Martyr Vermigli: At the Crossroads of Late Medieval Scholasticism, Christian Humanism and Resurgent Augustinianism," in Trueman and Clark 1999, pp. 62–79.

(2001). *Peter Martyr Vermigli and Predestination: The Augustinian Inheritance of an Italian Reformer*. Oxford: Oxford University Press.

James, Susan (1993). "Spinoza the Stoic," in Sorell 1993, pp. 289–316.

(1997). *Passion and Action: The Emotions in Seventeenth-Century Philosophy*. Oxford: Oxford University Press.

(1998). "Reason, the Passions and the Good Life," in Garber and Ayers 1998, vol. II, pp. 1358–96.

(2005). "Sympathy and Comparison: Two Principles of Human Nature," in Frasca-Spada and Kail 2005, pp. 107–24.

Jansen, Bernhard (1938). *Die Pflege der Philosophie im Jesuitenorden während des 17–18 Jahrhunderts*. Fulda: Parzeller.

Jardine, Lisa (1974). *Francis Bacon: Discovery and the Art of Discourse*. Cambridge: Cambridge University Press.

(1988). "Humanistic Logic," in Schmitt, Skinner, and Kessler 1988, pp. 173–98.

Jardine, Nicholas (1976). "Galileo's Road to Truth and the Demonstrative Regress," *Studies in History and Philosophy of Science* 7: 277–318.

(1988). "Epistemology of the Sciences," in Schmitt, Skinner, and Kessler 1988, pp. 685–711.

Jesseph, Douglas M. (2002). "Hobbes's Atheism," *Midwest Studies in Philosophy* 26: 140–66.

John Paul II, Pope (1994). *Crossing the Threshold of Hope*. New York: Knopf.

Johnson, Art (1994). *Classic Math: History Topics for the Classroom*. Palo Alto, CA: Dale Seymour Publications.

Jolley, Nicholas (1984). *Leibniz and Locke: A Study of the* New Essays on Human Understanding. Oxford: Oxford University Press.

(1990). *The Light of the Soul: Theories of Ideas in Leibniz, Malebranche, and Descartes*. Oxford: Oxford University Press.

(1999). *Locke: His Philosophical Thought*. Oxford: Oxford University Press.

Jones, Peter (1982). *Hume's Sentiments: Their Ciceronian and French Context*. Edinburgh: Edinburgh University Press.

Jonsen, Albert, and Toulmin, Stephen (1988). *The Abuse of Casuistry*. Berkeley: University of California Press.

Joy, Lynn Sumida (1987). *Gassendi the Atomist*. Cambridge: Cambridge University Press.

Kenny, Neil (2004). *The Uses of Curiosity in Early Modern France and Germany*. Oxford: Oxford University Press.

Kent, Bonnie (1995). *Virtues of the Will: The Transformation of Ethics in the Late Thirteenth Century*. Washington, DC: Catholic University of America Press.

Kerr, Fergus (2002). *After Aquinas: Versions of Thomism*. Malden, MA: Blackwell.

Keynes, John Maynard (1921). *A Treatise on Probability*. London: Macmillan.

Kneale, W. C., and Kneale, M. (1962). *The Development of Logic*. Oxford: Oxford University Press.

Knebel, Sven (1991). "*Scientia media*: Ein diskursarchäologischer Leitfaden durch das 17. Jahrhundert," *Archiv für Begriffsgeschichte* 34: 262–94.

(1996a). "Die früheste Axiomatisierung des Induktionsprinzips: Pietro Sforza Pallavicino SJ (1607–1667)," *Salzburger Jahrbuch für Philosophie* 41: 97–128.

(1996b). "Leibniz, Middle Knowledge, and the Intricacies of Word Design," *Studia leibnitiana* 28: 199–210.

(1998). "Antonio Perez SJ (1599–1649) in seinen Beziehungen zur polnischen Jesuitenscholastik," *Forum philosophicum* 3: 219–23.

(2000). *Wille, Würfel und Wahrscheinlichkeit: Das System der moralischen Notwendigkeit in der Jesuitenscholastik 1550–1700*. Hamburg: Felix Meiner.

(2001). "Pietro Sforza Pallavicino's Quest for Principles of Induction," *The Monist* 84: 502–19.

Knowlson, James (1975). *Universal Language Schemes in England and France, 1600–1800*. Toronto: University of Toronto Press.

Knox, Ronald A. (1950). *Enthusiasm: A Chapter in the History of Religion*. Oxford: Oxford University Press.

Knuutilla, Simo (2001). "Schweden und Finnland," in Helmut Holzhey et al. (eds.), *Die Philosophie des 17. Jahrhunderts*, vol. IV/1 (Uberweg): *Das Heilige Römische Reich, Deutscher Nation Nord- und Ostmitteleuropa*. Basel: Schwabe, pp. 1227–45.

Kondylis, Panajotis (2002). *Die Aufklärung im Rahmen des neuzeitlichen Rationalismus*. Hamburg: Felix Meiner.

Kors, Alan C. (1990). *Atheism in France*. Princeton: Princeton University Press.

Kovecses, Zoltan (2000). *Metaphor and Emotion: Language, Culture and Body in Human Feeling*. Cambridge: Cambridge University Press.

Kraye, Jill (1988). "Moral Philosophy," in Schmitt, Skinner, and Kessler 1988, pp. 303–86.

Kraye, Jill, and Saarinen, Risto (eds.) (2004). *Moral Philosophy on the Threshold of Modernity*. Dordrecht: Kluwer.

Kremer, Elmar J. (1994). "Grace and Free Will in Arnauld," in Elmar J. Kremer (ed.), *The Great Arnauld and Some of his Philosophical Correspondents*. Toronto: University of Toronto Press, pp. 219–240.

Kretzmann, Norman (1967). "History of Semantics," in Paul Edwards (ed.), *The Encyclopedia of Philosophy* (8 vols.). New York: Macmillan, vol. VII, pp. 358–406.

(1968). "The Main Thesis of Locke's Semantic Theory," *Philosophical Review* 77: 175–96.

Kretzmann, Norman, Kenny, Anthony, and Pinborg, Jan (eds.) (1982). *The Cambridge History of Later Medieval Philosophy*. Cambridge: Cambridge University Press.

Kristeller, Paul Oskar (1992). *Medieval Aspects of Renaissance Thought*. New York: Columbia University Press.

Krolzik, Udo (1990–92). "Jungius, Joachim," in F. W. Bautz (ed.), *Biographisch-Bibliographisches Kirchenlexikon* (17 vols.). Hertzberg: T. Bautz, vol. III, pp. 869–75.

Krook, Dorothea (1993). *John Sergeant and his Circle: A Study of Three Seventeenth-Century English Aristotelians*, ed. Beverley Southgate. Leiden: Brill.

Kuehn, Manfred (2001). *Kant: A Biography*. Cambridge: Cambridge University Press.

Kusukawa, Sachiko (1985). *The Transformation of Natural Philosophy: The Case of Philip Melancthon*. Cambridge: Cambridge University Press.

Labrousse, Elisabeth (1964). *Pierre Bayle: Hétérodoxie et rigorisme*. The Hague: Nijhoff.

(1983). *Bayle*. Oxford: Oxford University Press.

Lagerlund, Henrik, and Yrjönsuuri, Mikko (eds.) (2002). *Emotions and Choice from Boethius to Descartes*. Dordrecht: Reidel.

Lamberigts, Mathijs (ed.) (1994). *L'augustinisme a l'ancienne faculté de théologie de Louvain*. Louvain: Biblioteca Ephemeridum Theologicarum Lovaniensium.

Laudan, Larry (1981). *Science and Hypothesis*. Dordrecht: Reidel.

Lawn, Brian (1993): *The Rise and Decline of the Scholastic* Quaestio disputata: *With Special Emphasis on its Use in the Teaching of Medicine and Science*. Leiden: Brill.

Leahy, Louis (1963). *Dynamisme volontaire et jugement libre*. Bruges–Paris: Desclée de Brouwer.

Le Bachelet, Xavier-Marie (1931). *Prédestination et grâce efficace: controverses dans la Compagnie de Jésus au temps d'Aquaviva, 1610–1613: histoire et documents inédits*. Louvain: Museum Lessianum.

Lehmann, William C. (1960). *John Millar of Glasgow*. Cambridge: Cambridge University Press.

Leijenhorst, Cees (1998). *The Mechanisation of Aristotelianism: The Late Aristotelian Setting of Thomas Hobbes' Natural Philosophy*. Leiden: Brill.

Leinsle, Ulrich Gottfried (1985). *Das Ding und die Methode: Methodische Konstitution und Gegenstand der frühen protestantischen Metaphysik*. Augsburg: Maroverlag.

Lennon, Thomas M. (1993). *The Battle of the Gods and Giants: The Legacies of Descartes and Gassendi 1655–1715*. Princeton: Princeton University Press.

(2006). "Christ from the Head of Jupiter: An Epistemological Note on Huet's Treatment of the Virgin Birth," in Bonnie MacLachlan and Judith Fletcher (eds.), *Virginity Revisited: The Autonomy of the Unpossessed Body*. Toronto: University of Toronto Press.

Lenoble, Robert (1943). *Mersenne ou la naissance du mécanisme*. Paris: Vrin.

Lenzen, Wolfgang (1990). *Das System der Leibnizschen Logik*. Berlin: De Gruyter.

Lessnoff, Michael (1986). *Social Contract*. Atlantic Highlands, NJ: Humanities Press International.

Levi, Antony (1964). *French Moralists: The Theory of the Passions 1584–1649*. Oxford: Clarendon Press.

Lewalter, Ernst (1935). *Spanisch-jesuitische und deutsch-lutherische Metaphysik des 17. Jahrhunderts: Ein Beitrag zur Geschichte der iberisch-deutschen Kulturbeziehungen und zur Vorgeschichte des deutschen Idealismus*. Hamburg: Ibero-Amerikanisches Institut.

Lewis, C. I. (1918). *A Survey of Symbolic Logic*. Berkeley: University of California Press.

Lindberg, David C., and Numbers, Ronald L. (eds.) (1986). *God and Nature: Historical Essays on the Encounter between Christianity and Science*. Berkeley: University of California Press.

Lloyd, Genevieve (1996). *Routledge Philosophy Guidebook to Spinoza and the* Ethics. London: Routledge.

(1998). "Rationalising the Passions: Spinoza on Reason and the Passions," in Gaukroger 1998, pp. 34–45.

Loeb, Louis E. (1981). *From Descartes to Hume: Metaphysics and the Development of Modern Philosophy*. Ithaca, NY: Cornell University Press.

Lohr, Charles H. (1988). "Metaphysics," in Schmitt, Skinner, and Kessler 1988, pp. 537–638.

(1999). "Metaphysics and Natural Philosophy as Sciences: The Catholic and Protestant Views in the Sixteenth and Seventeenth Centuries," in Constance Blackwell and Sachiko Kusakawa (eds.), *Philosophy in the Sixteenth and Seventeenth Centuries: Conversations with Aristotle*. Aldershot: Ashgate, pp. 280–95.

Long, A. A. (2003). "Stoicism in the Philosophical Tradition: Spinoza, Lipsius, Butler," in Miller and Inwood 2003, pp. 7–29.

Losonsky, Michael (1989). "Locke on the Making of Complex Ideas," *Locke Newsletter* 20: 35–46.

(1992). "Leibniz's Adamic Language of Thought," *Journal of the History of Philosophy* 30: 523–43.

(1993a). "Passionate Thought: Computation, Thought, and Action in Hobbes," *Pragmatics and Cognition* 1: 245–66.

(1993b). "Representationalism and Adamicism in Leibniz," in Marcelo Dascal and Elhanan Yakira (eds.), *Leibniz and Adam*. Tel Aviv: University Publishing Projects, pp. 137–51.

(2001). *Enlightenment and Action from Descartes to Kant: Passionate Thought*. Cambridge: Cambridge University Press.

(2007). "Language, Meaning and Mind in Locke's *Essay*," in Lex Newman (ed.), *The Cambridge Companion to Locke's* Essay concerning Human Understanding. Cambridge: Cambridge University Press.

Lurz, Wilhelm (1932). *Adam Tanner und die Gnadenstreitigkeiten des 17. Jahrhunderts*. Breslau: Müller & Seiffert.

Lux, David (1991). "Societies, Circles, Academies, and Organizations: A Historiographic Essay on Seventeenth-Century Science," in Barker and Ariew 1991, pp. 23–43.

Maat, Jaap (2004). *Philosophical Languages in the Seventeenth Century: Dalgarno, Wilkins, Leibniz*. Dordrecht: Kluwer.

Maclean, Ian (1992). *Interpretation and Meaning in the Renaissance: The Case of Law*. Cambridge: Cambridge University Press.

(2001). *Logic, Signs, and Nature in the Renaissance: The Case of Learned Medicine*. Cambridge: Cambridge University Press.

Mahoney, Edward P. (1976). "Antonio Trombetta and Agostino Nifo on Averroes and Intelligibile Species: A Philosophical Dispute at the University of Padua," in Antonino Poppi (ed.), *Storia e cultura al Santo*. Vicenza: N. Pozza, pp. 289–301.

(1978). "Duns Scotus and the School of Padua around 1500," in Camille Bérubé (ed.), *Regnum hominis et regnum Dei: Acta quarti congressus scotistici internationalis patavii, 24–29 septembris 1976* (2 vols.). Roma: Societas Internationalis Scotistica, vol. II, pp. 214–27.

(1982). "Sense, Intellect, and Imagination in Albert, Thomas, and Siger," in Kretzmann, Kenny, and Pinborg 1982, pp. 602–22.

Mahoney, Michael S. (1975). "Peter Ramus," in Charles Coulston Gillispie (ed.), *Dictionary of Scientific Biography* (18 vols.). New York: Scribner, vol. XI, pp. 286–90.

Malcolm, Noel (2002). *Aspects of Hobbes*. Oxford: Oxford University Press.

Mamiani, Maurizio (2002). "Newton on Prophecy and the Apocalypse," in I. Bernard Cohen and George E. Smith (eds.), *The Cambridge Companion to Newton*. Cambridge: Cambridge University Press, pp. 387–408.

Manuel, Frank (1973). *The Religion of Isaac Newton*. Cambridge: Cambridge University Press.

Marcil-Lacoste, Louise (1982). *Claude Buffier and Thomas Reid: Two Common-Sense Philosophers*. Montreal: McGill–Queen's University Press.

Marcus-Leus, Elly (1995). *Johannes Wiggers Diestensis (1571–1639)*. Diest: Stedelijk Museum.

Marshall, John (1994). *John Locke: Resistance, Religion, and Responsibility*. Cambridge: Cambridge University Press.

Martinich, A. P. (1992). *The Two Gods of Leviathan: Thomas Hobbes on Religion and Politics*. Cambridge: Cambridge University Press.

(1999). *Hobbes: A Biography*. Cambridge: Cambridge University Press.

Martins, Antonio M. (1994). *Lógica e ontologia em Pedro da Fonseca*. Lisbon: Fundaçao Calouste Gulbenkian.

Mates, Benson (1972). "Leibniz on Possible Worlds," in Harry G. Frankfurt (ed.), *Leibniz: A Collection of Critical Essays*. Garden City, NY: Anchor Books, pp. 335–63.

(1986). *The Philosophy of Leibniz: Metaphysics and Language*. Oxford: Oxford University Press.

McClaughlin, Trevor (2000). "Descartes, Experiments, and a First-Generation Cartesian, Jacques Rohault," in Stephen Gaukroger, John Schuster, and John Sutton (eds.), *Descartes' Natural Philosophy*. London: Routledge, pp. 330–46.

McCool, Gerald A. (1977). *Catholic Theology in the Nineteenth Century: The Quest for a Unitary Method*. New York: Seabury Press.

McCracken, Charles J. (1983). *Malebranche and British Philosophy*. Oxford: Oxford University Press.

McGrade, A. S. (ed.) (2003). *The Cambridge Companion to Medieval Philosophy*. Cambridge: Cambridge University Press.

McMullin, Ernan (1998). "Galileo on Science and Scripture," in Peter Machamer (ed.), *The Cambridge Companion to Galileo*. Cambridge: Cambridge University Press, pp. 271–347.

Menn, Stephen (1997). "Suárez, Nominalism and Modes," in Kevin White (ed.), *Hispanic Philosophy in the Age of Discovery*. Washington, DC: Catholic University of America Press, pp. 226–57.

(1998). "The Intellectual Setting," in Garber and Ayers 1998, vol. 1, pp. 33–86.

Mercer, Christia (2001). *Leibniz's Metaphysics: Its Origins and Development*. Cambridge: Cambridge University Press.

Merl, Otho (1947). *Theologia salmanticensis*. Regensburg: J. Habbel.

Michalson, Gordon E. (1990). *Fallen Freedom: Kant on Radical Evil and Moral Regeneration*. Cambridge: Cambridge University Press.

Miller, Jon, and Inwood, Brad (eds.) (2003). *Hellenistic and Early Modern Philosophy*. Cambridge: Cambridge University Press.

Miller, Perry (1939). *The New England Mind: The Seventeenth Century*. Cambridge, MA: Harvard University Press.

Millet, Benignus (1964). *The Irish Franciscans, 1651–1665*. Rome: Gregorian University Press.

Milton, John (1984). "The Scholastic Background to Locke's Thought," *Locke Newsletter* 15: 25–34.

Mooney, Carice (1958). "The Writings of Father Luke Wadding, O.F.M.," *Franciscan Studies* 18: 225–39.

Moreau, Denis (1999). *Deux cartésiens: La polémique entre Antoine Arnauld et Nicolas Malebranche*. Paris: J. Vrin.

Mori, Gianluca (1999). *Bayle philosophe*. Paris: Champion.

Moriarty, Michael (2003). *Early Modern French Thought: The Age of Suspicion*. Oxford: Oxford University Press.

Morris, Christopher W. (1998). *An Essay on the Modern State*. Cambridge: Cambridge University Press.

Muller, Richard B. (1999). "The Use and Abuse of a Document: Beza's *Tabula praedestinationis*, the Bolsec Controversy, and the Origins of Reformed Orthodoxy," in Trueman and Clark 1999, pp. 33–63.

(2003). *Post-Reformation Reformed Dogmatics* (4 vols.). Grand Rapids, MI: Baker Academics.

Mundt, Lothar (1994). "Agricolas *De inventione dialectica*: Konzeption, historische Bedeutung und Wirkung," in Wilhelm Kühlmann (ed.), *Rudolf Agricola 1444–1485: Protagonist des nordeuropäischen Humanismus*. Bern: P. Lang.

Murdoch, John E., and Sylla, Edith D. (1978). "The Science of Motion," in David C. Lindberg (ed.), *Science in the Middle Ages*. Chicago: University of Chicago Press, pp. 206–64.

Murray, Michael (1995). "Leibniz on Divine Foreknowledge of Future Contingents and Human Freedom," *Philosophy and Phenomenological Research* 55: 75–108.

(2002). "Leibniz's Proposals for Theological Reconciliation among the Protestants," *American Catholic Philosophical Quarterly* 76: 623–46.

Nadler, Steven (ed.) (1993). *Causation in Early Modern Philosophy: Cartesianism, Occasionalism and Pre-established Harmony*. University Park, PA: Penn State University Press.

(1999). *Spinoza: A Life*. Cambridge: Cambridge University Press.

(ed.) (2000a). *The Cambridge Companion to Malebranche*. Cambridge: Cambridge University Press.

(2000b). "Malebranche on Causation," in Nadler 2000a, pp. 112–38.

(2001). *Spinoza's Heresy: Immortality and the Jewish Mind*. Oxford: Oxford University Press.

(ed.) (2002). *The Blackwell Companion to Early Modern Philosophy*. New York: Blackwell.

Northeast, Catherine M. (1991). *The Parisian Jesuits and the Enlightenment, 1700–1762*. Oxford: Voltaire Foundation.

Nuchelmans, Gabriel (1998). "Logic in the Seventeenth Century," in Garber and Ayers 1998, vol. I, pp. 103–46.

Nussbaum, Martha (1994). *The Therapy of Desire: Theory and Practice in Hellenistic Ethics*. Princeton: Princeton University Press.

Ogonowski, Zbigniew (2001). "Polen, §4. Die Schulphilosophie," in Helmut Holzhey et al. (eds.), *Die Philosophie des 17. Jahrhunderts*, vol. IV/1 (Überweg): *Das Heilige Römische Reich, Deutscher Nation Nord- und Ostmitteleuropa*. Basel: Schwabe, pp. 1,288–1,304.

Olivares, Estanislao (1984). "Juan de Lugo (1583–1660): Datos biográficos, sus escritos sobre su doctrina y bibliografia," *Archivo teológico granadino* 47: 5–129.

Olson, Mancur, Jr. (1971). *The Logic of Collective Action: Public Goods and the Theory of Groups*. Cambridge, MA: Harvard University Press.

O'Malley, John W. (1993). *The First Jesuits*. Cambridge, MA: Harvard University Press.

(1999). *The Jesuits: Cultures, Sciences, and the Arts 1540–1773*. Toronto: University of Toronto Press.

O'Neill, Eileen (1993). "Influxus Physicus," in Nadler 1993, pp. 27–55.

Ong, Walter J. (1983). *Ramus, Method, and the Decay of Dialogue*. Cambridge, MA: Harvard University Press.

Osler, Margaret J. (1993). "Ancients, Moderns, and the History of Philosophy: Gassendi's Epicurean Project," in Sorell 1993, pp. 129–43.

(2003). "Early Modern Uses of Hellenistic Philosophy: Gassendi's Epicurean Project," in Miller and Inwood 2003, pp. 30–44.

Oz-Salzberger, Fania. (2002). "Scots, Germans, Republic and Commerce," in Martin van Gelderen and Quentin Skinner (eds.), *Republicanism*, vol. II. Cambridge: Cambridge University Press, pp. 107–226.

Parkinson, G. H. R. (1965). *Logic and Reality in Leibniz's Metaphysics*. Oxford: Oxford University Press.

Pasnau, Robert (1997). *Theories of Cognition in the Later Middle Ages*. Cambridge: Cambridge University Press.

(2004). "Form, Substance, Mechanism," *Philosophical Review* 113: 31–88.

Pastine, Dino (1972). "Caramuel contro Descartes: Obiezioni inedite alle Meditazioni," *Rivista critica di storia della filosofia* 27: 177–221.

(1975). *Juan Caramuel: Probabilismo ed enciclopedia*. Florence: La Nuova Italia.

Penelhum, Terence (1994). "Hume's Moral Psychology," in David Fate Norton (ed.), *The Cambridge Companion to Hume*. Cambridge: Cambridge University Press, pp. 117–47.

Pereira, Miguel Baptista (1967). *Ser e pessoa: Pedro da Fonseca*. Coimbra: Universidade de Coimbra.

Pérez-Ramos, Antonio (1988). *Francis Bacon's Idea of Science and the Maker's Knowledge Tradition*. Oxford: Oxford University Press.

Peyrous, B. (1974). "Un grand centre de thomisme au XVIIe siècle: Le couvent des Frères Prêcheurs de Bordeaux et l'enseignement de J.-B. Gonet," *Divus Thomas* (Pl.) 77: 452–73.

Pinchard, Bruno, and Ricci, Saverio (eds.) (1993). *Rationalisme analogique et humanisme théologique: La culture de Thomas de Vio il Gaetano*. Naples: Vivarium.

Pink, Thomas (2004). "Suarez, Hobbes and the Scholastic Tradition in Action Theory," in Pink and Stone 2004, pp. 127–53.

Pink, Thomas, and Stone, M. W. F. (eds.) (2004). *The Will and Human Action: From the Ancients to the Present Day*. London: Routledge.

Pittock, Murray G. H. (2003). "Historiography," in Broadie 2003, pp. 258–79.

Platt, John (1982). *Reformed Thought and Scholasticism: The Arguments for and against the Existence of God in Dutch Theology, 1575–1650*. Leiden: Brill.

Pombo, Olga (1987). *Leibniz and the Problem of a Universal Language*. Münster: Nodus Publikationen.

Poole, W. (2003). "The Divine and the Grammarian: Theological Disputes in the 17th-Century Universal Language Movement," *Historiographica linguistica* 3: 273–300.

Popkin, Richard H. (1982). "Cartesianism and Biblical Criticism," in Thomas M. Lennon, John Nicholas, and John Davis (eds.), *Problems of Cartesianism*. Montreal: McGill University Press, 64–65.

(2001). "The Image of Judaism in Seventeenth-Century Europe," in Robert Crocker (ed.), *Religion, Reason and Nature in Early Modern Europe*. Dordrecht: Reidel, pp. 155–97.

(2003). *The History of Scepticism: From Savonarola to Bayle*. Oxford: Oxford University Press.

Poppi, Antonino (1962). "Lo scotista patavino Antonio Trombetta," *Il Santo* 2: 349–67.

(1966). *Causalità e infinità nella scuola padovana dal 1480 al 1513*. Padova: Antenore.

(1989). *La filosofia nello studio francescano del Santo a Padova*. Padova: Centro Studi Antoniani, pp. 169–78.

(2001). *Ricerche sulla teologia e la scienza nella scuola padovana del cinque e seicento*. Padova: Rubbettino.

Pyle, Andrew (2003). *Malebranche*. London: Routledge.

Quantin, Jean-Louis (1999). *Le catholicisme classique et les Pères de l'Eglise: Un retour aux sources (1669–1713)*. Paris: Institut d'Etudes Augustiniennes.

Quine, Willard V. O. (1980). *From a Logical Point of View*. 2nd ed. Cambridge, MA: Harvard University Press.

Quinto, Riccardo (2001). *Scholastica: Storia di un concetto*. Padova: Il Poligrafo.

Radner, Daisie (1985). "Is There a Problem of Cartesian Interaction?" *Journal of the History of Philosophy* 23: 221–36.

Ramelow, Tilman (1997). *Gott, Freiheit, Weltenwahl: Der Ursprung des Begriffs der besten aller möglichen Welten in der Metaphysik der*

Willensfreiheit zwischen Antonio Perez S.J. (1599–1649) und G. W. Leibniz (1646–1716). Leiden: Brill.

Richardson, Robert C. (1982). "The Scandal of Cartesian Interactionism," *Mind* 91: 20–37.

Riley, Patrick (1986). *The General Will before Rousseau*. Princeton: Princeton University Press.

Risse, Wilhelm (1964). *Die Logik der Neuzeit* (2 vols.). Stuttgart: F. Frommann.

Rogers, G. A. J. (1988). "Hobbes's Hidden Influence," in G. A. J. Rogers and A. Ryan (eds.), *Perspectives on Thomas Hobbes*. Oxford: Oxford University Press, pp. 189–205.

Rorty, Amelie Oksenberg (1982). "From Passions to Emotions and Sentiments," *Philosophy* 57: 159–72.

Rorty, Richard (1979). *Philosophy and the Mirror of Nature*. Princeton: Princeton University Press.

Roscic, N. (1971). "Mateo Frce (Ferkic, Ferchius): Un grande scotista croato," in *Studia mediaevalia et mariologica: P. Carolo Balić OFM septuagesimum explenti annum dicata*. Rome: Antonianum, pp. 377–402.

Rossi, Paolo (1960). *Clavis universalis: Arti mnemoniche e logica combinatoria da Lullo a Leibniz*. Milan: R. Ricciardi.

Rozemond, Marleen (1998). *Descartes' Dualism*. Cambridge, MA: Harvard University Press.

Ruello, F. (1963). "Christian Wolff et la scolastique," *Traditio* 19: 411–25.

Russell, Bertrand (1937). *A Critical Exposition of the Philosophy of Leibniz*. 2nd ed. London: Allen and Unwin.

Rutherford, Donald (1995a). *Leibniz and the Rational Order of Nature*. Cambridge: Cambridge University Press.

(1995b). "Philosophy and Language in Leibniz," in Nicholas Jolley (ed.), *The Cambridge Companion to Leibniz*. Cambridge: Cambridge University Press, pp. 224–69.

(1999). "Salvation as a State of Mind: The Place of *Acquiescentia* in Spinoza's *Ethics*," *British Journal of the History of Philosophy* 7: 447–73.

(2004). "On the Happy Life: Descartes vis-à-vis Seneca," in Strange and Zupko 2004, pp. 177–97.

Rutherford, Donald, and Cover, J. A. (eds.) (2005). *Leibniz: Nature and Freedom*. New York: Oxford University Press.

Ryan, J. K. (1948). "The Reputation of St. Thomas Aquinas among English Protestant Thinkers of the Seventeenth Century," *New Scholasticism* 22: 1–33, 126–208.

Sarasohn, Lisa (1996). *Gassendi's Ethics: Freedom in a Mechanistic Universe*. Ithaca, NY: Cornell University Press.

Saunders, Jason Lewis (1955). *Justus Lipsius: The Philosophy of Renaissance Stoicism*. New York: Liberal Arts.

Scaramuzzi, D. (1927). *Il pensiero di Giovanni Duns Scoto nel mezzogiorno d'Italia*. Rome: Ed. Pontifici.

Schmaltz, Tad M. (1996). *Malebranche's Theory of the Soul: A Cartesian Interpretation*. New York: Oxford University Press.

(1997). "Descartes on Innate Ideas, Sensation, and Scholasticism: The Response to Regius," in Stewart 1997, pp. 33–73.

Schmidt, James (ed.) (1996). *What Is Enlightenment?* Berkeley: University of California Press.

(2003). "Inventing the Enlightenment: Anti-Jacobins, British Hegelians, and the *Oxford English Dictionary*," *Journal of the History of Ideas* 64: 421–45.

Schmitt, Charles B. (1983a). *Aristotle and the Renaissance*. Cambridge, MA: Harvard University Press.

(1983b). "The Rediscovery of Ancient Skepticism in Modern Times," in Myles Burnyeat (ed.), *The Skeptical Tradition*. Berkeley: University of California Press, pp. 225–51.

Schmitt, Charles B., Skinner, Quentin, and Kessler, Eckhard (eds.) (1988). *The Cambridge History of Renaissance Philosophy*. Cambridge: Cambridge University Press.

Schmitt, Jean-Claude (1989). "The Ethics of Gesture," in Michel Feher, Ramona Naddaff, and Nadia Tazi (eds.), *Fragments for a History of the Human Body* (3 vols.). New York: Zone, vol. II, pp. 128–47.

Schmutz, Jacob (2000a). "Bulletin de scolastique moderne (I)," *Revue thomiste* 100: 270–341.

(2000b). "Juan Caramuel y Lobkowitz (1606–1682)," in F. W. Bautz (ed.), *Biographisch-Bibliographisches Kirchenlexicon* (17 vols.). Herzberg: T Bautz, vol. XVII, pp. 224–32.

(2001). "Juan Caramuel on the Year 2000: Time and Possible Worlds in Early-Modern Scholasticism," in Pasquale Porro (ed.), *The Medieval Concept of Time: Studies on the Scholastic Debate and its Reception in Early-Modern Philosophy*. Leiden: Brill, pp. 399–434.

(2002a). "Un Dieu indifférent: La crise de la science divine durant la scolastique moderne," in Boulnois, Schmutz, and Solère 2002, pp. 185–221.

(2002b). "Du péché de l'ange à la liberté d'indifférence: Les sources angélologiques de l'anthropologie moderne," *Les études philosophiques* 2: 169–98.

(2002c). "L'héritage des subtils: Cartographie du scotisme du XVIIe siècle," *Les études philosophiques* 1: 51–81.

(2002d). "Le miroir de l'univers: Gabriel Vazquez et les commentateurs jésuites," in Bardout and Boulnois 2002, pp. 382–411.

(2002e). "Sebastián Izquierdo: De la science divine à l'ontologie des états de choses," in Bardout and Boulnois 2002, pp. 412–35.

(2003). "Dieu est l'idée: La métaphysique d'Antonio Pérez (1599–1649) entre néo-augustinisme et crypto-spinozisme," *Revue thomiste* 103: 495–526.

(2004). "Science divine et métaphysique chez Francisco Suárez," in *Francisco Suárez, éste es el hombre: Libro homenaje al Profesor Salvador Castellote Cubells*. Valencia: Facultad de Teología San Vicente Ferrer, pp. 347–59.

Schneewind, J. B. (1998). *The Invention of Autonomy: A History of Modern Moral Philosophy*. Cambridge: Cambridge University Press.

(ed.) (2003). *Modern Moral Philosophy from Montaigne to Kant*. Cambridge: Cambridge University Press.

(ed.) (2004). *Teaching New Histories of Philosophy*. Princeton: The University Center for Human Values, Princeton University.

Schneiders, Werner (1990). *Hoffnung auf Vernunft*. Hamburg: Felix Meiner.

Schüßler, Rudolf (2002). *Moral im Zweifel*, vol. I: *Die scholastische Theorie des Entscheidens unter moralischer Unsicherheit*. Paderborn: Mentis.

Scruton, Roger (1994). *Modern Philosophy: An Introduction and Survey*. New York: Allen Lane.

Secada, Jorge (2000). *Cartesian Metaphysics: The Scholastic Origins of Modern Philosophy*. Cambridge: Cambridge University Press.

Shanley, Brian J. (2002). *The Thomist Tradition*. Dordrecht: Kluwer.

Shapin, Steven. (1996). *The Scientific Revolution*. Chicago: University of Chicago Press.

Shaver, Robert (1996). "Grotius on Scepticism and Self-Interest," *Archiv für Geschichte der Philosophie* 78: 27–47.

Shea, William R. (1986). "Galileo and the Church," in Lindberg and Numbers 1986, pp. 114–35.

Shuger, Debra K. (1988). *Sacred Rhetoric: The Christian Grand Style in the English Renaissance*. Princeton: Princeton University Press.

Sidgwick, Henry (1954). *Outlines of the History of Ethics for English Readers*. 6th ed. London: Macmillan.

(1967). *The Methods of Ethics*. 7th ed. London: Macmillan.

Simmons, A. John (1993). *On the Edge of Anarchy: Locke, Consent, and the Limits of Society*. Princeton: Princeton University Press.

Sinnema, Donald (1999). "The Distinction between Scholastic and Popular: Andreas Hyperius and Reformed Scholasticism," in Trueman and Clark 1999, pp. 127–44.

Siraisi, Nancy G. (1990). *Medieval and Early Renaissance Medicine: An Introduction to Knowledge and Practice*. Chicago: University of Chicago Press.

Skinner, Quentin (1978). *The Foundations of Modern Political Thought* (2 vols.). Cambridge: Cambridge University Press.

(1988). "Political Philosophy," in Schmitt, Skinner, and Kessler 1988, pp. 389–452.

Slaughter, M. M. (1982). *Universal Languages and Scientific Taxonomy in the Seventeenth Century*. Cambridge: Cambridge University Press.

Sleigh, Robert C., Jr. (1990). *Leibniz and Arnauld: A Commentary on their Correspondence*. New Haven: Yale University Press.

(1996). "Arnauld on Efficacious Grace and Free Choice," in Elmar J. Kremer (ed.), *Interpreting Arnauld*. Toronto: University of Toronto Press, pp. 164–75.

Sleigh, Robert C., Jr., Chappell, Vere, and Della Rocca, Michael (1998). "Determinism and Human Freedom," in Garber and Ayers 1998, vol. II, pp. 1195–1278.

Smeets, Uriel (1942). *Lineamenta bibliographiae scotisticae*. Rome: Commissio Scotistica.

Sommerville, Johann P. (1988). "The New Art of Lying," in Edmund Leites (ed.), *Conscience and Casuistry in Early Modern Europe*. Cambridge: Cambridge University Press.

Sorell, Tom (ed.) (1993). *The Rise of Modern Philosophy: The Tension between the New and Traditional Philosophies from Machiavelli to Leibniz*. Oxford: Oxford University Press.

Sousedik, Stanislav (1981). "La obra filosófica de Rodrigo de Arriaga," *Ibero-Americana Pragensia* 15: 103–46.

(1996). "Der Streit um den Wahren Sinn der Scotistischen Possibilienlehre," in Ludger Honnefelder et al. (eds.), *John Duns Scotus: Metaphysics and Ethics*. Leiden: Brill, pp. 191–204.

(ed.) (1998). *Rodrigo de Arriaga: Philosoph und Theologe (Prag 25–28 Juni 1996)*. Prague: Karolinum.

South, James B. (2001). "Suárez on Imagination," *Vivarium* 39: 119–58.

(2002). "Singular and Universal in Suárez's Account of Cognition," *Review of Metaphysics* 55: 785–823.

Southgate, Beverley (1993). *Covetous of Truth: The Life and Work of Thomas White, 1593–1676*. Dordrecht: Reidel.

Spellman, W. M. (1988). *Locke and the Problem of Depravity*. Oxford: Oxford University Press.

Spruyt, Hendrik (1994). *The Sovereign State and its Competitors*. Princeton: Princeton University Press.

Stegmüller, Friedrich (1935). *Geschichte des Molinismus*. Munster: Aschendorff.

(1959). *Filosofia e teologia nas universidades de Coimbra e Évora*. Coimbra: Universidade de Coimbra.

Steinmetz, David C. (1995). *Luther in Context*. Grand Rapids, MI: Baker Academic.

(1997). *Calvin in Context*. Oxford: Oxford University Press.

Stewart, M. A. (ed.) (1997). *Studies in Seventeenth-Century European Philosophy*. Oxford: Oxford University Press.

Stone, M. W. F. (1999). "The Adoption and Rejection of Aristotelian Moral Philosophy in Reformed Ethics," in Jill Kraye and M. W. F. Stone (eds.), *Humanism and Early Modern Philosophy*. London: Routledge, pp. 59–90.

(2000). "The Origins of Probabilism in Late Scholastic Moral Thought: A Prolegomenon to Further Study," *Recherches de théologie et philosophie médiévales* 67: 125–68.

(2002). "Aristotelianism and Scholasticism in Early Modern Philosophy," in Nadler 2002, pp. 7–25.

(2004a). "Making Sense of Thomas Aquinas in the Sixteenth Century: Dominic de Soto O.P., on the Natural Desire to See God," in Caroline Macé and Gerd Van Riel (eds.), *Platonic Ideas and Concept Formation in Ancient and Medieval Thought*. Louvain: Leuven University Press, pp. 211–32.

(2004b). "Michael Baius (1513–1589) and the Debate on 'Pure Nature': Grace and Moral Agency in Sixteenth-Century Scholasticism," in Kraye and Saarinen 2004, pp. 51–90.

(2004c). "Moral Psychology before 1277: The Will, *Liberum Arbitrium*, and Moral Rectitude in Bonaventure," in Pink and Stone 2004, pp. 99–126.

(2004d). "The Scope and Limits of Moral Deliberation: *Recta Ratio*, Natural Law, and Conscience in Francisco Suárez," in Lodi Nauta and Detlev Pätzold (eds.), *Imagination in the Later Middle Ages and Early Modern Times*. Louvain: Peeters, pp. 37–59.

(2004e). "Scrupulosity, Probabilism, and Conscience: The Origins of the Debate in Early Modern Scholasticism," in Harald Braun and Edward Vallance (eds.), *Contexts of Conscience in Early Modern Europe, 1500–1700*. London: Palgrave Macmillan, pp. 1–16, 182–88.

(2005a). "Moral Philosophy and the Conditions of Certainty: Descartes's *Morale* in Context," in Ricardo Salles (ed.), *Metaphysics, Soul, and Ethics in Ancient Thought: Themes from the Work of Richard Sorabji*. Oxford: Oxford University Press, pp. 507–50.

(2005b). "The Nature and Significance of Law in Early Modern Scholasticism," in Fred D. Miller, Jr. (ed.), *A History of Philosophy of Law from the Ancient Greeks to the Scholastics* (*A Treatise of Legal Philosophy and General Jurisprudence*, vol. vi). Dordrecht: Kluwer, pp. 564–606.

Stone, M. W. F., and Van Houdt, Toon (1999). "Probabilism and its Methods: Leonardus Lessius and his Contribution to the Development of Jesuit Casuistry," *Ephemerides theologicae lovanienses* 82: 359–94.

Strange, Steven K., and Zupko, Jack (eds.) (2004). *Stoicism: Traditions and Transformations*. Cambridge: Cambridge University Press.

Strauss, Leo (1988). *Persecution and the Art of Writing*. Chicago: University of Chicago Press.

Sutton, John (1998). *Philosophy and Memory Traces: Descartes to Connectionism*. Cambridge: Cambridge University Press.

Talon-Hugon, Carole (2002). *Descartes, ou les passions rêvées par la raison*. Paris: Vrin.

Tavuzzi, Michael M. (1997). *Prierias:The Life and Works of Silvestro Mazzolini da Prierio, 1456–1527*. Durham, NC: Duke University Press.

Thorndike, Lynn (1951). "The *Cursus Philosophicus* before Descartes," *Archives internationales d'histoire de la science* 4: 16–24.

Trentmann, John (1982). "Scholasticism in the Seventeenth Century," in Kretzmann, Kenny, and Pinborg 1982, pp. 818–37.

Trevor-Roper, Hugh (1989). *Catholics, Anglicans, and Puritans: Seventeenth-Century Essays*. London: Fontana.

Trueman, Carl R., and Clark, R. Scott (eds.) (1999). *Protestant Scholasticism:Essays in Reassessment*. Carlisle: Paternoster.

Tuck, Richard (1982). *Natural Rights Theories: Their Origin and Development*. Cambridge: Cambridge University Press.

(1983). "Grotius, Carneades, and Hobbes," *Grotiana* 4: 43–62.

(1987). "The 'Modern' Theory of Natural Law," in Anthony Pagden (ed.), *The Languages of Political Theory in Early-Modern Europe*. Cambridge: Cambridge University Press, pp. 99–122.

(1993). *Philosophy and Government, 1572–1651*. Cambridge: Cambridge University Press.

Tyacke, Nicholas (ed.) (1997). *The History of the University of Oxford*, vol. IV: *Seventeenth-Century Oxford*. Oxford: Oxford University Press.

Urbach, Peter (1987). *Francis Bacon's Philosophy of Science: An Account and Reappraisal*. La Salle, IL: Open Court.

Vacant, Alfred, and Mangenot, Eugene (ed.) (1923–50). *Dictionnaire de théologie catholique* (15 vols.). Paris: Letouzey et Ané.

Van Asselt, Willem, and Dekker, Eef (2001). *Reformation and Scholasticism: An Ecumenical Enterprise*. Grand Rapids, MI: Baker Academic.

Van Ruler, J. A. (1995). *The Crisis of Causality: Voetius and Descartes on God, Nature and Change*. Leiden: Brill.

Velarde Lombraña, Julián (1989). *Juan Caramuel: Vida y obra*. Oviedo: Pentalfa.

Velleman, J. David (2000). "The Possibility of Practical Reason," in J. David Velleman, *The Possibility of Practical Reason*. Oxford: Oxford University Press.

(2006). *Self to Self: Selected Essays*. Cambridge: Cambridge University Press.

Verbeek, Theo (1992). *Descartes and the Dutch: Early Reactions to Cartesian Philosophy, 1637–1650*. Carbondale, IL: Southern Illinois University Press.

(1995). "The First Objections," in Ariew and Grene 1995, pp. 21–32.

Vereecke, Louis (1957). *Conscience morale et loi humaine selon Gabriel Vazquez*. Paris: Desclée.

Vienne, Jean M. (1991). "Malebranche and Locke: The Theory of Moral Choice, a Neglected Theme," in Stuart Brown (ed.), *Nicolas Malebranche: His Philosophical Critics and Successors*. Assen: Van Gorcum, pp. 94–108.

Voak, Nigel (2003). *Richard Hooker and Reformed Theology: A Study of Reason, Will, and Grace*. Oxford: Oxford University Press.

Walton, D. N. (1999). "Peter Ramus," *Argumentation* 13: 391–92.

Watkins, John W. N. (1973). *Hobbes's System of Ideas*. 2nd ed. London: Hutchinson.

Westfall, Richard S. (1986). "The Rise of Science and the Decline of Orthodox Christianity: A Study of Kepler, Descartes, and Newton," in Lindberg and Numbers 1986, pp. 218–37.

Whitehead, Alfred North, and Russell, Bertrand (1997). *Principia Mathematica to *56*. Cambridge: Cambridge University Press.

Williams, Bernard (1978). *Descartes: The Project of Pure Enquiry*. Harmondsworth: Penguin.

Wilson, Catherine (1989). *Leibniz's Metaphysics: A Historical and Comparative Study*. Princeton: Princeton University Press.

(2003). "Epicureanism in Early Modern Philosophy: Leibniz and his Contemporaries," in Miller and Inwood 2003, pp. 90–115.

Wilson, Margaret (1999a). *Ideas and Mechanism: Essays on Early Modern Philosophy*. Princeton: Princeton University Press.

(1999b). "Skepticism without Indubitability," in Wilson 1999a, pp. 3–9.

(1999c). "Superadded Properties: The Limits of Mechanism in Locke," in Wilson 1999a, pp. 196–208.

(1999d). "Superadded Properties: A Reply to M. R. Ayers," in Wilson 1999a, pp. 209–14.

Wippel, John (1984). *Metaphysical Themes in Thomas Aquinas*. Washington, DC: Catholic University of America Press.

Wolf-Devine, Celia R. C. (1993). *Descartes on Seeing: Epistemology and Visual Perception*. Carbondale, IL: Southern Illinois University Press.

Wolterstoff, Nicholas (1996). *John Locke and the Ethics of Belief*. Cambridge: Cambridge University Press.

Wood, Thomas (1952). *English Casuistical Divinity during the Seventeenth Century*. London: SPCK.

Woolhouse, R. S. (1993). *Descartes, Spinoza, Leibniz: The Concept of Substance in Seventeenth-Century Metaphysics*. London: Routledge.

Wundt, Max (1939). *Die deutsche Schulmetaphysik des 17. Jahrhunderts*. Tübingen: Mohr.

Yaffe, Gideon (2000). *Liberty Worth the Name: Locke on Free Agency*. Princeton: Princeton University Press.

Zagorin, Perez (1998). *Francis Bacon*. Princeton: Princeton University Press.

Zanta, Léontine (1914). *La renaissance du stoïcisme au XVIe siècle*. Paris: Champion. Repr. Geneva: Slatkine, 1975.

Zuckert, Michael P. (1994). *Natural Rights and the New Republicanism*. Princeton: Princeton University Press.

INDEX

Page references in **bold type** indicate short biographies of major figures.